A Short History of

Philosophy

A Short History of
Philosophy

ROBERT C. SOLOMON
KATHLEEN M. HIGGINS

New York   Oxford
OXFORD UNIVERSITY PRESS
1996

Oxford University Press

Oxford   New York
Athens   Auckland   Bangkok
Calcutta   Cape Town   Dar es Salaam   Delhi
Florence   Hong Kong   Istanbul   Karachi
Kuala Lumpur   Madras   Madrid   Melbourne
Mexico City   Nairobi   Paris   Singapore
Taipei   Tokyo   Toronto

and associated companies in
Berlin   Ibadan

Published by Oxford University Press, Inc.
198 Madison Avenue, New York, New York 10016

Oxford is a registered trademark of Oxford University Press, Inc.

Library of Congress Cataloging-in-Publication Data
Solomon, Robert C.
A short history of philosophy / Robert C. Solomon,
Kathleen M. Higgins.
p. cm.   Includes bibliographical references.
ISBN 0–19–508647–3 (cloth).—ISBN 0–19–510196–0 (pbk.)
1. Philosophy—History.
I. Higgins, Kathleen Marie.   II. Title.
B72.S66   1996
109—dc20   95-12578

Excerpts from Plato's *Republic* translated by E. M A. Grube, and from
Plato's *Symposium* translated by Alexander Nehemas and P. Woodruff,
are reprinted with the permission of the Hackett Publishing Company,
copyright © 1974 and 1989 respectively.

5 7 9 8 6 4

Printed in the United States of America
on acid-free paper

For our friends and colleagues at
The University of Auckland,
in gratitude for their hospitality,
camaraderie, and conversation

Preface

The concepts that lie at the heart of philosophy antedate historical record by thousands of years. The concept of immortality, in one form or another, probably extends back at least to the Neanderthals some tens of thousands of years ago. They seem to have developed some notion of an afterlife, as is evident in their burial sites and symbolism. In prehistory, magic also displays unmistakable philosophical underpinnings: it appeals to causes unseen and not yet understood. Abstraction and idealized forms can be traced back to the Cro-Magnon, who lived more than ten thousand years ago. The ghastly practice of human sacrifice, which already indicates some complex set of beliefs about the world, can be traced back at least this far.

When did people first envision gods and goddesses who must be appeased? When did they first believe in forces behind the scenes and mysteries in the very stuff of life? When did they begin to speculate about the creation of the world, and in what terms? When did they move beyond the "facts" of nature to speculation, to spirituality, to wonder? When did these beliefs and speculations begin to consolidate into that cantankerous discipline that the Greeks called philosophy? How did the numerous gods and goddesses of the early ancient world become one? In 1370 B.C.E., the Egyptian pharoah Akhenaton (Amenhotep IV) proclaimed belief in one God, centuries before the birth of Moses. Abraham, we are told, had such a belief in a single God five hundred years earlier. How much of philosophy is an effort to come to terms with that demand for unity and concern for that which is "beyond" us?

In the pages that follow, we have tried to write a short history of philosophy that is simple and straightforward but captures the complexity and diversity of the subject. The reader may rightly wonder how we can justify calling "short" a book of roughly 300 pages. No doubt it could have been shorter, with broader brush strokes, omitting some figures and leaving out non-Western traditions altogether. But when we tried to cut, it was not our authorial egos that were bruised but our history. What is sufficiently inessential to omit? Of course, we have made such decisions, thousands of them, but, nevertheless, the richness of the subject was persuasive. At the risk of massive oversimplification, we have tried for inclusiveness. And we took heart as we read our

German philosophical counterpart, Hans Joachim Störig, whose "short history" weighs in at 750 pages.

We have tried to keep our own biases out of the text—not always successfully. We have also tried to glean some sense of a global perspective on philosophy, but we have not made a false attempt to avoid taking a distinctively "Western" perspective in doing so. There is no point in apologizing for this. We have also tried not to offend, not very easy these days. In the chapters on theology and religion in particular, we have bent over backward to be sensitive and nonsectarian. As for the rest, we trust that the reader will allow us an indulgent wisecrack, a criticism or two. Philosophy, wonderful as it may be, should not be taken *too* seriously.

Special thanks to Stephen Phillips, Roger Ames, Paul Woodruff, Harald Atmanspacher, Baird Callicott, David Hall, Harold Liebowitz, Janet McCracken, Eric Ormsby, Robert McDermott, Graham Parkes, Thomas Seung, Jacqueline Trimier, Jorge Valadez, Lucius Outlaw, Peter Kraus and Robert Gooding-Williams. We are grateful for the spectacular hospitality of the Villa Serbelloni at Bellagio and for wonderful friends and facilities at the University of Auckland in New Zealand. Thanks to our many friends at the University of Texas at Austin for their encouragement and stimulation. Special thanks to Angela Blackburn, who originally signed the project, and to Cynthia Read, our longtime friend and excellent editor at Oxford. Thanks to John Corvino for preparing the index.

Austin, Texas　　　　　　　　　　　　　　　　　　　　　R. C. S.
February 1995　　　　　　　　　　　　　　　　　　　　　 K. M. H.

Contents

IV. From Modernism to Postmodernism: The Twentieth Century, 243

Biographical Chronology

Abraham	(early 2nd millennium B.C.E.)
Moses	(14th–13th century B.C.E.)
David	(ca. 1000–962 B.C.E.)
Zoroaster	(ca. 628–ca. 551 B.C.E.)
Thales	(625?—547? B.C.E.)
Anaximander	(610–ca. 545 B.C.E.)
Pythagoras	(ca. 581–ca. 507 B.C.E.)
Siddhārtha Gautama (Buddha)	(ca. 563–ca. 483 B.C.E.)
Xenophanes	(ca. 560–ca. 478 B.C.E.)
Confucius	(551–479 B.C.E.)
Anaximenes	(fl. ca. 545 B.C.E.)
Heraclitus	(ca. 540–ca. 480 B.C.E.)
Lao-tzu	(6th century B.C.E.)
Parmenides	(ca. 515–450 B.C.E.)
Anaxagoras	(ca. 500–428 B.C.E.)
Empedocles	(ca. 490–430 B.C.E.)
Protagoras	(ca. 490–420 B.C.E.)
Zeno of Elea	(ca. 490–ca. 430 B.C.E.)
Gorgias	(ca. 483–ca. 376 B.C.E.)
Mo-tzu	(ca. 470–391 B.C.E.)
Socrates	(ca. 470–399 B.C.E.)
Democritus	(ca. 460–ca. 370 B.C.E.)
Hippocrates	(ca. 460–ca. 377 B.C.E.)
Plato	(ca. 428–348 or 347 B.C.E.)

Chuang-tzu	(4th century B.C.E.)
Aristotle	(384–322 B.C.E.)
Theophrastus	(ca. 372–ca. 287 B.C.E.)
Mencius	(ca. 372–ca. 289 B.C.E.)
Pyrrho	(ca. 360–ca. 272 B.C.E.)
Epicurus	(341–270 B.C.E.)
Zeno the Stoic	(ca. 335–263 B.C.E.)
Diogenes	(d. ca. 320 B.C.E.)
Chrysippus	(280–206 B.C.E.)
Hsün-tzu	(ca. 298–ca. 230 B.C.E.)
Cicero	(106–43 B.C.E.)
Lucretius	(ca. 100 to 90–ca. 55 to 53 B.C.E.)
Jesus Christ	(ca. 6 B.C.E.–30 C.E.)
Philo	(1st–2nd century C.E.)
St. Paul	(d. between 62 and 68 C.E.)
Epictetus	(ca. 55–ca. 135 C.E.)
Marcus Aurelius	(121–180)
Galen	(129–ca. 199)
Plotinus	(204–270)
St. Augustine	(354–430)
Hypatia	(370–415)
Muhammad	(ca. 570–632)
al-Kindi	(ca. 800–866)
al-Razi	(865–ca. 925)
al-Farabi	(ca. 878–ca. 950)
Sei Shōnagon	(966 or 967–1013)
Ibn Sina, or Avicenna	(980–1037)
St. Anselm	(1033–1109)
Peter Abelard	(1079–1144?)
Ibn Rushd	(1126–1198)
Chu Hsi	(1130–1200)
Moses Maimonides (Moses ben Maimon)	(1135–1204)
Dōgen	(1200–1253)

Thomas Aquinas	(1225–1274)
Meister Eckhart	(ca. 1260–1327?)
Duns Scotus	(1266?–1308)
William of Ockham	(ca.1285–1349?)
Marsilio Ficino	(1433–1499)
Erasmus	(1466?–1536)
Niccolò Machiavelli	(1469–1527)
Wang Yang-ming	(1472–1529)
Thomas More	(1478–1535)
Johann Faust	(ca. 1480–ca. 1540)
Martin Luther	(1483–1546)
Paracelsus	(1493–1541)
John Calvin	(1509–1564)
Teresa of Avila	(1515–1582)
Michel de Montaigne	(1533–1592)
Francisco Suárez	(1548–1617)
Francis Bacon	(1561–1626)
Mulla Sadra	(ca. 1571–1640)
Thomas Hobbes	(1588–1679)
René Descartes	(1596–1650)
Blaise Pascal	(1623–1662)
Baruch Spinoza	(1632–1677)
John Locke	(1632–1704)
Sir Isaac Newton	(1643–1727)
Gottfried Wilhelm von Leibniz	(1646–1716)
Giambattista Vico	(1668–1744)
Bishop George Berkeley	(1685–1753)
Montesquieu	(1689–1755)
Voltaire	(1694–1778)
Israel ben Aliezer	(ca. 1700–1760)
Jonathan Edwards	(1703–1758)
Benjamin Franklin	(1706–1790)
David Hume	(1711–1776)
Jean-Jacques Rousseau	(1712–1778)

Adam Smith	(1723–1790)
Immanuel Kant	(1724–1804)
Moses Mendelssohn	(1729–1786)
Thomas Jefferson	(1743–1826)
Johann Herder	(1744–1803)
Jeremy Bentham	(1748–1832)
Johann Wolfgang von Goethe	(1749–1832)
Mary Wollstonecraft	(1759–1797)
Friedrich Schiller	(1759–1805)
Johann Gottlieb Fichte	(1762–1814)
Georg Wilhelm Friedrich Hegel	(1770–1831)
James Mill	(1773–1836)
Friedrich Schelling	(1775–1854)
Arthur Schopenhauer	(1788–1860)
Auguste Comte	(1798–1857)
Ralph Waldo Emerson	(1803–1882)
John Stuart Mill	(1806–1873)
Harriet Taylor	(1807–1858)
Charles Darwin	(1809–1882)
Søren Kierkegaard	(1813–1855)
Frederick Douglass	(1817–1895)
Henry David Thoreau	(1817–1862)
Karl Marx	(1818–1883)
Friedrich Engels	(1820–1895)
Fyodor Dostoyevsky	(1821–1881)
Leo Tolstoy	(1828–1910)
Charles Sanders Peirce	(1839–1914)
William James	(1842–1910)
Friedrich Nietzsche	(1844–1900)
Gottlob Frege	(1848–1925)
Josiah Royce	(1855–1916)
Sigmund Freud	(1856–1939)
Edmund Husserl	(1859–1938)
John Dewey	(1859–1952)

Henri Bergson	(1859–1941)
Alfred North Whitehead	(1861–1947)
George Santayana	(1863–1952)
Miguel de Unamuno	(1864–1936)
Max Weber	(1864–1920)
Benedetto Croce	(1866–1952)
W. E. B. Du Bois	(1868–1963)
Mahatma Gandhi	(1869–1948)
Nishida Kitarō	(1870–1945)
Bertrand Russell	(1872–1970)
Ghose Aurobindo	(1872–1950)
Max Scheler	(1874–1928)
Nikolai Berdyayev	(1874–1948)
Albert Einstein	(1879–1955)
Teilhard de Chardin	(1881–1955)
Karl Jaspers	(1883–1969)
Mao Tse-tung	(1893–1976)
Ludwig Wittgenstein	(1889–1951)
Martin Heidegger	(1889–1976)
Gilbert Ryle	(1900–1976)
Nishitani Keiji	(b. 1900)
Jean-Paul Sartre	(1905–1980)
Léopold Sédar Senghor	(b. 1906)
Maurice Merleau-Ponty	(1908–1961)
Simone de Beauvoir	(1908–1986)
A. J. Ayer	(1910–1989)
J. L. Austin	(1911–1960)
Albert Camus	(1913–1960)
Frantz Fanon	(1925–1961)
Malcolm X	(1925–1965)
Michel Foucault	(1926–1984)
Martin Luther King, Jr.	(1929–1968)

Part I

✍

The Search for World Order:
Ancient Philosophy

The "Axial Period" and the Origins of Philosophy

Somewhere between the sixth and fourth centuries B.C.E.,[1] a remarkable development was occurring in a number of far-flung places around the globe. In areas north, south, and east of the Mediterranean, in China, India, and areas in between, ingenious thinkers began to challenge and go beyond the established religious beliefs, mythologies, and folklore of their societies. Their thought became more abstract. Their questions became more probing. Their answers became more ambitious, more speculative, more outrageous. They attracted students and disciples. They formed schools, cults, and great religions. They were "philosophers," seekers of wisdom, dissatisfied with easy answers and popular prejudices. All at once, they seemed to be everywhere. Although we don't know much about the intellectual world that preceded them, nor even very much about them, we can be fairly sure that since them the world has never been quite the same.

Some appeared on the eastern shores of the Mediterranean, in Greece and Asia Minor (what is now Turkey). These small groups of curious and sometimes curmudgeonly philosophers called into question the popular explanations of nature in terms of the whims of gods and goddesses. They were sages, wise men, confident of their own intelligence, critical of popular opinion, persuasive to those who followed them. They renewed ancient questions about the ultimate origins and the nature of all things. They were no longer satisfied by familiar myths and

1

stories (as exciting as they may have been), about sex between the earth and the sky, about Venus springing up from the sea and Zeus throwing his thunderbolts. They began to reject the popular conceptions of gods and goddesses in favor of less human (less "anthropomorphic") forms of understanding. They began to challenge commonsense notions about "the way things are" and to distinguish between "true" reality and the way things merely *appear* to be.

Meanwhile, the question, "How should we live?" moved from the realm of mere prudential concern and obedience to laws and customs within a particular society to the very general question, "What is the right way to live as a human being?" The abbreviated answer to that question was to be found in the notion of *wisdom,* and those who searched for it, those who loved it, were accordingly called *philosophers* (from *philein* = love, *sophia* = wisdom). They enriched the intellectual life of Asia Minor, Greece and Italy for a good part of the sixth and fifth centuries. Perhaps the greatest of them was Socrates (470–399 B.C.E.), who was executed for his teachings and for his politics. He insisted that the truly good man could come to no harm, and he died, in part, as if to make an extreme and dramatic demonstration of that belief. With his death, philosophy became an obsession for generations—of first Greek, then Roman, then European ponderers.

In roughly the same period an unhappy young aristocrat named Siddhārtha Gautama (563–483 B.C.E.) was wandering across India in search of a way to face mortality and the considerable suffering that he saw all around him. Eventually, he found an answer. He taught peace and tranquility in a time of radical change and continuing violence. After having a mystical experience, "as if awaken from a dream," he became known as "the Buddha," the "awakened" or "enlightened" one. His ideas challenged "Hindu" thought and changed India, all of eastern Asia, and eventually, the world.

In renouncing worldly goods and pleasures, he was part of a long tradition of seekers. Drawing from ancient themes in the Hindu scriptures, the Vedas and Upanishads (*Vedanta*), the Buddha developed the view that our ordinary picture of the universe and of ourselves is a kind of illusion. For several centuries, Indian philosophers had defended a conception of absolute reality, or *Brahman,* which some insisted was utterly independent of and unknown to ordinary human experience. The Buddha was certainly familiar with that viewpoint—and so was his contemporary, Mahavira, who is usually identified as the founder of Jainism. But both ultimately rejected the notion. Like the Jains, the Buddha argued that human suffering could only be transcended by seeing through the illusions of worldly reality and the individual self and by cultivating a personality that is free from the deluded desires and passions that cause suffering. In his name, the Buddha's followers developed rich theories of knowledge, of nature, of the self and its passions, of the human body and its ailments, of the mind and its afflictions, of language and our ways of conceiving of reality. So too did the Jains and many generations and many different schools of various philosophers of Brahman.

Meanwhile, in China, a man named Confucius (Kong Fuzi) (551–479 B.C.E.), a minor statesman who became known as one of the greatest educators of all time, attracted a following because of his good advice and deep understanding of the way people worked and lived together. China was already a highly advanced political culture. But it was also in turmoil, and the central aim of Confucius's teachings was to define and help cultivate the Way *(Tao)* to a harmonious society. During this period, the Chinese world consisted of fourteen "houses" under the nominal rule of the House of Zhou, and it became clear to everyone that the only alternative to a united empire was destruction and catastrophe. Confucius provided the philosophical basis for that unity.

The foundation of Chinese culture was the family. The family and what we today call "traditional family values," however, were in serious trouble (in 500 B.C.E.!), corrupted by power politics. Confucius's philosophy, accordingly, was almost entirely concerned with social and political issues, the issues of proper rule and government, the values of family and community. He talked about harmonious relationships, about leadership and statesmanship, about getting along with and inspiring others, about self-examination and self-transformation, about cultivating personal virtue and avoiding vice.

What Confucius did not talk about, in contrast to his philosophical colleagues to the west, is equally worth mentioning. He did not talk about nature or the nature of things, except by way of analogy to human relationships. He did not particularly concern himself about the ultimate nature of nonhuman reality, and, unlike the Buddha, he did not seem to consider the possibility that what we think we know as "reality" might be mere appearance or illusion. He did not talk of gods and goddesses, or, for that matter, much about anything other than personal virtue, human relationships, and the good society. Confucius had no intention of founding a religion and no ambition to overwhelm his countrymen with abstract philosophical brilliance. He says, modestly but prophetically, "There are men who seek for the abstruse, and practice wonders. Future generations may mention them. But that is what I will not do." After his death, however, he was admired and even deified by whole societies, and Confucianism—or some variation of it— is now the philosophy of one-third of the world.

Legend has it that it was also in sixth-century B.C.E. China that a second sage (or possibly a number of sages) called Lao-tzu developed a very different vision of a Way to peace and enlightenment.[2] Unlike his contemporary Confucius, Lao-tzu did attribute great importance to nature and, correspondingly, less to human society. Confucius thought certain passions "unnatural," for example, which meant (essentially) that they should play no part in the proper life of a gentleman. Lao-tzu had much more faith in nature and much more trust in the passions of uneducated, uncultivated men.[3] For Confucius, the way to the good life is to participate in the traditions of honor and respect set down by one's ancestors. For Lao-tzu, the Way is more mysterious. It cannot be spoken. It cannot be spelled out. It cannot be explained in a recipe or guidebook or a philosophy. (From the *Tao Te Ching:* "The Tao that can be followed is not the true tao; The name that can be named is not the true name.") But that does not mean that one cannot try to find it and try to live according to it.

Between them, Confucius and Lao-tzu defined Chinese philosophy. Both emphasized *harmony* as the ideal state of both society and the individual; and each insisted on a large view of one's life. Personal character was the goal in life, but

the personal was not to be defined in isolated, individual terms. For the Confucian, the personal was the social. For the Taoist, the personal was one's accord
with nature. Whatever their disagreements about the relative importance of nature and society, the Chinese thinkers shared this common framework.

The nature–society debate (provoked by Confucius and the Taoists) became a
perennial philosophical battleground in both the East and the West. The Chinese
pondered the interrelations between the natural and the human orders; the ancient Hebrews debated what was "natural"; and the Greeks began a debate that
continues today: What is natural and what is not in "human nature"? The medieval church and Islam were wholly caught up in the debate; thousands of tribes
and traditional societies from the South Pacific and much of Africa to South and
North America engaged in similar debates and discussions. Japan, philosophically
the most eclectic of societies, combined Lao-tzu's Taoism, Confucianism, and
Buddhism and carefully separated philosophical conceptions of nature, society,
and the soul and developed an indigenous philosophy of life uniquely their own.

The dialogue between Confucianism and Taoism or, more globally, between
the emphasis on society and tradition, on the one hand, and the emphasis on
nature, on the other, is itself a product of certain social conceptions and cultural
ideas. It is built on cultural notions about our place in nature, on the very distinction between nature and culture and, consequently, on what is considered to
be "natural" and what is not. The early Hebrews insisted that it was not "natural" to cook a baby goat in its mother's milk, perhaps qualifying their carniv-
orous diet with a modicum of early sensitivity to the dignity of the animals they
ate. The ancient Hebrews and then the early Christians set an agenda for the
twentieth-century U.S. Supreme Court when they argued about which sex acts
are natural and which are not. Aristotle thought loaning money for interest (*usury*)
was "unnatural," whereas most business people today would say that making
money is the most natural thing in the world. What is natural, one would think,
is simply what is given to us by the world. In fact, "nature" will prove to be
one of the most contested and controversial concepts in philosophy.

Back in the Middle East, in Persia—what is now present-day Iran—a man
named Zarathustra of Balkh, or Zoroaster (ca. 628–ca. 551 B.C.E.), began to move
toward a comprehensive moral monotheism. We can speculate to what extent
Zarathustra was influenced by the ancient Hebrews and the early Egyptian monotheist Akhenaton, perhaps even by the Vedas, and one might well deny that he
really was a monotheist, strictly speaking, for he did believe in a number of gods.
Nevertheless, he insisted on the exclusive worship of the most powerful of the
gods, Ahura Mazda. (It is worth noting that the Old Testament does not deny
the existence of other gods either. The Hebrew Bible is just brutally clear about
the superiority of Jehovah, who insists, "Thou shalt have no other gods before
me.")

Zarathustra also defended a powerful sense of ethics as a conflict between
metaphysical forces in the world. Ahura Mazda was on the side of the Good, in
opposition to the utter darkness that was Evil; and both good and evil are born
into all of us, according to Zarathustra. He worried at length—a thousand years
before the problem would be taken up in North Africa by St. Augustine—about

what has come to be called "the problem of evil." How is it that an all-powerful God can allow so much suffering and wrongdoing in the world? Zarathustra's answer was that both good and evil were created by God. Later, in the hands of the Manicheans (who were influenced by Zarathustra but considered heretics by the Zoroastrians), this moral dualism would become a cosmic battle between Good and Evil. Later Zoroastrians would turn their religion into an effective political force, and Persia would become one of the most powerful empires in the world.

The ancient Hebrews were a philosophical force in the world but no single Hebrew philosopher (before Jesus) stands out with the stature of Confucius, the Buddha, Socrates, or Zarathustra. Nevertheless, we have a whole book, one of the most influential books in history, about them, and by them as well. The Hebrew Bible or Old Testament (in particular Genesis) is, to be sure, first of all a work of religion, but it is also one of the most important books in philosophy. It is also history, mythology and, some would say, science. The ancient Hebrews did not invent the idea of the one God, nor were they the first ancient people to have an extensive body of law or to believe themselves "chosen." Akhenaton, the Egyptian, and later Zarathustra, also worshiped a single god; the Babylonians under Hammurabi had an extensive legal code from which the Hebrews borrowed freely; and the members of almost every tribe and society seem to have thought themselves special—as we still do. The outstanding success of the ancient Hebrews lay in their skill at creating and telling their own story, a story of a hearty people with a contract with God who had undergone all kinds of tragedies and disasters, supposedly of their own making, who nevertheless endured and continued to flourish. A long, self-made history is one great advantage that accrues to a people who honor their writers and thinkers, and who live to tell the tale.

Thus, philosophy, broadly conceived, came into the world, not once but a number of times, in various places. Yet we should avoid the temptation to celebrate just these pockets of known innovation to the exclusion of all others, as if, according to the too-familiar, self-congratulatory picture, the world was generally dark and uncivilized until the appearance of a few bright lights—the "miracle" of Greece and those two or three other miracles further away. We should be cautious about accepting any people's celebration of their culture as a haven of civilization surrounded by "barbarians." The Greeks spoke of the Persians that way, and the Persians responded in kind. The Hebrews dismissed all others as "Gentiles," and they were later rejected by Christians who no longer accepted their former Jewish identity. The Chinese philosopher Yu Ying Shih spoke similarly of the tribes at the outer reaches of China, including the "barbarian" tribe of what we now call Japan, one of the most sophisticated societies in the world. So, too, the Egyptians demeaned the Nubians to the south and the Romans displayed their contempt for the people to the north. In more modern times, the English looked down on the French, and the French the Germans, the Germans the Poles, the Poles the Russians—and the Russians the Siberians and the Chinese. One culture's "barbarians" are as often as not another flourishing civilization and fruitful source of ideas.

Only our own ignorance and prejudice prevent us from entertaining the possibility that rich schools of philosophy and sophisticated argumentation once flourished throughout the world. Many societies had intricate oral cultures which used more-intimate and often more-effective methods than writing to hand knowledge from one generation to another. Face-to-face storytelling is captivating and personal. Literacy was often rare. The written word was hard to come by and "cool," distant, and impersonal by comparison. Elders in oral societies passed along their wisdom in poetry and song. When those cultures disappeared, however, their ideas—and whole civilizations, in effect—were lost to us.

Even ancient Greece was an oral culture before it became so "philosophical," that is, before philosophers began writing down their ideas and requiring their students to read them. The *Iliad* and the *Odyssey* were not the work of a single author named Homer, and it is a matter of considerable luck that these have been passed on to us in such remarkable (though certainly not original) form. Much of Spartan philosophy was sung rather than written, and it is probably due to the literacy of the Athenians—and of Plato in particular—that Athens ultimately triumphed as the philosophical center of the world. (The great Socrates, for that matter, also wrote nothing, and it is only due to Plato that we [think we] know so much about him and his ideas.)

So, too, it is highly probable that much of Africa has been inhabited by tribes with complex and sophisticated ways of thinking about the world. Indeed, listening to human beings talk and speculate from one end of the earth to the other, in rural villages as well as urban cafés, it is hard to believe that any people did not or do not "do" philosophy, in some form or another. They wonder, what are the stars? Why do things happen? What is the significance of our life? Why do we die, and what happens to us when we do? What is really good, and what is evil? There is no reason to suppose that such questions and the thoughts that follow them were limited to those cultures that eventually employed written language and thus preserved texts for future generations to read and study.

Meanwhile, the Americas, which would later be "discovered" as "the New World," were already populated both north and south, and in the warmer parts near the equator people were developing remarkable civilizations and philosophies of their own. The Inca, Maya, and Aztec civilizations had long been operating in full form by the time the Europeans landed in the early sixteenth century. Native American tribes kept little by way of historical documents, but they may have developed ecologically sensitive systems of thought thousands of years before the mythology of Manifest Destiny marked their homelands for exploitation. The "aboriginals" in Australia have lived for tens of thousands of years according to their philosophical conception of "dreamtime," the time when the world was created by ancestral beings, who taught law and ritual to their human descendants before they disappeared into nature.

Needless to say, these developments were entirely unknown (and geographically unimaginable) to the ancient Greeks and Chinese, as they would be to another hundred generations of Europeans. But why should we assume that these cultures were less thoughtful, less "philosophical," less imaginative than those that are well preserved and self-consciously philosophical? It is well and good to celebrate the known beginnings of the intellectual twists and turns which we (somewhat presumptuously) consider "our own" philosophical tradition. But it is equally important to realize that we have been celebrating but one version among many, or perhaps one part of a much larger human project with many faces.

The "Miracle" of Greece

Long before the sixth century B.C.E., there were already flourishing civilizations in the eastern Mediterranean, the Middle East, Asia, and Africa. The Greeks (or Hellenes) were a group of nomadic Indo-Europeans who came down from the north and replaced a people already settled by the Aegean Sea. (This displaced people moved and founded a great civilization on the island of Crete. We've completely lost their language, but it is hard to believe that they didn't have a profound and complex philosophy. After all, they even had indoor plumbing.) Greece was mostly destroyed about 1200 B.C.E. (soon after the siege of Troy) and it remained largely "uncivilized" until the sixth century B.C.E.

The Greeks traded throughout the Mediterranean, borrowing freely from other cultures. From the Phoenicians they acquired an alphabet, some technology, and bold new religious ideas. From Egypt they obtained the ideas that defined what we call Greek architecture, the basics of geometry, and much else besides. From Babylon (now Iraq) they partook of astronomy, mathematics, geometry, and still more religious ideas. Greece was not a "miracle" (nor was ancient India): it was a lucky accident of history and the product of many unattributed lessons from neighbors and predecessors.

As part of this process, the Egyptian god Osiris became the Greek demigod Dionysus, and a powerful mystery cult of Dionysus spread across Greece in the sixth century B.C.E. According to the "Orphic" mysteries, giants (Titans) ruled the land. They were born of Gaia, the earth, who gave birth to Zeus, king of the gods and father of Dionysus. Dionysus was killed by the Titans, and Zeus killed them in return. Humans rose from their ashes. Accordingly, human nature is part nature, part divine. This was taken to mean, among other things, that we have eternal life—not an unwelcome idea in a world in which life is often, in the phrase of Thomas Hobbes, "nasty, brutish and short." The Orphic mysteries would cast a long shadow in Greek philosophy, no matter how "rational" it would pretend to be.

Greek philosophy emerged from this mixture of mythology, mysticism, mathematics, and the disturbing perception that all was not well with the world. The first Greek philosophers found themselves both in enviable and extremely vulnerable circumstances. Their culture was rich and creative, but it was surrounded by jealous and mutually competitive enemies. It was not at all unusual for great cultures to be suddenly invaded and virtually wiped off the map of the known world. And what was not destroyed by war would often be devastated by nature. Epidemics swept through the cities like silent armies. Life was unpredictable, often tragic, and therefore both precious and lamentable. ("Better to have never been born," claimed the cheerful figure Silenus, "and next best to die soon.")

In a world in which one had so little control, the concept of *fate* naturally played an important role. But whereas the Greeks at Troy and then the Greeks of Homer's time attributed fate to the whimsical decisions of the gods and goddesses, the philosophers of the sixth century B.C.E. looked for an underlying order to things, some stable and understandable basis for existence. Religion had opened the way to the "beyond" for thousands, perhaps ten thousand years, but it was philosophy that would demand order in the beyond. In place of the whims and passions of the gods, there had to be principles. In place of the apparent uncertainties of fate, there had to be *logos*, some reason or underlying logic.

The first Greek philosophers were the Milesians of Asia Minor. Miletus was a great city founded by Athenians but later conquered by the Lydians and then the Persians. Indeed, it was Persian culture in particular that gave the Milesians access to ideas about the unity of the cosmos, the beauty of mathematics, and certain religious ideas. Among these were the doctrines of Zoroastrianism: monotheism, the immortality of the soul, and the dichotomy of Good and Evil. The early Greek philosophers, as we shall see, put great stock in the importance of a unified theory of the cosmos *(cosmology)* and in the special status of mathematics as the ideal kind of knowledge. They also sought basic explanatory theories, such as the fundamental idea that the world is composed of ordered "oppositions" between competing elements and properties (hot and cold, wet and dry). Ultimate reality could be comprehended in terms of certain basic principles, and human life and its fate could and should be lived and understood in those terms.

The dramatic turnabout marked by the sixth-century thinkers probably seems more abrupt in retrospect than it actually was. Philosophy, like virtually every human endeavor, does not pop up from nowhere, and neither do philosophers. The cultures of the eastern Mediterranean, India, and China were already thriving civilizations; they were in the midst of unsettling changes; and this combination of tradition and change was the soil that sprouted philosophical ideas that had to be taken seriously. Hinduism was thousands of years old, and it was rich not only with fabulous stories and much folk wisdom but it also possessed of a legacy of sages and speculation and deep insights into the ways of the world. (The word "Hindu" refers not to a religion but to a place, "east of the Indus River.") The Hindu Vedas date back to 1400 B.C.E., and the Upanishads, which follow upon and comment on the Vedas (and are called "Vedanta," or commentary) date from 800 B.C.E. Free-thinking arguments and a penchant for mysticism were already prevalent in India when the Buddha emerged to challenge (some of) those ideas. It seems not at all unlikely that these exotic ideas also traveled to the busy ports of Asia Minor and Athens.

By the sixth century, the mythology of Greece was already becoming a bit tired and increasingly problematic. The stories of the gods and goddesses and their various victims and escorts were no longer taken all that seriously or literally. In that gap between the mundane and the fantastic the idea of "the Truth" started to arise. Suppose that we simply "made up" our gods and goddesses, complained Xenophanes (ca. 560–ca. 478 B.C.E.). "If oxen and horses and lions had hands and could draw as man does, horses would draw the gods shaped as horses and oxen like oxen, each making the bodies of the gods like their own."

In any case, Xenophanes went on, why should we worship beings who have such notoriously bad manners, such flabby morals, and such childish emotions? Xenophanes thus recommended, about the same time that the first books of the Hebrew Bible (or Old Testament) were being assembled, the belief in "one god, greatest among gods and men, in no way like mortals in body or in mind."

We do not know how far these doubts extended through Greek society, but it is very clear that they were in the air. Monotheism was certainly known through the Hebrews, for there was considerable contact between the Hebrews and the Greeks. Monotheism must have appealed to the Greek sense of unity, despite their plurality of deities. Judaism, which can be traced back almost to the third millennium B.C.E. (Abraham lived around 2000 B.C.E.), was rich in philosophy and philosophical disputation, particularly in the works of the prophets (ninth–eighth centuries B.C.E.) and the extensive writings and laws that became the Talmud and the Mishnah. King Solomon (1000 B.C.E.), despite a degenerate reign, nevertheless dropped pearls of wisdom for which he would long be remembered. In 750 B.C.E., Israel was enjoying one of its rare golden ages (which ended with the invasion of the Assyrians in 721 B.C.E.). This era produced new laws and new prophets, who denounced the poverty they saw in the midst of affluence. Philosophical argument became so basic to the life of the ancient Hebrews that there was no need to call it "philosophy." To be sure, the early Hebrew philosophers were not much interested in theology, in metaphysics, or in the epistemology of belief, compared to later centuries of Christian thought. Like Confucius, at the other end of an enormous continent, they were more interested in questions about how to live, questions about justice and the good society. Above all, they asked an overwhelming question: How are we to please our all-powerful, not always predictable God?

Also in the vicinity of Greece, the Babylonians under Hammurabi (eighteenth century B.C.E.) had long ago developed the first known codes of law and the first system of jurisprudence. The Hebrew Decalogue (Ten Commandments) was already well known and probably part of a larger canon of law. To the north, there was a Spartan constitution under Lycurgus and a thriving, progressive civilization, typically demeaned, of course, by the then less progressive Athenians. And we have already noted the importance of the great civilizations to the south of the Mediterranean, especially in Egypt and possibly in Nubia (present-day Ethiopia) and the Sudan and even further along the Nile. These cultures had sophisticated systems of astronomy, advanced mathematics, complex and thoughtful views of the nature of the soul, and an obsession with the question of life after death. Many of the leading ideas of Greek philosophy, including the all-important interest in geometry and the concept of the soul, were imported from Egypt. Indeed, it might be more enlightening to view the "miracle" in Greece not as a remarkable beginning but as a culmination, the climax of a long story the beginnings and middle of which we no longer recognize.

The culmination of this ancient story, however, and its central hero, is the figure of Socrates. He was not the first philosopher, by any means. Nearly two centuries and several generations of profound and persuasive philosophers preceded him in Greece. Nor was he the only philosopher to argue so vigorously, to disturb the platitudes of the day, to etch a vivid representation of "the philosopher" into the consciousness of the West. But, whatever his merits and virtues, and they were many, he owes his unique place in Western thinking to a fate both happy and tragic. In 399 B.C.E., Socrates was brought to trial, charged with "corrupting the minds" of his students, and famously condemned and executed. It was, no doubt, one of democratic Athens's most trying and embarrassing moments. But it established Socrates not only as "the philosopher" but as a martyr—a martyr for the truth, a martyr for his calling. "I would rather die than give up philosophy," he announced to the jury, virtually guaranteeing his own execution. Socrates set the standards for what philosophy should be, and they were very high standards indeed.

It was Socrates' happy fate, however, to be blessed with a student who was one of the most brilliant writers in the history of the species. Plato was an excellent student, an ardent admirer, a keen listener, a witty journalist, a skilled propagandist, an accomplished dramatist, and a philosophical genius in his own right. Plato first recorded, then elaborated, then embellished and transformed Socrates' many conversations, beginning with the circumstances of his trial. The resulting dialogues are the first full body of work we have in philosophy, and they are such astounding documents that it has been memorably noted that all of philosophy is nothing but a footnote to Plato. But Plato remains in the background. Socrates is the hero of the dialogues. If it were not for Plato, of course, Socrates would be little but a footnote in the archives of Greek history, for he himself published nothing. But if it were not for Socrates, we probably would have no Plato, and without Plato no Aristotle, through whom we know most of what we know about the philosophers who preceded Socrates (the "pre-Socratics"). The "miracle" of Greek philosophy would never have happened, as far as we would know.

Socrates, like his near contemporaries Confucius and the Buddha, was interested almost entirely in the concept of the good life—the life of virtue, a life in civilized society, the happy life. He had very different ideas than they did, and very different ideas than many of his Greek contemporaries and predecessors. Indeed, the most prominent idea associated with Socrates is the idea of Socrates himself as the embodiment of wisdom. This presents us with a certain problem, one which divides philosophers to this day.

Socrates dedicated his life to thinking about, teaching, and exemplifying virtue. He seems to have been not at all interested in the great cosmological questions of the day, only minimally interested in mathematics and geometry as subjects in their own right, and only perfunctorily interested in or respectful to the established religion of Athens (which was one of the other charges against him). But Plato, certainly, and the several generations of philosophers preceding him, were keenly interested in such matters, so the challenge in trying to paint a brief but not wholly inaccurate portrait of ancient Greek philosophy is to explain this apparent discontinuity, a serious disagreement concerning the very notion of "philosophy" itself. Is philosophy, as exemplified by Socrates, a very personal, very social and sociable, very practical concern about living well and teaching others (or, rather, helping them) to do so as well? Or is it a protoscientific, very abstract, and often abstruse attempt to understand the ultimate nature of the universe, an effort that seemed to be of little interest to Socrates, Confucius, and the Buddha?

The two tasks are not necessarily opposed or incompatible, of course, and most of the great philosophers, notably Plato and Aristotle, try to combine the two. But a tension exists between these two stances that has not yet been resolved. Is philosophy an impersonal search for the truth, or is it still in fact tied to the more ancient schools of the sages, wise men (and sometimes women) who *themselves* exemplify wisdom? Is the lionization of Socrates essential to the history of philosophy, and is philosophy itself the history of heroes, of individuals who, through their work, have come to define philosophy (Buddha, Confucius, Socrates, Plato, Aristotle, Jesus, St. Augustine, Ibn Rushd, Descartes, David Hume, Immanuel Kant, Gandhi, and so on)? Or is it the history of ideas, in their development or disclosure, a history in which the actual existence of individual figures is at most an interesting contingency? When we now survey the history of Greek philosophy, for example, to what extent do we or should we make Socrates the centerpiece of our study? To what extent is he merely a historical celebrity who might deserve some credit for the remarkable success of philosophy but is nevertheless ultimately a distraction from the real history of the subject? In the pages that follow, we will try to be as even-handed as possible about these matters.

Philosophy, Myth, Religion, and Science

In introducing philosophy, particularly the early philosophy of ancient Greece, it is now standard to say that philosophy began when it separated from mythology—the folk religion of Greek popular culture. That religion included the pantheon of Olympian gods and goddesses (such as Zeus, Hera, Apollo, and Aphrodite) as well as the mythological heroes and quasi-history of the many Greek legends. Note that we typically refer only to *other* people's beliefs as "mythology." But the Greeks had some sense of the distinction between philosophy and myth, and they applied it to themselves.

There were many levels of "belief" in sophisticated Greek society, which ranged from literal acceptance of mythical accounts to rather extravagant, poetic, allegorical interpretations. A poetic sensibility was considered essential to wisdom, which was not to be confused with mundane truths. Belief in the existence of gods and goddesses may have been more-or-less literal. (One of the charges that led to Socrates' execution was that he did not believe "in the gods of the city.") The historical fables of Hercules, and Jason and the Argonauts and the like, however, were regarded by most as worthy of a measure of playful skepticism. Oedipus was probably a real person, and there is little doubt that the characters (at least the human characters) of the *Odyssey* and the *Iliad* were real as well.

What did the Greeks make of the myths that reported intrigues between the Olympians and mere mortals? Allegedly, women were variously courted and raped by Zeus, who assumed the form of a swan, a bull, a cloud, and even the

exact form of one woman's own husband (a fascinating philosophical perplexity
in its own right. Was she thereby unfaithful to her husband?). Mythic characters
were turned into trees or flowers, and some were victims of divine vindictive-
ness—for example, Prometheus (who had his liver chewed daily by a vulture as
a punishment for giving fire to the human race) and Sisyphus (who had to spend
all eternity pushing a rock up a mountain, whence it would roll back down of
its own weight). Educated Greeks appear to have considered these to be morality
(or immorality) tales, not theological doctrines. This should make us wonder just
what less educated people really believed. Were the first philosophers combating
superstition (the popular view of philosophers in the Enlightenment, who saw
themselves repeating the process), or were they, rather, participating in a more
common enterprise? Perhaps the folk of ancient Greece simply enjoyed the play
of these ideas and images, and the philosophers who followed them just expressed
this skeptical view more explicitly.

In order to understand the birth of Western philosophy it is important to be
very careful regarding this much-abused distinction between philosophy and
myth, a distinction which the philosophers of the time promoted to underscore
their own importance and originality. It is said as a matter of course that the
sophisticated philosophy of Greece emerged out of and replaced popular ("vulgar") myth. It is, we are told, the difference between unthinking myth and
thoughtful philosophy that marks the end of one era and the beginning of another, the first emphasizing gods and goddesses, the second defending "naturalistic" explanation. Myth involves anthropomorphism, the projection of human
attributes onto (what we consider) lifeless natural forces. Thus, the ancient Egyptians and most of the other eastern Mediterranean cultures typically explained
the origins and the nature of the universe in terms of the behavior of humanlike
beings. The ancient Greeks explained origins and the nature of the universe in
terms of the actions and emotions of very human gods and goddesses. But beginning with Thales (625?–547? B.C.E.) and the other pre-Socratic Greek philosophers, the commonplace story goes, the explanations became more scientific,
more "naturalistic," more materialistic. These early Greek thinkers celebrated a
hard-headed rationality and an emphasis on material causes rather than speculative poetry and the behavior of divinities behind the scenes.

This simplified and self-congratulatory view, however, does not hold up to
scrutiny. The first Greek philosophers were steeped in mythology as well as the
new rationality inspired by geometry, and some of the greatest breakthroughs in
philosophy—made by Pythagoras, Parmenides, and Plato, for example—involved
the flat rejection of materialist explanations of the world. They often wrote in
riddles and allegories, and they more often sounded like mystic poets than contemporary science professors. The idea that philosophy, like science, provides
literal truths has always been open to doubt. Modern philosophers (like Kant
and Hegel) are fluent in metaphor and analogy, too. Of course, whether science
itself rests on metaphor, rather than literal description, is a theme that would
take us far beyond the confines of this history.

To be sure, the origins of philosophy in Greece were also the origins of
Western science, but philosophy is not science (at least not exclusively), and

mythology—the endowing of the cosmos with personality as well as rational explicability—is hardly without its charms, even for philosophers. Not surprisingly, poetic and mythological thinking continues in philosophy to this day.

The same point applies to other cultures, especially to those that did not and perhaps do not take science as seriously as we do. China has a technological tradition that goes back further than the Western tradition. (The Chinese invented gunpowder, noodles, and eyeglasses, for example, centuries before the West.) But China has always taken a pragmatic, practical view of science, and Confucian philosophy, in particular, esteems scientific theory far less than social harmony. The remarkable history of technology in Asia has much less to do with the frequently idealized "search for truth" than with a healthy social pragmatism. For all of its emphasis on nature, Taoism has virtually nothing to do with science, and Buddhism sees not only science but the very idea of progress in the knowledge of nature as just another of humanity's great illusions.

In religious philosophy, especially, the distinction between mythological deities and real flesh-and-blood individuals has often been made more stark than the ambiguities of divinity require. Greek and Hindu deities alike were ambiguously human and super- or inhuman. They often changed from one to the other. Confucius and the Buddha, like Moses, Jesus, and Muhammad, were certainly real people. (Lao-tzu, if not a single person, was—like Homer—a small number of real people.) Even in the singular case of Jesus as God incarnate, the apparent paradox of Jesus as man and Christ as God has caused intellectual ulcers throughout most of the history of Christian theology.

Ambiguity and analogy are the essence of Chinese philosophy. At the same time, the "deities" of Confucianism and Buddhism are individual human beings, not God incarnate like Christ, and not gods who once descended in human form to teach us noble truths. So, to say that these gods are anthropomorphic is quite obviously beside the point. Although ancient China certainly did have its myths, containing such colorful creatures as dragons, in Confucianism and Buddhism the very basis of the distinction between philosophy and mythology simply does not apply. The story of the Buddha, like the story of Jesus, is much more significant as symbolism than as history.

It is a far more complex story in early India. Hinduism is populated with fantastic creatures and divinities at least as imaginative as anything to be found in Greek mythology. A central trinity of gods is fundamental to classical Hindu mythology. These are Brahma (the creator god), Vishnu (the god who maintains the universe), and Shiva (the god of destruction). But these are, we are told, the faces of one God, one reality rather than many. Indeed, the Hindu pantheon is far larger and more complex than anything to be found in Greece, on the one hand, but far more explicitly unified, on the other. It is the polymorphism of the gods, rather than their individual identities, that is most striking to the Western reader.

The familiar depiction of Shiva with six or more arms is only the beginning of a bewildering complexity: the gods routinely take on various forms and manifestations, adopt different personae, serve very different functions, and have, accordingly, any number of different names. Shiva's consort Parvati, for example, is also the maternal Amba, the destructive Kali, and Shakti, who is understood to be Shiva's source of power. Indian myths also vary among cities and subcultures, and Indian folklore and literature consist of many diverse stories, much like the earliest versions of the Greek myths, which Hesiod, in particular, tried (unsuccessfully) to unify and synthesize. In Hinduism, the attempt is virtually unthinkable, as many an expert in mythology will attest.

The long history of ancient India (like the considerably shorter history of ancient Greece) is especially rich in quasi-historical heroes who are also philosophical exemplars. Of particular note is the hero Arjuna in the *Bhagavad-Gita* (Song of the Lord), a religious text attached to the epic *Mahabharata* (The Great Epic of the Bharata Dynasty). Arjuna pauses before the beginning of a battle. He is unwilling to fight the hostile force that opposes his own, for the enemy army consists of his own kinsmen. Although it is his own family, Krishna, the Supreme God (posing as Arjuna's charioteer), tells Arjuna that it is his duty to go to battle, and that as a duty, this should be performed selflessly, with one's heart fixed on God.

Such a moral dilemma may seem incomprehensibly horrifying to us—that is, the very idea that there might be circumstances in which it would be one's duty to kill one's own family. But similar horrors can be found in the Hebrew Bible, in Greek mythology and in every civil war. Is the point of such horror stories merely to entertain us (in the manner of a Godzilla film)? Or are these profound moral tales that engage us in deep philosophical quandaries that go right to the heart of human morals and experience? Gandhi interpreted Arjuna's crisis as the battle between good and evil in each one of us. When Krishna reveals his divinity to Arjuna, our ordinary world is spun around. The myths are in fact the fodder of philosophy, the fuel of speculative thinking that does not necessarily appear in literal form.

Along with the flamboyant tale of the *Bhagavad-Gita* comes a deep, thoughtful commentary, philosophical in every sense, but expressing little interest in (the early Western fascination with) literal, naturalistic explanations. However, as we shall see, the early Greek philosophers were often not very literal minded themselves, and while they rejected anthropomorphism in its cruder and literally incredible forms, they nonetheless held onto the intentional ambiguities and the animated vision of the world portrayed by the old mythologies.

Most evident and appealing in Hindu mythology is its imaginative playfulness and relative lack of inhibition in comparison to Western mythology. (Zeus might turn into a bull, but this is merely a temporary ploy. He nevertheless remains Zeus.) According to one of the favorite Hindu myths, for example, Shiva goes to war when his son Ganesh is quite young. He returns many years later and discovers a handsome young man in the company of his wife. Taking the young man to be a rival, Shiva beheads him, only to discover that he has beheaded his own son. Horrified, he vows to restore his son to life by giving him the head of the next creature he sees, which turns out to be an elephant.

Are such stories to be taken literally? Are they merely fanciful? Or is it more likely that they present profound insights in playful form, interpretations of reality in more palatable but less predigested form than the protoscience of early Western philosophy? In fact, we suggest, the bewildering imaginative variation of Indian mythology expresses the very same ideas that will dominate Indian philosophy throughout most of its history. In even the most playful Hindu tales, we recognize the enduring themes of renewal and continuity of life. Above all, however, there is the decisive theme of "the oneness of the universe," however many manifestations or appearances it may take on. In philosophy, this one absolute reality will take on the name "Brahman." But in early mythology, the plurality of gods who are in fact manifestations of one god expresses much the same theme. From mythology to philosophy is not a grand leap in logic so much as a shift to a less picturesque language.

That difference, however, should not incline us away from myth and toward philosophy. Both have their merits. Myth involves a narrative—a story—and while the characters may be fanciful, it is the story itself that is of ultimate importance, and that story becomes especially important when we envision ourselves as the characters. Philosophy is more concerned with systematic theory than story; but when philosophy leaves out the historical narrative—when it seems to leave us out of the picture altogether—the result is too often a bare set of concepts devoid of context, falsely construed as eternal truths. A mythological narrative can embrace contradictions and even absurdities, but these may add charm and capture the real confusions of the world rather than subtract credibility and consistency. (The American Walt Whitman was not the only sage who celebrated his contradictions rather than lament or try to "resolve" them.) A philosophy, by contrast, incorporates contradictions and incoherence only at its considerable peril, and most philosophers of every culture are anxious to avoid them, even when (like the German philosophers Hegel and Nietzsche and some great philosophers of the Zen tradition) they see contradiction and incoherence as an essential part of both life and philosophy.

Perhaps we should pay attention to Nietzsche when he warns us to beware of the unrecognized myths of modern philosophy, "cause," "substance," "free will," "morality," and, of course, "God." Philosophy has its own mythic assumptions, no less so because they are impersonal. This does not mean that we are obliged to give up these notions, but what it does mean is that we should not so readily accept them literally while consigning other people's concepts to the realm of mythology. One might continue to insist that myth leads to edification and philosophy to understanding, but the best myths, like the best philosophy, surely do both.

Similarly, one should carefully consider the relationship between religion and philosophy. Some of the ancient Greeks cautiously separated the two, but for most of the past two thousand years Western philosophy has been inseparable from the Judeo-Christian tradition, even in the case of those philosophers who spend their lives attacking that tradition. It is only in the past two hundred years that many American and some European philosophers have presupposed a separation, and in many other cultures, the identity of religion and philosophy remains entirely intact. In many societies, including most tribal cultures, the religion defines the philosophy. In others, the philosophy defines the religion, notably in Confucianism and Buddhism, which are both nontheistic religions—religions without a god. One might try to distinguish religion and philosophy according to the fuzzy demarcation between myth and philosophy or via the dismissive distinction between critical thought and mere "dogma," but this often means misunderstanding the dynamic thoughtfulness of religion. To be sure, philosophy can play a considerable role both within and beyond the bounds of religion, but it is a mistake to conclude that religion, theology, and religious philosophy (as opposed to the more secular and critical "philosophy of religion") lie outside the bounds of philosophy.

One should also carefully consider the relation between science and philosophy, taking care not to conclude too hastily—while trying to distinguish philosophy from religion—that if philosophy is not religion then it must be science or, at least, scientific. There is much to think about in life—one's personal and social identity, our relationships with others, our political responsibilities and concerns, the beauty or delightful intricacy of works of art, even the wonders of nature as such—which need be neither science nor religion. Indeed, the modern idea that philosophy ought to be scientific is only a few hundred years old and mainly a product of the European Enlightenment. This idea has also been contested since its inception, and most other cultures are not particularly concerned with it—which is emphatically not to say that they are unenlightened. Science, to be sure, has a special claim to objectivity. But when science and the scientific method(s) are taken to *define* the notion of objectivity, as they often are, this assumption deserves philosophical scrutiny. Certainly, the impersonality and detachment required in science need not be recommended for philosophy, and accordingly many philosophers (of both East and West) have properly stressed that philosophy is an art, a skill, a discipline, or a practice distinct from, or at least more pervasive than, science.

Even philosophers who virtually worship science recognize its limitations. Thus Immanuel Kant, one of the greatest modern philosophers and an enthusiast of Newton's physics, declared that two things filled him with "awe"—"the starry skies above and the moral law within." Kant also recognized the beauty of art, the piety of religion, the marvels of mathematics, the company of his neighbors and a good glass of wine, as well as the value of science. Newton himself did not by any means confine his philosophy to "Nature." He spent the last twenty years of his life developing a theology to complement and embrace his physics. Friedrich Nietzsche, often an enthusiast of (nineteenth-century) science, recognized that scientific "truth" described only a narrow sliver of our experience, and he considered what he called "aesthetic truth" to be more important and relevant to philosophy.

Nevertheless, there is something salutary and essential in the link between philosophy and science, something more than their mutual emphasis on objectivity and rationality and their shared pursuit of the truth. But for many years—including much of the time when some philosophers were arguing that philosophy should be considered either a part of science or a janitorial service, mopping up the loose ends of science—some of those philosophers were overly adamant that philosophical problems were distinct from science. On this view, philosophical problems did not require any evidence from experience or need the latest in scientific research—or indeed, any evidence or research at all. In philosophical jargon, these problems could be and could only be solved a priori—that is, independently of any experience or experiment, perhaps by appeal to logic and language, perhaps by appeal to a special sort of intuition.

The result was, and in some quarters still is, a fatal impoverishment of philosophy. Questions not prone to solution "through reason alone," through pure, unaided thinking, were dismissed as "merely empirical" or as "psychology, not philosophy." Along these lines, some recent Anglo-American philosophers have argued at great length about the relation between the mind and the body, for example, without bothering to learn anything at all about the brain, which would seem to have some real relevance to the issue. Some philosophers debate the essential nature of science and nature without ever talking to a physicist, and many still argue at great length about human nature without bothering to read more than a few lines of Freud. Happily, this is changing.

The lesson to be learned is that philosophy is continuous with science. It is not, as many philosophers have suggested, science's mother, nor is it merely a conceptual janitor, cleaning up messy terms and concepts once the scientists have done their thing. In the pursuit of any number of topics, there is no strict dividing line between philosophy and other disciplines. This is especially true in all of those fields called "The Philosophy of _____" (whether of science, social science, art, or religion). Nor can one sharply separate the experiential and the knowledgeable from the a priori, the insider from the outsider. Of course, this cooperation and respect needs to go on in both directions. In 1932, Einstein employed a maternal analogy but insisted, "Philosophy is like the mother who gave birth to and endowed all the other sciences. Therefore, one should not scorn her in her nakedness and poverty, but should hope, rather, that part of the Don Quixote ideal will live on in her children so that they do not sink into philistinism."

Philosophy is continuous with science as it is continuous with mythology and religion, although this does not mean that these are all the same. It is with these cautious distinctions between philosophy, mythology, religion, and science in mind that we can now approach the beginnings of philosophy. In the West, philosophy was nurtured in the bosom of cosmology or, more properly, of *cosmogony*, the study of how the world came to be as it is.

Meaning and Creation: Cosmogony and the Origins of Philosophy

As in Egypt and the Fertile Crescent, the Greeks' dependence on agriculture led them to study geography and meteorology, to speculate about what would entice the earth goddess, Gaia, to yield up her fertility. On the seas, astronomy provided a powerful new tool for navigation. Primitive wonder about the complexity of the heavens eventually led to the careful study of astronomy, to the practical, if not always dependable, predictions of astrology, to the imaginative products of mythology and religion, to the population of the heavens with divinities. Such speculations led quite naturally to questions of cosmogony: Where did all of this come from? And how did the world come to be as it is?

Despite the centrality of such questions to science, it would be a mistake to think that these were first of all scientific or protoscientific questions. The first cosmogonists sought meaning and edification as well as explanation. They asked of whatever they encountered: What is it for? What is its purpose, and what does this forebode? For the Greeks, and for many of the peoples of the ancient world, the quest for cosmic explanation took the same form as a quest for the explanation of human behavior, a question about *agency*. *Who* did this, and *why* did he do it? A "cause" is first of all an *intention*, some primordial project that needs to be comprehended.

The Greeks were not so much curious as they were frightened and desperate. They wanted to feel secure and comfortable in a world they did not understand. They wanted some explanation, some consolation for the wounds and illnesses, the tragedies and deprivations they suffered, and, ultimately, for death. The phenomenon of death has struck people as mysterious and disturbing from very early times. The prehistoric Neanderthals buried their dead and made primitive icons for the dead a hundred thousand years before the philosophers of the Mediterranean started speculating about the immortality of the soul. It is in that dreadful sense of wonder that philosophy is born. We may have developed our enormous brains to inform our remarkable thumbs and allow us our upright posture, as physical anthropologists tell us, but we use our brains to cope with questions that are not entirely an obvious boon or an evolutionary advantage. We use those very brains to fill the world with wonder.

It is as important as it is impossible for us to try to imagine what it must have been like for those who first asked such questions. Children now ask their parents, who all too often give them some digestible nonsense, send them to the library, or send them out to play or to clean up their rooms. But when human beings first asked them, there was no one there to answer. There were no books and only a few self-appointed priests or wise men. What would the first philosophers and their contemporaries even make of the question, "Where did everything come from?" The first answer, no doubt, was one form or another of "It's just there, that's all" or "It's always been there." But in time the answers became more imaginative and the questions were taken more seriously. Early philosophers (or pre-philosophers, if you insist) suggested that the universe was born of two primordial beings, who mated and laid a cosmic egg. Others suggested that these primordial beings were gods, working out their rather dysfunctional family relations. Other cultures similarly suggested violent family relations as the archetype for creation.

In Greek cosmogony, the world was envisioned as a flat, round disk, covered by a bowl, which we see as the heavens. At the bottom, somewhat like a tree trunk, the world had its roots in Hades, "the underworld," and Tartaros, Hades' lowest level. Surrounding the earth was a "mighty river," Oceanos, an image that was probably borrowed from Egypt and Mesopotamia. Oceanos was said to be the source of all things, including the gods, both by Homer, in the *Iliad*, and by Thales, often described as the first philosopher. The Greeks also speculated about the significance of night or darkness, personified by Homer as terrifying, even to Zeus.

According to the poet Hesiod, first of all there was *Chaos*, which did not mean "utter confusion" (as it usually does today) but rather formlessness, or strictly speaking, a gap, perhaps between the sky and the earth. (Aristotle suggests that "chaos" means space; the Stoics took it to be the atmosphere.) With Chaos came Gaia, the earth, and *eros*, or love (envisioned as rain or heavenly semen). Out of Chaos came night, and from night came the *ether* (the fiery upper atmosphere) and the day. From the earth came the sky, Ouranos, and from their union came Oceanos, the sea.

The relationship of sky and earth is the key to the cosmogonical story, separating and conjoining. Hesiod writes, "Great Ouranos came bringing night with him, and over Gaia, desiring love, he stretched himself and spread all over her." Aeschylus's description is similar: "Holy sky passionately longs to penetrate the earth, and desire takes hold of earth to achieve this union. Rain from her bedfellow sky falls and impregnates earth."[4] Sex and mayhem abound in these early accounts of the origin of the universe. After their union, the sky and earth separated. All of their children were hated by their father, who tended to murder them. One of the sons, with a "jagged-toothed sickle," castrated his father, and from the "severed parts," Aphrodite was born. Such stories are frequently cited by Homer (ninth century B.C.E.) and the poet Hesiod (eighth century B.C.E.), who tried to synthesize them and render the various versions consistent in his *Theogony*.

In Egyptian myth, the god Set mutilated his father, Osiris; his widow, Isis, rejoined the pieces and thereby restored him to life. In the Hindu Rg Veda, the creator god, Brahma, creates a second being, who is his daughter. As "Heaven" and "Earth," they have incestuous sex and spawn other beings.[5] So, too, in early tales from the South Pacific, Maori legend has it that Papa (the earth) was given female form and fertilized by her son Tane. The Zuni Indians of New Mexico tell of Awonawilona, the Maker of All, who conceived of himself in the infinite darkness of space, made himself real, and impregnated the waters to give birth to Awitelin Tsita, the Earth Mother. Awonawilona and Awitelin Tsita together conceived all of the beings of the earth.

None of these early cosmogonies suggests that the world emerges from nothing. The world is created by some primordial Creator, whose first act is often the creation (that is, the manifestation) of himself. Or, the first act is a division of a formless prior unity or chaos. In Maori legend, the first step in creation is the separation of the earth (Papa) and the sky (Rangi). In the Hindu Upanishads, the world before creation is "just water," but creation organizes already-existing energies to give form to the breath of life. Breath gives movement to the water, from which everything else emerged.

Similarly, according to Genesis, which sees the world as the work of a single eternal God, creation began when God separated the day from the night and the heaven from the earth. (This basic plot line seems to have worked its way into early Greek cosmogony as well. The image of the earth as dark boundless water, then the separation of the waters into the waters of the sky and of the earth, was defended by Thales.) The theory of the single creator had the great advantage of unity, without the need for primordial sex and warfare. But the Genesis story of creation, some might argue, thereby lost a good deal of the excitement evident in other creation accounts. (Perhaps that is why physicists today find the image of the Big Bang theory of the universe so appealing. It maintains the intense drama without yielding to anthropomorphic familial violence.)

It is worth noting that some similar concepts appeared in China, but with significantly different meanings. *Cosmos* is the Greek word for unity, while in Chinese the comparable character (referring to the universe), means "ten thousand things." So, too, whereas *chaos* in Greek meant formlessness, in Chinese the comparable term *(hun-tun)* meant "the sum of the orders of the ten thousand things." Chaos implies innocent spontaneity and original harmony, not disorder. In Greek cosmogony the world originates from the victory of Cosmos (form) over Chaos (formlessness). In China Chaos might also be defeated, but this loss would be seen as a crisis. The Taoist Chuang-tzu tells the story of Chaos dying when human beings tried to give him human senses. "The rulers of the Northern and Southern oceans, Shu and Hu, tried to treat Chaos to the seven senses, digging a different hole in him every day, until he died."

The question of cosmogony or past origins is also tied to the question of the future. In the Judeo-Christian tradition there is a good deal of concern and debate about the end, rather than simply the beginning, of the world. In Christianity, the end of the world is the single most important event in history. In Hindu cosmology, by contrast, the world recurrently comes to an end and is perpetually recreated. Even the gods die at times, but they, like everything else, are also reborn. The specific form of rebirth depends on one's *karma*, tendencies established in previous lives. So, too, the cosmos itself: After each destruction, the cosmos reappears, emerging from the latent energies remaining from earlier creations. Such abstract cosmological theses can have direct and serious social consequences. Hindu mythology thus treats one's social circumstances (health, illness, wealth, and poverty) not as a matter of luck but as determined directly by the nature of reality itself. Accordingly, one's fulfillment of *dharma*, the duties required by each particular social role, is considered to be essential to the maintenance of order in the universe.

It is marvelous to imagine how—between these early myths of Creation and the supposedly literal concepts of modern science—the first philosophers came to construct the most basic concepts of our understanding. Our understanding of *time*, for instance, is the product of a long development of conceptual sophistication. Of course, many conscious creatures have some sense of the passage of time. Every human society has some way of marking and measuring time, whether simply the days and nights or the seasons or years. Many societies have a name for Time, or at least for the time-keeper (for example *Chronos* in Greek mythology). But none of these is quite the same as having a concept of time. Commentators on early philosophy sometimes refer to such pre-philosophical notions of time as "merely poetic" or as a failure of objectivity, and note that the notion of Time as a subject for analysis does not appear until Aristotle. It is sometimes suggested that not only the question

"What is time?" but the very concept of time as a linear phenomenon to be understood in terms of individual experience does not come into being until St. Augustine in the fourth century C.E.

And yet, we should be impressed by the remarkably varied and imaginative conceptions of time that we find in virtually all societies. In ancient America, for example, time was conceived of as a three-part phenomenon of historical, divine, and mystical time. The aboriginal Australians refer to the "dreamtime," before the creation of human beings. The ancient Middle Eastern conception of circular time, or "eternal recurrence," was picked up by the early Greeks and much later celebrated by the German philosopher Nietzsche. The ancient Hindus had a remarkable sense of time as not only recurrent (in four distinct stages) but as fantastically extended. A cycle of time, called a Great Yuga, is 4.32 million years, a thousand of which equal one day for Brahman, the Absolute reality. After one hundred Brahman years (some 300 trillion years), a new Brahma (the God) appears and a new cycle begins. Given the scope of such calculations, one need not wonder why human life seems so pitifully insignificant to those committed to this special arithmetic of time. In early Christianity, by contrast, time has a definitive end as well as a beginning, even if God, at least, is eternal, and the total time from beginning to end, according to one standard calculation, would be less than six thousand years. When as in Augustine the focus moves to the individual soul, this, perhaps, might be time enough.

Although it is not properly speaking a cosmological or cosmogonical notion, it would probably be good to say something here (in a preliminary way) about the *soul* (or *psyche*). The soul, needless to say, will be one of the recurring themes throughout the history of philosophy. In early Greek philosophy the soul is considered just another thing, and a pretty insubstantial thing at that. It has no moral significance. Indeed, it is rather pathetic, a source of life only when it is embodied. Otherwise, it is like a shadow, insubstantial, a mere "breath." A similar view led the ancient Egyptians, in particular, to insist that a soul could enter the afterlife only if the body were preserved. They took great pains to ensure bodily preservation of the dead (and to accompany the body with all of its accoutrements, luxuries, and servants).

The soul is a rather "thin" concept in the thought of many ancient cultures. This would also suggest a reason why the early Christians took the resurrection of the body to be essential. The ancient Hebrews, by contrast, talked very little of the abstract soul as such, more or less restricting their concern to the concrete character of the individual human being. So, too, the Chinese spoke of the "soul" of a person only with his or her personal character and social identity in mind, with no abstract metaphysical remainder. For the Buddhists (and many Hindus), either the soul was one with the rest of the universe or it was an illusion to be overcome. The Jains, by contrast, did believe in the individual soul—and they believed even insects and vermin had souls that were eternal. Hindus were divided on such matters, but they too believed in the continuity of the soul after death, through reincarnation or rebirth. (The debates between Hindus, Jains, and Buddhists are intriguing on this matter, needless to say.) Heraclitus, one of the most imaginative early Greek philosophers, suggested that the soul was "fiery" and made up of the same stuff as the stars. But before we think this view too elevated, we should remind ourselves that Heraclitus thought of the stars as being just little pockets in the sky, and not very substantial either.

Vedas and Vedanta: Early Philosophy in India

We have often referred to the philosophy of ancient India, and in particular referred to something called "Hinduism," but it is time to be a bit more precise. Strictly speaking, there is no single set of philosophies—or, for that matter, no single religion—called Hinduism. As we mentioned earlier, "Hindu" is originally an Arabic word, referring merely to a place (east of the Indus River). "Hinduism" refers rather indiscriminately to an enormous variety of beliefs, some of them theistic, some of them not, some of them very spiritual, others not, some of them steeped in ancient Indian mythology, others not, and it refers to a particular social system, the caste system, although this is often justified (or rationalized) with a cosmological theory.

As a philosophy, however, Hinduism is best identified by reference to a set of writings—first of all to those commonly known as the Vedas. The earliest Vedas, the Rg Veda, may have been written nearly 1500 years B.C.E., hundreds of years before Moses and six hundred years before Homer. The Vedas are a combination of poetry, hymns, mythology, and cosmogony, among other things. Vedic cosmogony is an account of the "personal" origins of the universe. Later commentaries on the Vedas, the Upanishads—which are known as *Vedanta* (or "fulfilling" the Vedas)—further focus the story of creation on *Brahman* (Absolute reality), and the ritualistic practices usually known as Hinduism might accordingly be called Brahmanism, and its practitioners Brahmans, the highest priestly caste.[6] However, we will continue to refer to the philosophy of Brahman as Vedanta.

The Vedas pose the cosmogonical question, "Why is there anything?" It is worth noting that even the earliest Vedas display a certain skepticism about whether such ultimate questions are answerable at all. "Whence this creation has arisen—perhaps it formed itself, or perhaps it did not—the one who looks down on it, in the highest heaven, only he knows—or perhaps he does not know."[7] There is also the question of nothingness, what it was like before the creation (perhaps not even nothing) or, for that matter, whether the world is itself an illusion, or nothing. It is in India that we first hear the story of the "cosmic egg" and the familiar stories of an original progenitor who creates the world and all things in it. The sexual imagery is candid, and it would not be inaccurate to see early Indian cosmogony, like most of the cosmogonies of the ancient world, as a personification of the cosmos, an attempt to understand creation as such through the more immediate understanding of human procreation. Indeed, the Rg Veda even casts the universe itself as a *Purusha*, a cosmic person, who is both immortal and sacrificed for the sake of the world. "The *Purusha* has a thousand heads, a thousand eyes. . . . He is the ruler of immortality . . . they divided the *Purusha* . . . the moon was born from his mouth, the sun from his eye, from his two feet came the earth."[8]

This basic concern with the "person" pervades Indian philosophy, and it is nowhere more evident than in the perpetual concern for the self, the soul, and the true nature of the individual person. The same concerns will preoccupy Jainism and Buddhism, which will emerge from Hinduism several hundred years later. On the one hand, there is the conception of the individual soul, or *jiva*, which distinguishes each individual as a unique being. Whether or not this *jiva* is genuine, however, or in any way sufficiently substantial to survive the death of the body is a matter of considerable imaginative debate. The self is also referred to as *atman*, which might more generally be understood as the principle of life that exists in all (as well as in each) human being. Thus one might see each and every individual as a *jiva* vitalized by an *atman*, or, quite differently, one might come to see *jiva* as a false self and *atman* as the true self. Nevertheless, the Vedas make clear that we are not to think of *jiva* and *atman* as two selves fighting for superiority within a person. Rather, they are like "two birds, companions who are always united, clinging to the self-same tree."[9] Nevertheless, the relationship is obviously problematic, and the true nature of the self, *jiva* or *atman*, will continue to be one of the focal points of philosophy in India for the next 2,300 years.

The Upanishads developed the themes of the Vedas in a clearly philosophical direction. The ultimate principle of existence—which in the Vedas was sometimes described (as in more Western literature) as "the word"—became known (as we have mentioned) as Brahman, or absolute existence. Vedanta, like the rich mythology of earlier India, was shot through with ambiguity and contradiction, not by way of perversity, but all to the end of making a single point (one that would not be at all opposed to the earliest philosophy of the Greeks). That idea is that there is one reality (Brahman) albeit with infinitely many manifestations. The idea that there are many gods, all of whom are manifestations of the same God, is no doubt bewildering to monotheists, or to polytheists who think of being godlike as an inherently stable quality. But so, too, Indian philosophy will seem bewildering or incoherent to those who insist on not only the singularity but the ultimate rationality of reality, or its inherent (if not eternal) unchanging existence. But Brahman is unchanging only in the sense that it is always changing, and even the gods are born anew every three hundred trillion years or so.

None of this, however, is quite to say what Brahman is, or, for that matter, how we relate to Brahman. Can we know Brahman? If so, how? Are we part of Brahman? Aspects of Brahman? Irreconcilably opposed to Brahman? Here we can locate what is best known (in the West) about Indian philosophy—its *mysticism* and that familiar set of exercises known as *yoga*. It would be an enormous mistake to think of Indian philosophy, even in its most ancient forms, as *nothing but* mysticism—a formulation which allowed many generations of Western philosophers to ignore Indian philosophy altogether. But it would be equally a mistake to deny the central role of mysticism in philosophy, as many current advocates, in reaction, have done.

The skeptical doubts of the oldest Vedas continue throughout Indian philosophy, but they frequently tend to focus not on the possibility of knowledge as such but on the idea that Brahman can be comprehended through reason or reflection alone. Knowledge of Brahman comes essentially through experience, and in particular that form of all-embracing, unifying experience known as *mystical* experience. But one does not simply have such experiences, as some unprepared Christians, notably Paul on his way to Damascus, have claimed to have visions of Christ or the Virgin or the Holy Grail. One needs ample preparation, which includes, among other things, a thorough study and understanding of the Vedas and Upanishads, certain ascetic (self-denying) practices such as *meditation* and yoga. (Yoga may in fact precede Sanskrit India by centuries. The word is somewhat confused in Indian philosophy by the fact that there is a classical school of philosophy also named "Yoga," from the *Yoga sutras* by Patanjali—second century B.C.E.) To have the experience of Brahman, *brahmavidya*, one must be "fit." But this does not refer primarily to health or body tone (although such matters are not ignored), nor is relaxation as such a proper aim of yoga. It is self-discipline, the spiritual self-discipline that will allow a person to reach a "deeper" reality and have a blissful experience in doing so.

This blissful experience lies at the heart of almost all Indian philosophy, especially in ancient times, although it goes by various names and it is approached by very different doctrines and techniques. Buddhists refer to it as *Nirvana*, Jains as "liberation from suffering" Hindus as *mukti*, although they place very different interpretations on its nature and its significance. Some would say that what we call reality is an illusion (*samsara*, or "the veil of *maya*") and the mystical experience of Brahman allows us to perceive the really real for the first time. Others would allow that our everyday world is real enough, real enough for an everyday world, that is, but it is a superficial reality. Reality has many levels and depths, and at bottom, it is Brahman, the One. In almost every case, the ultimate aim is to achieve a certain aloofness from the troubles and concerns of everyday existence. On a more metaphysical level, such "liberation" results in freedom from the recurrent cycle of death and rebirth to which all beings are bound.

The experience of Brahman might also be described as a sense of "selflessness," which in Indian philosophy, as we have anticipated, has potentially profound meanings. To be sure, popular (albeit "transcendental") meditation may provide us with a relaxed feeling of well-being in which selfish thoughts—and most other thoughts—are systematically ignored or relegated to the margins of consciousness. But the "selflessness" understood by Indian philosophers is far more profound than this. It is the recognition that what we ordinarily call the self is unreal, an illusion. In Sanskrit terms, we are not *jiva*. We are *atman*, where *atman* is considered an aspect of Brahman. Nevertheless, the relationship between Brahman and atman remains one of the main points of debate in classical Indian scholarship. In the oldest of the Upanishads, one of the highest gods describes *atman* as "the self which is free from evil, free from old age, free from death, free from grief, free from hunger and thirst, whose desire is the real, whose thought is the real. He who understands and has found out about that self obtains all worlds and all desires."[10] In later Vedanta, the emphasis is far more on "release" from the world and desire. Atman, however, remains quite opposed to the contingent, transient self of everyday life. It is the animating principle in all of us. It is life itself.

The First (Greek) Philosopher

Who was the first Western philosopher? Even if we limit our focus to the rocky shores of ancient Greece, the answer to that overly competitive question is by no means obvious. The standard answer is Thales, who lived in Miletus in the seventh century (625?–547? B.C.E.). In fact we know very little about him and possess none of his writings. What little we do know of him comes from the not-always-reliable Aristotle. Thales suggested that the world is surrounded by and ultimately born of water, an idea that very likely came from earlier Greek cosmogony and other cultures. The conversion of this idea into a cosmological thesis, however, was probably due to Aristotle, who for his own purposes wanted to view Thales' theory as akin to the theories of his successors, and thus recast it as concerning the fundamental "stuff" of the universe.

Thales does not quite say that everything is *made of* water. He argues, along with many other thinkers of his times, that the world is surrounded by water, and he seems to suggest that in some sense the *source* of all things is water, but this is something less than the physical theory that everything is essentially water. Still, in breaking with the mythological tradition that explained all of nature in terms of gods, goddesses, and other spirits, Thales adopted what we might call a *naturalistic* outlook, a scientific viewpoint, an explanation of natural phenomena in terms of other straightforward natural phenomena. Accordingly, or at least according to some, he deserves to be called the first philosopher.

But there are reasons to doubt this attribution, and this raises the question of what we mean by this prestigious label, "philosopher." If philosophy is an attempt to understand order in the world, to explain why things happen and why they ought to happen, if philosophy is the effort to understand, for instance, what it is to be a human being, where we fit into the universe, what happens to us when we die, then philosophy surely precedes Thales by many centuries. So understood, philosophy goes back to the ancient poets, Homer and Hesiod, and further back to the ancient Minoan civilization on Crete, and still further back to the ancient civilizations of Egypt, Sumeria, and Babylon, among others.

If, however, philosophy is to be understood on the model of the natural sciences, as the attempt to explain the world without any reference to gods, goddesses, and spirits, then Thales was not the first philosopher either. Thales clearly believed, in his own words, that "there are gods in all things." Indeed, we have to wait several centuries before we find philosophers who are not, similarly, *animists*, seeing all things as in some sense alive—"animated." Indeed, even Aristotle, the greatest scientist–philosopher of the ancient world, was an animist, and one of his most exciting ideas was that the world as a whole, the cosmos, was ultimately alive and divine. But we should distinguish the claim that something is alive in the sense of an animal (perceiving, feeling, and being capable of movement and reproduction) and a weaker sense, in which something is alive if it is simply "self-moving." The Greeks would sometimes shift along a continuum between these two very different meanings. They would also shift between three quite different animist claims: (1) everything is alive (even rocks, stars and water); (2) life permeates everything; and (3) the cosmos as a whole is alive. It is not always clear in Thales or in Aristotle, for instance, which of these claims is intended.

Many contemporary philosophers hold yet another view of philosophy. Philosophy, they contend, consists of arguments and deep thoughts about the nature of reality (a philosophical enterprise called "metaphysics"). On this view, the mantle of "first philosopher" probably belongs to a fellow named Parmenides, an extremely difficult thinker who lived in the fifth century (ca. 515-450 B.C.E.). Parmenides argued in a more abstract and obscure way than any of his predecessors or contemporaries. He himself called his efforts a "new way of thinking" concerning the nature of "being as such." Crucially, Parmenides *argued*. That is, he not only stated bold (and extremely contentious) claims; he attempted to demonstrate his claims, and he expected, indeed, invited, counterarguments in return.

Parmenides defended views about the nature of existence, about what exists, about what does not. Parmenides was not concerned with the particular composition of things, unlike his scientific predecessors. He was not worried whether things were ultimately made of water or some other sort of element. Parmenides' claims and arguments were abstract in an entirely different way. For example, he argued that "what you can speak of and think of has to be, since it can be while nothing cannot be. Think about that." This is often considered to be the first philosophical argument and Parmenides, accordingly, the first metaphysician, the first true philosopher.

Of course, one could challenge this conclusion. People have been arguing as long as (and possibly before) they spoke a language, and there is a sense, at least, in which even the most ancient thinker–poets and prophets were concerned about the riddles of existence, their own existence, and the existence of God or gods, good and evil, worlds beyond this one, life after death. Moreover, Parmenides presented his own argument (as did many of the ancient philosophers, both in Greece and throughout the Middle East) in the form of poetry, a form of writing that would become philosophically unacceptable with Plato and, for the most part, remains so today. Still, Parmenides opened up philosophical thinking to a new (and some would say incomprehensible) level of abstraction. If extreme abstraction and argumentation is the mark of true philosophy, Parmenides would seem to be our man, the first philosopher.

If, on the other hand, it is profound obscurity as such that we're looking for, the mantle goes instead to Parmenides' contemporary, Heraclitus (ca. 540–ca. 480 B.C.E.). The "dark sayings" of Heraclitus are virtually unmatched in philosophy for their profundity and unintelligibility (at least until the twentieth-century German philosopher Martin Heidegger, who borrowed generously from his illustrious predecessor). While other philosophers were trying to get to the bottom of nature, Heraclitus announced that "nature loves concealment." He himself loved puzzles, paradoxes, and puzzling word play that concealed his own meanings. He suggested, often and always to the irritation of his contemporaries, that nature makes itself known only to the very few. And while he taught that there was an underlying order to the world, a *logos* that moves through all things, he kept reminding his colleagues that they would "never understand it, neither before nor after they have heard it."

Heraclitus was also famous for his seemingly obvious observations which on second thought become deep and obscure conundrums,—for example, "The way up and the way back are the same." As for the question of life after death, he said, unhelpfully, "All that we see when awake is death," and "Men do not expect or imagine what awaits them at death." To a civilization desperate for peace in the wake of continuous war, he insisted, "War is father and king of all." But Heraclitus, unlike his contemporary Parmenides, did not argue for these doctrines. He gave no *reasons* for believing them, although he no doubt had thought about them a great deal. He was content to be viewed in the traditional role of the sage, the prophet, the wise man, a human version of the oracle.

If one must choose, however, our own nomination for the first (Greek) philosopher goes to a figure familiar even to most high school students. His name is Pythagoras (ca. 581–ca. 507 B.C.E.). He was a generation older than Heraclitus and Parmenides and a contemporary of Thales' best Milesian students. Among many other things, Pythagoras thought up and proved a theorem, one of the mainstays of geometry, to the effect that, in a right triangle, the square of the hypotenuse (the long side, for those of you who forget) is equal in length to the sum of the squares of the other two sides. He made other significant discoveries in mathematics, including the notion of "irrational numbers"—numbers that cannot be evenly divided by one integer into another. (Egyptians and Babylonians had already calculated the value of *pi*, one of those "irrational" numbers, at 3.16 and 3.125, respectively.)

But Pythagoras was first of all a philosopher, a mesmerizing philosopher who had theories about the nature of the universe and the making of music, who had exotic beliefs about the nature of the soul and the best way to live (many of which he imported from Egypt, along with much of his geometry). Plato, in the *Republic*, would praise Pythagoras, who "presided over a band of intimate disciples who loved him for the inspiration of his society and handed down a way of life which to this day distinguishes the Pythagoreans from the rest of the world." Indeed, Plato himself, by some accounts, was an unacknowledged but devout Pythagorean.[11]

Pythagoras lived and worked in what is now southern Italy, far away from the other philosophers in and around the Greek peninsula. His studies of geometry were but a small part of a grand view of the world and the cosmos, one in which mathematics defined the basic order of all things. Everything, he said, is defined by numbers. This is, of course, a view very sympathetic to that of many physicists working today, who insist that mathematics is the key to understanding the universe. Pythagoras further used his theory of proportions to explain, among other things, the nature of music and the movements of the stars. He surmised that the stars made a great deal of noise (audible only to the gods) which he called "the music of the spheres." Most important of all, Pythagoras developed a complex vision of the soul, the afterlife, and the right way to live.

He adapted and developed a considerable number of other spiritual and occult ideas that he learned from Egypt and Asia, including reincarnation (an idea Plato probably got from him). He gathered together many followers, among them many of the first women philosophers, who joined him in his thoughtful, highly intellectual search for the spiritual life. Because he was a cult figure, however (and because his members were very successful in keeping their secrets), we do not know much about his teachings. Founding a cult, of course, is not usually thought of as the mark of a philosopher, and we can lament the fact that the first philosopher was not willing to make his wisdom more generally available. But perhaps the strongest argument for calling Pythagoras the first (Greek) philosopher is simply this: he was (we have very good reason to believe) the first of these many thinkers to actually *call himself a "philosopher,"* that is, a "lover of wisdom." And since philosophy is a kind of self-reflection and self-understanding, we should surely pay some attention to what the philosophers actually thought of themselves.

It is important to note that being a *lover* of wisdom does not necessarily mean that one is wise. Indeed, when asked if he were a wise man, Pythagoras replied, "No, I am *only* a lover of wisdom." It is the search, the query, the activity of the mind that makes one a philosopher, not the summary answers, which are too easily reduced to unthinking dogma and bumper-sticker slogans and may require no thought or understanding at all. That is why we can so confidently count as philosophers many of these early thinkers, despite the fact that we have barely a sentence of their actual opinions. We do know, through Aristotle and other sources, that they were seekers, that they loved the activity of thought and thinking, that they were not willing to merely accept popular opinion and the established beliefs at face value but insisted on going beyond and sometimes against them. And that, too, is why we should be generous in granting the status of philosopher to many of those other thinkers whose names may be unknown to us, whose customs and modes of expression are very foreign to us, but whose efforts indicate that they were also seekers, actively engaged in the search.

Perhaps the only difference between a philosopher and anyone else is the simple fact that he or she *thinks through* the questions and the too glib answers provoked by the contingencies and uncertainties of life. Whether he or she writes down the answers, or for that matter ever reaches them, and whether those answers survive, are secondary concerns. The first philosophers set the tone, established the seriousness of a kind of thinking that was new, often mysterious, against the grain of popular platitudes and, often self-consciously, "useless." They practiced their art first and foremost with each other and with their students. They talked. They thought hard. They only rarely wrote it down. "Publish or perish" may be the sign above the door of the University, but that is the self-made obsession of academic professionals. It has nothing to do with philosophy or being philosophical.

Pythagoras lived in the sixth century B.C.E., and he was therefore part of what is usually considered the second generation of philosophers in ancient Greece. Because he was in Italy rather than Asia Minor, there was limited contact. But Pythagoras did meet his younger contemporary Heraclitus (who later had many bad things to say about him, as he did about almost everyone). Pythagoras was also an exact contemporary of Xenophanes, the imaginative critic of popular Greek religion. But it is time for us to go back to the so-called first generation of philosopher–scientists, beginning with Thales, for their story is well worth telling as one of the beginnings, though by no means *the* beginning, of philosophy. The qualification is not so much because Thales and his immediate followers now seem to be more scientists than philosophers; indeed, there is not all that much point to distinguishing these roles at this early point in history. Nor, for that matter, is it very helpful to try to separate philosophy from religion and mythology in early philosophy, although, to be sure, such distinctions and tensions were starting to appear.

Briefly, Thales was followed by Anaximander, who was followed by Anaximenes, who was followed by Pythagoras, Heraclitus, and Parmenides and his student, Zeno, who threw everything into confusion. Then came "the atomists," Empedocles, Anaxagoras, and Democritus, a contemporary of Socrates. After Socrates and Plato came Aristotle, who wrapped up the science of his times and defined most of the sciences for many centuries to come. There were dozens of other figures, of course, many of them merely commentators and kibitzers, most of them forgotten, but the image of smooth progress that emerges from the standard account (largely invented or, perhaps more fairly, superimposed by Aristotle) is an illusion. Instead of a steady improvement over time we have a rich, torn, and tangled tapestry of conflicting viewpoints, excited argument, wild speculation, and heated disagreement. Unlike the owl of wisdom, which Hegel tells us flies quietly at dusk, we find these aggressive and seemingly fearless songbirds bringing with them a strange new dawn.

The Pre-Socratic Philosophers (I): The Stuff of the World

Before we attempt to review the progression of Greek philosophers before Socrates, it is important to locate them in place in their society. The watchword of their philosophy was to explain the unknown in terms of the familiar rather than by appeals to the divine or mythology (a fancy way of admitting, "I do not know"). If their reliance on "common sense" sometimes seemed to turn against common sense, we shall see that this is not at all unusual in the history of philosophy. But the sixth and fifth centuries B.C.E. in Greece were in fact innovative and productive in other ways besides philosophy. Most important was the explosion of technology.

Into the midst of an essentially feudal agrarian society of wealthy landowners and peasants came a new class of craftsmen, tradesmen, technicians. (It is worth noting how often the tradesman serves as an example for Plato and Aristotle.) Inventors were numerous and inventions were plentiful. New farming and navigation implements appeared. So did new techniques and new crafts. The geometry and other mathematical systems the Greeks had imported from Egypt and Babylon allowed them to make breakthroughs in navigation and cartography. Most important of all, certainly from a practical and humanistic viewpoint, the science and practice of medicine flourished. The great physician Hippocrates (ca. 460–ca. 377 B.C.E.) summed up the new consciousness of the age, saying, "Men think [a disease] divine merely because they do not understand it. But if they called everything divine which they do not understand, why, there would be no end of divine things."[12]

Thales' speculation found itself quite at home in the midst of this explosion of innovation and technology. New ideas, new inventions, a herd of tradesmen, a battalion of new craftsmen were making their mark in Athens and in the Athenian colony of Miletus. (Athenians founded Miletus after the Trojan War. The Lydians and Persians would not take over until the end of the sixth century B.C.E.) The scientific speculation which was supposedly invented by Thales did not happen in an intellectual or a social vacuum. Similar ideas had been floating around the eastern Mediterranean for many years. In particular, philosophical speculation reflected society's new fascination with *techne*; the new skills that grounded the new technology stimulated new questions and inspired a new, more "nuts-and-bolts" way of looking at nature. Plato and Aristotle often employ the notion of *techne* as an analog to the virtues. These were exciting times when all sorts of new thoughts and experiments were going on. Philosophy would simply be one of them.

The speculations of the pre-Socratic philosophers also had a political dimension, whether or not this is evident in what remains of their works. The philosophers were not allowing their minds to fly off to the heavens. They were rather bringing thought back to earth. It was during this period of Greek history that Solon was "modernizing" Athens, establishing democracy, giving the vote to free males and freeing some of the slaves (those slaves who were native Athenians and had been forced into servitude by debt or disgrace). After Solon, Athens would return to tyranny, experience a devastating invasion by Sparta, and suffer a local revolution. Democracy would reappear, but this was not, as we would fancifully like to believe, an easy or nonviolent process. We must place the first philosophers within this often violent context in order to understand their passion for order and understanding.

Thales' naturalistic account of the cosmos in terms of the basic element of water might not sound particularly promising or profound to us. But, unlike its predecessors, it presented a nonanthropomorphic account of the world in terms that we would call "scientific." And, unlike the admittedly colorful but quite ad hoc stories of dozens of gods and goddesses and their exploits, Thales' account gave us a unified and singular view of the world. Even the idea that the world rests on water would have been a dramatic suggestion. But if Aristotle was right in interpreting Thales as claiming that the world is essentially made of water, this provided a startling answer to the question of cosmogony. It also provided a new beginning for the more particular questions of cosmology and what would eventually become the physical sciences. What sorts of things are there? Thales' hypothesis may seem rather simple-minded to us, as it did to Aristotle. But it marked a new way of thinking, a new kind of search for origins, and it was not, in the context of the times, all that implausible. We now know that the human body, reduced to its basic ingredients, is something like 98 percent water. Squeeze a fruit, a log, even a rock with sufficient pressure, and out comes some liquid. Common observations would lend support to the idea that water was the basic substance.

We do not know much else about Thales' ideas, but we know that he had a remarkable reputation for both intelligence and eccentricity. The story goes that Thales, his eyes on the heavens, fell into a well. It is also said that he used his extensive knowledge of the heavens to correctly predict the olive harvest. He invested in Ionian olive presses, cornered the market and became the equivalent of a millionaire in his time. Such little anecdotes signify the odd and sometimes ironic role of the philosopher (and philosophy) in the Western tradition.

On the one hand, this tradition is woven around charismatic personalities, brilliant eccentrics. On the other hand, it is in the nature of Western philosophy that ideas have a life of their own, even if they also betray some deep concern of the philosopher. By contrast, the stories told about Confucius and the Buddha are hardly separable from their philosophy. Confucianism and Buddhism are about Confucius and Buddha in a way that Greek philosophy is not about Thales and his followers, or even Socrates, the most exemplary of them all. Philosophy was, from the first, about the ideas, and so it should be no surprise, in the centuries to follow, that the ideas should take on a life of their own and become the center of focus. Biographies of the philosophers, accordingly, are considered just so much gossip.

The Western philosophical tradition is always reinterpreting, reinventing, and challenging itself.[13] More than occasionally, philosophers within that tradition reject it altogether. Indeed, it is one of the more charming peculiarities of the Western philosophical tradition that so many great philosophers have begun their greatest works by claiming that virtually all of what their predecessors have said is just plain wrong. Many of these same philosophers have also declared that they have finished with philosophy altogether, settled (or eliminated) the questions, gotten things right once and for all. And yet there are always new philosophers, new critics, new ways of looking at things, even if the greatest philosophers, however "mistaken," remain at the center of the conversation.

This was true even at the beginning. Philosophy is always open to question: this is one of the most dramatic and important ways in which Western philosophy differs from mythology and religion. It explicitly invites challenge and revision. It is, to anticipate two important terms, *dialectical* and not *dogmatic*.[14] Thales, in particular, was taken to task by his younger Milesian contemporary Anaximander (610–547 B.C.E.), who rejected his elder's view of a world made of water and suggested a different vision. His view was so much more complicated and systematic (and so much more of his writing endured) that many scholars have suggested that he, not Thales, deserves the much disputed mantle of "first philosopher."

Anaximander helped organize the traditional Greek cosmology, distinguishing earth, air, fire, and water and explaining how their various properties—the hot and the cold, the wet and the dry—acted upon and opposed one another to produce nature *(physis)*. Pressed for an answer to Thales' question about which of these is the most basic, fundamental element, Anaximander's answer was, "None of these." The ultimate source of the universe and the basic ingredient of all things is something which we cannot, as such, perceive. He called it *apeiron*, which we might just call "basic stuff," although the word in Greek means "unbounded" or "unlimited." In terms of the history of science, this is perhaps the first significant instance of a theoretical postulate, something purported to exist in order to explain perceivable phenomena although it is itself not perceivable. (Electrons and genes are more current examples.) But, like Thales' water, Anaximander's *apeiron* was neither inanimate nor without spiritual substance. It too was divine and eternal, although, needless to say, it would not become any part of the pantheon of gods and goddesses in whom ordinary Greeks believed.

Anaximenes, also of Miletus, was a student of Anaximander. Therefore, it was incumbent upon him to criticize his teacher's mysterious and unperceivable *apeiron* and move back into the order of ordinary experience. Accordingly, Anaximenes argued that air was the most essential of the elements, condensing and evaporating, heating up and cooling off, thickening and thinning.

Thales, Anaximander, and Anaximenes—the "Milesians"—made a major move beyond the old mythologies and folktales of Greece. Yet we should be cautious about describing this change too quickly in terms of such loaded notions as "philosophy" and "rationality." They set the stage for what we have come to call "philosophy" (as well as much of what we have come to call "science"). But it is against the background of Thales, Anaximander, and Anaximenes that we can appreciate the far more radical departures of their successors, notably Pythagoras, Heraclitus, and Parmenides.

The Pre-Socratic Philosophers (II): The Underlying Order

Thales, Anaximander, and Anaximenes provided "naturalistic" accounts of the cosmos—that is, accounts which emphasized perceivable elements (or, in the case of Anaximander, a postulated element) in their explanation of why the world is as it is. Yet it is also important to appreciate just how minimal these accounts were, not only in contrast to the rich and exciting myths that they were intended to supplant, but in contrast to other, less down-to-earth accounts that would soon be available. Thales, Anaximander, and Anaximenes were all *materialists,* in the sense that the world, for each of them, was made up of some basic kind of stuff, whether it be water or air or *apeiron*. What was missing?

Pythagoras, by contrast, insisted that the basic ingredients of the cosmos were numbers and proportions, not "stuff" at all but rather forms and relationships. It was *order as such* that claimed our philosophical attention, not the material ordered. To be sure, the Milesian materialists intended to avoid the traditional supernatural accounts (despite their continuing animism). But "natural" does not mean "material" only (much less the lifeless matter of modern chemistry). It is with Pythagoras in particular that the central problem of ancient (and then medieval) ontology becomes focused. This is the question of how the abstract order or form of things manifests itself in the multitude of actual things in the world, a concern that is often summarized simply as "the Problem of the *One in the Many*" (or, sometimes, "the One and the Many").

Mathematics, as the Greeks soon appreciated, differed from all other forms of knowledge. It possessed an elegance, a purity, an attractive *universality* and a *certainty* that was to be found nowhere else, especially in the messy business of everyday life. The propositions of mathematics and geometry were true, true everywhere, and they could be known to be true, and proved, for certain. A right triangle in Egypt or Persia had exactly the same formal properties as a right triangle in Athens or Italy. The proof of the Pythagorean theorem was valid, not here or there, but everywhere. Ever since Pythagoras, the elegance, purity, and certainty of mathematics has remained an ideal for philosophers, the ultimate demonstration of rationality at its best, a systematic display of the abstract form of a perfect philosophy.

It is in contrast to the Milesian materialists, too, that we can appreciate the murky but monumental philosophy of Heraclitus. On the one hand, Heraclitus could be viewed as an early philosopher–scientist who embraced yet another of the natural elements, fire, and declared it primary. In many ways, he speaks of fire in the same sort of way that Milesian materialists had talked about water, air, and *apeiron*. He saw lightning (thunderbolts) as divine and fire as their underlying stuff: "Fire lives the death of earth and our lives the death of fire." But the element of fire played a *symbolic* role in Heraclitus's thought that the other elements did not play for the Milesians.

Fire is violent. A flame is constantly changing, flickering. For Heraclitus, the world was constantly changing, "in flux," and apparent stability was assuredly an illusion. Switching metaphors, it was Heraclitus who insisted, famously, that one cannot step in the same river twice. (Actually he said, "Upon those who step into the same rivers, different and again different waters flow."[15]) But his language is so metaphorical that it is hard to think of Heraclitus as merely another materialist. He was making a much larger point—that the apparent constant in the universe is change. And yet, the world is eternal: "The cosmos which is common to all was not made by god or man but it forever was, is and will be, an ever-living fire kindled in measures, going out in measures."[16]

Moreover, the world is one, according to Heraclitus. All things are connected, if primarily in opposition, and behind the multitude of things in the world is a single unity, the *logos*. The logos unites all apparent opposites, which gives order to chaos, which provides laws for change and allows us, or a very few of us anyway, to understand that unity, that order, those laws. Here, of course, Heraclitus's unflattering warnings to his philosophical peers strike home. There is an order beneath the apparent chaos, but only a few brilliant seers are capable of appreciating it. Here we can see an important continuity with Anaximander, in the postulation of the unseen, but we can also see how dramatically Heraclitus altered the program of his materialist predecessors. The *logos* is not just another kind of stuff. And the difference between the way the world appears to be, in our ordinary view of things, and the way it really is, according to the wisest of philosophers, had never been greater.

At which point we come, again, to Parmenides. There are those, as we said, who consider him the first philosopher, and, indeed, even one of the greatest philosophers.[17] Parmenides and his student, Zeno of Elea, shifted the focus in philosophy to the technique of argumentation—to logic and the analysis of the most basic bits of language (e.g. "is" and "of"). In doing so, they removed philosophy from the hands of mere sages, visionaries, and speculators and turned it into a discipline, a difficult set of skills to be mastered only with considerable intelligence and patience. Some might argue that Parmenides and Zeno were the originators of a great deal of mischief and distraction, setting generations of philosophers down the path to pointless puzzle-solving. They tie and untie logical knots and then tie new ones in their stead, forgetting about the basic business of philosophy, which is to answer real questions and solve real problems of real people.

What Parmenides did, however, was to shift the emphasis in philosophy to a new level of abstraction. His arguments were riddled with paradox but based on the supposedly most basic of all concepts or categories, that of Being, and accordingly his thought has much to do with the most fundamental aspect of our language, the verb "to be."

Let us pass over the fact that not all languages have a verb "to be" or anything much like it. Let us avoid pointing out again that whole philosophical traditions, in China, for instance, have managed to proceed for thousands of years without such puzzles and paradoxes (on which basis, of course, some philosophers would deny that they are at all philosophical).[18] The point is rather to appreciate, at least for the moment, the ingenious contribution of Parmenides and his most famous student, Zeno, to the ongoing story of philosophy. Without them, what we now think of as philosophy would no doubt be very different indeed.

When we review the work of Parmenides' predecessors, several central themes come to mind. First is the attempt, never really complete, to free accounts of the cosmos from supernatural and mythological explanations. Second is the growing sense of divorce between reality or truth, on the one hand, and mere appearance, the world as it looks to us ordinary folk, on the other. Third is an obsessive, if often unstated, insistence by these thinkers on unity, whether it be the insistence on a single fundamental element in the Milesians or the underlying unity of the *logos* in Heraclitus. (Pythagoras is a bit less clear on this matter than the others, but his emphasis on the singularity of mathematics, the purity of the soul, and harmony in the world all certainly point in this direction.)

Fourth is the turn away from both mythology and materialism to immaterial forms of order, again, in Heraclitus and Pythagoras. (It is important to note that the pre-Socratics themselves would not have recognized this distinction between the material and the immaterial.) And fifth is an insistent sense of *necessity* about these cosmic arrangements, so obvious in mathematics and the *logos*, but evident in the Greek belief in *fate* as well. Sixth, whatever there is, it seems, must be eternal, for although things can certainly change (by way of transformation and rearrangement, for instance), the idea of creation from nothing or destruction into nothing is simply too difficult to explain.

Finally, the notions of reason and rationality have been evolving through this history, first, perhaps, as an emphasis on thinking and dialogue, but increasingly as the concept of a special faculty or medium for comprehending the truth. Reason becomes increasingly distinct from experience and ordinary knowledge. Put these seven themes together, and the philosophical world is ripe for an argument to the effect that the world as we "know" it is not the true world.

The details of Parmenides' argument, which plays on the verb "to be," is extremely complex and obscure, and its meaning is a matter of bitter scholarly controversy even today. It has been argued that his entire argument rests on a colossal confusion of grammar, logic, and metaphysics, even though none of these fields had in fact yet been invented. But in rather everyday terms, it amounts to this: if something can be thought of at all, it must exist, and so it does not make any sense whatever to speak about nothing (or something that does not exist, does not yet exist, or no longer exists). Therefore, whatever is must be eternal; it cannot come into being and it cannot be destroyed. (This insistence on the enduring nature of the underlying reality of things had been evident in the earlier pre-Socratics as well.)

From this, Parmenides concludes that there can be no such thing as change.[19] What is already is. And nothing can come to be out of what is not. He further concludes that there can be no time, that our sense of time passing is an illusion, and that space is an illusion too. What we call reality is nothing but "the deceitful ordering of words." The true reality, however, is absolutely unitary, unchanging, eternal, "the one." (It is worth nothing that Vedantists and the Buddha were also proposing arguments concerning unity, change and permanence, although not in the same style or context.)[20] This reality is not the one we live in.

Despite his flamboyant rationality and his attempt at deductive rigor, Parmenides suggests in his philosophical poem's opening that his insights have been derived from magic, by way of revelation. The fact that he writes his thoughts in the form of a poem suggests a somewhat mystical intent, again, not so different from some of the early mystical writers of ancient India. The largely negative conclusion of Parmenides' poem was conjoined with a confident certainty on his part of its truth. Coupling denial that we can know the world as it really is with certainty of that denial greatly impressed many future philosophers—among them, Plato and Aristotle, both of whom speak of Parmenides with great respect.

The long evolution of *skepticism* (beginning with the Greek skeptic Pyrrho and continuing in philosophy up to this day) can find its ancestry in Parmenides, despite Parmenides' own confidence in his position. (The disconcerting figure of the confident skeptic will often appear in philosophy.) Parmenides also indicates two future directions for philosophy: "Analytical" philosophers who consider deductive arguments to be the "lifeblood" of philosophy find in Parmenides their first practitioner. But so, too, do those who seek in Western (as well as Eastern) philosophy a privileged or *esoteric* realm, the claim of a "higher consciousness," accessible to only a few. Thus, there has always been in philosophy a not always polite tension between those who insist that "the love of wisdom" is a formidably technical or private domain and those who would put that love on the best-seller list. (We will meet some of the latter in a few moments.)

Immediately after Parmenides, however, there were only so many ways for future philosophers to respond. One way, of course, was to simply agree with

him, and this was the case with his student Zeno. The latter invented a series
of ingenious arguments to "prove" that, indeed, the very notions of time and
change were utter nonsense. The most famous of these were a group of paradoxes, in the form of arguments "to absurdity" (*reductio ad absurdum*), whose
point was to show that if one assumes that there really is time or change, then
nonsense follows. Therefore, there can be no time or change. The most familiar
of these paradoxes, perhaps, is the paradox of the arrow. If an arrow moves from
bow to target, it must traverse some portion of its trajectory. But to do that, it
must traverse some smaller portion, and to do that, some smaller portion, and
so on ad infinitum. Thus, as a philosophy professor in Tom Stoppard's play
Jumpers concludes, "The arrow never arrives and Saint Sebastian [who was martyred by the Romans by being shot through with arrows] died of fright." The
tricks and sleights necessarily involved in such "proofs" need not detain us here.
Suffice it to say that they perplexed many a bright young (and not so young)
philosopher in the fourth century B.C.E. and challenged many of them to try
(unsuccessfully) to refute them.

The Pre-Socratic Philosophers (III): The Pluralists

Another way of dealing with Parmenides and his argument was to ignore him,
an approach we shall consider shortly. A more philosophical way of dealing with
Parmenides, however, was to attack him. This strategy was pursued not so much
by way of refutation as by undermining the premises of his argument and further
developing the scientific cosmology of the Milesians. One of those premises,
which Parmenides simply took over from the earlier pre-Socratics, involved their
pervasive sense of unity. Three philosophers in particular chose to attack the
idea that the cosmos is essentially One, a doctrine that has been called *monism*
and dates back to the earliest pre-Socratics (with obvious affinities to the monotheistic religions and cosmologies that preceded and surrounded them). Empedocles, Anaxagoras, and Democritus, by contrast, were all *pluralists*, who did not
assume that the world was based on any one element or unified by any one order.
Empedocles surmised (as did Anaximander and Heraclitus before him) that the
world was structured by *conflict*. Moreover, there was no underlying element or
order, just endless conflict between the forces of *love* and *strife*.

In most accounts of the pre-Socratics, Empedocles gets rather short shrift
primarily because his modest pluralism is so obviously inadequate to counter
Parmenides' sophisticated gimmickry. But once we look beyond the limited confines of philosophical cleverness, we find that Empedocles was one of the most
complex, colorful, and remarkable individuals of antiquity. He was an astute
politician, a brilliant orator and rhetorician, a medical doctor, a poet, an imaginative historian, and a powerful religious thinker. He just wasn't much of a
metaphysician, and he therefore received little attention from Aristotle. Consequently, he was more or less ignored in the main line of Greek philosophy.

Anaxagoras seems to have been far more promising in terms of pure cosmology, and he established—even if he did not invent or follow through—some of
the most important features of later Greek cosmology. As a pluralist, he held

that there are many kinds of things; indeed, each thing is of its own kind. Against all of the prior pre-Socratics, Anaxagoras suggested that there were as many elements as there were kinds of stuff, not only earth, air, fire and water but paper, flesh, pulp, wood, wine, bone, bronze—the list is virtually endless. And since nothing can come from nothing, each of these elements must have always existed.

Still, according to Anaxagoras, not everything is an element. A person is not an element but rather a very complex mixture of elements. An element, however, can also be cut and divided indefinitely. Thus, Anaxagoras claims (oddly) that there is "everything in everything," bits of every element interspersed with every other. It has taken considerable gymnastics for readers both ancient and modern to try to make sense of this.

Anaxagoras at least toyed with the idea of mind (or *nous*) as an organizing agency, a view that would attract a great deal of attention several hundred years down the philosophical road. But he had little idea about what mind was supposed to be (but, then, none of the Greeks employed anything like the special concept of "mind" that is part and parcel of modern philosophy). It might be worth noting that Buddhism was developing just such a notion of "interiority" at about this time.

Moreover, with this concept of mind as an organizing agency, Anaxagoras naturally started thinking of the cosmos not only in terms of order but also in terms of some cosmic purpose or end. Again, he seems not to have followed through on this insight, as would Aristotle just a century later. Once again, this was an idea whose time had not yet come. (In nineteenth-century German philosophy, it would become an idea that all but obliterated everything else.)

This emphasis on the divisibility of all things inspired two other philosophers, Leucippus, about whom little is known, and Democritus, his student. They pursued the idea of smaller and smaller pieces of "stuff" until they landed upon what would later become one of the most important ideas of modern times. This is the concept of the *atom*.

Democritus was a pluralist in the extreme. The world consists of any number of various "particles," differing in sizes and shapes, but, as elements, having one distinctive feature in common. They cannot be cut or further divided. (The word "atom" etymologically implies this, for it stems from *a* = not and *tom* = cut.) Thus, Democritus countered Anaxagoras's insistence on infinite divisibility by directly contradicting him. The basic unit of reality is the atom, which cannot be divided. Directly contradicting Parmenides as well, Democritus declared that there does indeed exist *nothing*, namely, the *void*, the empty space in which atoms move and combine.

The idea that atoms move, of course, was also a direct contradiction of Parmenides, but the extent of their disagreement should not blind us to the one way in which Parmenides and Democritus ultimately agreed. This lies in the idea of the One, eternal and unchanging. But for Democritus, there were many, indeed, infinite versions of the One, each of them an atom. Every atom was eternal, and it could be neither created nor destroyed. There was no space *within* an atom, and it was thus that they could not be cut or divided. This basic move, taking a vision of the cosmos as a whole and translating it into an account of discrete but independent bits, is a move that we will see again and again. (So, too, of course, we have already seen how speculation encourages interpretations of the cosmos in much more extravagant visions.)

With Democritus, the attempt to deanimate and demythologize the world was complete. His idea of the universe was thoroughly material, devoid of any imposed order or intelligence, devoid of a *logos*, a purpose, a mind. The old ideas about fate, controlling our destiny, about gods and goddesses who rule the world, even the idea of the soul or psyche, which might survive us after death, all of this disappeared. With Democritus, what we would call a purely "materialist" theory of the world, devoid of spirits and animation, came into the world. Indeed, even the human soul, a matter of mystery to most of the pre-Socratics, was for Democritus just one more material atom not particularly important in a universe of material atoms.

Looking at the history of pre-Socratic philosophy as the development of science, we can readily appreciate a progression that moves from the first glimmer of speculation about the ultimate nature of things to an ambitious theory which wholly exorcises all talk of gods and mythology, the human soul, and the mysteries of religion. But it is important to ask ourselves what is lost in this development, even if much is gained. How much more comfortable might be a world that was ruled by intelligence, even if mysteriously so, in which our fates are decided (even if we did not or could not know how), in which we could be confident that our souls continued after death, perhaps to continue the journeys we had begun in our lives?

We should not be surprised to find that many thinkers (and most ordinary people) felt an enormous loss when such notions were threatened. Before Christianity was even a glimmer on the horizon and before the three great philosophers of ancient Athens came on the scene, the poverty of the emerging philosophy was already a matter of concern. By the nineteenth century, in Germany, this nostalgia had become something of an obsession, and philosophers as different as Hegel, Nietzsche, and Heidegger all shared in it. Indeed, Heidegger, in this sense the most extreme of those three, went so far as to declare that our very ability to philosophize had been lost sometime soon after the fifth century B.C.E..

Yet Democritus's cosmology, in particular, had another upsetting aspect, which would have serious ramifications for modern philosophy. Atoms were colorless, tasteless, odorless, and this meant, in another important sense, that the world as we experience it in everyday life is not the world as it is in itself. Democritus worried about the thesis that the properties we perceive in things could not be located in the atoms themselves, which had only spatial properties. This means that perceptions of color, taste, texture, and so on, are not truly properties of reality at all and become such only in interaction with the perceiver. One can discern here the beginning of a long tradition, culminating in John Locke in the seventeenth century, distinguishing between "primary" and "secondary" qualities. Primary qualities are those that adhere in things as such, while secondary qualities are rather "in us" (although Democritus did not make and could not have made the distinction in quite this way). The troubling idea for those who were paying attention to this new philosophy was that reality itself now seemed tasteless and colorless, eclipsed in the philosophical mind by the excitement of theory.

With Democritus, Greek science approaches its high point, and one might well think that it would be a short step from the ancient atomists to modern scientific philosophy. But, ironically, it is soon after this, when Greek science reaches its epitome with Aristotle, that the drive for general scientific knowledge seems to come to a sudden halt. The choice between Parmenides, who was sure that the world was unified, eternal and unchanging but also insisted that we could never know it, and Democritus, who insisted that the world was a multitude of tasteless, colorless atoms, hardly appealed to people who had much to do besides listen to the speculations of philosophers. And so, philosophy took off in other directions, and science was marginalized, despite scientific geniuses who were either ignored or martyred, for another fifteen hundred years.

The greatest of Greek scientists was Aristotle (384–322 B.C.E.). He would look back at the progress and the attempts of the pre-Socratic philosophers, make his own contributions, summarize the whole of science, and encapsulate it. It is because of him, in particular, that we know much of anything about the early Greek philosophers, but it is also arguably because of him that we now have science at all. His views on the natural sciences, most of which he invented, were to remain in place as the final word, all but unchallenged, for well over a thousand years. Aristotle, accordingly, is viewed by scientists of the last few centuries with very mixed feelings. On the one hand, he was probably the greatest scientist that ever lived. On the other hand, he also became an enormous obstacle to scientific progress. His brilliance made him so central to the doctrines of the all-powerful medieval church from the thirteenth through the sixteenth centuries that further theories in science were discouraged until modern times.

But we are getting ahead of our story. Back we go to Parmenides and his argument to the effect that we can never know the world. What, then, can we know? And what can we do with philosophy if it brings us to that abrupt and final conclusion? One possibility: spend the next two thousand years attacking the premises, criticizing and refining the logic, clarifying and extrapolating the terms "existence" and "is," reinterpreting the conclusion, reaffirming the conclusion, reconstructing the argument, translating the argument into theology, converting the theology into ontology, redefining ontology and reducing it to semantics, redefining semantics and returning it to the language of common sense once again, then challenging or ridiculing common sense and turning it back into paradox, further refining the logic, generating new and even more puzzling paradoxes. . . . Or,

Enter the Sophists

Another way of getting around Parmenides and his argument, as we mentioned, was to ignore him. And this was the way taken by a new generation of philosophers who saw how absurd the conclusions (and the responses to the conclusions) had become but felt no particular urge to respond to them. The suggestion that we can never know the real world, that the world of our daily experience is in some sense an illusion, obviously set philosophers against common sense in a most dramatic way. Such puzzles and paradoxes may provide an intellectual challenge, but they may also provoke a shrug of the shoulders. They did, however, open up room for all kinds of argument and free young minds from the dogmatism of received opinion.

Some of these younger philosophers, called *Sophists (sophistes,* meaning "practitioners of wisdom"), used the new techniques of argumentation to belittle and parody the Parmenidean philosophy. Others exploited the skepticism about our ever knowing the truth and used Parmenides' arguments to advance radical ideas in religion and morality. Such ideas included the suggestion that all human knowledge and values are merely "relative" and not ultimately "true" at all. In ethics, it was similarly argued that our ideals are in fact nothing more than the ideals of those who rule and that justice is nothing but the advantage of those already in power. Other Sophists simply taught the tools themselves, teaching eager and ambitious young Athenians how to win arguments, score points, tie their opponents in verbal knots, impress the public and make political careers for themselves in the new democracy.

With the Sophists, in other words, philosophy became thoroughly *practical*, a way of making one's way in the world. Enough of the origins of the world and the nature of ultimate reality. Enough dark sayings and impossible arguments. Let's get down to the business of living, of using philosophy to make something of ourselves, and, not to be too disrespectful, for having a little fun.

Among the various Sophists, we might mention Gorgias, who imitated Parmenides' style of argument and "proved" the following rather striking conclusions:

1. Nothing exists.

2. If anything did exist, it would be unintelligible.

3. If something were intelligible, one could say nothing about it.

Now, one could imagine that Gorgias took this sequence of absurd propositions and the arguments for them seriously, but one would probably conclude that he must have been a lunatic. Alternatively, one could take this sequence of propositions and arguments as a challenge, another puzzle to be solved. But it would seem much more reasonable to interpret these propositions and arguments as they were probably intended, as a parody, and as a demonstration, not of the absurd conclusions themselves, but of the rather different thesis that this whole business of "proofs" is really just nonsense. Given sufficiently abstruse, arcane, or ambiguous premises and a good deal of cleverness, a smart philosopher can "prove" just about anything.

On this view, so-called proofs and arguments are really just another form of *rhetoric*, the tools of persuasion, perhaps of trickery. So conceived, they may actually work in the sense of persuading an opponent of one's point of view. But they may also lead us down the royal road to nowhere. Parmenides was a parody of himself, and Zeno of Elea one of the great philosophical tricksters of all time. Given an issue that is sufficiently mysterious, e.g., the nature of Time, and concepts that are not well understood (for instance, the concepts of infinity and infinitesimal), one can "prove" all sorts of nonsense. And when what is at stake is the way things *really* are, distinct from common sense and the evidence of the senses, then it is hard to see what would count against these arguments. Certainly, it would not be common sense or experience. It could only be another argument, equally detached. (The only cure for philosophy, in Wittgenstein's twentieth-century diagnosis, is more philosophy.) But in the clash of conflicting claims about the world beyond our experience, there is no ultimate proof or demonstration, only rhetoric and opinion, more or less skillfully presented.

Gorgias's arguments raise a further question, however, which will be of some importance to us as we go on to consider the writings of other philosophers. How much of our understanding of a philosophical text depends upon our knowledge of the intentions of the philosopher who wrote it? Does it matter whether Gorgias wrote his "proofs" tongue in cheek while Parmenides was dead serious about his? (Or could it be that Gorgias, on the verge of a psychotic break, was fully sincere in his work while Parmenides was just having a good time?) Of course, in most cases we have corroborating accounts of the philosophers and their attitudes, but this is not always the case. Once we have insisted on the independence of ideas and their worth quite apart from any knowledge we might have of the philosopher who articulated them, the arguments seem to stand alone, a challenge to future generations, no matter how intentionally absurd the thesis.

Does it matter who articulates a philosophical thesis and argument? Protagoras, perhaps the original and in any case one of the most elegant of the Sophists, thought that it did matter. It was Protagoras who said that "man is the measure of all things." This is sometimes quoted as an early statement of humanism, that is, the insistence on paying attention to human needs, human concepts, human interests, and it is, accordingly, taken to recommend a kind of pragmatism, the view that we should believe what is useful to us. It also suggests the opinion—considered blasphemous at the time—that there is no divine view, that there are, in fact, no gods.

However, this maxim is much more often taken to indicate a kind of skepticism, that is, a pervasive and irrefutable reason for doubting all claims about reality. Thus, this familiar interpretation goes, the point does not concern human beings as the source or the subjects of knowledge (concepts which themselves would not become central to philosophical thinking in the West for another thousand years or so) but rather concerns the *limitations* of all human knowledge. Our knowledge is constrained by our five human senses and restricted by the capacities of human intelligence, which are determined by the biases and prejudices of human beings. We cannot know what really *is*, in other words, but only *what seems to us to be*. Nor can we know "what is not," but only *what seems to us not to be*. "Man is the measure" on this view means human beings are limited to their own viewpoint, and this viewpoint does not allow us to know things as they are in themselves.

But there is a less skeptical way of interpreting Protagoras so that his statement becomes a statement of confidence rather than doubt. We do know the world, on this interpretation, *because* we view it in human terms. The implications of this view would not be worked out for another two thousand years, but suffice it to say for now that the philosophy of Protagoras the Sophist does not have to be read as "sophistry" in the narrow sense of argument for its own sake. It can be interpreted as a keenly insightful view into the nature of knowledge. As a response to Parmenides, it relocates the concerns about ultimate reality and human knowledge, "bringing it all back home."

Protagoras is also viewed by some as the father of "relativism," the view that all knowledge is "relative" to a source, a context, a culture, a people, a person. But in one sense, relativism is obviously an innocent and innocuous charge. It says only that knowledge essentially requires a knower. That surely does not block the possibility of knowledge, nor does it even suggest that there is no truth to be known. It could be further argued, however, that all knowers (except perhaps divine knowers) have built-in limitations so that any (ordinary) knower can understand reality only from his or her own perspective. This does qualify the sense in which we can be said to know reality, but it does not by any means eliminate the possibility of knowledge. Nor does it undermine the notion of truth. The truth on this view is what everyone truly knows (or fails to know) from his or her own perspective.

One can make the view more problematic by insisting that knowing the truth from a perspective means, necessarily, knowing less than the whole truth and, in that sense, not really knowing the truth. One can further argue that since one can never get outside of or beyond one's perspective, there is no way of knowing whether there is any truth, apart from our particular "take" on it. Moreover, one might push the view clearly beyond what Protagoras ever intended and suggest that "man" here means not just human beings but particular, individual human beings, each of whom is somewhat different (and people from different cultures may be very different from one another indeed). Then truth becomes "relative" not only to human understanding, but to each and every human being.

Still, one might argue that there is no reason to suppose that these many individual perspectives must be significantly different from one another in any fundamental sense, nor is there any reason to conclude that the knowledge of a learned scholar is no "better" than the untutored opinions of a below-average student. Protagoras probably did not intend anything nearly so radical as this conclusion, yet he is dismissed by most philosophers as irresponsible and implausible. The truth is that "relativism" is a fully respectable thesis that has rarely had its fair run (although it can be argued that Protagoras gets the best of Socrates in the Platonic dialogue that carries his name). Protagoras the Sophist has been the victim of sophistry more than its perpetrator.

Among the Sophists, a few other figures deserve a mention, if only because they, too, would so often serve as the butt of philosophical abuse in the years to come. Thrasymachus, who serves as a character in the first book of Plato's *Republic*, was a real person who really did argue, in effect, that justice is nothing but what those in power see to their advantage, and he probably did have the same blunt style of argument caricatured by Plato. Then there was Callicles, who insisted on the natural expressions of power and was rather cynical about the role of other ideals in human affairs. (The modern philosopher Friedrich Nietzsche is often said to resemble him.) Another philosopher–poet of the period was an aristocrat named Critias. Critias was installed as a tyrant by the Spartans, and in addition to spinning out a few lines of thoughtful verse, he murdered thousands of admitted and suspected democrats in Athens. He did not come to a happy end. Plato, we might mention, was his cousin.

One other real-life figure in Athenian history is worth a brief mention as well. He is the infamous figure Alcibiades. Alcibiades was one of the best known young aristocrats in Athens. He was notoriously handsome, talented, and treacherous. He was an outspoken enemy of democracy and twice a traitor to Athens. (He once joined the Spartans and later the Persians against his hometown.) He was famous as a lover, a heartbreaker, an adulterer, and a blasphemer. He was also one of Socrates' prize students.

It is important to remember that democracy in Greece did not appear at once. No single spontaneous uprising of citizens could create such a system (and one can be sure no king or tyrant would simply command one into existence). The ancient Dorians, who invaded Greece around 1200 B.C.E., already ruled themselves with a popular assembly, and Athens, which managed to remain independent even while most of Greece was conquered by foreign armies, had a long tradition of popular rule, officiated for a while by Solon, but it took a genuine revolution to establish a democracy ruled by a popular assembly in Athens, just around the turn of the fifth century B.C.E. Even then, "democracy" was limited to a relatively small number of (male) citizens, most of them rich and members of old aristocratic families.

In 463 B.C.E., there was a further move by radical democrats to extend the vote to the lower classes. Under Pericles (who reigned as "the leading citizen" during the "Golden Age" of Athens), the popular assembly swelled to 18,000, governed by a council of 500, who were chosen by random draw. Even generals were elected, and trials had juries of 501 and more (making bribery and lobbying almost impossible). But democracy was never without its challengers. Rich aristocratic families resented the loss of power and privilege, and they organized secret societies to undermine the always-fragile democracy. At the time of the Sophists, Athens was already traumatized from the plague of 430–429 B.C.E. which killed a fourth of the population (including Pericles) and by devastating losses to Sparta in the ongoing Peloponnesian War. It was to the young men of the secret societies, including the youthful Alcibiades, that Socrates, the wisest and cleverest of the Sophists, appealed.

Socrates

Western philosophers have always taken Socrates as their hero. Indeed, he has always been considered our philosophical ideal, the man who was unyielding in his search for the truth, virtually unbeatable in an argument, and who, in the end, died for his ideals. All of this may be true, but it is impossible to understand Socrates and his philosophy unless we also understand his politics and the political situation in which he inserted himself. He was by no means the pure, detached philosopher, the absent-minded and socially indifferent professor whom we have come to know and celebrate or ridicule. He was a man with a mission, and while his most important mission may have been to "save his soul," as he always said, he had a political mission as well. That included his opposition to democracy, but he seemed equally opposed to all forms of government administered by men not "expert" at ruling.

According to Plato, at least, Socrates envisioned the ideal of a perfect state, a "republic" that would be ruled by philosophers. In fact, the Athens that Socrates knew was far from ideal. The city had been ruled by the "Thirty Tyrants," who systematically executed their fellow citizens in a reign of terror. The leader of the Thirty was Critias, one of Socrates's students. When the Thirty were overthrown and Critias was killed, the restored democracy turned its vengeful eyes to Socrates. An amnesty law prevented prosecution for past political crimes, but then as now there were roads around the law. Socrates was accused of "not believing in the gods of Athens and corrupting the youth." The charges seem trumped up and absurd, but only so long as we fail to take account of the larger political picture.

Socrates was put on trial. The jury, however, was made up of the very citizens who had been humiliated and offended by Socrates during his long career. (He was already seventy.) There is no question that his response and self-defense— more or less faithfully recorded in Plato's *Apology*—were brilliant, arrogant, sarcastic, and quite beside the point, for how can a man defend himself against charges that are not the real charges? Socrates brashly suggested that the jury grant him a pension, and they responded by sentencing him to death. No doubt the jury, with their eyes on history if not on justice, would have rather sent him into exile. But Socrates sealed his own fate with his rather sarcastic speech, and in 399 B.C.E. he was executed.

This was a truly traumatic event in the history of philosophy. When Socrates was executed for "corrupting the minds of the youth," Athens was the most democratic city-state (or *polis*) in Greece, and Socrates had already gained a reputation as one of the greatest philosophers. Ever since, he has exemplified the ideal of a lone thinker defending lofty ideals and exemplifying them as well. Socrates taught, among other things, that virtue is the most valuable of all possessions, that the truth lies beyond the "shadows" of our everyday experience, and that it is the proper business of the philosopher to show us how little we really know. It is often said that he died to exemplify those virtues and so as not to betray the ideas which he had taught so long and so well.

Well, yes and no. Socrates may have died a virtuous man, but his political affiliations, now mostly forgotten, certainly colored the picture at the time. And he himself insisted that he died in his own self-interest, "for the good of his soul." He was an ambiguous as well as a brilliant figure.

Socrates did not try to set down his ideas in thematic order, nor is it evident that he had anything like a philosophical system. In many ways, he could be said to be in the same tradition as the Old Testament prophets, and he is often compared to Jesus. He was a sage, a wise man, a "gadfly." He argued his philosophy personally and publicly in the marketplace of Athens, exemplifying his own virtues and offending the authorities. What we know of him we know through the reports of others, and what we know is mainly his "method"—that is, his inquisitive conversation, those demanding dialogues in which he refutes one view then another, his *dialectic*.

And yet, as we know, Socrates was only one of a substantial number of such brilliantly argumentative gadflies in fifth-century Athens. Like the other Sophists, he excelled in logical as well as rhetorical tricks and twists, many of them borrowed from the ingenious Parmenides and the exceedingly clever Zeno. Socrates knew how to make a seeming truism collapse in on itself in paradox, how to turn a platitude into a contradiction, how to twist an argument, its sharpest barbs pointing back at its propounder. He knew how to think up and if need be invent possible cases, to counter any generalization with "counterexamples," and he knew how to ask the hardest questions, promote the most provocative theories, and parody the most respectable lines of argument until they were reduced to nonsense, or worse.

Socrates' point, however, was not just to demolish other people's claims and arguments, even though he rarely gave them the answers to his own questions. The point was to force others to seek the answers themselves, and Socrates, unlike some of the Sophists, seemed confident that there was, in fact, an answer to these questions.

We have already noted that, in their twists and turns of argument and their skillful displays of rhetoric, the Sophists often made profound points. If today their reputation has made them into "tricksters" and their arguments mere "sophistry," the truth is that they had a good deal of value to teach. Indeed, they claimed to teach virtue. Socrates disagreed. Virtue cannot be taught, he said. Nevertheless, he agreed with them on the importance of virtue, and he emulated their methods. Together, they provided a healthy antidote to the abstract and sometimes abstruse perplexities of pre-Socratic philosophy and the absolute confidence that so often went with them, promoted by Parmenides and Zeno, in particular. Ironically, "sophistry" has since been seen as a contrast to Socrates, who was cast by Plato as the hero of all philosophers and the nemesis of the Sophists. Indeed, Plato cast many of the Sophists as Socrates' victims, his "interlocutors," the comedian's foils. They rarely got the best lines, which were almost always reserved for Socrates alone.

In truth, however, Socrates was not opposed to the Sophists. Rather, he bested them with their own rhetorical arguments. He accused them of too quickly claiming knowledge. He faulted them as teachers when they could not pass his rigorous dialectical tests. Socrates set high—perhaps impossibly high—standards for knowledge. Accordingly, he always admitted his own ignorance, and he excelled, above all, in revealing the ignorance of others. He was the best of the Sophists. He also believed in something. And—as fate would have it—he had the best public relations agent in history.

Socrates' student Plato (ca. 428–348 or 347 B.C.E.) transcribed the activities and teachings of his teacher. Luckily for us (and for Socrates' reputation), Plato was a devoted pupil, a (more or less) faithful reporter, and a brilliant writer. In his later writings, Plato would start adding more than a few opinions and ideas of his own. Indeed, to this day a lively and unresolvable debate continues about how much of what we know of Socrates is Socrates and how much of Socrates is really pure Plato. But, on the assumption that much can be gleaned of the original from the early writings of Plato (and less faithful descriptions by the historian Xenophon and other writers), we can imagine ourselves in what must have been one of the liveliest episodes in the history of philosophy, when philosophy took to the streets of the *agora* (or marketplace) of Athens and resembled more an Olympic contest than a staid philosophy seminar. Let us put Socrates' politics and his death in the background and try to understand just why his students and ultimately so many thinkers from his time to ours have come to view him as *"the philosopher."*

Socrates' undisputed title of "first philosopher" refers not, of course, to priority in time, but to his status. Indeed, it is no small recognition of his unique position in philosophy that all of the philosophers who came before him (including Democritus, who was actually his younger contemporary) are collectively known as "pre-Socratics," that is, before Socrates. They are consigned to virtual prehistory so far as the standard history of philosophy is concerned. And yet, when it comes to many of the mainstay standards often used to assess the pre-Socratics as philosophers—systematic thinking, a controversial central thesis (preferably written down in some form), freedom from literary and ordinary conversational constraints, an interest in the ultimate questions of cosmology and cosmogony—Socrates would seem to fail every test.

The Socratic dialogues display no single line of thought and very little by way of philosophical theories—only Socrates' inimitable style and personality. Scholars debate to this day whether Socrates held any consistent thesis at all or whether he simply dispatched the arguments of everyone around him, leaving only questions in return. Socrates never wrote down his philosophy but instead employed it in animated conversations with his students and other philosophers who were his contemporaries. He presented very little that would readily count as a philosophical thesis, although he was ingenious and often insightful in his arguments. And, he seemed to display no interest whatever in the heady questions that had so moved his predecessors.

Nevertheless, we have ample documentation of his teachings in the writings of Plato and Xenophon.[21] Socrates did defend something of a theory, at the core of which was a very special notion of *virtue*. The virtues represented what was best about a person, and foremost among these were the philosophical or intellectual virtues. Socrates' death might be said to reflect this sense of virtue. As Aristotle was later to argue, the first virtue of philosophy is the need to do philosophy. Yet Socrates also argued that he gave up his life "for the sake of his soul." Here we find one of those philosophical nuggets that would obsess moralists for the next two thousand years. Does this mean that Socrates was, as he teasingly suggested, being *selfish*, looking after his own interests (the interests of his soul)? Alternatively, is acting (dying) for the sake of one's soul the ultimate virtue? Or is this dilemma a false one, as is the opposition on which it depends?

Socrates was notoriously equivocal on what we might call the boundaries of the self. Socrates claimed to have an inner voice, a *"daemon,"* which kept him in line.[22] This daemon told him, over and over again, how much he didn't know, how ignorant he was, and yet—how knowledge alone would save his soul. The Oracle at Delphi had told Socrates, nevertheless, that he was the wisest man in the world. Put those two voices together, and you can draw the conclusion that wisdom begins with the stark realization that you don't know much of anything. By comparison, Socrates thought that his fellow citizens, especially those uneducated democrats who thought they knew so much, were virtual morons. He also took it upon himself to make sure that they knew this. Asking them such questions as "What is virtue?," "What is knowledge?," and "What is justice?," he deftly demonstrated both the difficulty of these philosophical queries and the doltishness of his democratic colleagues.

Now it might seem odd that we have given so few details about Socrates' actual philosophy. The reason, again, is that he asserted very little. He taught that the most important thing in life is to save your soul, that the mark of a good soul is virtue, and that the most important goal is to gain knowledge, that is, wisdom. And yet, he argues that virtue cannot be taught. Indeed, he made very little attempt to "reach" his own students. He seems to have believed not only in the immortality of the soul but also in reincarnation. Probably he was influenced here by Pythagoras. He certainly believed in his own ideals and the power of reason. Throughout the dialogues, as in his life, Socrates continues to insist on both his own ignorance and his own virtue, despite the fact that the one crystal-clear thesis throughout his philosophy is his insistence that virtue is knowledge. But beyond this, Socrates made few positive claims.

His concept of the soul, for instance, is notoriously indeterminate and open-minded. It is not clearly religious and seems to presuppose no metaphysical or theological doctrines. Nor does it involve any naturalistic or physical commitments, such as the traditional view that the soul is animating "breath." Indeed, it is not even obvious that he is seeking agreement about his contention that the soul is immortal, and in the *Apology* he only says how nice it would be *if* that were so. Living (and dying) for the sake of one's soul has purely to do with personal character and integrity and nothing to do with any expectations of future reward. Socrates' concerns are strictly ethical, without a hint of the cosmological intrigue that had fascinated his predecessors.

So, too, the all-important notion of virtue (and the analysis of the virtues) that emerges from the various Socratic dialogues is at best a disorganized series of examples and counterexamples coupled with the continuing insistence that virtue is essential to being a good person and living a good life. There is hardly anything that one might call a "theory" of the virtues or, for that matter, even a clear list of what counts as a virtue and what does not. As for the details, Socrates doesn't tell, even when his victim is thoroughly defeated and seems in desperate need of some enlightenment. Socrates insists that one find out for oneself, and so we get very little from him. Even when he seems to assert a position, he often takes it back or contradicts it—occasionally in the same dialogue.

In the dialogue *Crito*, for example, Socrates argues energetically with his friend and intended liberator Crito. Is it right for him to break the laws of Athens by escaping from prison, even if, under the circumstances, he had been falsely accused and unjustly sentenced? He seems to insist that a citizen has an absolute obligation to obey the law of the land, even when that law is unjust and turns against him. But several years earlier, when Socrates had been commanded by the tyrants to arrest an (innocent) fellow citizen, he had refused to do so. No such argument, it seems, had been forthcoming then.

So, too, Socrates will refute a definition of courage or justice, for example, in one dialogue or book (the *Laches*, for example, or Book I of the *Republic*) and then he himself will put forward a similar definition in another dialogue or book (the *Protagoras*, for example, or Book X of the *Republic*). In some dialogues, Socrates seems to be arguing for what, in Plato's terminology, is usually called "the theory of Forms." But in others, Socrates expresses the gravest doubts about any such theory and raises some of the keenest objections against it.

Scholars, perhaps, can sort out and resolve these apparent contradictions, which must confuse most readers. What does come through, in every dialogue, is the astounding personality of Socrates. What is so admirable about Socrates is not the nature or the persuasiveness of any particular claims but the charms of the man himself and his method. Socrates truly practiced philosophy. He lived it. And whatever he may or may not have believed by way of theory, he showed us how a philosopher should be.

One can, however, discern in Socrates two very different influences on the future of philosophy: his character and his method. He was very personal and personable. He loved conversation and argument, and undoubtedly enjoyed winning, tripping up his opponents, baiting them into further discussion, giving them a bit of encouragement and then tripping them up again. Watching Socrates at work is like watching a verbal kung-fu master. He had endurance that even impressed the young warriors (who were his students). He was also funny, extremely ironic, and playful. He was earthy, passionate, enthusiastic. He had charms that made him a legend among the youth of Athens. And, of course, he talked all the time.

But Socrates also has a method, which also emerges as his philosophy, especially in some of the later dialogues of Plato, where Socrates becomes less of a character and more of a "pure philosopher." (Here is where the "Socrates or Plato" question becomes really important, and frustratingly unanswerable.) That method, which is the primary focus of much of the commentary on Socrates in the past century or so, can and has been described as a "method of irony"— because he keeps claiming not to understand when, in fact, he clearly understands better than anyone. Or, perhaps better, it is a method of cross-examination, the creation of perplexity (*aporia*). Socrates begins by seeking "definitions" but then rejects virtually every definition that is given. But by "definition," Socrates does not mean a mere dictionary definition of how words (like "justice," "virtue," or "courage") are used. He is looking for the "thing" itself—justice, virtue, or courage—in its purest form. Thus, his method would seem to suggest that when all of the inadequate definitions are cast aside, what will be left, by the process of "dialectic" (or, simply, vigorous conversation), will be true. That true definition, in turn, will point us to the ideal itself (of justice, virtue, or courage).

Thus Socrates seems to believe in ideals which themselves lie beyond normal human experience.

These ideals define virtue and determine the worth of one's soul. More surprising, Socrates insists that they are known by the soul, even at birth. But these ideals are by no means merely "in us." They belong to a world of ideals which only the wise man, the philosopher, can comprehend. That is why only the philosopher is ultimately fit to rule, and why the unenlightened must be made aware of their unfitness.

The method and its implications point back to earlier Greek philosophy, before Socrates, to the belief or hope in the existence of an ideal, unchanging world, beyond the world of flux and mere appearance—in other words, back to the wild cosmologies of Pythagoras and Parmenides. But Socrates seems to have been mostly indifferent to their ideas,[23] and he was hostile, as were all of the Sophists, to any claim to absolute knowledge. If we are to appreciate the impact of the pre-Socratics' ideas, it seems, we will have to go beyond Socrates to Plato. But there, we will find, the questions only become more complicated.[24]

Plato: Metaphysician or Sublime Humorist?

Plato was the greatest writer in philosophy, and a genius of a dramatist. Of course, he was fortunate to have so much of his work survive. (This applies only to his philosophical writings, however. Plato destroyed his plays when he decided to devote himself to philosophy.) Plato also founded a school, the Academy, to make sure that his writings and ideas (and the teachings of Socrates) were kept alive.

Compared to virtually any philosopher before or since, Plato was more brilliant, more moving, funnier, and more profound. Consider the following two brief excerpts, from the *Republic* and the *Symposium*, respectively:

SOCRATES: Come then, Thrasymachus, answer us from the beginning. You say that complete injustice is more profitable than complete justice?

THRASYMACHUS: I certainly do say that, and I have told you why.

SOCRATES: Well then, what about this: you call one of the two a virtue and the other a vice?

THRASYMACHUS: Of course.

SOCRATES: That is, you call justice a virtue, and injustice a vice?

THRASYMACHUS: Is that likely, my good man, since I say that injustice is profitable, and justice is not?

SOCRATES: What then?

THRASYMACHUS: The opposite.

SOCRATES: Do you call being just a vice?

THRASYMACHUS: No, but certainly high-minded foolishness.

SOCRATES: And you call being unjust low-minded?

THRASYMACHUS: No, I call it good judgment.

SOCRATES: You consider the unjust then, Thrasymachus, to be good and knowledgeable?

THRASYMACHUS. Yes, those who are able to carry injustice through to the end, who can bring cities and communities of men under their power. Perhaps you think I mean purse-snatchers? Not that those actions too are not profitable, if they are not found out, but they are not worth mentioning in comparison with what I am talking about.

SOCRATES: I am not unaware of what you mean, but this point astonishes me: do you include injustice under virtue and wisdom, and justice among their opposites?

THRASYMACHUS: I certainly do.

SOCRATES: That makes it harder, my friend, and it is not easy now to know what to say. If you had declared that injustice was more profitable, but agreed that it was a vice or shameful as some others do, we could have discussed it along the lines of general opinion. Now, obviously, you will say that it is fine and strong, and apply to it all the attributes which we used to apply to justice, since you have been so bold as to include it under virtue and wisdom.

THRASYMACHUS: Your guess is quite right.

SOCRATES: We must not, however, shrink from pursuing our argument and looking into this, so long as I am sure that you mean what you say. For I do not think you are joking now, Thrasymachus, but are saying what you believe to be true.

THRASYMACHUS: What difference does it make to you whether I believe it or not? Is it not my argument you are refuting?

SOCRATES: No difference. . . .

from The Republic, trans. E. M. A. Grube

SOCRATES: A man or anyone else who has a desire desires what he does not have, and what he is not, and that of which he is in need; for such are the objects of desire and love.

AGATHON: Certainly.

SOCRATES: Come, then, let us review the points on which we've agreed. Aren't they, first, that Love is the love of something, and, second, that he loves things of which he has a present need?

AGATHON: Yes.

SOCRATES: Now, remember, in addition to these points, what you said in your speech about what it is that Love loves. If you like, I'll remind you. I think you said something like this: that the gods' quarrels were settled by love of beautiful things, for there is no love of ugly ones. Didn't you say something like that?

AGATHON: I did.

SOCRATES: And that's a suitable thing to say, my friend, but if this is so, wouldn't Love have to be a desire for beauty, and never for ugliness?

AGATHON: Yes.

SOCRATES: And we also agreed that he loves just what he needs and does not have.

AGATHON: Yes.

SOCRATES: So Love needs beauty, then, and does not have it.
AGATHON: Necessarily.
SOCRATES: So! If something needs beauty and has got no beauty at all, would you still say that it is beautiful?
AGATHON: Certainly not.
SOCRATES: Then do you still agree that Love is beautiful, if those things are so?
AGATHON: It turns out, Socrates, I didn't know what I was talking about in that speech.
SOCRATES: It was a beautiful speech, anyway, Agathon. Now take it a little further. Don't you think that good things are always beautiful as well?

from *The Symposium*, trans. A. Nehamas and P. Woodruff

The fate of Socrates overshadowed every dialogue, lending poignance to every exchange and giving dignity to every argument. Indeed, the use of Socrates, first as the dramatic hero, but later on as a philosophical mouthpiece, was so successful that Plato continued using him, even when it became clear that the ideas supposedly being articulated and argued by Socrates were actually Plato's own.

This raises the familiar problem: How do we know when Plato is being more or less faithful to Socrates or simply using Socrates as his rhetorical and philosophical spokesman? When can we assume the two are in agreement, and when should we assume that the theses being recommended are those of Plato alone? To make matters even more complicated, the difficulty with the dialogue form is that there is no assurance whatever that the author (Plato) agrees with the speaker in the dialogue. In the *Symposium*, for instance, Plato presents us with more than a half-dozen speakers contradicting one another, and it is by no means clear that he himself agrees with any of them, including Socrates. (In a few late dialogues, Socrates disappears altogether.)

Plato's philosophy began, first of all, with a credible if overly admiring and uncritical account of Socrates, particularly Socrates' last days. Socrates' trial, imprisonment, and execution are reported in the *Apology*, the *Crito*, and the *Phaedo*, respectively. Plato also creates extensive conversations—dialogues—in which Socrates holds forth with some of the cleverest (and a few not so clever) thinkers of his time, including Aristophanes, Alcibiades, Parmenides, Zeno, Protagoras, and Gorgias. Through Socrates' refutation of their various arguments, Plato begins to suggest his own views. It is probably safe to say that Plato's earlier dialogues, those that are especially concerned with ethics and being a good person and the definition of the virtues, are a fair but obviously much embellished account of Socrates' views. The later dialogues, those that are more concerned with problems of knowledge and cosmological issues, are almost certainly Plato's own philosophy.

Plato's cosmological concerns include the Pythagorean view of the world as number, the Heraclitean view of the world as flux and as *logos*, and the Parmenidean vision of an eternal, unchanging, unknowable reality. Central to Plato's philosophy, though at most implied by Socrates, was his theory of Forms. This theory entailed a "two-world" cosmology. One world is our everyday world of change and impermanence. The other is an ideal world populated by ideal "Forms" or *Eidoi* (from the singular *eidos*). The first, the "World of Becoming," was in flux, as Heraclitus insisted, but the latter, the "World of Being," was eternal and unchanging, as Parmenides demanded. What made Plato's new vision so appealing was that, first of all, the two worlds were interrelated, not unrelated as Parmenides and some of the Sophists had suggested. The World of Becoming, our world, was defined by ("participated in") the World of Being, the world of ideal Forms. Thus the idea of an unchanging *logos* underlying the everyday world could be understood as the ideality of the Forms, defining the world despite the fact of continual change. Furthermore, this ideal world of Forms was not, as in Parmenides, unknowable. According to Plato, we could get a glimpse of this world, at least, through reason.

Ready examples of such glimpses into the ideal world are available in the fields of mathematics and geometry. Take, for example, a geometrical proof of a theorem having to do with triangles. The triangle that we draw on the blackboard or on paper is an untidy thing. In fact, given the way the lines are smudged and crooked and the way the corners do not quite come together, it really isn't a triangle at all. And yet, by using this poor drawing of a triangle, something essential about triangles can nevertheless be proven. How can this be possible?

Pythagoras had already led the way in his theory that the essence of the world could be found in number, in proportion or *ratio*. What was most real, Pythagoras suggested, was not the matter of things but their *form*. The study of mathematics and geometry, accordingly, was the study of the essential structure of reality, whatever the passing fate of particular beings and relationships. And so, one might say, the study of mathematics and geometry allows us to "see through" the everyday flux of the world and understand something essential, unchanging. So, too, we "see through" our badly drawn triangle to the idea or form of *triangle-as-such*. What we prove is not so much a theorem about our badly drawn triangle as it is a theorem about all triangles, insofar as they exemplify the triangle-as-such. Of course, our badly drawn triangle conforms to the theorem, too, insofar as it is indeed a representation of a triangle. But that is just to say it is a triangle by virtue of the fact that it is a representation of something else, triangle-as-such, which is not in this world. And yet, we can evidently know triangle-as-such, that is, the ideal Form of The Triangle. We come to understand it through our reasoning.

Likewise, all things in this world are representations, for better or worse, of ideal Forms. Looking back to the historical Socrates (as opposed to Plato's character), we can now see in what sense he anticipated (whether or not he actually believed in) a theory of Forms. When he was looking for a "definition" of virtue, he was in fact seeking the ideal Form, virtue-as-such. When he was asking for a definition of courage, or justice, or wisdom, what he was seeking were the ideal Forms. And when Socrates went looking for "the Good," what he sought was the Form behind all good things, good acts, good beings. Thus we can understand why the Socratic method of intense cross-examination and reasoning through various attempted definitions was so important, but we can also see why Socrates was so ironically adamant about his own ignorance and why he insisted that he could not teach these definitions or the virtuousness that such revelations produced. One had to work these matters out, one had to "see" these Forms for oneself. Socrates, we can be sure, had his mind's eye on the ideal Form of virtue all the way, whether or not he ever gave us a singular definition as such. That is why he was so confident and unswerving, even in the face of death.

Perhaps the most memorable image of the Forms and their ability to dazzle the philosopher who sees them is the vision that Plato provides for us in Book VII of his masterpiece, the *Republic*. There he spins an allegory, "The Myth of the Cave," which is both an allegory concerning the relationship between the World of Being and the World of Becoming—the Forms and the things of this world—and a warning of the dangers facing the philosopher. Plato presumably refers to his teacher Socrates, who tried to explain or expose these Forms to the general populace.

The Myth begins with the image of a number of prisoners shackled in a cave with their faces to the wall. What they see, and what they consider to be reality, are the shadows cast on the wall. So, too, Socrates goes on to explain (as he narrates the allegory), what we all take to be reality consists ultimately of shadows. It is not that these are unreal. They are real shadows, but they are shadows of things that are even more real. So the distinction here is not, as in Parmenides, between reality and illusion. It is the distinction between more and less real, a superior and an inferior world.

Now suppose that one of those prisoners, a philosopher, were to break free and turn around, casting his eyes, for the first time, on the genuine objects that cast the shadows and the bright sun that does the casting. Would he not be dazzled? Would he not immediately see how imperfect are the shadows of everyday reality compared with the reality he now observed? So, too, the philosopher is dazzled when he sees the perfect Forms of virtue, justice, and courage, compared to the imperfect and usually confused ideas and actions of ordinary men and women. How much "higher" then his aspirations will be. And if such a philosopher were then to turn back to the cave and try to tell his fellows how impoverished their world was, how inadequate their ideals, would they not turn on him and kill him? The reference to Socrates' own fate is unmistakable, but the allusion to the Forms is of much more general and profound significance.

The theory of Forms makes Plato's philosophy sound very abstract and cosmological. In fact, it was first of all a political philosophy, and the *Republic* was a political and very polemical book. But it was not mere politics either. Defending and redefining the Greek city-state required an entirely new cosmology—a new religion, in effect, to take the place of Zeus and his gang. (Among the charges against Socrates was his rejection of the gods of Athens and his introduction of "new gods.")

The republic described by Plato had much in common, needless to say, with the Athenian city-state, but it also displayed some disconcerting differences, many of which we still find extreme. To begin with, it was not a democracy. On this point, Plato and Socrates are certainly in agreement. Rule is in the hands of those who know best and have insight into virtue—and that means philosophers. In the *Republic* Plato gives us the image of philosopher-kings, which was no doubt received with as much ridicule then as now. (The absentminded philosopher joke had been around at least since Thales.)

Plato's republic is oddly authoritarian, hierarchical, and egalitarian in turns. It is a "natural" aristocracy, based on talent, the fortunes of birth, and upbringing. It is a benign dictatorship in which everyone, including the "guardians," knows their place. It is not a society that caters to individuals or to individual interests but in which the individual and individual interests are expected to be subordinated to the common good. Plato advocates the use of artistic censorship, for example, contending that the stimulating influence of art should be limited to the role of instilling appropriate social attitudes and behavior. It is a society in which people are not entitled to own property and are not even free to bring up their own children, who would be educated, instead, by the state. But it is a society in which women are to be given as much power as men—a daring suggestion in those times. The well-being of the least citizen is to be considered as important as the well-being of the greatest. Even the rulers are given no special privileges and are not expected to be happy, given their awesome responsibilities. Happiness, Plato tells us, is not for any privileged class of citizens but for the city-state as a whole.

It is difficult to reconcile this antidemocratic vision of the good society and Socrates's almost saintly example of the good but eccentric gadfly. But the *Republic* is not just a political model of a merely imagined state. It also advocates a new way of thinking about ourselves and the world. We might reject the authoritarian and inegalitarian aspects of the republic described without dismissing the *Republic*'s worldview. (Indeed, Plato rejects this model of the republic himself, defending a far more ambivalent conception of politics in his very late dialogue the *Laws*.) So, too, we might reject the metaphysical extreme of believing in another world of absolute ideals without letting go of the ideal of virtuousness and the importance of the cultivation of the virtues, in part, through philosophy. But Plato, following Socrates, had something more to promise us than a utopian city-state and a rather incredible metaphysics. He also gave us an inspiring picture of the soul, which now had to navigate an entirely new way of looking at the world.

As we mentioned earlier, the Greeks, from Homer to Democritus, "believed in" the soul only to a minimal extent. They admitted that something, call it "breath" (which is the original meaning of the word *psyche*), was needed to animate the body, and departed the body with death. But, according to this picture, the soul needed the body just as much as the body needed the soul. Without the soul, the body was dead, but without the body, the soul was just a pathetic shadow, with no meaning and no value. But for Socrates the soul had moral significance. It was also more important than the body. Socrates believed that the soul outlives the body in a significant sense. (In this, he is obviously kin to—if not borrowing from—Pythagoras and the Pythagorean doctrines of the immortality and transmigration of the soul.)

In the *Apology*, Socrates fantasizes the joy of thinking philosophy all of the time in the afterlife, without interruptions or distractions. It was as if he faced death as the prospect of a vacation, even treating it as a cure.[25] Plato's later vision gives us a vehicle for understanding this conception of the soul. The soul, unlike the rest of us, belongs (in part) to the World of Being, the eternal world. Its loss of the body is therefore only a partial loss (or no loss at all, depending on how you look at it). That is why, according to Socrates, a truly good man can ultimately suffer no evil, despite physical harm or even death.

Moreover, if the soul belongs (in part) to the World of Being, then it already contains the knowledge of the Forms. Thus our knowledge of virtue, beauty, and the good does not depend on learning, much less being taught about them. We are born with this knowledge. It is "innate" (literally "born into" us). In the *Phaedo*, Socrates says, "In order to know anything absolutely, we must be free from the body and behold actual reality with the eyes of the soul alone." The soul thus becomes the conduit of intellectual as well as moral life. Quite literally, it is the one thing in life truly worth worrying about.

One of the most memorable and deservedly famous of all of the Socratic dialogues is the *Symposium*, a mainly fictitious and delightful account of an after-dinner party in which Socrates and several poets and playwrights discuss and debate the virtues of *eros*—erotic love. Among the symposiasts is the comic playwright Aristophanes. Plato perhaps gets even for the drubbing Socrates had received in Aristophanes' *Clouds*. (Aristophanes suffers from hiccups, for instance.) There is also Pausanias, and Agathon, a talented young tragedian and the host of the party. Perhaps most dramatic of all is Alcibiades, who shows up late, very drunk, and is pointedly snubbed by Socrates. In the *Symposium*, Socrates argues that love is not just the desire for a beautiful body or even a beautiful person, but something much more—the love of Beauty itself. "Beauty itself," of course, is one of the Forms. And that makes the true lover the lover of wisdom, the philosopher.

The emphasis on Beauty in the *Symposium* reflects an important feature of Plato's thought. Aesthetic concerns about beauty and order are central to Plato's philosophy as a whole. Beauty was the Form that embodied human beings could most easily recognize, and a glimpse of beauty was often the initial motivation that incited a person to pursue philosophy. Moreover, virtue, for Plato, is akin to beauty. Virtue makes the soul harmonious, as beauty orders the elements of a face or a scene. Even Plato's ideal republic involves the aesthetic notion of harmoniously organized parts. The centrality of aesthetic notions in formulating ethical and political ideals continues in Aristotle's philosophy, and it reemerges at various points in later philosophy, although rarely with the straightforwardness of the ancient Greeks (or the early Chinese).

The *Symposium* has several special features that are worth mentioning. First, in this relatively early dialogue, Plato is not wholly represented by Socrates, and the upshot of the dialogue is by no means Socrates' view alone. Aristophanes gives a fanciful speech that, no matter how much it is ridiculed by Socrates, is particularly memorable and poignant as an account of the origins of love. (This is the ancient story of human double-creatures who are split in half by Zeus, and ever since have been "trying to find their other half.") Other speakers point out the more humorous and practical features of love.

At the end of the dialogue, Alcibiades comes crashing in, making fun of Socrates and abusing him as a heartbreaker. But Alcibiades also demonstrates an important point which directly contradicts Socrates' own teaching. He shows by his behavior (but does not actually argue) that love is not directed toward a Form but toward a very particular individual, and, furthermore, that the beauty and virtue of that individual are of no particular relevance to love. (Socrates may have been virtuous, but he was notoriously not good-looking. Alcibiades, on the other hand, was extremely handsome but notorious.) It would seem that Plato's own measured opinion of *eros* was that it exemplified some of the ideal features that Socrates suggested, but it also has a metaphysical, mythological, and obsessional nature that Socrates ignores.

The *Symposium* is also the only dialogue in which Socrates clearly states that he is not ignorant. The one thing he knows about for certain, he claims, is love. This is, of course, because he is already a lover (of wisdom), which does not imply that one *has* wisdom. Nevertheless, Socrates will not even claim that what he knows about love is something he has discovered for himself. He rather attributes this knowledge to a muse named Diotima. (Whether Diotima was real or not is not nearly as interesting as the fact that she is a woman, and Greek philosophers almost never took philosophical advice from a woman.[26])

Finally, it should be said that the *Symposium*, for all of its insights, is first of all fun and funny.[27] It demonstrates once and for all that philosophy can be profound without being unbearably serious. Unfortunately, that lesson didn't really take hold, and one would never guess from most of the tribute paid to Plato that he was philosophy's most sublime humorist as well as a great metaphysician.

The Philosopher's Philosopher: Aristotle

As a student of Plato, Aristotle was naturally concerned with his teacher's theory of Forms, which he rejected. As the "grand-student" of Socrates, he was also particularly interested in his teacher's concept of the virtues, and here he could heartily agree. But this agreement could not extend to the otherworldly notion of Virtue-as-such, Virtue as an ideal Form. A virtue, according to Aristotle, is a concrete aspect of human character, of individual characters, and not an abstraction or an ideal that is in any sense detached from the people who exemplify that virtue.

Thus, in Aristotle we find a "one-world" philosophy which has its feet firmly planted on the ground. Like Plato, his aim is to find his way through the ingenuity and obscurities of the pre-Socratic philosophers in order to develop an adequate theory of both human nature and nature in general. Like Socrates, he is centrally concerned with the cultivation of the virtues—although contrary to Socrates and in agreement with the other Sophists, Aristotle claims that these can be taught. But that does not mean that they can be taught in a philosophy seminar or a book. An individual has to be brought up with the virtues, trained so that they become second nature. No philosopher and no philosophy book can do that. Here, as always in Aristotle, the bottom line comes down to the individual. There is no place and no need for a theory of Forms, a theory of another world, a theory of the migrating soul.

And yet, no philosopher is more steeped in cosmology and the sciences of this world than Aristotle. He not only studied but summarized and reinterpreted the cosmologies and cosmogonies of the pre-Socratics. Indeed, as we have noted, it is mainly through Aristotle that we know of their work and even of their existence at all. And Aristotle not only incorporated the science of the past; he pursued almost all of the sciences into the future—indeed, very far into the future. Many of his views went virtually unchallenged for another fifteen centuries, and they were not for the most part rejected for another three hundred years after that. He was a cosmologist, an astronomer, a meteorologist, a physicist, a geologist, a biologist, a psychologist, and the first logician of any importance. The one science that he seems not to have tackled, interestingly enough, was mathematics.

Moreover, Aristotle was a poet, a literary theorist, a rhetorician, a politician, a political theorist, a statesman and a tutor to statesmen, notably, the young Alexander, soon to become "the Great." (Aristotle's father was the court physician to Philip of Macedon, Alexander's father. As Alexander's tutor, Aristotle came vicariously close to being Plato's philosopher-king.) Aristotle was by far the most advanced intellect of his time, and in virtually every field. We could fill this book with just a list of Aristotle's various theories and achievements, but we must be much more modest. As with Plato, we shall try only to fit him into the long and complex story we are telling.

What we will stress are a couple of themes in Aristotle's metaphysics which have had particular power and influence over the years, and his ethics, which still stands today as one of the great contributions to that field. He does not write about religion as such, perhaps because his views on that subject were so progressive and, no doubt, dangerous to him at the time. (The shadow of Socrates' fate was certainly still in view.) Our first and main point has to do with Aristotle's attack on Plato's theory of Forms, and with it, his response to the cosmologies of the pre-Socratics, especially the views of Heraclitus and Parmenides.

Aristotle, unlike the pre-Socratics, has no problem accepting the reality of change. At the same time, he agrees that there must be some fundamental "stuff" if knowledge of the world is to be possible. He does not feel compelled to choose, as the early pre-Socratics did, some one basic element (water, air, fire, *apeiron*). Nor did he feel compelled to choose between the priority of form and matter. Obviously, he says, things require both. But neither was there any need— or intelligible reason—to separate them, as in Pythagoras and Plato.

Although the history of philosophy has been described in terms of the dueling legacies of Plato and Aristotle, Aristotle never intended a full-scale split with Plato, his teacher and friend for twenty years. Aristotle agreed with Plato that the form of things is of the utmost importance. But Aristotle maintained that the form *of* something was also *in* the thing, not somewhere above or beyond it. He was much more of a scientist than Plato, often more of a scientist than a philosopher, in the sense ordinarily conveyed by those labels. Thus his orientation was very different. The sign above the door at Plato's Academy allegedly instructed all entrants to first of all learn geometry. Aristotle's Lyceum, on the other hand, was filled with scientific exhibits, collections of rocks, plants, animal remains. Unlike earlier philosophers, he did not distrust the senses but *used* them, to observe, to collect specimens, and to experiment, although it must be said that, in some instances, he put more faith in reason than in actual experiments. (It was many centuries before Galileo showed that, contrary to reason—that is, Aristotle's untested expectations—a large stone falls no faster than a small stone.)

Like his teacher Plato, Aristotle sought the essence of things, and this in turn was the business of reason. Aristotle therefore spends a good deal of philosophy analyzing the ways of reason and reasoning—in logic, in categorizing and interpretation, in "dialectic" (or conversational debate), even in rhetoric. But to explain reason in terms of the Forms, Aristotle says, is to fall back on "empty words and poetic metaphors."

And yet, Aristotle's philosophy also involved a "reaching beyond," not beyond sensible experience but beyond the actual state of things. His emphasis was not on what things currently are but on their *potential*. Aristotle, as we noted, did not shy away from the obvious fact of change in the world. Rather, he embraced it, and he gave special place in his philosophy to a certain kind of change, namely, self-realization, growth, and development. He was, above all, a biologist. Even Aristotle's account of Greek tragedy in the *Poetics* draws from biology. The elements of the play should work together like the organs of the body, in Aristotle's "organic" model of art.

Aristotle's status and his insistence on naturalistic explanations did not prevent him from hanging onto the old sense of animism, of "gods in all things," as Thales put it. But these "gods" were ultimately the animating principle of the thing itself, its own *form*, where "form" here includes what Aristotle calls a thing's *function*. A seed cannot be fully understood by reference to the matter that makes it up and its current shape and features. A seed must be considered in terms of its potential to grow into a certain sort of plant, and in order to understand this it must be understood to have an internal principle, a blueprint of sorts, that would direct that development. Aristotle did not know, of course, of the substance we know as deoxyribonucleic acid, or DNA, nor did he even know of the more primitive concept of "genes." But he certainly knew that certain sorts of seed dependably grow into certain sorts of plants, that animals give birth only to their own kind, and that human children look and often behave strikingly like their parents.

Thus the central feature of Aristotle's philosophy (one that he in fact shared with Plato, who did not so emphasize it) is *teleology*, the purposiveness of things. Stones, to be sure, have rather simple and dull-witted purposes—notably, to just sit there, or, to fall to the ground whenever they have the chance. (One should not think that they deliberate and decide to do so, needless to say, and the thought that rocks might be conscious was not one that Aristotle would have taken seriously.) Plants and animals have increasingly complicated purposes, and the parts of plants and animals have increasingly complex functions (their common purpose, to keep the plant or animal alive).

People, of course, act for all sorts of purposes, but their ultimate purpose, the purpose of human life, is by no means to be understood as simply what particular people or even whole societies of people *think* that they want. Here the Socratic project comes back into view, to show people that many of the things they want are not ultimately worth wanting, at least not as such. There is a purpose to human life, according to Aristotle, and not surprisingly it is just that purpose that was promoted by Socrates: to realize one's capacities as a rational animal, to live a virtuous life in accordance with reason.

But before we get into Aristotle's ethics, it is important that we appreciate his ingenious metaphysics, which, in competition with Plato's theory of Forms, set the agenda for at least sixty generations. The basic principle of his philosophy, his teleology, shifts the emphasis away from cosmogony, the attempt to account for the origins of the cosmos, and leads instead to questions about the nature of the universe and all the things in it. Indeed, Aristotle did not have a cosmogony at all, for in his opinion the universe has existed eternally and had no beginning. But he does need to explain the idea of a thing's potentiality—what it can and will become—and its internal principle, which defines and guides that potential.

Whereas for Plato the Forms that defined individual things were quite distinct from them, for Aristotle the forms of things just are these guiding internal principles. And whereas Plato sometimes said that there would be one Form for infinitely many individuals "participating" in that Form (the pre-Socratic problem sometimes called "the One in [and] the Many"), Aristotle insisted that what ultimately exists is nothing other than each individual thing, *this* horse, *this* tree, *this* man. There is no superreality, no world of Forms, insisted Aristotle, but only the individual things of this world.

Aristotle called these individual things by the specialized name *substances*. An individual human being—for instance, Socrates—is a substance. A horse, a tree or a dog is a substance. To understand Socrates or a horse, a tree, or a dog, one need not get a glimpse of anything (such as a Form) besides Socrates, a horse, a tree, or a dog. Of course, a thing consists of parts. Socrates, the horse, and the dog all have legs, hair, eyes, and a nose. The tree has leaves, a trunk, branches, and roots. But all together, these parts form a whole, a complete individual. Again, the biological paradigm is evident.

It is important to appreciate the significance of both Aristotle's emphasis on the existence of individual things as complete in themselves and the importance of the seemingly obvious idea of a thing having features or properties. The pre-Socratics believed that things were made up out of basic ingredients, but then the question of how things change, how they can turn from one thing into another, became a bit of a puzzle—indeed, an apparent contradiction. Aristotle avoided this problem. On his account, a substance is a substratum that *has* properties. The substance itself does not disappear when one claims that the stove is no longer hot but cold, or that Socrates once had hair but now is bald.

Not all of the properties of a thing are of equal weight or importance. Some are *essential*—definitive of the substance as such. Others are "accidental"—contingent, inessential. They might be present in the thing but, if they were not, the thing would still be the thing that it is. When Socrates loses his hair, he is still Socrates. But if Socrates became a frog—not a peculiarly articulate and virtuous Socratic frog but a perfectly ordinary croaking frog—that frog would not be Socrates. The *essence* of a thing consists of those properties that make that thing what it is, without which it would not be that thing. The essence of Socrates, for example, includes the fact that he is a man and a philosopher. Socrates' haircut, by contrast, is a merely accidental property of Socrates, irrelevant to his true nature. This down-to-earth talk of individual substances and essences is central to Aristotle's philosophy, and it eliminates any need to appeal to Plato's mysterious Forms.

Looking back at the pre-Socratics, we can appreciate just how far Greek thought has come from their early speculations about the nature of things and the nature of reality. In response to the stark reductionism of the early materialists and the bland pluralism of the atomists, Aristotle has restored the world to its original, commonsense richness, but without sacrificing the probing insights that the pre-Socratic philosophers had provided. He took their various suggestions concerning the ultimate "stuff" of the universe, appraised their progress, and noted that they had been unduly narrow in their interpretation of the world. Some had overemphasized matter and neglected the importance of form. In response to the troubling arguments by Parmenides and Zeno, Aristotle had joined with Heraclitus in maintaining the reality of change. Parmenides had confused two different senses of the verb "to be," Aristotle argued, the first indicating existence but the second "the 'is' of predication," the "is" which asserts that a substance has a property or feature. To be sure, nothing comes out of nothing. But the "is" of existence is compatible with any number of different applications of the "is" of predication, so that what exists may now be cold but can *become* hot. What is now an acorn can *become* an oak tree. There is becoming as well as being. It is equally real, and not paradoxical at all.

Heraclitus had postulated that underlying all change is the *logos*. In place of the *logos* Aristotle postulates "principles of motion and rest," principles of change (which themselves do not change) *within* each and every being. But at least one notion in Aristotle does seem to correspond to Heraclitus's *logos*, and that is his concept of God, the ultimate principle of all motion, "the prime mover." With Aristotle more than with any Greek before, we get an explicit idea of God that is totally devoid of anthropomorphism, a principle rather than a person. Xenophanes had suggested a concept of the One to replace the anthropomorphic pantheon of popular Greek religion. Parmenides can certainly be interpreted in a religious way, and Plato has Socrates put forward conceptions that have often been interpreted as theological. But it is Aristotle who gives us what will later be called (without praise) "the God of the philosophers."

It must not be thought that Aristotle's God is a mere physical principle, a "first cause" that initiates the development of the universe, like the God of the eighteenth-century "Deists." God did not just appear and then go out of existence. And as always in Aristotle, the concept is above all teleological. Every activity has a *telos*, an ideal that lies at its end, not outside in the World of Being but within the activity itself. Nevertheless, in retrospect, Aristotle can be interpreted as providing an excellent foundation for later Christian conceptions of God. The ultimate end of the cosmos itself, the only form which exists in itself and apart from any matter, is God. God is the unmoved mover, who keeps the stars and planets in their paths, who maintains life in the universe. God is eternal and complete in Himself. He is all actuality, the final end, the aspiration, the purpose toward which all things move and (try to) realize their potential. Meanwhile, God is fully realized activity, the activity of pure thinking, "thought thinking itself." What such a deity has in common with the God who will reign over Christianity is a difficult and debatable question, one which continues to this day.

The difference between a purely physical notion of God as a first cause, who simply sets the world in motion, and a teleological notion of God, understood as the world's ultimate purpose, underscores the complexity of the central Aristotelian concept of "cause." Indeed, one could argue that the word "cause" is misleading and unfortunate, insofar as the word "cause" has become the cornerstone of physical theory and is often used today precisely in order to exclude teleological notions. For example, a causal account in biology is typically intended to replace a purposive account. The theory of evolution and natural selection was intended to replace traditional theories of creation as an expression of God's will and as intending toward some natural goal. So, too, a person may be said to be "caused" (as in "compelled") to respond in a certain way when one means to deny that he chose to act for reasons of his own.

Aristotle distinguishes between four different kinds of "causes," but for Aristotle a "cause" is an explanatory principle, any "reason," any "because." What we usually refer to as a cause, a more or less immediate, typically physical cause, is only one of these. The four causes are: the *material* cause, which is the matter that makes up a thing or goes into an activity; the *formal* cause, which is the form, the blueprint, the essence, the internal principle which guides and explains development; the *final* cause, which is the end, the *telos*, "that for the sake of which," toward which the activity is aimed; and finally the *efficient* cause, which is what we usually call the cause, the immediate trigger or "push" that sets an activity in motion or stops it.

In the more recent history of causality, particularly with the modern scientific revolution, "the cause" of an event will generally be understood as that change in conditions immediately prior to an event which best explains the occurrence. The cause of the eight ball moving toward the corner pocket was its being hit by the five ball. The cause of the stampede was the fact that the dog had gotten loose in the corral. The cause of her failure was the incompetent advice of her advisor. (Or, somewhat dubiously, the cause of the cloudburst, a soaked colleague complains, is the fact that we had forgotten our umbrella.)

Aristotle's material cause, by contrast, is only occasionally still cited as a cause, as in "the cause of the blanket's bursting into flame is the fact that it is made of a highly flammable material." Aristotle's formal causes are even more rarely cited as causes in this contemporary sense except, perhaps, in such explanations as "the plan was screwed up from its very conception." Numerologists might also cite formal causes (as in "13 is an unlucky number, and you were in row 13"), but the status of such explanations as "causal" explanations is dubious at best.

Final causes are no longer acceptable in science, and this, perhaps, is where Aristotle's scheme differs most strikingly from modern thinking, and not just in mere terminology. We mentioned the theory of evolution as one arena in which teleological explanations have been jettisoned in favor of purely (efficient) causal accounts. Almost any area of biology would display the same tendency. A layman might say that a plant turns its leaves toward the sunlight in order to receive more of the sun's rays, but a good botanist will point out that the amount of water in the cells of the stem increases in such a way that the plant is twisted in a certain direction. A layman says "the purpose of the heart is to pump blood through the body," but a physiologist would insist that the heart is nothing but an electrically stimulated muscular organ that, in its contractions, pumps blood through the body. A layman (or the narrator of the television series *Nature*) might say that antelopes have antlers in order to protect themselves, engage in a mating ritual, and attract females of the species. But any hard-headed biologist would insist that since antelopes happen to have developed antlers, these antlers now can be used for protection; females happen to be more attracted to bucks with antlers, and consequently more males are born with genes for bigger antlers and more females are born with an attraction for bucks with bigger antlers.

(Aristotle, of course, would reject such evolutionary arguments. Species do not evolve. Each species is eternal, and the idea that a species came into existence through the contingencies of natural selection would have struck Aristotle as nonsense.)

Where the explanations do not involve living things, there is no longer any dispute. No modern student of science would suggest, as Aristotle did, that rocks tend to fall to their rightful place, that the planets and stars move by desire, or that magnetic stones literally "attract" bits of metal. But even human behavior is now suspect when it comes to accounts in terms of "final causes," that is, teleological explanations. Self-consciously scientific psychologists insist that human behavior is all a matter of stimulus-response, that is, cause and effect. Desires are reinterpreted not in terms of their ends (that is, what is wanted) but as states initiating behavior. Indeed, a powerful movement in contemporary "philosophy of mind" suggests that desires are not real at all but simply a "folk psychology" leftover from Aristotle's archaic explanations. In the future, these theorists argue, we will explain all behavior in terms of neurological states and occurrences—in other words, in terms of nothing but Aristotle's efficient causes.

It might be encouraging for a perplexed reader to hear that formal causes and final causes are difficult to distinguish, even for experts, given Aristotle's teleology. The end, or *telos*, of an activity may simply be its definition—in other words, its formal cause. Consider the activity of fishing. Fishing is, by definition, trying to catch a fish. But the end, the purpose of fishing, is catching a fish. Since most or at least many human activities are defined in terms of their aims, the formal cause will simply be the final cause. But mathematics provides us with infinitely many examples of formal causes, which is why Aristotle mentions Pythagoras as the philosopher who discovered formal causes. And in Plato the Forms are the (formal) cause of all the things that "participate" in them.

The discovery of material causes, quite naturally, is credited to the early pre-Socratics—Thales, Anaximander, Anaximenes, and Heraclitus. As we have suggested, this is probably not a fair representation of any of these philosophers;

but this claim allows Aristotle to interpret the entire prior history of philosophy as a sequence of discoveries leading up to his own. His emphasis on teleology or final causes allows him both to incorporate much of what Plato had to say and to explain not only all of human behavior but nature in general in terms of its ultimate purposes (including the cosmos as such). This inspirational picture, even if "unscientific," has moved philosophers and nonphilosophers alike, and it still moves people today.

Before we finally turn to Aristotle's ethics, perhaps we should once again come back to that recurrent character in our philosophical drama, the human soul. We have noted that, in both early Greek thinking and in Egyptian thinking, the soul was a somewhat pathetic being incapable of existing in any significant sense unless it was embodied. For some Greek philosophers, notably Democritus, the soul was nothing very significant at all, just another atom or combination of atoms. But with Pythagoras and the Orphic cults, the soul took on new significance. It may have still needed a body, but it found new ones, through reincarnation. And with Pythagoras, Socrates, and then Plato, the soul became the seat of the intellect as well as of virtue. It became part of the world of Forms and eternal in its own right. Aristotle, however, rejected the world of Forms. What, then, did he think about the soul?

Well, first of all, Aristotle took the soul to be the form, not just of human beings, but of every living thing. Animals, in particular, had forms. It was their form (not their matter alone) that allowed them to live. Their form, of course, included their various functions, which included eating, breathing, moving and sensing. But Aristotle had no hesitation about calling the form of an animal a "soul," or *anima*. So, too, plants had forms, although their functions were somewhat more limited. (To his credit, Aristotle recognized from his extensive field experience that the line dividing plants from animals was not easily discerned.) But plants, too, had souls insofar as they have the capacity to function as living beings.

Human beings have souls, then, insofar as they have forms, and each and every human being does have a form. But these are not distinct or separate from them, as in Plato's theory. The forms of people are *in* them. They define their essence, and the human essence is *rationality*. Insofar as we think, therefore, we have souls, and while we are thinking, especially thinking about thinking (as we are doing now), we are immortal. This might not be as satisfying as the more dramatic immortality suggested by Pythagoras and by Plato's heavenly World of Being. It might not be so inspiring as Socrates' fantasy about pursuing philosophy without interruption for all eternity. But it is what we would expect of Aristotle, with his utter refusal to separate the soul from the body, form from matter, biology from psychology and theology, this world from any other. The soul is not itself a substance (that is, an independently existing thing). It is the form of a substance. We will have to be satisfied, therefore, with our moments of immortality—for example, when we are engaged in philosophy.

* * *

Aristotle's teleology had practical application in his ethics and in his politics. Strictly speaking, there is no separating the two. The good life, which is the focus of Aristotle's treatment of ethics, requires participation in a good society, which is the focus of Aristotle's treatment of politics. But here we should pause for a somber moment of political reflection, because the organization of Aristotle's good society was one that we cannot accept. The foundation of Athenian affluence was the vile institution of slavery.

In Aristotle's Athens there were forty thousand or so male citizens. Some of them, a truly leisure class, disdained work, and this freed them full-time to be philosophers, statesmen, poets, and inventors. There was also a growing middle class of talented tradesmen, and there was, of necessity, a large army. But women, for the most part, were confined to the household, and most of the work, including the most important industry, agriculture, was done by slaves. There were at least three times the number of slaves as free citizens in Athens, and with Athens' military conquests there were always more slaves available. Aristotle's Athens depended upon slavery.

Aristotle, in this context, developed an ethical theory that is concerned primarily with the virtue and well-being of an extremely privileged class of people. And his politics, for all of its merits (he is far more democratic than Plato, for example), virtually begins with a defense of the institution of slavery. Yet in both ethics and politics Aristotle has much to say to us. His views are not just a matter of historical curiosity, as is the case for most of his science and much of his metaphysics. They are there for our serious consideration for current, practical application. It is necessary, therefore, to pry the ethics loose from the morally indefensible social structure that contains it, which is what we shall be doing here.

Aristotle's ethics is, again, strictly teleological. It is defined in terms of "the ends of being human." People have purposes. They have not only immediate purposes—to catch that bus, to earn a promotion on the job, to get to the top of the mountain—but an ultimate natural purpose, a purpose which, Aristotle tells us, is generally agreed to be "happiness" or, more accurately, "doing well." (The Greek word is *eudaimonia*, often translated as "doing well" or "flourishing.") Aristotle's *Nicomachean Ethics*, accordingly, is the analysis of the true nature of happiness and its essential components—notably, reason and virtue. Happiness, Aristotle tells us, is really just the name for the good life—that is, whatever sort of life fulfills the proper "function" or achieves the natural "ends" of man. The real question is, what sort of life is that?

Some people think that it is the life of pleasure, the enjoyable life. Aristotle quickly dispatches that view. Some pleasures are degrading and humiliating, but, more important, pleasure is just an accompaniment of satisfying activity; it is not an activity's end or goal. One lives well and consequently enjoys oneself; one does not live well in order to get the pleasure.

Others think that the good life is a life of wealth and many belongings. Aristotle responds that wealth is just a means to happiness, not happiness itself.

Still others believe that the good life is honor, power, or success. But these cannot be happiness, Aristotle says, because they depend on the whims of others, and happiness, properly understood, should be self-contained, complete in itself.

"Some philosophers," Aristotle coyly suggests, define the Good in terms of the Forms, but Aristotle will have none of that. Once again, he lays out his refutation of Plato's theory.

Finally, Aristotle characterizes happiness as the life of virtuous activity in accordance with reason. Each part of this characterization deserves careful attention. First of all, we note that the good life is an active life, a life filled with activity. A good life is filled with friends, and in his discussion of friendship (the longest single discussion in his entire ethics) Aristotle declares that "no one would choose to live without friends." It is a life of participation in the community. It is a life of accomplishment and, also, the philosophical activity of contemplation. Not just any activity will do. The good life is not, for Aristotle and his fellow Athenians, merely a busy life. Indeed, busy-ness, and especially business, are utterly antithetical to the good life, as is work of any kind.[28] (Aristotle has mixed views of tradesmen, who are prized for their skills and contributions but nevertheless lack the leisure time to lead the good life as he defines it.)

The most important activities that Aristotle recommends are those that are expressions of the virtues. It is important to note that the Greek word for virtue *(areté)* can also be translated as "excellence," and a virtue is one of those traits of character that make a person excel. In this sense, of course, there are all sorts of virtues, such as strength in wrestling, speed in racing, artistic talent in making a painting, calculating ability in accounting, cleverness in debating, having an excellent voice in singing, and so on. The virtues that occupy Aristotle's attention are more general virtues, however—those which make a person an excellent human being, not an excellent athlete, artist, or doctor. Such general virtues are courage, temperance, a sense of justice, a good sense of humor, being truthful, friendly, and, in general, just being someone who is easy and interesting to live with. Notice that there is nothing peculiarly "moral" about this list of virtues, and it is worth noting that neither Aristotle (nor any of the Greeks) had that rather specific sense of "morality" (as a definitive code of principles) that makes up so much of the core of ethics today.

What defines a virtue and virtuous activity, according to Aristotle, is *reason*. But here we should proceed with some caution. Reason may define the virtues, but reasoning is not the way to learn or exercise the virtues. We must be brought up to be virtuous. This usually includes being rewarded when we act properly and punished when we act badly, but as children we are not usually given a rational explanation as to *why* this form of behavior is right or wrong. First we learn to behave correctly. Later on, when we study ethics with Aristotle, we learn to explain in rational terms why we ought to behave the way we do.

Moreover, a virtuous person does not usually take time to reason and deliberate his or her virtuous actions. A courageous person spontaneously acts bravely, and a generous person spontaneously gives money when it is needed. To stop and think about such acts, to wonder whether or not one should be courageous or generous, is already to indicate that one is something less than either. Furthermore, a virtuous person *enjoys* being virtuous. There is no conflict between what one should do and what one would like to do, no tension between virtue and self-interest. These features of Aristotle's ethics are quite different from the way many of us have been brought up to think about ethics and morality, where obligation is often counter to self-interest and doing what one ought to do is often measured not by one's enjoyment but by the amount of temptation one overcomes.

None of this is to say that acting correctly is not a matter of rationality, but the role of rationality is more subtle than the calculation of what one ought to do. Rationality first of all defines the nature of the virtues themselves. Aristotle's rationality involves a sense of proportion, and he argues that the virtues are all "means between the extremes." This is more than the usual Greek plea for "moderation." Virtue involves optimum balance and measure in one's behavior, much as beauty involves symmetry and order, on Aristotle's scheme. For example, courage is the mean between the extremes of fearfulness and cowardice on the one side and foolhardiness and recklessness on the other.

Rationality also refers to the way we come to understand the virtues. To be a fully mature human being is not just to act correctly and virtuously, like a well-trained dog, but to understand and appreciate what one is doing, to be able to talk about it and explain it to others. (Two centuries earlier, Confucius had developed a remarkably similar way of talking about ethics in China; see Part II.) Rationality, for Aristotle, involves both the "know-how" of behavior in accordance with the goal of a fulfilled human life and the understanding of that life. Despite his mixed feelings about tradespeople, Aristotle here asserts the importance of *techne*, or "know-how," and applies the widespread enthusiasm for the expertise of tradespeople to the more general concerns of ethics. This same device serves him well in his discussion of the arts. Aristotle's influential treatise on tragedy, the *Poetics*, describes the techniques he observed to be effective in arousing the "pity and fear" of the audience and in achieving "catharsis" (purgation or purification). Rationality is practical skill as well as deliberation. It is proper emotional response as well as intellectual understanding.

If ethics, as a philosophical study, can only come after one has been brought up correctly, then that means that the philosophical study of ethics, by itself, cannot do much for us. One must already have the good fortune to be brought up in a good family, with good teachers and the right friends. One would also need to have good health, a decent amount of wealth, a good family name with power in the *polis* (the Greek city-state), intelligence, and, if one is to do philosophy, a decent grounding in the sciences. If not, there is nothing much to be done.

In this sense, Aristotle is an unabashed elitist. He is writing an ethics only for the aristocracy, those who are "the best" (but also the luckiest). Not for Aristotle the supposedly happy life of poverty, such as that preached by Socrates' other student, Antisthenes, the cynic. Happiness, the good life, may not be the life of pleasure, power, and wealth, but these are nevertheless its preconditions. Aristotle did not consider this to be unfair, but neither did he find social inequities as disturbing as we would. In keeping with the view of his society, he believed that human beings were vulnerable to many exigencies of fate. Even though his ethics presents a system for putting one's life "under control," he believed that fate could undermine the best human efforts. This fatalism (evident particularly in Athenian tragedies) contrasts markedly with the overly optimistic outlook of some contemporary Western societies. The idea of "taking control of one's life" is often a mix of responsibility and *hubris*.

The nature of the specific virtues and the role of reason in coming to understand ethics are beyond the scope of our treatment here. But it would be good to note one important complication in Aristotle's ethics which he himself seems not to have resolved. We began this analysis by saying that the happy life is the life of activity, but we also mentioned that one of these activities, in fact one of the most important and most "divine," according to Aristotle, was the activity of contemplation (thinking, reflection, philosophy). In fact, Aristotle praises the life of contemplation above all others, for it is, he says, most godlike and, as we noted, the only kind of immortality we can expect to enjoy. But the idea of a life of contemplation does not sit well with the alternative idea of an active social and political life, and Aristotle, with his various moves from academic philosopher to vicarious philosopher-king with Alexander, seems to have felt the pull of both of these.[29]

Furthermore, the harmonious social and political life that Aristotle describes is as much a matter of nostalgia as it was an accurate description of the Greek city-state at the time. The devastation of war, the incorporation of Athens and all of the other Greek city-states into the empire built by Alexander, the apparent failure of traditional codes of honor, loyalty, and family values, all were contributing to the decline of the glory that was Greece. As Nietzsche (a classics scholar as well as a philosopher) would later insist, Socrates, Plato, and Aristotle were already "decadents," spokesmen for a society in rapid decline. In such a situation, it is not surprising that the part of Aristotle's ethics that would be grabbed up most greedily by his own followers would be the ideal of a life of contemplation. The ideal of detached reason, which became elevated in Greek philosophy to the most essential and even divine feature of human nature, would come to dominate the Western tradition for virtually its entire future. It would often provide the primary means of escape—like "liberation" in the East—from a chaotic and unhappy world.

After Plato's death, Aristotle had left the Academy for Macedonia. He later returned to Athens and founded the Lyceum in 335 B.C.E.[30] But after Alexander's death twelve years later (at the age of thirty-three), Aristotle found himself to be unpopular in Athens. The old charges of "impiety," which had been used to silence Socrates, were raised once again. Unlike Socrates, Aristotle fled, "to prevent the Athenians from committing a second sin against philosophy." It was not an unwise decision.

A Footnote to Plato (and Aristotle)

Alfred North Whitehead famously suggested that the entire Western philosophical tradition is but a footnote to Plato. A bit more generously, one might describe it as an elaborate extension of the debate between Plato and Aristotle. Plato is speculative, suggestive, poetic. His known works—most of them in dialogue form with Socrates as the main character—are as much drama as philosophy. The ultimate ideas remain half hidden like a great secret glimpsed by the very few. Aristotle, in contrast, is through and through a scientist, and although he may have written dialogues (now lost), what we know of his work is rather dry, clear, and cautious, thoroughly analytic and only rarely speculative. Of course, one can discern many suggestive analyses and arguments in Plato, and Aristotle has some spectacular philosophical visions, but their differences in style and substance define two different temperaments that are interwoven throughout the Western tradition.

In Christian philosophy, for example, Augustine will follow Plato, Aquinas will follow Aristotle, to whom he will refer simply as "The Philosopher." In modern times, those philosophers who call themselves "rationalists" often look back to Plato in their appeal to reason as the faculty that can see "beyond" mere experience and seek absolutes. Those who call themselves "empiricists" often resemble, even if they do not follow, Aristotle the scientist, the careful observer, suspicious of any idea that does not rest on the testimony of experience and common sense, always open to revision. The nineteenth-century German idealists and many twentieth-century European philosophers shared Plato's speculative sensibilities even if they rejected his philosophy, while twentieth-century "analytic" philosophy clearly follows Aristotle in its demand for precision, thoroughness, and clarity.

Philosophers, accordingly, have adopted different images for themselves, beautifully depicted by the Renaissance artist Raphael in a mural near the Sistine Chapel in the Vatican. Plato points upward, his mind on the heavens. Aristotle pushes his own hand down toward the ground, suggesting his own earthy temperament, indisposed to flights of speculation. Here are the two greatest philosophers in the West—teacher and student, intimate friends, virtually kin—disagreeing about the nature of philosophy in the deepest possible way. Even in the limited context of fourth century B.C.E. Athens, philosophy is anything but a singular enterprise, a single "discourse" or "discipline." Today there are philosophers who pride themselves on their bold ideas, their breadth, their sensitivity, their outrageousness. There are philosophers who pride themselves on their logic and hardheadedness. Unfortunately, too much of philosophy has been a not always amiable and self-righteous conversation about the "proper" way of doing philosophy. But if Plato and Aristotle are to teach us anything, it should, first of all, be the role of different temperaments and the need to find one's own style of philosophizing. There is still a great deal of philosophy to come, and little of it can be dismissed as mere "footnotes."

Tough Times: Stoicism, Skepticism, and Epicureanism

After Aristotle, philosophy became more and more a rivalry of various schools, not only between Plato's Academy and Aristotle's Lyceum (both now in other hands), but among new competing schools as well. Despite the "academic" settings, many of these philosophies were primarily concerned with the basic human question of *how to live*. To be sure, many followers of Plato pursued important investigations into the nature of numbers and geometry (as well as his theory of the Forms), and students of Aristotle pursued their various interests in logic and the sciences. We will not trace those developments here. Instead, we will concentrate on the very different paths that philosophers took in response to increasingly tough times—including the collapse of the Greek city-state, meaningless wars between ambitious monarchs, persecutions and massacres in Egypt, the overrunning of Greece by Rome, and the notorious decadence and decay of that great empire.

Plato's Academy lasted, and would play a significant role in philosophy, for several hundred more years. But the amazing breadth of Plato's and Aristotle's philosophy and the world of the *polis* that nourished it came to a sudden end with the triumph and death of Alexander. "Political" philosophy came to an end. Much of Greek science migrated south to the ports of Alexandria and Pergamum. The philosophies that followed the death of Aristotle were surprisingly free of his influence, although the "Academics" influenced by Plato (and Socrates, of course) continued to be a force in philosophy. Both the Stoics and Epicurians rejected Aristotle as well as Plato (to whom they owed a far greater debt) in favor of a more materialistic conception of the world. But cosmology was not their primary concern. The "Hellenistic" world that followed the deaths of Alexander and Aristotle (323 and 322 B.C.E., respectively) became largely preoccupied with questions of ethics.[31] It was also significant for the proliferation of "schools," a phenomenon that would dominate philosophy throughout the Middle Ages and even influence contemporary philosophy. Accordingly, philosophy became something of a team sport as well as a search for the good life. Perhaps it is worth noting that it was in the Greco-Roman world that philosophy gradually became a "popular" enterprise as well.

Another remarkable aspect of the Hellenistic period was its cosmopolitanism, its universalism. This was due, in part, to the forced unification of Greece and the conquest of both Egypt and Persia. The Hellenistic world was (more or less) a single world, not unlike the Roman Empire that was to follow. Special mention should be made of the Egyptian city of Alexandria, at the mouth of the Nile. After the death of Alexander, Ptolemy (one of Alexander's generals) took charge of Egypt, which then flourished as a center of culture and philosophy. Because of the monumental library in Alexandria, the classics of Greece—and also the texts of the Hebrews—were preserved and studied. But the reign of Ptolemy's dynasty was a mixed blessing. Alexandria became the main bastion of Greek culture under Ptolemy I, but toward the end of the second century B.C.E., under Ptolemy IX (nicknamed "Fat Belly" by the Greeks), a series of persecutions and massacres scattered the scientists, poets, and scholars around the Mediterranean. Eventually Rome conquered Greece and Greek culture, as it did Egypt as well.

In Alexandria, the cross-currents of religion from the East increasingly affected the thinking of the Greeks and then the Romans. Alexandria was a meeting place for Greeks and Jews. The philosopher Philo was one of the first to combine classic Greek philosophy with the Old Testament teachings of the Hebrew prophets, preparing the way for Christianity. The Greek Bible was an Alexandrian creation. One zealous philosopher even went so far as to claim that Plato had the same philosophy as Moses. Out of this confluence of cultures emerged much of the metaphysics that would later emerge as medieval theology.

But back in Athens, Hellenistic philosophy encouraged the flourishing of many schools, including the school of Epicurus, an atomist of sorts, a follower of Democritus, and the founder of *Epicureanism*. Epicurus (341–270 B.C.E.) has gotten quite a reputation, which he would no doubt deplore, as the ultimate party animal. An epicurean today is a person who takes special delight in the senses, who enjoys luxury, even to excess. Nothing could be further from the original. Epicurus was, in fact, a rather private individual, and the members of his school generally avoided the heated debates of the time. What they really believed in was peace of mind. Epicurus thought that the pursuit of pleasure and the delights of the senses were perfectly "natural." (He did not disdain or denounce them like some of the Cynics, but he did not encourage them, much less promote them as the purpose of life.) His main concern was freedom from anxiety—tranquility *(ataraxia)*. The wise man, said Epicurus, would have nothing to fear from life, even in the worst situations. Epicurus claimed that the truly wise man could be happy even under torture. Pain, he insisted, never lasts forever.

Death, according to Epicurus, is utterly nothing, just the separation of the atoms that make up our bodies and our psyches. As such, it is nothing to fear. For those who might have lingering anxieties about being judged and punished by the gods for their deeds, Epicurus assures us that the gods are not concerned with us at all. One should not conclude, however, that Epicurus was sour on life, a mere cynic. Quite the contrary, he did insist that pleasure was easy, and that we should enjoy it. He defended virtue, but not (like Socrates) as the highest end. Virtue was just another means to peace of mind. The virtuous person has fewer enemies, does not have to worry about being sued or arrested, and generally has less cause for anxiety.

Above all, Epicurus recommended friendship as the key to the good life, much like Aristotle forty years before him. Indeed, one of the most glaring if unnoted shifts from ancient ethics to our own is the diminished importance attributed to friendship in discussions of the good life. Philosophers today talk a great deal about morality, the public good, and the sanctity of contracts. The more vulgar philosophers talk about wealth and power. They rarely talk about the importance of friends. One might argue that modern philosophers are more prone to simply take friendship for granted and not consider it worth philosophical concern, but even this is revealing. For Epicurus, friendship was the centerpiece of a decent life, and perhaps this more than anything brought him recognition and respect as a philosopher. Later, in Rome, Epicureanism would become one of the two most influential philosophies, eclipsing those of Plato and Aristotle. (The other was the philosophy of Stoicism, which we will consider shortly.)

The Roman philosopher Lucretius, who wrote in the first century B.C.E. became Epicurus's most devoted and famous follower (if only because his works alone survived). While his *De Rerum Natura* (The Way of Nature) is often read primarily as a thesis in materialist metaphysics (a version of atomism), his deeper intention was to define again and defend the "settled, sweet, Epicurean calm" of *ataraxia*, particularly against superstition and unnecessary fear of the gods. Neither Epicurus nor Lucretius denied the existence of the gods. Indeed, Epicurus considered the existence of the gods a palpable fact, and Lucretius even declares that the gods come to visit us in dreams. But the true life of the gods is, on their accounts, calm and serene, free from anxiety of any kind, and (accordingly) unaffected by human behavior and unconcerned with human affairs. *Ataraxia*, and not the meddlesome ways of Zeus and Hera (or Jupiter and Juno, their Roman counterparts), is the truly divine life of the gods.

The second great Hellenistic school, *Stoicism,* was the single most successful and longest-lasting movement in Greco-Roman philosophy. Some Stoic philosophers appeared soon after Aristotle, notably Zeno the Stoic (ca. 335–263 B.C.E.—not to be confused with Zeno of Elea, the disciple of Parmenides), and then Chrysippus (280–206 B.C.E.). Later Stoics taught during the height and the disintegration of the Roman Empire. Their "life is tough" theme affected not only those who were down and out, like the slave Epictetus (ca. 55–ca. 135 C.E.), but even those at the pinnacle of power. Indeed, one of the Stoics, Marcus Aurelius (121–180), was the emperor of Rome.

The Stoics are characterized by an almost fanatic faith in reason. In particular, they intensify the ancient antagonism between reason and emotion.[32] Plato distinguished among different parts of the soul (the appetitive, the "spirited," and the divine or rational), and Aristotle, too, had clearly distinguished between reason and emotion. But, although Socrates had warned his followers not to let emotions cloud their reason, Plato praised the ideal harmony of all three parts of the soul. Aristotle made emotion, just as much as reason, an essential part of virtue, character, and the good life. (A person who did not get angry when provoked, he said, would be a "fool.") But with the Stoics, reason and emotion part company.

Emotions, the Stoics suggested, are forms of irrational judgment, the sort that makes us frustrated and unhappy. As the Buddha had taught a few centuries earlier and more than a few thousand miles to the east: minimize your desires and you will minimize your suffering. Epictetus similarly declared, "Demand not that events happen as you wish, but wish them to happen as they do happen, and you will get on well."[33]

The Stoics looked around and found themselves in a world that had gone haywire, a social world in which vanity, cruelty, and foolishness reigned supreme. And yet they believed in a rational universe, however irrational or absurd it may seem to us. They also believed in the power of human reason, a "spark of the divine," to enable us to see through the cruel and petty foolishness of human concerns in order to appreciate that larger rationality.

Chrysippus, referring back to Aristotle's notion of cause, insisted that we should only be concerned with what he called *principle* (formal or final) causes—that is, those determinations of our world which are to be found *in us,* in our character. We should ignore those merely accidental (efficient) causes external to us. In general, the Stoics taught that we should live "in conformity with nature," but nature was now to be viewed "in accordance with reason," not according to our feelings. Indeed, the philosophical ideal of the Stoics could be summarized as "indifference" (*apatheia,* or apathy). Thus, they rejected human vanity and pride. They taught that anger is pointless and can only be self-destructive, that love and even friendship can be dangerous, and that the wise man forms only limited attachments and should not be afraid of tragedy or death.

The practical Romans had less love of philosophy than the more spiritual Greeks, and philosophers often had a hard time of it. Exemplary is the tragic fate of Seneca, one of the leading philosophers of Rome. He was a statesman in dangerous times. He barely escaped execution under the mad emperor Caligula only because of his ill health, and he got into serious trouble with Claudius (whose claims to divinity Seneca mercilessly ridiculed). But it was while serving under Nero, one of the more cultured of a long string of corrupt and dysfunctional emperors, that Seneca was ordered to commit suicide (for alleged conspiracy), and he did. The philosophy of the Roman Stoics was designed to cope with such tragedies and injustices, and one of its continuing themes, accordingly, was the importance of detaching oneself from the absurdities of life through reason.

Stoicism was an extreme philosophy but one that would serve many souls well in difficult and troubled times. It became an immensely popular philosophy in Rome and throughout the Roman Empire. Indeed, the Stoics' defense of asceticism and their vision of a larger rationality in a seemingly irrational world were picked up by the early Christians and became an essential part of their philosophy as well.

Finally, there was the even more extreme philosophy of *Skepticism,* which can be traced from Pyrrho (ca. 360–ca. 272 B.C.E.) to Sextus Empiricus (third century C.E.) in Rome. Pyrrho taught that the avoidance of belief is the way to tranquility. (It is worth noting that he may well have brought the ideal of tranquility [*ataraxia*] from India.) Epicurus was surely influenced by him, as were generations of Skeptics. Stories have circulated ever since antiquity about how Pyrrho would almost walk off cliffs or into the path of horses and chariots, how he would eat erratically and incautiously, surviving only because of the keen watchfulness of his friends and pupils. (Given that he lived to be somewhere around ninety, these stories are almost certainly false.) Needless to say, Pyrrho did not bother to write anything down. (There are limits to how far a philosopher will contradict himself in practice.) What would be the point of such a vain activity?

Sextus Empiricus, however, was an energetic if not very eloquent writer, a powerful dialectician and, we are told, an excellent physician. He asserted very little, but he ruthlessly questioned everything and everyone. (Skeptics discovered, as did Socrates, the immense argumentative advantages of a position that does not assert anything but at the same time demands ample justification and proof from others.) Earlier Skeptics, from Plato's old Academy, went against the Stoics (whom they considered "dogmatic") and argued that belief of any kind, including belief in reason, is a source of discontent and disharmony. Unlike the modern movement that goes by that name, the ancient Skeptics were concerned almost entirely with ethics, not the possibility of knowledge and its justification.

Whatever its arguments about the nature and justification of belief, skepticism was first of all a philosophy of life. It was primarily concerned with the question of how to live in such a way that one can cope with an often brutal, tragic, and unjust universe. The Skeptics' insistence on the suspension of belief *(epoché)*, was above all a form of therapy, a way of detaching oneself, a way of achieving *ataraxia*—serenity and freedom from anxiety. It was quite different, therefore, from the skepticism that would flourish in modern times. The latter still continues in university life and books as a troublesome and apparently insoluble paradox concerning the justification of belief, but it is little concerned with the practical implications of such matters. For the ancient Skeptics, pervasive doubt was wisdom, a reasonable way of life. The idea of a merely intellectual skepticism, especially when coupled with dogmatic political or religious convictions, would have struck them as hypocritical and absurd.

The tradition of Skepticism, especially in its opposition to Stoicism, owes a great deal to the leaders of the "new" period of Plato's Academy. Beginning in the early third century B.C.E., they launched an all-out attack on the Stoic theory of knowledge by means of an expanded application of Socratic skepticism, the claim that one does not—and perhaps cannot—know anything. It was the Socratic method, as much as Platonic metaphysics, that the Academy pursued.

Perhaps the most famous proponent of this new Socratic method was the Roman statesman and orator Marcus Tullius Cicero (106–43 B.C.E.). Although he found much to admire (and sometimes even borrowed) from the Stoics (conversely, he found much to ridicule in the Epicureans), given his role in public controversies,[34] he felt that the confrontation of different viewpoints applauded by the Skeptics was both engaging and extremely practical. Not surprisingly, he became a champion of rhetoric and what we today would call "applied ethics," approaches to the everyday problems of politics and commerce. (If you are selling a house with a leaky roof, do you have an obligation to inform the buyer?) Like the other Skeptics, he did not formulate a "system" of philosophy so much as he made a sport—but a serious one—of confronting other views on their own intellectual ground. Accordingly, he was one of the inventors of the art of *casuistry* (the gathering together of principles convenient to making a particular argument in a particular context), an art that, like its earlier counterpart "sophistry," has unjustly acquired a bad name over the years.

Nevertheless, in the best Socratic Academy tradition, they held up knowledge as an ultimate ideal (and in the last century B.C.E., the Platonic Forms would enjoy the beginning of a long revival). The "Academics" considered the Stoics (and the Epicureans) "dogmatic." Indeed, both Stoics and Epicureans display a remarkable continuity in doctrine, however controversial their internal variations. This "dogma," however, also provided a source of solace—belief in larger meanings and the paradoxical combination of self-sufficiency and fate—and in the Stoicism of Emperor Marcus Aurelius we can find many of the attitudes that would become essential to early Christianity.

A vociferous opponent of skepticism, in turn, was the Greek physician Galen (129–ca. 199). (The Skeptic Sextus Empiricus would also be a physician-philosopher.) In addition to his many contributions to medicine and medical theory, Galen was an outspoken critic. How can a teacher teach, he complained, when he begins by depriving students of the very foundation of education, namely, a teacher who knows something? But he also challenged the strong views of the Stoics, who put so much emphasis on the voluntary aspects of emotions and character. Since emotions are far more a matter of physiology than of choice, he argued, to hold a person responsible for his or her passions was misguided. When one observes young children, for example, one cannot but be struck by how early a sense of character has already been clearly established. There are definite limits to how much choice one has, how he or she should live, or who he or she will be. In the midst of the most flamboyant philosophies, one can always find such voices of common sense and practicality. Philosophy thrives in the exchange—even the shouting—among them.

Mysticism and Logic in Ancient India: Nagarjuna and Nyaya

Stoicism and Skepticism were desperate philosophical responses to desperate circumstances. At the same time that the Roman Empire was colonizing the farthest reaches of Europe (as far as England), Asia (virtually to India), and Africa (from Egypt to Algeria), its central government was disintegrating in scandal and corruption. Emperors such as Nero and Caligula were among the most demented rulers in history. Marcus Aurelius, another emperor who was also a Stoic philosopher, was something of a saint by comparison. He, of course, was murdered. The Empire weakened within and around its many borders. Rebellions were put down without mercy. But by the fourth century C.E., pagan Rome had been won over by Christianity, and by the end of the fifth century, it was gone, conquered by "barbarians."

Of course, we have insisted that one culture's barbarians may be another's civilization. But there can be little comparison between the Eternal City, the center of authority and culture with over one million citizens, and the decimated ruins with merely forty thousand inhabitants at the middle of the millennium. The Germans, Saxons, Celts, and Franks would eventually earn their own place at the center of Western civilization, but, for now, they were indeed the destroyers. Thor's hammer was not yet a sufficiently delicate instrument to supplement the philosophy, arts, and literature, not to mention the good life, of the Rome that was.

Civilization, however, was not dead. It was not even in eclipse. It had just been relocated, to the east. The Christian Roman Empire survived and flourished in Byzantium (now Istanbul), and soon Islam would extend its Semitic empire across Africa and throughout the Middle East. Indeed, the following chapters of Western philosophy would all be sketched in the non–Indo–European languages of the Middle East (Hebrew and Arabic), even if they would continue to receive their formal codification in Greek (see Part II).

Further East still, however, philosophy in India was and had long been flourishing. In ancient India, poets and philosophers had been developing the deep insights of the Vedas and sophisticated philosophical theses and arguments in Sanskrit,[35] which strongly resembled Latin and Greek (thus *Indo*-European). Sanskrit was the language of the Vedas and the Upanishads and of all classical Indian philosophy. "Hinduism"—or, more accurately, Vedanta—had developed an immensely complex philosophy before the time of Plato. The Buddha had appeared in the sixth century B.C.E. and Jainism dates back at least that far. Both Buddhism and Jainism had formulated deep and intriguing accounts of the soul and human (and, in the case of the Jain, nonhuman) nature. Hindu pundits,[36] Buddhist and Jain sages, and scholars had created a rich philosophical world in India by the second century B.C.E. (Jain scholars, because they insisted on having no doctrinal axes to grind—they sometimes defended a philosophy called *"maybe-ism"*—are for that reason among the most reliable reporters of ancient Indian philosophy.)

The period following the collapse of Alexander's empire proved to be a golden epoch for Indian politics, culture, and philosophy, beginning with the Mauryan dynasty in 320 B.C.E. and culminating in the classical age of 320–550 C.E.

In China, meanwhile, the Chou dynasty (1120–256 B.C.E.) had produced Confucius (551–479 B.C.E.) and then his very different followers, Mencius (ca. 371–ca. 289 B.C.E.) and Hsün-tzu (ca. 298–230 B.C.E.) as well as the Taoists and other schools of flourishing thought (see Part II.) Over the next several hundred years in "the East," philosophical productivity, both in volume and originality, would overtake philosophy in the West.[37]

Some of these topics (including Brahmanism, Buddhism, Jainism, Confucianism, and Taoism) will be covered and compared with their Western religious counterparts, namely, Judaism, Christianity, and Islam in Part II. Nevertheless, it would be a mistake to leave the ancient world with the idea that philosophy in the East was exclusively or primarily religious philosophy. True, philosophy and religion are never really distinguished in India and China as they are by many Western philosophers, but in China much of what is called religion is extremely secular by Western (Judeo-Christian) standards, and in India religious concerns sparked an enormous amount of what in the West would be called metaphysical and epistemological speculation about the nature of reality and human knowledge.

Perhaps what is most striking to the Western reader is the powerful combination of mysticism and logic in India, two fields of philosophy (insofar as either is considered to be "in" philosophy) that are usually considered as far apart as possible, indeed, flatly opposed to one another.[38] But in India, mysticism in one form or another, would become the focal point of all three major religions—Hinduism, Buddhism, and Jainism. Indeed the Sanskrit word for "philosophy" is "seeing" *(darsana)*. All three traditions would develop powerful logics and arguments both in support of this experience and as weapons against those who would compromise the possibility or integrity of such experiences through over-intellectualization or excessive attachment to the things of the everyday world and the categories of common sense.

Vedanta thrives on ambiguity and contradiction in order to make a single point, the unity of the One Absolute Reality (Brahman) despite its infinitely many manifestations. Vedanta, which develops from roughly the earliest Upanishads (800 B.C.E.) to its reinterpretation in recent times,[39] is primarily concerned with the understanding and elaboration of this primal unity, which can be "seen" ultimately only in mystical revelation. But along with this obviously metaphysical concern (and the puzzles of knowledge that accompany it) is a central concern with the good life, the best life, what the Greeks called *eudaimonia* and then the Romans called *summum bonum* and what in Sanskrit was called *parama-purusha-artha*, "the supreme personal good." The common view of Indian philosophy, Hinduism in particular, as extremely impersonal and indifferent to everyday joy and suffering, could not be further from the truth. The aim of Vedanta and the experience of Brahman is precisely to achieve one's supreme personal good, which is to find the ultimate joy (*mukti*) and free oneself from unnecessary suffering.[40]

To this end, it is first essential that one free oneself from illusion, and in particular, the illusion of one's special individual place in the world. The mystical experience of *bramhavidya* is the essence of this insight, but its ground can be best prepared, according to many pundits, with a healthy dose of logic. With logical analysis or "discrimination" (*samkhya*), the illusory nature of our ordinary commonsense categories can be shown to be utterly confused and contradictory. Thus Indian logicians explored the complex world of logical paradoxes 2,500 years before Bertrand Russell and the British Raj, about the same time that Parmenides and Zeno were making their remarkably similar first forays into this conscientiously confusing territory.

It would take us far beyond our topic to explore these logical puzzles and paradoxes here, but what we can do briefly is look at the role and relationship of logic to the central doctrines of Vedanta. In Vedanta (as in Heraclitus and some of the other pre-Socratic philosophers) Brahman is the ground, the value, and the essence of everything. This ultimate unity is therefore a coincidence of opposites (hot and cold, dry and wet, consciousness and world), which is incomprehensible to us. Brahman is "beyond all names and forms," and "Brahman" (like "Yahweh") is a name for the unnamable, a reference to what cannot be understood or analyzed. (Brahman is always "not this, not that.") But Brahman can be experienced, in meditation and mysticism, and Brahman is ultimately identical to one's true self *(atman)*. It is thus the awareness of Brahman, most importantly, that is every person's supreme personal good. One of the obstacles to this good, especially among the learned, is the illusion of understanding. For some of the most exciting philosophers in India, the play of paradoxes was the key to unlocking this illusion.

The single most famous practitioner of this play of paradoxes was the Buddhist philosopher Nagarjuna (flourished ca. 150–200 C.E.). He might rightly be called the Socrates of India, because he was one of the most diabolically clever "dialecticians" in the history of philosophy. In Buddhism as in Brahmanism there were strong intellectual currents in favor of analysis and keen intellectual diagnosis of the illusions of everyday selfhood. The Buddha himself had strong doubts about such an intellectual approach. He famously asked, "When your house is on fire, is it wise to discourse on the nature of fire? No, it is wise to put it out."[41]

Nagarjuna used the intellect against itself. He argued, for instance, that every attempted justification invites the demand for another justification, thus resulting in an endless regress which provides no justification at all. He elaborated a theory of what philosophers in the twentieth century would call the problem of reference and the nature of "nothingness," marking off some deep implications of the seemingly simple fact that some terms in language (for example, "nothing") do not seem to refer to anything. He also pointed out some of the problems of motion that, partly because of the similar grammar of the language, were puzzling the Greek philosophers, too. ("How indeed could it occur that there be a moving belonging to something that is currently being moved?"[42]) Several of Nagarjuna's arguments thus paralleled the arguments of Parmenides and Zeno.

By pointing out the absurdities in the intellectuals' various positions, Nagarjuna cleared the way to pure (but not, therefore, uninformed or unlearned) experience. By emphasizing the practices of Buddhism instead of intellectual understanding, he expressed what he considered to be the true message of the Buddha. And, not coincidentally, he saw in his own cleverness a manifestation of wisdom, one of the Buddha's essential "perfections," the mark of a bodhisattva, a Buddhist saint.

Despite Nagarjuna's effort to discourage intellectual speculation, Buddhist logic became increasingly rich in succeeding centuries. So did the logic of Vedanta in attempting to unravel similar paradoxes in the philosophical explication of Brahman. In the next millennium, there would be a virtual festival of Indian philosophy, often combative, often brilliant. In particular, the tradition called *Nyaya* ("logic") would become an influential counterbalance to the "illusionism" of many Brahmanists and skeptics. The *Nyaya yikas* rejected the notion that the everyday world was an illusion. They consequently had doubts about the emphasis on mysticism and the religious orientation assumed by most Hindus. These doubts led to a debate that has lasted for seventeen centuries, in both Buddhism and Brahmanism. We will look at some of their consequences in Part II.

Part II

God and the Philosophers: Religious and Medieval Philosophy

The relationship between philosophy and religion has always been both intimate and delicate. In an overly narrow sense, perhaps, religion preceded philosophy by thousands of years—that is, if one takes philosophy to be essentially critical and "naturalistic" and religion to be merely a matter of belief in the supernatural. But the truth is that religious belief has probably always been surrounded and permeated by doubts and disputation, and philosophy has almost always had its eye on the larger, suprahuman, if not supernatural, aspects of the world. The close identification of philosophy with science during certain periods has encouraged the sharp opposition of philosophy and religion, but it is worth remembering that many of the greatest scientists and mathematicians, Pythagoras and Isaac Newton, for example, refused to accept that opposition.

The difference between philosophy and religion is often captured in the distinction between reason and faith, but this distinction, too, tends to disintegrate on examination. The history of logic during most of the Middle Ages was motivated and often based upon theological questions which, though matters of faith, called for the most exquisitely precise employment of our reasoning faculties. The effort of many of the greatest philosophers has been to bring reason and faith together, to show that faith is or can itself be rational, or at any rate to show how reason and faith function together to give us a more edifying picture of the world.

The very distinction between philosophy and religion, as well as the distinctive notions of reason and faith, is a rather Western conception. Indian thought, both in its mythological and extremely sophisticated logical manifestations, recognizes no such distinction and speaks very little of any such narrow concept of reason or such a concept of faith. Indian mystics (for example, Nagarjuna) were among the world's keenest logicians. Confucianism and Taoism, while often listed among the world's great religions, do not talk about faith (as opposed to, say, harmony) as in Western religion. In most cultures, the supposedly sharp difference between thinking through questions by way of reasons and accepting a doctrine on faith or authority is difficult to discern. Where people talk and think together in line with a tradition, where critical inquiry is not encouraged as such but group participation and consensus are expected, the very individualistic dilemmas and choices that (eventually) give rise to such Western notions as "the leap of faith" are not to be found.

Before we get to the big three "Western" religions—all of which were founded in what was considered until very recently the "East"—we should certainly say a few words about the philosophy of religion and a few of the other great religions of the world. Judaism, Christianity, and Islam have dictated and defined the terms of a great deal of Western philosophy, from the legitimation of the Christian Church in Rome in the fourth century C.E. to the success of the "new Science" at the beginning of the modern era, and much of contemporary metaphysics too. But other religions have also made their mark on the thought of the world. It is all too easy, from within the Western perspective, to take the religious and metaphysical dimensions of Western philosophy for granted and deny or ignore the very different shapes of both philosophy and religion elsewhere in the world (and here at home as well).

In contrast to the three Middle Eastern religions, other religious traditions, in Asia, for example, had very different concerns. The philosophical worldviews of ancient China and India, although cited in any list of major world "religions," are not focused on humanity's relationship to a single God. (The presence of various "deities" and divine figures should not be immediately assimilated to the Western monotheistic conception of God.) Thus the dominant Judeo-Christian-Islamic questions of accessibility and revelation are all but irrelevant, although many Asian traditions (especially Buddhism and Confucianism) have essential texts or Scriptures. One might be tempted to say that these Eastern traditions tend to focus instead, like the Greeks and the Romans, on the appropriate way to live in this world. But that already introduces a distinction between the secular and the sacred which is a Western, not an Eastern, way of thinking. In Confucianism, for instance, the distinction between heaven and earth, although thematic, is not a dichotomy between radically different orders of being; and that between religion and daily ethics is not pronounced, insofar as it can be made out at all. We begin, accordingly, with a few speculative comments about the nature of religion in general and several (of many) remarkable religions in Asia.

Religion and Spirituality: Three Philosophical Themes

In a perhaps overly bold attempt at an overview, we might suggest that the world's religions—and their philosophies—share three central themes, without thereby suggesting that these receive anything like the same treatment in all traditions or, for that matter, within any single tradition. The first theme is the no doubt prehistoric, primordial sense that *we share our world with other beings.* In so-called "primitive" religions, these beings may be the familiar creatures around us, carefully observed and perhaps enveloped in creative narratives. They may be the local animals, birds, snakes, and spiders, or perhaps the easily identified shape of the nearby mountain. It might be the spirit of the soil itself or the nutritive and perhaps curative power of local plants and trees. The python, for example, is the creator of the human race in one of the myths of aboriginal Australia. The ancient Egyptians attributed godlike status to cats, among other creatures. The Hindus recognize divinity in all kinds of local creatures, from the very familiar cow to the slightly more exotic monkeys. They also recognize a large number of deities, many of whom inhabit the everyday world and should not be thought of as "otherworldly."

These other beings may be fabulously mythological creatures, or personifications of natural forces, of "mother" earth herself. Belief begins with empathy, an essential (but not unique) human trait: we recognize or project onto others the same sorts of feelings and thoughts we recognize in ourselves. Whether it is recognition or projection may be a matter of dispute, of course, even in our ordinary attributions of feelings and thoughts to each other and to such animals as our dogs and cats. But with empathy comes the natural tendency to understand other beings as importantly similar. A few killjoy philosophers and scientists may insist that such empathy is legitimate only for other human beings (if even for them). But the truth for most people and most philosophers, too, is that the world is rich with animated inhabitants.

These other inhabitants may be Olympian gods and goddesses—divine but invisible neighbors with prying eyes and ears and an all too familiar tendency to intrude. Or, there may be but one significant nonhuman inhabitant and the focus may be wholly unitary, if we owe our existence to a single, all-embracing, transcendent God. That transcendent world (and this world too) may be further populated by angels, devils, muses, spirits of all kinds. And in virtually every tradition, we share the world in some way with our ancestors. Whether they are envisioned as looking down at us from Heaven or, as among the Kaluli of Papua New Guinea, as surrounding us and singing to us, as birds, it is hard to deny the appeal of the idea that we are not alone, that we are still watched over and cared about by those who came before us. In many African cultures, the ancestors are thought to be quite palpable presences. In Confucianism, the ongoing significance of one's ancestors is a central theme of this very secular religion. The presence of ancestors enriches our own existence and provides us with the wisdom to live well.

The second major theme is, in a single Western word, *justice,* the idea that the world is affected by us and our efforts and we have expectations in return.

In many cultures, the existence of ancestors is already sufficient to establish traditions of fair exchange, debt and revenge. Indeed, in Old Norse tales and in the myths of ancient Greece, such relationships and expectations hold even among the gods. In the Judeo-Christian-Islamic tradition, justice is assured by an all-powerful, loving, and sometimes wrathful God. In Hinduism, justice emerges in the law of *karma*, which briefly says that what goes around comes around, that good and evil are repaid in kind, that one's deeds are not ephemeral but carry weight over time. Of course, one aspect of this concern for justice is caution against always expecting just returns, whether because the gods are fickle or trying to "test" us or because, in the larger scheme of things, our actions and our individual lives are of little or no importance. But it is against the backdrop of this primal belief in justice that most religions must be viewed.

The theme of justice, in turn, suggests the demand for a certain social order. Every religion, no matter how unworldly, has its worldly, political counterpart in the lives of its adherents. The Egyptian pharaohs, and most royalty ever since, claimed a divine right to rule. The primary connection between the Hebrews and their God was the Law, and they, like the Muslims succeeding them, lived the details of their daily life according to the Will of God. Christ said "render unto Caesar what is Caesar's," but Christianity has rarely been shy about taking on the role of Caesar and asserting itself as the state religion. Taoists generally dismiss political authority (itself a political position), but for Confucianism a proper political order lies at the very heart, not in the mere implications, of religion.

Every religion, in other words, finds some political orders more acceptable than others, and, we should say, some more advantageous than others. It would be naive to think, for example, that the tensions between the Pharisees and the Sadducees around the time of Christ did not have a political undertone. The Greeks raided Troy only with the (rather complicated) blessings of the gods. The Hebrews clearly used their status as the Chosen People to justify what today would be recognized as invasion and massacre, and so, too, did both Christians and Muslims, culminating in four monumental "crusades," which lasted from the eleventh until the thirteenth century. But while it will be necessary to recognize such political agendas in the otherwise ethereal discussions of matters of the spirit, it is just as important not to give them too much weight and to fully recognize the power of religious philosophical ideas in their own right. One of these ideas, typically disadvantageous to those in power, was the insistence on equality—the idea that, in the eyes of God or the Law, all people are equal. This was an important element in Judaism and later in Christianity and Islam. Indeed, it came to signify the core of the Western ideal of justice.

At the other extreme, the Hindu caste system, which is first of all a religious and not a social or political concept, invokes the law of karma to suggest that each of us is rightly born to our proper position in life, whether as rich or poor, fortunate or unlucky, healthy or sick or crippled. It is also a matter of karma whether one is born (or reborn) human or not. One's status is thus not contestable. It was against this harsh and incontestable Hindu insistence on "natural" inequality that the Buddhists and the Jains rebelled, putting in its place an all-encompassing egalitarianism. (The Jains, for example, are so insistent on every sentient being's equal right to life that they will not even swat a mosquito.) Similarly, the early Christians rebelled against the supercilious Pharisees and against the hierarchical aristocracy of Rome, even though they soon established a church which embraced a similar hierarchy. Confucius did not dispute the hierarchical organization of his society, but he nevertheless defended the equality of all citizens under the Law.[43]

Third and finally, virtually all religions embrace as a theme some *possibility of a personal essence which continues after death* and, perhaps, lives again. Socrates, for example, clearly embraced this possibility, although its general status in ancient Greek religion remains somewhat murky. Some ancient Hebrews and virtually all Christians, Muslims, and Hindus believe in some form of the soul surviving the biological death of the body. In its most straightforward form, this belief holds that one's personal self survives the death of the body. Without the animate body, however, the idea of a personal self seems rather abstract, and the nature and the vehicle of continued existence becomes a problem for speculation. From the ancient Egyptians to contemporary Christianity, such hopeful speculation has spurred an enormous number of ingenious theories. The Egyptians preserved the original body, together with all of its trappings, implements, and enjoyments, in the expectation that it would return to life. The Yoruba of Nigeria believe that the human person is a conjunction of three souls as well as a body. In the afterlife, the person continues as an ancestor spirit; but the person can simultaneously reappear in living descendants (whose physical features often resemble those of the returning ancestor). Christians have long speculated about the nature of continued existence, and the doctrine of the eventual resurrection of the body suggests that the immortal soul, even after death, is most properly housed in a body.

Some traditions have not been so adamant about the continuation of the distinctively human soul, however. The Kaluli believe that the spirits of the dead are reborn as birds. The Hindus are among many peoples who believe that the soul may be reborn in any number of forms as another human being or as an animal. Reincarnation thus raises all sorts of fascinating questions about the nature of the soul or spirit and the possibility of its continued existence. What is the soul, the self or essence of a human being, such that it might survive death and enter into another being? How much of what we think of as our *selves* could survive such a transformation? In what sense would one still exist as oneself if reborn as a butterfly, a cow, a child of a different race, sex, and culture? Indeed, in what sense does one survive even in the genes and memory of one's grandchildren? For most Jews, continued existence in genes and memory is enough.

The idea of continued essential life can take other forms as well. For example, the Buddhists believe that the individual self is an illusion, so the questions just raised can only be treated as confusions. Not only do we not survive as individuals; we do not even exist as individuals at present. At the time of death we lose our illusions of individuality and return to our original nothingness. What's more, many traditions do not consider continued existence an obvious blessing. Eternity in Hell is hardly a happy promise for Christians, and, for Buddhists, Jains, and

Hindus, death ideally results in release from the cycle of rebirth that religion proclaims, not in eternal existence. Nevertheless, what has always been hard to believe, for the Neanderthal as well as sophisticated moderns, is that the selves we know so well, our own and others', simply disappear at death. It is hard to imagine ourselves not existing, and this has led people in many traditions to the conclusion that it is more plausible (as well as, usually, more pleasing) to imagine ourselves continuing to exist than not.

The most important implication of this idea of a personal essence, however, does not concern the possibility of life after death but rather the possibility of an essential *transformation* of the self during life. This is put in different ways by different religions, whether in terms of "salvation" or "enlightenment," whether through prayer, group song, or private meditation. The self of everyday life, we are assured by the various traditions, is not necessarily the real self. The self that is too often selfish, that is too readily caught up in its own personal ambitions and interests, may in fact be—as we sometimes suspect it to be—a distorted self, a deluded self, a self that is neither one nor at peace with itself. Thus, Socrates sought the transformation of his self through philosophy, Jesus through suffering, and the Buddha through an awakening. For some religions, the purpose of life itself becomes the achievement of such a transformation. For some, it may happen in a moment, like St. Paul's conversion on the road to Damascus. For others, it may take a lifetime of ritual and practice, like Tibetan monks, whose self-discipline is legendary. For still others, the true self may be nothing more than total immersion in the group, including a joining together with one's ancestors. But the self to which religion and philosophy refer is not necessarily the everyday self, and the effort to discover or realize this essential self is one of the central aims of religion—and philosophy.

One might lump these three themes and their variations under the single title "spirituality," although this term is too often claimed by one or another religious tradition as its own. Sometimes, the term is restricted to those who believe in a transcendent God. Others limit the term to certain inner feelings and emotions. Still others insist that the term refers to an irreducibly *social* dimension of religious life. The truth, however, is that there are many ways of thinking of spirit and spirits, many conceptions of soul and of the perhaps unseen beings with whom we share our world. The spiritual may refer to the transcendent beyond, but it may not. It may also refer to a distinctive and deep sense of social order, determined by our ancestors and given over to us with their blessings. This, too, is religion (itself an overly textbookish classification that tends to homogenize and overly organize the many worlds of spirituality). But with this multi-faceted view of spirituality in mind, let us turn to the very spiritual philosophies of Asia.

The Wisdom of the East (I): Hinduism, Jainism, Buddhism

The three indigenous religions of India—Hinduism, Jainism, and Buddhism— share a great many evident similarities, including the notable ways in which they differ from the monotheistic religions of the West. Indeed, what is most striking, from the point of view of that comparison, is the lack of apparent rigor and dogmatism in the religions of southern Asia, at least in their many concepts of the divine. In Hinduism, in particular, there is nothing like the compulsory monotheism of the West. ("Thou shalt have no other Gods.") Concepts of the divine are greatly varied and richly imaginative, and, in contrast with the solemnity that characterizes the three Western religions, Eastern concepts of God are often strikingly playful and mischievous. Different areas (and in many cases each village) have their own favorite gods or goddesses. Buddhism, in general, is a religion without God (although it is quite full of divinities).

There is, however, a complex tradition of monotheism in India, although the status of the divine is much debated and by no means accepted by most Hindus. Even within Vedic monotheism—for example, in the "illusionist" school called *Advaita Vedanta*—even the status of God is very much in question in the philosophical literature; it is not at all the dogma upon which the entire religion rests. (Indeed, even God turns out to be an illusion.) As we insisted in Part I, Hinduism is not, as such, a religion in the sense of a distinctive set of beliefs. It is rather a wide variety of philosophies, folk myths, practices, rituals, and social structures, many of which are based on the Vedas. Some Vedanta scholars take Brahman to be the one God. Others do not. But despite a long history of disputation and argument, the Hindus have not, for the most part, been proselytizing or competitive. This is not to deny, of course, that members of various sects within India (as in most parts of the world) found frequent occasions for mutual slaughter, but until the arrival of Islam and the Europeans, the many myths and philosophies of Hinduism peacefully coexisted and often mixed and blended with Buddhism and Jainism and other local religions.

One can overplay the differences between the religions of the West (that is, Asia Minor and the "Middle" East) and the East (especially India and the "Far" East) as well as overplay the similarities within Asia. Eastern religion is not, for example, all about mysticism, although, to be sure, mysticism plays an important role in all three major Indian religions. (In China, it plays a much smaller role in Taoism, and virtually no role in Confucianism.) In Indian philosophy, the Vedas remain the point of departure for all three major religions, but both Buddhism and Jainism ultimately reject the Hindu interpretations of the Vedas and, in particular, the abhorrent caste system which the Vedas have been taken to justify. Similarly, Buddhists generally reject both the notion of Brahman and the notion of self (atman) that are so central to much of Hindu thought.

Even within Hinduism and Buddhism, there are deep divisions and disagreements on these issues. Despite the fantastic plethora of gods, goddesses, and other deities and divine creatures, it would be false to simply summarize Hinduism as a polytheistic religion (in other words, a religion with many gods). Traditional Hindu mythology makes much of the idea that all of the deities are in some sense manifestations of the one God (*henotheism*), and some Vedanta philosophers have further elaborated the argument that Brahman is the only God—indeed, the only substantial being. Others (for example, the Nyaya) attempted to prove the existence of God as creator in a fashion that resembles (and long anticipated) some of the best-known arguments of medieval Christian philosophy. Buddhists reject the idea of God altogether, but even there, we find considerable room for disagreement and dissension.

All three religions have as central themes the suffering of life (*dukkha*) and the notion of "release" or "liberation" (*nirvana* in Buddhism, *moksha* in Hinduism and Jainism). The different sects' visions of the way to liberation are enormously varied, however. In some Buddhist sects or cults, years of intensive training and discipline are required for enlightenment. In some forms of Hinduism, by contrast, the advice is, rather, "Whatever works for you." We have noted that all three religions are deeply concerned with the nature of the soul or self, but, in particular, all three accept that peculiar form of causality involving and defining the self called karma and some version of the belief in continued life through reincarnation through which karma shows its effects.

And, yet, in the West too much is made of this exclusive emphasis on life as suffering in Indian philosophy and religion. Insofar as life is suffering, we can readily understand the desire to escape it. The belief that life happens not just once but repeatedly only makes the need for liberation all the more imperative and difficult. Nevertheless, the emphasis is on the release, not the suffering.

The first "Noble Truth" of Buddhism is the truth of suffering, but favorite representations of Buddha show him very much at peace, even dancing. Jains are devoted to the need to prevent suffering as far as possible. In Hinduism, the combination of the philosophy of karma and the brutality of the caste system tends to underscore the prevalence of suffering, but what is often underemphasized is the central role of joy, bliss, and delight in Indian philosophy. Hinduism, in particular, sees the world as something like a playground, and the joyful antics of the gods and goddesses exemplify this attitude. Mystical experiences are typically described in terms of *bliss* and Buddhist tranquility is by no means to be understood simply in the negative terms of "escape." Indeed, if the Indian tolerance for suffering seems sometimes excessive to Christian eyes, it must also be said that the playfulness of Indian philosophy and religion is somewhat foreign as well. Philosophy and religion do not have to be "serious" business, even if one's very soul is at stake.

If we may be permitted to greatly oversimplify this enormously rich tapestry of religious beliefs, we might best begin with Hinduism and trace the reactions of both Buddhists and Jains to Vedanta in particular. The similarities and differences emerge regarding four major issues: (1) the question of self, soul *(atman, jiva, anatman);* (2) the question of the highest good and its relationship with God, Brahman, the One; (3) the question of karma and suffering; and (4) the question of liberation (and the experience of liberation).

With regard to the first question, there is considerable agreement that the individual material self is not the ultimate self, what we would call the "soul." But whereas most Vedanta philosophers would argue that the true self is Brahman, a transpersonal, all-embracing self which includes us all, Jains still maintain that the true self is nonetheless individual, while Buddhists reject the idea of the self altogether in favor of *anatman,* no-self. Still, at least some Indian philosophers (*Carvakas*) take a straightforward materialist position, insisting that the self is nothing but the individual material self, a natural organism that will die and disappear, and that is the end of it.

The answer to the question of the highest good depends on how the self is understood. In Vedanta, the highest good (*parama-purusa-artha*) is self-recognition—that is, recognition of oneself as *atman.* An important distinction is made between the individual living being, *jiva,* and the larger self, the principle of existence within all of us, *atman.* While jiva is usually translated as "soul," there is considerable disagreement within Vedanta as to whether jiva is in any sense independent of the particular living organism and whether it survives the death of the person. Jiva is usually construed simply as the particular collection of physical features, memories, thoughts, activities, and feelings of a distinctive individual. When the person dies, jiva ceases to exist. In any case, jiva should not be construed as the "real" self, the self that endures. That role belongs to atman. Thus, the highest good is self-recognition, not as one's individual self, but as the larger all-encompassing self that is atman. Atman is not distinctively individual. Atman is immortal and impersonal. And yet, jiva and atman are bound up together in the living person *(purusha),* at least until death.

After death, atman remains undiminished. It remains the principle of life, continuously manifested in other beings. The more difficult and controversial question is what happens to jiva, the distinct individual person. Although the Indian materialists consider death the end of jiva, most Hindus (including most Vedanta scholars) believe that the individual continues to exist and is eventually reborn as a different person, perhaps of a different caste and possibly even as a member of a different species. The key to this transmigration is neither jiva, which remains distinctively individual, nor atman, which remains emphatically general, but karma, which one might think of as the "residue" of the actions and activities a person performs over his or her lifetime. It is karma that is the key to rebirth and reincarnation.

In Vedanta, recognizing oneself as atman is at the same time recognizing one's true self as Brahman. An individual person is really just one aspect, one of infinitely many transient manifestations, of the One. But this central belief leaves ample room for interpretation, for example, as to whether Brahman is to be considered as God who created those manifestations or rather is identical to them, or who is incomprehensibly different from them. This in turn gives rise to very different conceptions of the individual and reality. Advaita Vedanta, for example, can be viewed as both monotheistic and atheistic since it recommends devotion to God as a prop for developing the mystical awareness that everything, including God, is an illusion (*maya*). One's highest good, accordingly, is "seeing" the world of everyday needs and desires as illusory and recognizing spiritual self-awareness (*bhakti*) as the fulfillment of life. Nyaya, however, accepts the world as real and takes God as an impersonal metaphysical principle, not unlike Aristotle's "prime mover." One's highest good, accordingly, does not involve rejecting the world, but neither does it necessitate any sort of personal sense of divine participation. Carvakas dispense with God along with the idea of the soul and an afterlife. Their conclusion, accordingly, is that one should get as much out of life as one can.

Hindus, Buddhists, and Jains all accept some version of the continuation of life through rebirth, and all three entertain serious doubts about the ultimate reality of both the individual material self and the material world. But their different views on the nature of self lead them to different conceptions of the highest good. Most Hindus believe in the importance of seeing oneself as not only part of but identical with the larger whole, Brahman. Their highest good, accordingly, is to recognize this larger self (whether Brahman is God or not) and to reject the "illusion" of the individual self. Buddhists, by contrast, reject the idea of any self, including atman or Brahman. Hence, they see liberation as an extinction of self, not an identification of oneself with something larger. Many Buddhists still have a notion of the One, but this is a strictly impersonal One, not atman *(anatman)*.[44] Jains, however, hold onto the belief in an individual self or soul, not only in human beings but in every living thing. That is why their respect for all life is so extreme. (They also believe, like many Hindus, that human souls may be reborn in animals.) After death and with liberation, according to the Jains, the soul floats free, "like a balloon" according to one classical commentator.

This brings us to our last two issues, karma and liberation. Karma is one of the best known but most often misunderstood concepts in Indian philosophy. It is central to all three religions, but it has its origins in the Vedas. Hinduism, Buddhism, and Jainism are often conceived in the West as religions of resignation, religions that put little emphasis on actions and "good works." In fact, questions of behavior as well as a concern for rituals and various practices are central to all three religions, although the most important behavior, particularly in Buddhism and Jainism, is *not doing*—namely, not doing harm to others. Some Jains aspire to not even breathe (or they wear masks) to avoid unintentionally killing tiny insects in the air. But in Hinduism, especially, what one does in his or her life reaps its rewards or punishments later in life, or in the next one. This "afterlife," however, is not Heaven or Hell (although some such notions are not entirely absent from Hindu thinking), but in rebirth. Every action bears some fruit, and the fruition of one's total actions define one's karma. Some of the rewards and punishments that follow good and bad actions, respectively, are evident in this life, even immediately. But "bad" karma not only shows its ill effects in a lifetime. It also alters the cosmic causal network into which one is reborn. Thus one may suffer not only from a diminished or more lowly life, but one will also prolong *samsara*, the ordeal of life and continued rebirth which itself is suffering.

Karma is often discussed as a version of fate (much like the concepts of fate in archaic Greece and the tragedies of the great Greek playwrights). However, the concept of karma, as far back as the *Bhagavad-Gita,* includes the notions of free will and responsibility. This is immensely complicated, however, by the Hindu ideal of acting "with detachment"—that is, not egoistically and not with concern for oneself. Thus, freedom is not understood as unconstrained individual agency, as it typically is in the West. Buddhism, too, diverges from Western thought on this matter, and special attention is given to "selfless" (or "mindless") actions.

The doctrine of karma includes the belief that one can also affect karma by willfully undertaking virtuous and compassionate actions toward others. In Hinduism, duty *(dharma)* defines virtue and is especially conducive to enlightened living and liberation. Westerners often underestimated just how much emphasis Hindu society places, in particular, on both the duties of citizenship and the duties of family. (This is reflected in the myth that Brihaspati, the Lord of Heavenly Wisdom, issued two sets of instructions to Indra, the king of the gods, one on good rulership, the other on having a happy marriage.) India's great twentieth-century leader, Mohatma Gandhi, built his radical liberation philosophy on a conception of dharma, based on the Vedas. His concept of liberation, however, included the whole of society.

Hinduism prescribes no single way to liberation, and it is on this theme that we find the greatest disagreements and controversies. For some theorists, notably the Nyaya, liberation comes through understanding. According to the *Yoga sutras,* by contrast, the way to liberation is spiritual discipline, meditation, and mystical insight. (Yoga here is a philosophy, not just relaxation exercise.) Enlightenment and liberation come from an extreme form of detachment—a trance, complete emotional disengagement, "mental silence." In Hindu thought from the *Upanishads* (the earliest of which dates back to 800 B.C.E.), liberation is, at least in part, bound up with practices for the transformation of consciousness, which involves a different way of seeing the world, a profound experience of selflessness, an "oceanic experience" *(samadhi).* A twentieth-century sage, Aurobindo, describes this form of *bhakti* as "commiting adultery with God, the perfect experience."

Buddhism, the "newest" of these three ancient Indic religions, deserves special attention with regard to its elaborate speculations on the nature of suffering, the self, and liberation. Siddhartha Gautama, the Buddha, was deeply concerned about the horrible suffering he saw all around him, and he insisted on social reform. He denounced the caste system and the excesses of the Hindu priesthood as inhumane and destructive institutions. The Buddha's basic philosophy, however, is concerned primarily with the individual's *inner* transformation, achieved by means of insight into the *Four Noble Truths* of Buddhism:

1. All of life is suffering.
2. Suffering arises from selfish craving.
3. Selfish craving can be eliminated.
4. The elimination of selfish craving results from following the right way.

This right way to liberation or enlightenment is called the *Eightfold Path* of Buddhism, which consists of:

Right way of seeing
Right thinking
Right speech
Right action
Right effort
Right way of living
Right mindfulness
Right meditation

The aim of Buddhism is to free oneself from deluded belief in the ego and all that goes with it, desire and frustration, ambition and disappointment, pride and humiliation, and to gain enlightenment and the end of suffering, a condition called *nirvana*. Although *nirvana* is typically described in terms of the negation of the egoistic perspective, as the cessation of suffering, it can be more positively understood as *bliss*, although it would be misleading to characterize the aim of Buddhism as anything like the Western ideal of "happiness." The Buddhist conception of life is primarily concerned with suffering and its relief; but what the Greeks would call "flourishing" is not as such a Buddhist idea.

Buddhists, more emphatically than most Hindus, believe that all of life is impermanent. Reality amounts to a series of successive momentary existences; there are no enduring substances. This doctrine of impermanence helps to explain the pathos of our situation, as described in the Four Noble Truths. We desire objects that are themselves impermanent, with the result that we never get (or get to keep) what we want. But until we recognize that the things we want are only momentary existences, we will tend to take them seriously as goals, harming ourselves and others in our efforts.

One might note a contrary tendency in the Judeo-Christian-Islamic tradition to take religion as a *means* to getting what you want, whether here or in the afterlife. ("Believing in God will make you happy and more secure." "Faith will make you successful." "Martyrdom will get you into the garden of delights that is Heaven." "Jesus *wants* you to have that Cadillac!") Nevertheless, it would be a mistake to treat Asian religion as essentially ascetic. In Hinduism *dharma* and *moksha* are only two of four *purusharthas*, or natural human aims: the others are wealth and other material interests *(artha)* and pleasures and emotional fulfillment *(kama)*. In Confucianism, especially, the three great pillars of hope are prosperity, progeny, and longevity. Buddhists do not by any means eschew material comforts, but there is a strict separation of these illusory "needs" and the desire for liberation. The meeting of secular wants and spiritual needs is not a contrast between East and West but rather a fascinating fault line within virtually every religious tradition, a line which is often masked by the word "spirituality."

Like the delusion that anything endures, Buddhists say, a delusion leads us to believe that our egos have reality. In fact, there is no permanent self or soul. A human being is just a temporary composite of body, feeling, thoughts, dispositions, and consciousness. There is no underlying substance, a "self" or soul in addition to this composite. There is not even a larger eternal self, atman. There is only anatman, no atman, no self. Recognition of the impermanence of both self and all objects of desire is a step toward insight and the end of misery. In the Judeo-Christian-Islamic tradition (as well as in some Greek philosophy), the soul is the essential self, and the question is only *which* desires are right to pursue. (The Stoics, notably, rejected desire *as such*, and in this they greatly resembled— and may have even been inspired by—the Buddhists who lived so far to the east of them.)

Although all Buddhists share certain basic beliefs, Buddhism has developed many schools of thought. It became more and more diverse as the religion spread into eastern and northern Asia, not only Japan and China, where it was integrated and synthesized with Confucianism and Taoism, but also Tibet and Nepal, Indonesia and Indochina. Early on, there was a serious separation of Southern Buddhists, mainly in and near India, and Northern Buddhists (in China, Tibet, Nepal, Japan, and Korea). The Southern Buddhists focused their attention on personal enlightenment, the loss of all individual personality, and impersonal bliss. They believed that enlightenment is to be found in an extremely ascetic and isolated monastic life, and that enlightenment is thus limited to a relatively small percentage of humanity.

The Northern Buddhists, by contrast, insisted on the primacy of compassion and regard for other. They demanded that everyone must be freed from suffering and spiritual ignorance and those who are already enlightened must "stay back" to help those who live more or less ordinary lives, outside of monasteries and in the hurly-burly everyday world. The Buddha, they argued, could have blissed out but stayed around out of compassion for others. A person who follows this example of the Buddha is a *bodhisattva*. Bodhisattvas do not enter the state of nirvana when they reach enlightenment. Instead, they remain active in the world to help others to extinguish suffering by sharing their insights. Thus *compassion* becomes a central virtue for (Northern) Buddhists, as it would become for much of the Judeo-Christian world as well.

The Wisdom of the East (II): Confucius and Confucianism

Confucius, like the Buddha, was moved by the plight of the people and the society around him, but rather than prescribe any form of philosophical escape or transcendence, he urged participation in society and human improvement. His philosophy is largely focused on the ethical and social conduct that would be conducive to a harmonious community. The metaphor "harmony" is particularly important here (as it was for Plato), and Confucius often uses the harmony of music as an intuitive analogy for social and personal well-being. The wise ruler, the sage, will orchestrate society. But the harmony of society depends upon individual virtue. (Again, the comparison with Plato and Aristotle is tempting.) Confucius's philosophy, accordingly, is largely an exhortation to virtue.

The single most important virtue for any society is good leadership. Good leadership requires the personal development of the ruler, who in turn inspires virtue in his subjects. The Confucian urge to self-realization should be understood in this social context. It is not individual enlightenment or personal perfection. It is through and through a *social* concern, and the emphasis is always on social relationships—above all, the relationships of the *family*. Society as a whole, in Confucian thought, is like a gigantic extended family, even such an enormous society as China.

Confucian philosophy, however, is not entirely taken up with social thought. Long before Western philosophy became fascinated with language, the Chinese philosophers recognized the central definitive role of language in the determination of our way(s) of seeing the world. Whereas the pre-Socratic Greeks primarily asked such questions as "What is reality?" and "Why is there something rather than nothing?" the classical Chinese philosophers recognized the role of language in our efforts to understand and affect our world. Classical Chinese asks not so much what something really is but rather "How should we call something?" It is through language that we define and evaluate the world around us, especially the social world. For example, calling a man "independent" (in English) is not only to describe his social relations but (in our society) to praise him. In Chinese, this notion of independence would be incomprehensible. A man without social attachments or a recognition of his many dependencies on other people and the community in general would be called "antisocial," a profound criticism. The difference is not just one of value, but the very nature of language. According to Confucius, "the rectification of names" is essential for any society to be a good society. Words have ideals built into them, and to call someone a "leader," for example, is not so much to *describe* his role in society as it is to *prescribe* the values and actions that should define his behavior. In other words, things should be made to correspond to their names. Confucius did not simply mean that words should be used with attention to what we today would call "honesty in advertising." He also meant that human beings in their practices should live up to their ideals, the ideals that were built into the language itself. Taking care in using language is a primary way of taking care of the world.

The emphasis on personal character and the virtues within the context of a harmonious society is extremely important for understanding Confucianism, but it also provides an important link with the West. Two centuries later, in Greece, Aristotle would develop a similar conception of ethics, in which personal virtue was primary but presupposed one's role in a harmoniously functioning city-state (polis). The primary importance given to virtue should be contrasted with, for example, the primary importance given to law in Judaism, which is emphatically *not* to say that Judaism does not also have a strong conception of virtuous character or that Greek and Chinese philosophy do not recognize the importance of law. But the differences between the two visions of society and the individual that is captured by these different emphases are significant, not least in the fact that the Jewish law presupposes the presence of an all-powerful God who both dictated those laws and sanctions them. Both the Greeks and the Chinese see the sole end of ethics as the promotion of a harmonious society, quite apart from any external judge or lawgiver. Confucius does refer to the will of Heaven; but this is usually interpreted as a reminder that although human beings can influence their circumstances, they cannot control them and they cannot assure their success or failure. (In this respect, too, Confucianism can be compared and contrasted with Greek thought, with its emphasis on human beings' vulnerability to fate.) Thus the highest achievement for the Confucian is to be "in tune" with the harmony of society and the universe, not necessarily "in control."

So, too, the Confucian emphasis on virtue and self-realization must always be understood in terms of its value for social harmony, not primarily in terms of individual achievement. By comparison, Judaism, Christianity, and Islam, while much more concerned with obedience and God's law, tend to be more individualistic and more concerned with the well-being of the individual soul (Christianity especially so). In Confucianism, there is no atomistic "soul" in the Western sense, for the individual cannot be distinguished from his or her social roles and relationships. When Confucius speaks of "the superior man," he is still not speaking of the individual as such but rather celebrating personal virtue as the means by which society can be transformed and harmonized.

The Confucian perspective is centered in human experience, and it understands experience as embodied, not in terms of an abstract spirit or immaterial soul. Our physical natures are as important for responding to the flow of our world as more intellectual awareness. Disciplined physical exercise, such as the martial arts, is seen as a means of attaining spiritual mastery over oneself by inducing rhythmic breathing, emptying the mind of distractions, and equilibrating the emotions. As in other Asian traditions, mind and body are considered complements, not opposites, in Confucian thought. Physical exercises, in fact, are understood as means of heightening one's mental acuity and clearing the mind in such a way that one is apt to become more intuitive.

The central Confucian virtue, which encompasses other virtues within it, is *jen* (pronounced "ren"), which can be translated as "humanity" or "humaneness." Included within this notion are the ideals of love and magnanimity; and at times *jen* is used to refer to "virtue" generally. Although Confucius believed that *jen* is inherent in human beings, he insisted that a human being is not what he or she is but rather what he or she does. In Aristotle's terms, a virtue must be actual, not merely potential. A virtue is an achievement. It must be cultivated and developed. In a child, *jen* is developed by observing filial piety, behavior in accordance with respect for one's parents. As a young adult, *jen* is manifested as more general social respect and piety. An important manifestation of *jen*, accordingly, is *li*, or ritual. But *li* should not be understood as repetitive behavior, a mere or empty ritual. A ritual must be focused and heartfelt, a true union of bodily action and mental concentration. Ceremony and music are particularly important, for not only do they bring society physically and spiritually together; they also provide the rituals through which *jen* is learned, practiced, and cultivated. This combination of music and social togetherness provides a striking confluence of "harmonies."

Because ritual, or *li*, involves more than the external observance of ceremonial forms, it involves an active sense of appropriateness to one's context, as well as grace in one's action. Confucian society is elitist, much like Plato's, in its accep-

tance of a culturally defined, hierarchical order with strong leadership. Accordingly, what is appropriate is largely defined by one's place in society, and the
relative dominance and subordination of a given individual's role depends on
one's personal education and the articulation of his or her place in the community. In many situations, elders have the predominant role, for they are (usually)
recognized as being wiser than younger people. In military activity, however,
younger individuals might play a dominant role because they are physically
stronger than their elders. Nevertheless, respect remains the essential virtue.
Confucian virtue, like Aristotelean virtue, involves a sense of appropriate measure
in one's behavior, and one should seek a sense of this appropriate measure—the
mean—within oneself. (Aristotle similarly described virtue in terms of a cultivated sense of the mean between extremes.)

In this summary sketch of Confucianism, we have said nothing about those
questions which dominate the Judeo-Christian-Islamic tradition, nothing about
faith or revelation, nothing about God as the cause or the cure for suffering,
nothing about the creation of the cosmos or Judgment Day. But like those Western religions, Confucianism may be defined by a set of Scriptures—namely, the
classic texts that precede Confucius (the *Book of Changes*, the *Book of Odes*, the
Book of History, Rites, Music, and the *Spring and Autumn Annals*, which provide
an historical account of Confucius's home state, Lu), the four great books of
Confucianism (the *Confucian Analects*, the *Book of Mencius*, the *Great Learning*,
and the *Doctrine of the Mean*), and the many commentaries upon them. These
books, however, are not considered to be divine revelations. Confucius is neither
a prophet nor a god. Confucianism has virtually nothing to say about cosmology;
and neither God nor Confucius sits or will sit in judgment over people. People
rather do that themselves, every day, in the social context in which they display
their *jen*, or fail to do so.

Not all of Confucius's immediate successors were satisfied with the emphases
and omissions in his philosophy. Mo-tzu (470?–391? B.C.E.), whose life began at
approximately the time Confucius's ended, was critical of Confucius for his endorsement of prevailing institutions (so long as they could be restored from their
corrupt condition). Mo-tzu contended instead that the institutions, rituals, and
arts received from tradition were themselves objectionable, since they drained
the community's resources and energy and secured the position of the aristocracy
over less powerful groups within society. Mo-tzu contended that rituals and
ceremonies were wasteful and unimportant. In contemporary terms, we might
say that the Mohists were something of "utilitarians," with an eye on practical
consequences and "utility." The ethical ideal of a good society could be achieved
only by means of universal love, a doctrine that Mo-tzu personally exemplified.

Somewhat surprisingly for a school that promoted all-embracing love, the
Mohists developed a crack military organization. The apparent paradox is resolved, however, when one realizes that Mo-tzu and his school opposed war and
considered military force warranted only for purposes of self-defense. (Then as
now, this is not always an obvious distinction in practice.) Mo-tzu was a pioneer
in the theory of military deterrence. He believed that if one could demonstrate
that every move of an opposing force could be countered by one's own side, the

opposing force would have no incentive to fight. The Mohist military operation, therefore, was developed with primarily pacifistic aims in mind. More idealistically, Mo-tzu contended that all-embracing love would secure peace. If people stopped distinguishing between their own states and those of others, they would never have any reason to attack another nation. Like the Confucians, the Mohists developed a keen interest in language and logic, for how one thinks and talks about territory or a particular piece of land determines how one acts concerning that piece of land. What is meant by and included in one's notion of "China" or "England," for example, obviously dictates an enormous number of actions and attitudes. Chinese social and military interests thus converge with the philosophical interest in the integrity of names and propositions.

Mo-tzu was sufficiently pragmatic to recognize that people would be more likely to adopt behavior in accordance with the ideal of all-embracing love if there were also sanctions behind the ideal. Accordingly, he played up folk wisdom about a personal God and spirits. All-embracing love was God's will, according to Mo-tzu; and God would punish those who defied his will. Mo-tzu also argued for a central, all-powerful state that would enforce the standard of universal love. Love would set everything right, according to Mo-tzu; but en route to this condition, force was unavoidable.

The Confucian school opposed Mo-tzu's doctrine of universal love, contending that it was quite appropriate that one's love for one's parents be greater than one's love for strangers. Given the need for authentic practice, Mencius (ca. 372–ca. 289 B.C.E.) contended that in order for love to be more than superficial, it should admit of gradations, with one's love for humanity at large a continuation of the more powerful love one feels for one's own family. Contending that human beings are essentially good, Mencius was optimistic about humanity's ability to be benevolent in their dealings with others. Although he considered training and commitment to be essential if goodness was to be realized in society, Mencius considered sagehood and moral goodness to be within the reach of anyone committed to acting like a sage. Wisdom and compassion were available to everyone.

The Confucian school was not in full agreement, however, about whether human beings are inherently good. Hsün-tzu (ca. 298–ca. 230 B.C.E.) contended just the opposite. Human beings, on his view, are naturally evil, with innate tendencies to pursue personal gain and pleasure. Fortunately, however, human beings are also intelligent, and with their intelligence they can cultivate goodness in themselves. In keeping with the doctrine of Confucius, Hsün-tzu stressed the importance of ritual and appropriate behavior toward those around us, particularly members of one's family. Morality was not grounded in nature, according to Hsün-tzu; instead, it was the invention of human intelligence, constructed to ensure social cooperation in the face of our more natural, selfish, desires.

In more contemporary terminology, Hsün-tzu's claim is that kinship and social relationships are socially constructed, not grounded in nature. In contrast to many Western philosophers who have suggested that "mere convention" indicates the arbitrariness or unimportance of such constructions, Hsün-tzu considered the fact that human relationships are socially constructed to be an indication of their importance. In the debate about the relative merits of culture and nature, therefore, Hsün-tzu consistently sides with culture against nature. Nature becomes valuable only by means of cultivation. In this respect, Hsün-tzu's position is in adamant opposition to the teachings of Taoism, the second major current in Chinese philosophy.

The Wisdom of the East (III):
Lao-tzu, Chuang-tzu,
and Taoism

Confucianism and Taoism are two of the major currents in Chinese thought and religion. We should not, however, imagine that the two traditions have spent more than two thousand years in competition with one another. Both have been central influences on subsequent Chinese thought, especially since the neo-Confucian thinkers of the Sung dynasty (960–1279 C.E.), who superficially rejected Taoist and Buddhist influences but in fact borrowed and synthesized a great deal from both traditions.

Nevertheless, Confucius and Lao-tzu, the two traditions' most prominent respective sages, had different conceptions of the proper relationship between the individual and society and different notions of the virtues that a person should pursue. Like Plato, Confucius located the individual's activity on the map of the social fabric. Lao-tzu[45] (more like Jean-Jacques Rousseau in the West) located it on the map of nature, understood as contrasting in certain respects from society's cultivated habits.

Although the actual existence and dates of Lao-tzu are disputed, the Taoist tradition most likely preceded the sage. The original Taoists were rather reclusive individuals who found harmful tendencies in society and believed that one should protect the life within oneself instead of trying to amass property. Arising within this tradition, Lao-tzu recognized the desirability of social harmony, but he considered such harmony more likely to prevail if sages ruled. Or rather, more accurately, rulers should not rule, for the wise ruler is one who rules as little as possible. In the West, the long-standing tradition of sages, or wise men, was largely eclipsed by the prophets in the Judeo-Christian-Islamic tradition and philosophers in Greece (where, for example, the sage tradition lived on in Heraclitus). Prophets were spokesmen for God rather than wise in their own right. The Greek philosophers were wise, but by virtue of reason. For Taoists, however, the tradition of the sage remained extremely important, and the idea of "inner wisdom," dictated by nature, took the place of both the word of God or reason, as taught in the West, and the dictates of a noble leader, the ideal defended by Confucianism.

Lao-tzu's philosophy was primarily focused on the means for achieving wisdom, which he believed to be a process of attuning the inner person to the rhythms of nature—the *Tao*, the Way of the universe. Confucius put his emphasis on society. Lao-tzu emphasized the natural context of human communities and a person's spontaneous behavior in accordance with his or her own nature. Simplicity, the avoidance of artificiality, is the way to wisdom, according to Lao-tzu. Even traditional moral concepts like "good" and "evil" can be obstacles to living in accordance with the Tao, on the Taoist view. Too often such concepts are understood so rigidly that they obscure more than they illuminate; and, in particular, they fail to reflect the subtle changes of the Tao.

The greatest virtue, according to Lao-tzu, is acting naturally and without resistance (sometimes translated as "nonaction," *wu-wei*). The ideal leader, paradoxically, does not lead. Lao-tzu was keenly aware of the foibles that can result from "overdoing it," especially where governmental policies and legal restrictions are concerned. Similarly, the ideal teacher does not teach. The virtuous individual does not act, in the sense of asserting him or herself. Avoiding all contentious effort, the wise individual "acts naturally," behaving spontaneously in accordance with nature as it exists within and without him or her. Such an individual adopts a stance of receptiveness, and this in turn allows the Way of the universe (the universal Tao) to act through him or her. In this way, the person expresses *Te*, his or her own natural power. (The *Lao-tzu*, the book attributed to Lao-tzu, is also known as the *Tao Te Ching*, literally *The Book of the Way and Power*.)

Nature and humanity are intertwined and interactive on the Taoist view. In Taoism, there is never the struggle between nature and culture, between nature and nurture, that plays such an enormous role in Western philosophy. Aspects of the human being correlate with aspects of the dynamic world around us, and ultimately the human being is an inextricable part of the surrounding world, not an independent being for whom the environment is either hostile or to be subjugated. To be wise is to realize this unity with nature and to live in conjunction with the rhythm of the world, the Way.

The Tao's rhythm is a spiral, cyclical, and every condition that is manifest at any given time will give way to other conditions, eventually to return. (The cyclical notion of "eternal recurrence" was also part of archaic Greek thought, but it lost favor with the beginnings of Western philosophy.) When the extreme case of any situation (whether wealth, power, or calamity) is reached, reversal will come about, according to the Taoists. Pursuing one's desires too avidly, for example, will inevitably lead to failure in one's efforts. To live well, therefore, one should avoid excesses in one's behavior and give even what opposes one's own goals its appropriate due.

Life and death are merely explanatory concepts that express this rhythm, so neither life nor death should be overemphasized. Nevertheless, Taoists diverge in their sense of appropriate emphasis in this connection. While philosophical Taoism emphasizes serenity toward death as well as toward all natural occurrences, religious Taoists—those who utilize the philosophy of Taoism in particular practices—attempt to utilize insight into nature practically by securing longer lives for themselves.

The Taoist contention that change or *flux* is the natural condition of existence is very much at odds with the underlying premise of much of Greek philosophy—true reality does not change. Within flux, however, there is significance in the specific configurations. The *I Ching* (the same ancient Chinese classic that became important to the Confucians) is seen by the Taoists as indicating intelligible moments of change within the larger flux of reality.

One can also contrast the Taoist insistence on flow and change with the Judeo-

Christian-Islamic tradition's insistence, for all things sacred, on the notion of *eternity*. Taoism has no concept of eternity, in the sense that the Tao's fundamental patterns are always provisional, always unique (like the grain in a piece of wood). The Tao, in fact, is sometimes described as "the constant" (*ch'ang*), which is not the same as "the permanent" or "the unchanging." Taoists consider a human being spiritual insofar as he or she is part of nature, flowing through time. In the Judeo-Christian-Islamic tradition, by contrast, one tends to be holy insofar as he or she is *not* part of nature and *outside* of time ("in the world but not of it," in one New Testament formulation). The Christian soul, in particular, is an intact bit of eternity in all of us. The Taoist soul is more like a drop of water in a stream.

The Taoist interest in cycles of change is reflected in the complementary notions of *yin* and *yang*, literally "the dark side" and "the sunny side," which can be used to describe any play of opposites within change. Deficiency in any quality (yin) gives way to sufficiency (yang) and then excess, and this will be followed by decline and deficiency again. The significance of patterns of waxing and waning was so apparent to Chinese thinkers—as it was to most people in largely agrarian China—that the complementarity of *yin* and *yang* eventually became a standard conception and an exemplary focus of wisdom throughout Chinese philosophy.

Lao-tzu was not the only significant sage of early Taoism. Chuang-tzu (fourth century B.C.E), a contemporary of Mencius, is perhaps as important a figure if one distinguishes the historical individual Lao-tzu from the influence of the work that bears his name. (The work known as the *Chuang-tzu* was probably not written entirely by Chuang-tzu himself; the later commentator who compiled the work seems to have included writings by some of Chuang-tzu's followers as well.) Chuang-tzu was an anarchist, dubious of all government. According to Chuang-tzu, governments are obstacles to human happiness, which depends on individual freedom to express spontaneously the nature within them.

In his efforts to attack the many impediments to happiness, Chuang-tzu developed fatalistic doctrines that resemble those of the Stoics (who were soon to appear in the Roman world). In particular, Chuang-tzu contended that many of the emotions that interfere with happiness could be dissolved by means of understanding the Way of nature. For example, if one recognizes that death is part of the cyclical movement of Way, one's distress at a loved one's death will be diminished or eliminated. Like the Stoics, Chuang-tzu believed that one was vulnerable to the extent that one depended upon external things and had unreasonable expectations: the course of wisdom was to minimize such dependence and such expectations.

The Stoics sought to achieve serenity by refining their sense of certain distinctions, such as the distinction between what one can affect and what one cannot. Chuang-tzu, by contrast, argued that the highest happiness could be attained only by transcending distinctions. The initial step in overcoming distinctions is to recognize the partiality and relativity of all viewpoints. If one really recognizes that one's own point of view is limited, one will not defend it against the views of others. Eventually, one will stop identifying with any limited point of view. Instead, one will identify only with the Tao. Ultimately, the sage "forgets" the distinction between the self and the Tao. In this mystical condition, the sage experiences a remarkable pervasiveness in both space and time (similar to Indian "enlightenment"). The personal self of the sage may die, but the Tao with which the sage identifies lives on.

Deep in the Heart of Persia: Zoroastrianism

The particular concerns of the three major Western traditions are historically linked through their shared history, a history that weaves in and through the ancient world and its great civilizations, in Babylon and Egypt, in Greece and in Rome. One pioneering version of Western monotheism, however, developed in Persia, in the philosophy of *Zoroastrianism*. Philosophically, Zoroastrianism is of particular interest because of its original confrontation with those philosophical problems associated with the conception of a single, all-powerful Creator God.

Long before the coming of Islam, Zarathustra, or Zoroaster (ca. 628–ca. 551 B.C.E.) was a prophet and the founder of the major religious tradition in Persia. In opposition to the practice of his contemporaries who worshiped two kinds of deities, the *devas* and the *ahuras,* Zarathustra denounced worship of the *devas* and devoted himself to the worship of a single *ahura,* Ahura Mazda. Zarathustra also credited this one God with the creation of the world.

Because he devoted himself to one God, Zarathustra is traditionally viewed as a monotheist. Zarathustra nevertheless acknowledged the reality of lesser deities who were created by Ahura Mazda and existed in union with him. These lesser deities were associated with particular aspects of nature, and Zoroastrians (the followers of Zarathustra) took themselves to be worshiping those aspects of nature when they worshiped these divinities. This worship of nature, of course, was one of the oldest forms of religion, and nature worship was evident, about the same time, in Greek and other Middle Eastern religions, often coexisting with anthropomorphic and more abstractly spiritual religions. The same is true of Zoroastrianism. Although devoted to Ahura Mazda as the supreme God, Zoroastrians consider worship of fire (and the Sun, as a creature of fire) as a duty. Zoroastrians were sometimes called "fire worshipers" as a consequence.

This compromise between monotheism and polytheism, naturalism and supernaturalism, anticipated a number of complex problems that would prompt a good deal of Jewish, Christian, and Islamic theology. The primary problem had to do with the relationship of the one God to Creation. Did God create a world that was independent of himself, or is the world to be considered to be divine as well? The pantheon of lesser divinities provided an intermediate answer for the Zoroastrians, for these deities were both attached to God and part of nature.

This still crude hierarchy would form the basis of a good deal of later philosophical thought—in particular, of the Neoplatonic theory of "emanations," which explained God's presence in all things in terms of the various orders of reality. Sometimes the problem came to be formulated in very abstract, quasi-Pythagorean terms: How did multiplicity emerge from the divine Unity, the Many from the One? In more concrete and personal terms, the nature of creation itself presented perhaps the most perplexing metaphysical question for the Western tradition. What was God doing before He created the universe? How did God create the universe? Why did he do it as he did it, and why, in particular, did he create people, "in his image" as the English translation of the Hebrew Bible puts it? What is his continuing relationship with them?

Zarathustra used the lesser deities' role within creation to help resolve the central issue he bequeathed to later Western religious traditions. This is *the problem of evil*, the question of how evil can exist if a good and all-powerful God created the world, and the question how reason can resolve this dilemma. Zarathustra explained evil as the consequence of a war between two twin spirits, the first of the spirits that Ahura Mazda created. One of these spirits is good; the other is destructive. The world is a manifestation of a battle between these two, between good and evil.

Zarathustra answers the problem of evil with the now familiar argument that human beings have a free moral choice, the choice to ally themselves with one or the other deity, the good spirit or the bad one. As a religion, Zoroastrianism engages the believer and encourages commitment to the good spirit in all thoughts, words, and deeds. This alliance will prove to be rewarding, Zarathustra promises, as he introduces yet another doctrine that would have enormous appeal to the traditions that follow: at the end of this world, Zoroastrian doctrine assures us, Zarathustra will lead those allied with the good spirit to an eternally blessed existence. The good, in other words, will triumph after all.

From Athens to Jerusalem: Judaism, Christianity, and Islam

The three major religions of the Western world, Judaism, Christianity, and Islam, can be thought of as a single family. All grew out of the same region of the Middle East, and all three centered their focus on the singular city of Jerusalem. All three claim the common ancestry of Abraham. And, most important of all, all three are profoundly monotheistic, devoted in their belief in one God. Christianity grew directly out of Judaism and incorporated the Hebrew Bible as the "old" Testament. Islam recognizes both Judaism and Christianity as its predecessors and accepts the Hebrew prophets and Jesus as precursors of Muhammad.

Philosophically, the three religions share a number of essential concerns, and not only because of their monotheism and their overlapping history. It is important to appreciate, historically, how revolutionary and philosophically overwhelming the idea of a single, all-powerful God must have been. Philosophically, the idea of a single, all-powerful God implied universality, a single set of rules and beliefs that would apply not only in this or that region or city-state, but everywhere, and to everyone.

One of the pharaohs of ancient Egypt defended the idea of a single God against great resistance. Amenhotep IV renamed himself "Akhenaton," after *Aton*, the Sun god, in the fourteenth century B.C.E. It is not entirely clear when the ancient Hebrews adopted their more durable notion of the one God, but it clearly followed a period during which they, too, acknowledged a plurality of competing gods and goddesses, one of whom became their favorite and who, in return, made them His[46] "chosen people." Before Akhenaton and the ancient Hebrews, most societies recognized a plurality of gods and goddesses. Each city had its favorite or favorites, although the deities themselves were often unpredictable or unfriendly, even to their own believers. It was also understood that they were often ruthless with one another and, especially, with their mortal enemies. The gods were demanding, and sacrifices, including human sacrifices, were a routine part of virtually every Middle Eastern religion. (The story of Abraham and Isaac is, in part, a basis for the Hebrew innovation that God does not require human sacrifices, and that these should be replaced by animal sacrifices.)[47]

There was considerable convergence in the recognition, identification, and conception of the various gods and goddesses as the various societies traded, battled, and otherwise intermingled with one another. Nevertheless, religious pluralism and polytheism insured considerable diversity. Monotheism, however, demands the convergence of belief and ideas. For many centuries, it may have been understood that God goes by many (even "infinitely many") names, and, like the deities of India, perhaps, took on many manifestations as well. But the disagreements about what to call the one God (complicated by the fact that the ancient Hebrews sometimes insisted that He not be called by name at all) were forced by the logic of the single reference into agreement, more or less. The difference between "God," "Jehovah," "Yahweh," and "Allah," for example, is generally acknowledged to be no real difference at all: they are merely different names for one and the same God. But what those terms refer to—the nature of the all-powerful being who is the single source/object of faith and worship—is a matter of continuing debate and disagreement. One could certainly argue, for example, that the differences between the Old Testament God of the Hebrews and the New Testament God of the Gospels are sufficient to suggest two very different deities.

The philosophical issues most vital to Judaism, Christianity, and Islam, however, emerge from the claim that all three worship the same single, loving, Creator God. These three religious traditions do not agree on the nature of God, nor, of course, do they always agree on the proper way of thinking about Him, approaching Him, worshiping Him, or satisfying His Will. Speculations about the nature of God utterly dominate Western philosophy from the earliest centuries C.E. until the fifteenth century (and their form and influence still dominate a great deal of philosophy).

One of the most inescapable problems, which we touched upon earlier, that pervades the philosophical writings of all three religions arises directly from the notion that God is both powerful enough to create the universe and is a loving God, concerned for His people. The problem is the problem of evil, and, as in Zoroastrianism, it is the question of how needless suffering, pain, and death can exist if in fact a good and all-powerful God created and watches over the world. If God were not good, if He were not in any sense a loving or a caring God, the prevalence of suffering and the inevitability of death would not present a theological problem. Indeed, mutilation and death at the hands of the Greek Olympian gods and goddesses were accepted as a matter of course, although one could ask, in any particular case, why the god or goddess in question had suddenly turned on the victim. The Hindu god Shiva was explicitly designated as the god of destruction. When he destroyed, accordingly, there was no philosophical paradox, no theological problem to be resolved. Shiva was just being Shiva. So, too, when the evil goddess Kave of the Caroline Islands caused destruction, no further explanation was necessary. Kave was just being Kave.

In the history of the Hebrews, however, questions about God's reasons were unavoidable. When the Hebrew God allowed his "chosen" people to be sold into slavery, allowed Jerusalem and the Temple to be destroyed (not once but several times), the Hebrews faced a profound and deeply disturbing choice. They could either conclude that their God had broken His covenant and abandoned them, or they could conclude that they themselves had broken the covenant and betrayed God's trust. The question was unavoidable. Why would He do this? Even Jesus asked, "Why have You forsaken me?" The philosophy of the Hebrews and much of Jewish history after can be found in their answer—in blaming themselves. Thus the prophets often celebrated the force of the enemies of Israel, not out of disloyalty (although such charges were often forthcoming) but because they so adamantly insisted that the people, not God, were to blame for their considerable misfortunes. The same question would repeat itself, three thousand years later, after the Shoah, or Nazi "Holocaust," in mid-twentieth-century Germany.[48] Jewish history is replete with disasters, each of which precipitated a religious crisis as well. Every political crisis and foreign invasion challenged the belief that God was protecting His people.

If God or Allah were not loving or caring, there would be no religious or philosophical problem (although suffering itself would still be a profound human concern, of course). On the other hand, if He were less than all-powerful, one might well imagine that God wanted to stop suffering, but for some reason he could not do so. One way around the problem of evil might be the introduction of a second powerful being—Satan, also known as the Devil. But if this malevolent being were strong enough to counter the will of God, the God of the three great Western religions would not only not be all-powerful but not the one God either. Or, if Satan is not strong enough to counter the will of God, then we are back to our original question: How could a loving God allow evil to take place?

Jewish, Christian, and Muslim believers have been perplexed and tortured by this thought—that a loving, all-powerful God allows His creatures (His creations) to suffer. In a sense, this is *the* problem that has dominated the religious philosophy of the West. If a philosopher does not believe in God (a position that has often been dangerous if not fatal to admit), the problem need not arise. If one believed in a plurality of gods, vying against one another (as in Greek and Norse religion), one could easily understand the damage to innocent (or not so innocent) bystanders along the way. If one sufficiently compromises his or her conception of God, or simply refuses to think about the question, the problem of evil might well lose much of its urgency. But one of the definitive features of Western philosophy has to do with the absolute and uncompromising belief in God—or, rather, *beliefs* in God, as these do in fact change considerably from century to century, from region to region, from sect to sect, and, of course, from Judaism to Christianity to Islam. But whatever the specifics, the problem remains: how can an all-powerful, loving God permit so much suffering?

A perhaps even more basic question is, "What is God's nature?" In many "primitive" religions, the local deities are also the local fauna, certain privileged animals who are quite familiar and very well known and understood. Or the deities are local leaders, whose presence is palpable and whose personalities are a matter of intimate knowledge. In such religions, questions about the "nature" of the divine are quite straightforward. So, too, when the gods and goddesses are very humanlike beings, with a few added blessings such as immortality and some magical powers, their "natures" are already largely familiar, based on ordinary knowledge of the psychology and intergroup dynamics of ordinary people. One need only add, as imaginative people have always done, certain fantasies of the "what if" variety. But as God becomes less accessible and the nature of God becomes less and less familiar, the question of knowing His nature becomes more and more problematic. On what do we base our beliefs?

Judaism, Christianity, and Islam are similar in believing that God has *revealed* himself to human beings, and that his revelations are recorded in sacred Scriptures (or texts). For this reason, all three religions are sometimes described as religions "of the book," in which sacred texts play an essential role in the expression and formation of religious belief. In many religions, the gods are silent or "speak" only through their actions (or, rather, the perceived effects of their actions). In the Judeo-Christian-Islamic tradition, God speaks to His people (more or less) directly. He reveals His own nature in Scripture. But this, too, raises deep philosophical problems—specifically problems of *interpretation* and *authority*. How are these texts to be read and understood? Who is in a position to understand them and say what they mean?

The centrality of Scripture raises some common questions for all three religions. Who has the authority to interpret Scripture? Can anyone do it? Must one be specially trained? Does one need a special gift or sensibility? This leads to the question, "What role, if any, should human *reason* play in interpretation?" Are we allowed to or expected to "make sense" of what Scripture tell us, when such an understanding diverges from the literal meaning of the text? If a concept or claim makes no literal sense to us, are we permitted to reinterpret it? Does reading Scripture presuppose faith or some special attitude or vision, or is care and intelligence alone sufficient for understanding? What is the relative importance of reason and *revelation* in knowing the truth? Is the notion of revelation compatible with more secular and rationalistic ("reasonable") traditions of thought—for example, scientific explanation of the miracles described in the Bible or sociohistorical explanation of why these people might have been motivated to believe this thesis at this particular time? Does it make sense (or is it allowed) to ask who *wrote* the Scripture? In interpreting Scripture, is it necessary to understand the people who first wrote it down and their cultural and political context? This is a special application of the more general question, "Does one need (or is it even relevant) to know or understand the philosopher in order to understand the philosophy?"

Furthermore, does it matter if Scripture seems to contradict itself, perhaps as the result of being put together from different books recorded by different people at different times? Is Scripture translatable, or is the original language itself sacred (as that of Islamic Qur'an is considered to be). The Christian Bible has been translated into virtually every language in the world, often from the English (King James) or German (Lutheran) versions. These were translations from the Latin, which were translations from the Greek, which were translations from the Hebrew, which were translations from the Aramaic. Are these equally "faithful" to the original, or does it really matter?

Sometimes it seems as if every culture (perhaps even every community) makes the Scripture "its own," interpreting certain passages in its own particular way, and thinking of God in one way rather than another. Are these different interpretations equally valid? Are some more "correct" than others? Or are all interpretations equally valid, so long as they inspire the appropriate belief in God? Is it possible to read Scripture without interpreting? What is the role of experts (rabbis, priests, ministers, mullahs) in Scriptural interpretation? More historically, what is the role of the *prophets* in coming to understand God and His ways? Can one justify this or that interpretation of the Bible as the only possible one, and therefore not a mere "interpretation" at all? All of this culminates in the question of the *accessibility* of Scripture to the understanding of the average person. Can an ordinary person read the Bible or the Qur'an and comprehend God's message, or does he or she need professional help?

As we make our way from the Mediterranean to the Middle East, from Athens to Jerusalem, we can explore the second source of "Western" philosophy. It would be an oversimplification, but not very far from the predominant view, to summarize the whole of Western philosophy as the synthesis of Greek philosophy (especially the philosophies of Plato and Aristotle) and Judeo–Christian–Islamic (but particularly Christian) philosophy. (Judaism, of course, set some of the main parameters of Western philosophy, not only through its contribution of monotheism but also with its strong conception of law. Islam played an extremely important but often neglected role, not only in the further development but also in the preservation of ancient Greek philosophy.)

Whereas Greek philosophy placed a very high premium on reason and rationality, however, the three great religions we are about to discuss tended to emphasize *faith* as well. These religious traditions also contrast with the Greek tendency to view their questions ahistorically. Although Judaism, Christianity, and Islam insist that God is eternal, each places a great deal of importance on the temporal histories of their people, the stories of their original prophets. Thus, the history of the Hebrews, the life of Jesus, and the story of Muhammad become central concerns in their religions. Our account of the three great religions, therefore, will be dominated as much by history as by philosophy. In Judaism, Christianity, and Islam, philosophy becomes a concrete cultural expression, perhaps with universal appeal, but focusing more immediately on such questions as, "What does it mean to be a Jew? A Christian? A Muslim?"

Nevertheless, abstract philosophy—in fact the most abstract philosophy—inevitably pervades the religious thinking of these traditions. The grand abstractions of Being and Becoming were fairly marginal in Greco-Roman philosophy (with the exception of Parmenides and especially Plato and Aristotle). The problems of Greek and Roman philosophy, especially since Socrates, had much more to do with finding order in the world, understanding human virtue, and making recommendations for living a good life. But when the overwhelming concept in philosophy becomes the presence and nature of an all-powerful but largely unknown and mysterious God, such metaphysical abstractions as Being and Becoming quite naturally move up to the forefront of the discussion. Accordingly, Judaism, Christianity, and Islam readily join up with the more metaphysical parts of Plato and Aristotle in the effort to comprehend the mysteries of an eternal yet historically present God.

The Hebrew People and the Origins of Judaism

Although the Western philosophical tradition owes much to Greek thought, it was cross-fertilized by the Hebrew (later to be referred to as Judaic, from the name of the Kingdom of Judah) tradition as well. Jewish thought was far more motivated by religion than was Greek philosophy: the Greeks made a self-conscious effort to divorce their new philosophy from their old religion; the Jews made an equally self-conscious effort to keep philosophy and religion together.

As the Jewish religion was defined by the notion of a single God, Jewish philosophy was mainly concerned with the nature of God, with the nature of His creation and the significance of the laws He had given to His people. The conception of a single God would have greatly appealed to the Greek sense of unity, and the idea that God, as the underlying reality, existed eternally would fit in well with the most basic assumptions of Greek metaphysics. But there were enormous differences as well, and however influential the "pagan" traditions of Greece and Rome may have been, they would eventually be absorbed by the religious ideas emerging elsewhere in the Middle East, particularly in Palestine.

Most obviously, unlike the other religions in the region (with the qualified exception of Zoroastrianism), the Hebrew religion was monotheistic, acknowledging a single God, as opposed to multiple deities. In the early books of the Hebrew Bible the Jewish God appears in competition with the gods of other people. So long as the Hebrews were victorious in their battles with these other cultures, they could believe with considerable confidence that their God had defeated the other gods. But as battles were lost and enemies triumphed the competition between God and the other gods shifted its terms. The other gods were declared to be "false," and eventually they were said not to exist at all. Jewish monotheism concluded that only one God existed, not only *above* all others but *instead of* all others.

The relationship between the Hebrew people and their God is, in an important sense, the whole philosophy of Judaism. "Hear, Oh Israel, the Lord our God, the Lord is one" summarizes the basic idea of Judaism. But this central, all-important conception implied at least two corollary concepts that help to explain both the history and the philosophical temperament of Judaism. One is the notion of exclusivity of the Jews as "the chosen people," favored by God above all others. And, in return for this favor, the submission to God was required of them, and, in particular, submission to the Law. The Law would become central to Hebrew and later Jewish religious thinking in a way that it did not to any other people, although several ancient cultures, including the Hittites, the Assyrians, and especially the Babylonians under Hammurabi, developed extensive legal systems.

The ancient Hebrew philosophy was largely defined by these three key concepts: the existence of a single God, the status of being favored or "chosen" by that God, and the importance of Law. The second, perhaps, might be dismissed as chauvinistic and too ethnically exclusive for philosophy, although it might be noted that almost every society (ancient and modern) has tended to think of itself as somehow "chosen" and therefore privileged. Many a nation has gone into battle assuming that God is on its side. The first and third concepts, the One God and His Law, however, not only define the philosophy of the ancient Hebrews but provide the framework for virtually the entire course of Western history and philosophy.

Although Judaism emphasizes the dignity of the individual, it began, we should remember, as a tribal religion. The individual has meaning and dignity, first and foremost, insofar as he or she is a member of the community. As in so many ancient societies, the formation of this community is not left to happenstance. Judaism traces its status as "chosen" to God's promise to the ancestor Abraham (ca. 2000 B.C.E.), who probably migrated from Ur (in Sumeria) to Palestine. God promised Abraham that his descendants would become a great nation. This gave Judaism an exclusive, even racial, character that would be firmly rejected by the early Christians. Jewishness is not so much adherence to a philosophy or a set of beliefs, according to this ancient viewpoint, as it is a matter of membership. Consequently, Jewish philosophy is not nearly as focused on the intricacies of theology and belief as on the meaning of membership in the Jewish community and the implications of that membership.

Because it is a religion largely defined by community membership, Judaism bears at least a superficial resemblance to certain aspects of Confucianism, which is also concerned with the practicalities of social life. As an expression and as an instrument of religious solidarity, *ritual* is extremely important in Judaism. But Jewish rituals, many of which are associated with particular dates in the calendar year, reenact historical events in the life of the Jewish people. God may be eternal, but his people are historical. In fact, one might say that Jewish philosophy begins with Jewish history, or rather, the *meaning* of that history. Its ideas are embedded in the carefully preserved memories of several thousand years of triumphs and disasters. And those ideas have to do with the ongoing relationship between the Jewish people and their God.

For example, one of the most important holy occasions, the week of Passover, annually commemorates the Exodus of the Jewish slaves from Egypt into Palestine, toward "the Promised land" of Canaan in the thirteenth century B.C.E. The Exodus is seen as a particularly significant event in the relationship of the Jewish people to God. It was during the Exodus that Moses ascended Mount Sinai and received the Law from God. The holiday (holy day) begins with a ritual "Seder" supper, involving prescribed prayers in conjunction with foods symbolizing various aspects of the Jews' experience in Egypt and their escape from it. The ritual service emphasizes history as a way of consolidating the religion. One can understand more contemporary Jewish commemorations of the horrors of the Shoah, or "Holocaust," in the same way.

The relationship between God and His chosen people is also a central theme in the Hebrew Scripture. The opening book of the Hebrew Bible, the book of Genesis, presents God as the all-powerful Creator, who created the different orders of beings in steps, on six consecutive "days," culminating with the creation of human beings "in God's own image." This departed from the common Middle Eastern tendency to see the world as subsequent to previous worlds and conditions. Even for the Greeks, the idea that the world could come into being *from nothing* was all but incomprehensible. By contrast, Judaism holds that God created the world *ex nihilo*—out of nothing. Needless to say, there has been a great deal of disputation about the proper interpretation of Genesis, beginning long before Charles Darwin added a radically new wrinkle with his notion of evolution. But what has been most discussed and debated in and after the Hebrew Bible is God's relationship to one of his creations, human beings. What is meant by the claim that human beings were created "in God's own image"? And if this claim is true, why would God seem to favor some human beings over others—for example, Abraham, whom He favored alone among the population of an already well-populated and civilized area, or Isaac, the son of Abraham, whom God chose over Ishmael, according to the Hebrew Bible, as Abraham's successor. (The Arab population within Islam traces its ancestry to Ishmael, whom the Qur'an presents as the favored son of Abraham. The divergence of these accounts has helped to precipitate one of the most hate-filled conflicts in the world, with the two antagonistic neighbors each claiming to be the "chosen" people, with special priority and special protection from "their" God.)

It is not irrelevant or uninteresting that the notion of the chosen people should have been embraced by a people who had no permanent homeland, who dreamed of settling down in the rugged and often hostile territory along the eastern shores of the Mediterranean. There was a period, during the reigns of David and Solomon, when Jerusalem was the capital of a mighty kingdom comprising twelve different Hebrew tribes. Israel was, for a time, one of the established nations. King Solomon devoted much of his attention to beautifying the capital city, and the culmination of his efforts was the construction of a lavish Temple. The building of the Temple was to become a central focus in Jewish history, for it was destroyed—and rebuilt—several times. During the period described in the Hebrew Bible, the ancient Hebrews were variously conquered, enslaved, and driven into exile. It is in the light of this tragic history (not to mention the troubles that would face the Jews later, when they were no longer together as a single people) that we must understand the unique system of ideas that bound this people to their God, and vice versa.

There is little by way of theology in the Hebrew Bible, but the personality of God, if we may call it that, is rendered as clearly as if in a novel. The God of the Hebrews is, by His own admission, a jealous God. He is sometimes an angry

God, a wrathful God. The large philosophical thesis—which is more than a little reminiscent of the Greek view of Fate—is that the Hebrews' all-powerful, protecting God was extremely unpredictable, tempestuous, even whimsical. He was easily enraged, and the disasters that befell the Hebrews were proof of this. On the one hand, the Hebrews were protected by their mighty God. On the other hand, however, this protection was by no means wholly dependable. It was the absence of God's protection that had to be explained.

The heart and the durability of Judaism can be understood in terms of this great fear. It has been argued that the Jews burdened themselves with a great yoke of Law, a not unfamiliar Christian critique of the strict Jewish rules concerning virtually every aspect of life. But the truth is that the so-called "covenant," the promise on the part of the Hebrews to obey God's Law, gave them considerable confidence, something by way of a guarantee. If they obeyed the Law, then God would protect them.

However, when disaster struck—as it so often did—the Jews did not doubt their belief in God but rather blamed themselves. The prophets would speak almost with pride of the forces amassed against Israel, not as proof of God's abandonment but rather as proof of His continuing concern, expressed through such signs of His displeasure at the Jewish people's infractions against the Law. The alternative interpretation, that they were being abandoned by God, was unthinkable to the Hebrews. Guilt was far preferable, and it might be said that the Hebrews gave to guilt its philosophical form.

There is no feature more central to Judaism and Jewish philosophy than the Law. The Law is conceived as being directly revealed by God. It should not be considered merely a code or a contract invented by human beings to hold their societies together. Neither should it be thought of as an invention or an instrument of power of those who rule. Indeed, it should not be thought of as an imposition but rather as a privilege, a blessing. God's revelation of the Law to them is precisely what made the Jewish people "chosen."

The Ten Commandments (the Decalogue) lie at the heart of Jewish law. According to Scripture, these were given to Moses on Mount Sinai in what is now known as the Gaza Strip. The obligations the Decalogue included were: to have no other gods besides the one God; to make no graven images or invoke no magical names to summon God's appearance; to observe the weekly Sabbath by abstaining from all labor; to submit to one's parents' authority; and to abstain from murder, adultery, theft, giving false testimony in court, and dispossessing another man of his spouse or household.

Further laws, derived from the Decalogue, specified how persons, even slaves, should be treated respectfully and nonexploitatively. In particular, help should be given to individuals in situations of misfortune. Justice ordained that those in more secure positions should try to ensure that assistance is given to those in need.[49] Thus the obligations of Law were conjoined with an emphasis on compassion and respect, not only for one's superiors but for everyone. Every individual has dignity and worth and is therefore worthy of respect, and everyone is equal before, and should be equally committed to, the Law.

The Law defines Jewish philosophy, but it seems to be the violation of the

Law that defines its history. According to the Jewish Scripture, the perfect order of God's creation was undercut by the first human beings. Genesis explains the origin of evil in the world in terms of human *sin*. The concept of sin has come to play a central role in the religious philosophy of the West. Sin can best be understood as the defiance of God's laws, a breach in the relationship between humans and God, caused by inappropriate behavior of which humans are guilty. Every culture has some concept(s) of wrongdoing, but "sin" implies a particular kind of wrong, an offense against God.

After He created Adam and then Eve as the first human couple, God warned them not to eat the fruit of a particular tree, the Tree of Knowledge of Good and Evil. A serpent tempted Eve to eat the forbidden fruit, claiming that it would make anyone who ate it God-like. Eve ate the fruit and offered it to Adam, who did likewise.

The story is revealing for what it says about human wrongdoing, and it has often been understood allegorically. The idea of an original innocence, replaced by the awful weight of knowledge, and with knowledge, the ability to make choices between good and evil, summarizes much of the moral plot of the Judeo-Christian-Islamic tradition and its approach to the problem of evil. Innocence is destroyed by knowledge. A primordial bliss is clouded by the need for morality, and with it the need for reflection and, one might add, philosophy. We might note that human curiosity, however, the temptation to know, is already evident in the condition of innocence. Thus the question of ultimate responsibility for sin enters the Judeo-Christian-Islamic tradition right from the outset. Did God knowingly create us with a nature that would inevitably yield to curiosity in this fashion?

Notice, too, that the participation of Satan (the serpent) suggests that monotheism has not yet dispensed with the notion that there are other quasi-deities (although far less powerful than God). These quasi-deities, as in Zoroastrianism, help to explain the existence of human suffering and misfortune in the world without attributing these directly to God.

God responded to the disobedience of Adam and Eve with anger, revealing a trait that is characteristic of God in the Hebrew Bible: his proneness to *wrath*. As a consequence of their sin, Adam and Eve were banished from the paradise in which they had previously resided. They now entered a world of sickness, suffering, and death. Their previous nature, made "in the image of God," had been damaged, and they themselves had done it by their own willful disobedience.

From then on, human beings would no longer be naturally disposed to godlike (good) behavior (although the original story already suggests a serious flaw in this natural disposition). Their actions were now a matter of choice, often a choice between good and evil. Accordingly, the philosophical writings of Judaism are therefore for the most part emminently practical, devoted to spelling out the correct reasons for making the right choices.

The Genesis account of the first sin, "the Fall," provided the foundation for the Jewish solution to the problem of evil. Genesis suggests that evil came into the world through human choice. Later Jewish thought frequently takes its cue from Genesis, seeking to explain suffering and misfortune as consequences of human failure and, in particular, human violations of God's laws. This was, for example, the contention of the prophets who explained the political havoc that followed Solomon's reign in terms of the Jewish people's failure to observe God's laws.

Prophets are philosophers, of course, but they were not, in general, abstract thinkers; they were, first of all, speakers for God. They were also cultural critics who interpreted the political devastation following Solomon's death as the consequence of sin and injustice, systematic violations of God's laws. Solomon's efforts to construct a beautiful and prosperous city were supported by burdensome taxation. The gap between the wealthy and the poor widened, and resistance and rebellion were followed by invasion. Palestine was divided into two unfriendly nations and Jerusalem was captured by the Egyptian pharaoh shortly after Solomon's death. As the wealth of the city was siphoned away to Egypt, there began a long period of turmoil and self-doubt.

The period of the prophets began in response to the economic inequities that had developed in Judea. They preached repentance and virtue, and they predicted disaster if their society continued in its sinful ways. The prophets' words, largely unheeded, anticipated a series of disastrous misfortunes that befell the Jews. After the Egyptian invasion of Jerusalem and the division of the Jewish state, the northern kingdom was taken by the Assyrians in 733 B.C.E., and two hundred thousand Jews were enslaved. Jerusalem (the capital of the southern kingdom) survived, but only after the uncertainty of a long siege. The situation reached a low point when Jerusalem was captured by the Babylonians in 586 B.C.E. This time the city was burned and the Temple was destroyed. The leading citizens were exiled, and Israel was absorbed into the Babylonian empire.

Once again, the interpretation that Jewish religious leaders gave to these events was that Israel was being punished for its sins, particularly the worship of foreign gods and the inhumane treatment of the poor. Because of Israel's unjust and unlawful behavior, God had justly removed His protection. It is worth emphasizing that ancient Jewish thought depicted the consequences of sin in terms of disasters on earth, not in terms of an afterlife. Judaism did not and does not, in general, promote the idea of personal immortality.[50]

During the Babylonian exile, the prophets proclaimed that God might again help the Jews, as He had in getting them out of Egypt, if they remained faithful to Him during that prolonged crisis. Such "tests" of faith under duress would be repeated many times in the history of Judaism, as well as in the histories of Christianity and Islam. Eventually, God seemed to fulfill the prophecy. Cyrus of Persia conquered Babylon and allowed the exiled Jews to return to Jerusalem. He also returned the remains of the wealth that the Babylonians had stolen from the Temple. The Temple was rebuilt, and its reemergence became a powerful symbol of the indestructibility of the Jewish religion.

But this indestructibility continued to face numerous tests, and the Temple was destroyed once again in 70 C.E., following a Jewish rebellion against Rome. The Diaspora, the dispersion of Jews through the Mediterranean and elsewhere, is considered by most scholars to have begun at this time. Again, the political disaster was given a religious interpretation. Misfortune resulted from human sinfulness and a failure of faith among the Jews. They had not succeeded in upholding the Law, and inequities in their behavior had once again brought disaster. The concept of responsibility and its consequences was by this time set deep into Jewish consciousness.

The presumed correspondence between responsibility and consequences was bound to be called into question. In Jewish literature itself, the connection between sin and disaster was challenged in a most dramatic way. The Book of Job (possibly written during the Babylonian exile, around 400 B.C.E.) tells the story of a good man named Job who is horribly punished despite the fact that he has faithfully obeyed all of God's laws. Satan taunts God, suggesting that Job behaves righteously only because God treats him well. God "tests" Job by allowing Satan to cause the worst personal disasters to befall Job and his family. Through it all, Job continues to live as piously as he always has, although he frequently implores God to help him. His friends assume that he must have sinned secretly and that his misfortunes are punishment for sin. Job, however, knows that he is innocent, and so does the reader. Despite the apparent injustice of his sufferings, Job affirms his belief in God.

God ultimately restores Job to his former happy state, but He insists that His ways need not be comprehensible to human beings and on the need for faith despite the apparent injustice in the world. This leaves the problem of evil horribly unresolved. Why should a just man suffer? In the story, there is no doubt but that God bears some responsibility for Job's suffering. Is this a case of God behaving "incomprehensibly"? Isn't it a clear case of unjust punishment? Isn't it possible, the story asks us, for one to be perfectly good and nevertheless suffer, not only under the watch but in the hands of an all-powerful loving God? Here, the problem of evil is presented in its most extreme version.

The Book of Job has had as provocative an impact on Jewish philosophy as many of the political disasters that befell the Jewish people, arousing centuries of dispute and volumes of commentaries. Like Christianity and Islam to follow, Judaism was and is a "religion of the book." Consequently, scholarship and argumentation are highly valued in the Jewish tradition and essential to Jewish philosophy. Indeed, the method and the manner of continuing disagreement and dialectic largely define that philosophy—like the philosophy of Socrates—and they are one of the great strengths that has kept Jewish ideas alive and resilient for thousands of years.

Greek Jew: Philo of Alexandria

Because Judaism is a religion of the book, it had to face those issues concerned with the proper interpretation of Scripture. Among these are such questions as: Who is capable of interpreting Scripture? Is the possibility open to everyone? Does proper interpretation depend on revelation? If so, how does one recognize when revelation is genuine? Between Jewish scholarship and debate and Greek philosophy, there arose a particularly significant perplexity concerning the role of reason in interpreting Scripture. Did reason provide a basis for interpretation? Could proper interpretation of Scripture ever result in teachings that conflicted with reason? If so, how should one settle the resulting controversy? Should faith give way to reason, or should reason give way to faith? The history of Judaism pointed to the conclusion that faith, above all, is essential. The dialectical activity of the rabbis and the Greek philosophers, however, indicated an important role for reason.

These issues quite naturally came to a head when the Jewish religion met Greek philosophy in the final centuries of the millennium. Philo (fl.20 B.C.E.,– 40 C.E.), was one of the first Jewish thinkers to draw upon Greek thought in his efforts to establish the proper approach for interpreting Scripture. He was particularly concerned with the issues of faith and reason. Philo was a Greek-speaking Jew of Alexandria who was educated in Hellenistic philosophy (that is, Greek philosophy as it developed around the Mediterranean after the Greeks dispersed in the wake of Alexander the Great's conquest of the region). Philo was particularly sensitive to the conflicts between the two traditions he inherited. As a Jew, he was committed to monotheism and resistant to assimilation. On the other hand, the culture and philosophical tradition in which he had been educated were distinctively Greek. This question, whether to maintain one's Jewish identity or to assimilate into the dominant culture, has fostered one of the longest debates in philosophical history, and the issue goes right to the heart of the question of self-identity.

Philo's philosophical response was to systematize Jewish thought in Greek terms and to harmonize it with reasoned argumentation. Jewish philosophy and history, as we have seen, consisted far more of stories than philosophical reflections as such. But Greek thought had been similar before the advent of "philosophy" with Thales and the Milesians. Homer had long been interpreted allegorically, and Alexandrian Jews before Philo had developed a tradition of allegorical interpretation, too, particularly of Genesis. Accordingly, Philo availed himself of these techniques and interpreted biblical tales as mythic statements about the nature of the human condition and humanity's relationship to the divine. He tended to see the characters in biblical accounts as representing abstract concepts. For example, he interprets Adam as reason and Eve as the senses. The serpent represents lust. Philo interprets the story of the first sin as an account of lust's power. Lust initially attracts the senses, but it can be the downfall of reason once the senses are subdued.

Philo went on to suggest that the Greek philosophers had been inspired by the same God who had revealed Himself through Scripture. Thus, truth could be found in their reasoned arguments as well as in Scripture—the same truth, the revealed word of God. Philo attempted, accordingly, to show that allegorical interpretation of Scripture brings its insights into conjunction with Greek thought. He underplayed the miraculous and those aspects of Scripture that mark off the Jews as the uniquely "chosen" people, emphasizing instead that God's power is manifested through the principles of nature. This was an idea that was palatable to the Greeks, and it did not set the one tradition against the other. This move toward giving Hebrew philosophy a universalistic interpretation would also be extremely important for the development of Christianity.

Philo appropriated a number of insights from Pythagoreanism, describing God as the One underlying all multiplicity. In particular, however, he drew from

Platonism and early Stoicism. With the Platonists, Philo contended that the material world was but a reflection of a higher, transcendent world. What Plato called the Forms (in the higher world) were really the thoughts of God, according to Philo. Like the Stoics, Philo conceived of God as pervading the world, so an inner divine spark was evident within every human being. Although God Himself is transcendent, he is nevertheless related to the material world through *logos* (the world's underlying structure), and in that sense God is immanent, within us. *Logos* turns out to be an image of God, and the human mind, in turn, is made in the image of *logos*. (The Christian Gospel according to John begins with a similar claim: "In the beginning, was the *logos*.") Because it shares in God's image, the human mind is able to know and love God, although human knowledge of God is limited. It is also *logos* that holds together the elements of the natural world. Philo also explains direct manifestations of God in the world (through, for example, the burning bush that appeared to Moses) in terms of *logos*.

According to Philo, Plato's philosophy was accurate in its portrayal of the highest good for human beings. Plato's Socrates had described the dazzling insight provided by even a glimpse of the Forms. Judaism similarly held that one should aim for a mystical vision of God. Plato was also correct in his view that the mind naturally leads in the right direction. God's essence, however, is beyond the power of the mind to grasp, according to Philo. Thus Philo's conception of human knowledge of God takes the form of a *via negativa*, a negative way. In other words, given our limited abilities, we can gain a sense of God's nature by specifying what God is not (not by offering positive descriptions). In particular, Philo maintains, God is not a limited, morally flawed being, like the traditional gods of the Greeks.

Despite his synthesis of Greek thought and Jewish theology, Philo recognized that there could still be conflicts between reason and revealed truth. He contended that such conflicts should be resolved in favor of revelation. Reason, he suggested, was unable to grasp some of the most profound truths inspired by faith. Reason could not, for instance, comprehend the unity of God. Nor could it comprehend the fact that God's essence transcends human (and thus rational) description. Philo thus expressed limits to his admiration for reason and claimed that mystical ecstasy was ultimately more important than philosophical and theological speculation. In this, too, however, Philo saw Plato as his ally. Although they both valued meticulous rationality, it was a vision of the True World that Plato and Philo both considered the ultimate human aim.

Finally, Philo also follows Plato in postulating a decisive division between soul and body, with the body presenting an obstacle to virtue. Philo describes the body as akin to a tomb and sometimes suggests that only the soul has virtue. This emphasis on the inner life of the soul coupled with disdain for the body links Philo to his early Christian contemporaries. Like the early Christians (and somewhat like Confucius), Philo emphasized inner virtue, suggesting that external ritual without appropriate inner attitude is worthless. He did not, however, conclude from this that ritual is unimportant. Instead, he emphasized the importance of approaching ritual with the right attitude. Perhaps because his emphases coincided more with those of early Christianity than with those of contemporary Palestinian Judaism, Philo was more influential for later Christians than for his own Jewish people.

The Birth of Christianity

Christianity developed around Jesus, the "Christ" ("the anointed one"), who lived approximately 6 B.C.E. to 30 C.E. in Palestine, then part of the Roman Empire. The Judaism into which Jesus was born was fragmented into a number of factions. Some, such as the Pharisees and the Sadducees mentioned in the New Testament, supported Roman rule, although for different reasons. The Sadducees, priestly families who had assimilated Hellenistic ideas, accepted Roman governance in the hope of retaining their relatively high social status. The Pharisees (literally, "separated ones"), by contrast, saw Roman rule as punishment for the sins of the people. They adopted dramatic ritual practices, notably practices of ritual purification, and they viewed themselves as more religious, more Jewish, than others. In doing so, however, they in fact deviated from traditional Jewish belief, accepting, for example, the nontraditional notion of an afterlife, perhaps as a compensation for the political disadvantages of their current life under Roman rule. The Pharisees were particularly influential on later Jewish thought because they supplemented the written law of the Hebrew Bible with a rich codification of interpretations that had developed through the oral tradition. They held that these traditional interpretations were as binding as the written law itself. The Pharisees were also the religious leaders who had sustained the Jews' sense of themselves as a people after the destruction of the Temple in Jerusalem in 70 C.E.

The Pharisees were conservative, but other Jewish factions, notably the Zealots, vigorously encouraged the revolt against Rome. Still others lived in isolated monastic communities. Among these were the Essenes, a sect that lived primarily in the area of the Dead Sea. (The Essenes have been linked by historians to the Dead Sea Scrolls—fragments of approximately six hundred ancient manuscripts that were stored in stone jars inside caves, discovered beginning in 1947 on the Dead Sea's northwestern shore. They include a wide range of Jewish religious and literary writings, including some documents regarding the religious community at Qumran, which some scholars believe was an Essene group.) The Essenes observed unusual dietary laws and made much of ritual bathing. They also were sexually ascetic (although they did allow marital intercourse for the purpose of procreation). The lifestyle of Essenes was agrarian and communal, and their religious lives centered around meditation. Although they were apolitical pacifists, they anticipated the arrival of a Messiah who would create a new kingdom on earth. (Despite their pacificism, they joined in the defense of Jerusalem in 70 C.E. and were virtually wiped out.)

The rivalries among these various factions, together with the running friction with Rome, made the early first century C.E. in Jerusalem an exciting and confusing place. To add to the confusion, a great many prophetlike figures were spreading various messages of foreboding and apocalyptic promises. Several of these aspiring prophets became prominent in the Jewish community into which Jesus was born. One of them, John the Baptist, was Jesus' cousin. (His odd diet of honey and locusts suggests that he may have been a member of the Essenes.) John preached "The end is near" and urged people to repent for their sins. He practiced the ritual of *baptism*, which involved purification by water, a sign of repentance. Jesus was baptized in the Jordan River by John at the age of thirty, and the practice of baptism was absorbed into Christianity as an initiation ceremony involving an affirmation of faith and a symbolic immersion into water. The appropriate age for baptism and the precise significance of the ceremony would become contentious issues within Christianity, both before and after the Protestant Reformation. (The baptism of an adult indicated a confirmation of faith, but the baptism of an infant was less clear in its significance.)

John was one of those prophets who clearly announced the coming of a Messiah. (The word "Messiah" also means "the anointed," as does the Greek word "Christ." The Messiah would be "anointed with divine spirit.") In Christian Scripture, accordingly, John is presented as a herald for Jesus. Most of John's disciples became Christians. John himself was imprisoned and executed by Herod, the Roman ruler in charge of Galilee. (Herod asked the dancing girl Salomé what she would like in return for pleasing him. Following her mother's cruel suggestion, she asked for "the head of John the Baptist.")

Like John, Jesus encouraged apocalyptic anticipations on the part of his disciples. According to the standard story circulating at the time, the Messiah would come from the family of David, which Jesus did, and most Jews expected him to be a warrior and a political leader. Jesus' reported miracles were taken as confirmation of his status as the Messiah. His teachings proclaimed that a new Kingdom of God was about to begin, effectively playing into the popular expectations about the Messiah.

In contrast to the portrayal of an often harsh and punitive God in the Hebrew Bible, Jesus stressed God's mercy and *forgiveness* rather than God's wrath, although Jesus, too, could be harsh and did not call into question God's sometimes-unpredictable justice. (He promoted the concept of God's bestowing "*grace*," for example, even though he also preached faith and the virtues. But God would not be *obligated* by anyone's behavior.) Despite his rejection of certain approaches to Judaism, however, many of Jesus' teachings encompassed themes that were already central to Jewish thought. His emphasis on love was presented as an interpretation already established in the Jewish tradition. Jesus also followed a standard theme in Jewish thought when he emphasized the importance of helping the unfortunate and when he described desire for wealth as a distraction from holiness. He taught the by no means orthodox thesis that the Jewish law could be summarized in terms of loving God with one's whole heart and one's neighbor as oneself. This emphasis on love is stressed by Christians as a new law, *a law of love,* based on inner disposition as opposed to external ritual and obedience to the letter of the law. But this distinction can be overtaxed. Jesus criticized those who made great shows of their holiness but had callous attitudes toward other people. Again this theme is a traditional Jewish theme, evident particularly in the teachings of the prophets. The God-given law and the love of God were never intended to be very far apart.

Emerging as a tradition within Judaism, Christianity absorbed many other Jewish theses as well. Like Jews, Christians believe that there is one God, who created the world out of nothing. Similarly, Christians emphasize God's enormous power, and they reiterate the Jewish emphasis on human dignity. Christianity, however, elaborated its own accounts of these originally Jewish themes. Embracing monotheism, the new religion nevertheless contended that the one God is three persons, *the Holy Trinity*. One of these, the Father, is characterized much as the Jewish God is characterized, with emphasis placed on His power and His role in creation.

The second, the Son, is God as manifest in the person of Jesus Christ, who is believed to have been God incarnate in human flesh. This great mystery of the God-man, who chose to be born and to die in time, is known as the *Incarnation*. This doctrine was particularly shocking after centuries of Jewish emphasis on God's difference from human beings, especially on His limitless power. The mystery is the very idea that the eternal God could become what seemed to be a perfectly natural human being, a man who could suffer, who could bleed, who could die. After centuries of philosophy in which the eternal was sharply distinguished from the temporal, in which the transcendent was contrasted with the ordinary, here was a shocking claim, which would motivate the efforts of philosophers and theologians well into the nineteenth century.

The third person of God is the Holy Spirit, often described as the immanence of God as he dwells among human beings. The person of the Holy Spirit, as the most abstract conception of the three, nevertheless played an essential part in creation, according to traditional Christian theology, and it would be this notion in particular which would exercise the imagination of a great many philosophers both before and after the reformation.

The doctrine of the Trinity would also create numerous tensions within the view that God is one. For many Christian thinkers, these tensions present a philosophical challenge to provide coherent accounts of the two doctrines to show how they are compatible. A good deal of Christian theology is devoted to this intricate, abstract puzzle. In what sense can the one God be three? Who or what is God that He can be both the eternal and live in time (in the person of the Son)? The tensions created by the doctrine of the Trinity sometimes presented an excuse for several divergent sects to make war on one another, allegedly in the name of theology, more often as a matter of accumulated hatred and, not infrequently, greed. In the eleventh century C.E. it would be invoked in order to split the entire Christian church in two.

The Christian doctrine of the *Virgin Birth* clarifies Jesus' role within the Trinity while also suggesting that Jesus was, from birth, marked for a supernatural destiny. The doctrine also embodied the traditions of the Essenes and the growing distaste of the Pharisees for matters of the body. According to this doctrine of the virgin birth, Jesus' mother Mary conceived Jesus directly, without a human father. God (in the person of the Holy Spirit) was literally Jesus' father. Thus, even at conception, Jesus was fully God, even if also human. The doctrine of the virgin birth also supports the literal interpretation of Jesus as "the Son of God."

Christianity, like Judaism and Zoroastrianism, was particularly concerned with the problem of evil, the prevalence of suffering in a world watched over by a caring (now loving) God. Christians, like Jews, explain the prevalence of evil in terms of human sinfulness. Christians thus embrace Genesis and the story of Adam and Eve's Fall as an account of how suffering came into the human world. The unique Christian contribution to this theory of suffering is the contention that humanity remained in a "fallen" position until Jesus Christ was crucified, although he himself was innocent, at the hands of Roman officials. Christians interpret the Crucifixion in terms of Christ having taken upon himself the guilt of humanity and the suffering necessary to expiate this guilt. It is a profound and, in the context of the long Jewish tradition of guilt and self-blame, an extremely relieving idea. It is also, in terms of ordinary notions of justice or redemption, an extremely difficult notion.

According to the Christian Gospels, Jesus rose from the dead three days after his crucifixion and appeared on several occasions to his disciples. The Crucifixion and Resurrection are considered by Christians to be essential to the salvation of humanity. Jesus is therefore seen as the fulfillment of God's ancient promise to the Jews and the culmination of what had always been an intimate relationship between humanity and God. In Jesus, God literally becomes one with His people, sharing their life. As part of God's punishment for the sin of Adam and Eve, death had entered the world and human beings had been blocked from paradise and eternal life. Jesus' sacrifice opens the way to salvation, now understood as eternal life in union with God. Thus, the Crucifixion is seen by Christians as putting things right between God and humanity.

The Resurrection of Jesus also represents the idea of triumph over death. Thus, although belief in an *afterlife* had never been an official doctrine among the Jews, it became one of the basic tenets of Christian doctrine. The risen Jesus promised his followers that they too would conquer death. When Jesus returns to earth, his "Second Coming" will signal the end of the world and the final judgment, in which the bodies of the dead will be reunited with their souls, and all individuals will be permanently admitted or denied admittance to heaven.

That is the story of the origins of Christianity, the "cult narrative" upon which all of the rest of Christian philosophy is constructed. But Christianity, like Judaism, is a religion "of the book," and its strength has rested, in part, on the centrality of Scripture and the dynamic interplay of differing interpretations. Christian Scripture includes both the Hebrew Bible, which is appropriated as the Old Testament, and the New Testament, which includes four different accounts of Christ's life. The accounts of Christ's life are attributed to the *Evangelists* Matthew, Mark, Luke, and John. Although these evangelists have traditionally been taken to be among the twelve *Apostles*, the inner circle among Jesus' disciples, scholars are fairly certain that these accounts were written later than the lifetimes of the Apostles and thus absorbed a good deal of legend and folklore.

The New Testament also includes the Acts of the Apostles, an account of the experiences of the early Christians, particularly the apostles Peter and Paul. The Epistles, letters from central religious leaders in the young movement, and the Apocalypse, make up the rest of the New Testament. The Apocalypse is a visionary prophetic work written by an author named "John," traditionally identified with John the Apostle.[51] The entire New Testament—and what Christians now know as the Bible—was formally fixed (in its Greek version) in 382 C.E.

Like Judaism, Christianity is rich in ritual (although the specific nature of those rituals has been much in dispute). And like Judaism, Christianity associates specific occasions in the year with specific, religiously significant events. But while Judaism focuses on significant historical events in the history of the Jewish people, Christianity focuses instead on significant events in the life of Christ, and these are steeped in abstract symbolism, typically concerning the nature of God.

The central such ritual is the ceremony of the *Eucharist*, the breaking and eating of bread in commemoration of Jesus' Last Supper (a seder for Passover) the night before his crucifixion. Jesus is reported to have taken the bread in his hands and said, "Take and eat, for this is my body," and to have said of wine, "Take and drink, for this is my blood." But this was no mere "reminder," as the ritual foods of Passover were reminders to the Jews of past trials and hardships. The Eucharist was interpreted literally as Christ's body and blood by the early Christians, as it is still by Catholics, who celebrate the Eucharist, or *Communion*, as involving the participants' mystical presence at Christ's Last Supper (experienced in ritual, extraordinary time). Thus the ritual of the *Mass* is considered a reenactment of the Last Supper, which involves the *transubstantiation* of bread and wine literally into Christ's body and blood.

Religious experience as such achieves central importance in most Christian thinking, together with the symbolic meanings that give what might otherwise be routine gestures (eating a wafer, sipping wine) profound significance. As in so many religions, Christian ritual and symbolism come to embrace not only deep philosophical ideas but the most mysterious metaphors as well. For someone who is not deeply engaged in these ideas and mysteries, it may be hard to understand the intensity, even ferocity, of the theological disputes in the fifteen hundred years to follow.

The Opening of Christianity: St. Paul

Early Christianity confronted a variety of challenges and practical concerns that had philosophical implications. One of the challenges was that Christianity was immediately recognized as a subversive threat by the ruling Romans, and many Christians were persecuted and killed in the early years of the religion. Many of the early Christians' concerns, however, had to do with who could or could not be considered a member of that persecuted group. Was Christianity to be (more or less) limited to Jews, or was the faith open to others as well? What would be the role of Hebraic law in the life of Christians? Christianity began, in effect, as a sect within Judaism. Many Christian Jews continued to worship at the Temple, seeing no conflict between their new beliefs and Jewish ritual. But as the appeal of Christianity began to reach a larger audience, tensions emerged between the various ethnic groups and, by the first half century of the new millennium, Christianity not only opened its doors but began to actively recruit new members, potentially everyone in the world.

The definitive figure and most influential philosopher in these early days of Christianity was (St.) Paul (died between 62 and 68 C.E.), who was among the best educated of the early Christian leaders. Like Philo, Paul was a Hellenized Jew. Although he was an enthusiastic persecutor of Christians in his early adulthood, he became an equally ardent defender of the faith after his conversion. This occurred, according to his own testimony, through a dramatic experience on the road to Damascus, where he was traveling to organize the persecution of some poor Christians. As Paul told it, he was knocked off his horse and temporarily blinded, and he heard a voice that asked, "Why do you persecute me?" Thus "seeing the light," he converted to Christianity.

The extent of Paul's influence is evident from the fact that he came to be considered an Apostle, even though he had not personally known Jesus. Paul encouraged a new understanding of apostleship, claiming that personal acquaintance was unimportant given the possibility of such overpowering experiences of Jesus as he had on his way to Damascus. Paul played a central role in the controversy over the relevance of the Jewish law to Christians, for he considered himself to have a special vocation to the "Gentiles," the non-Jewish population. He encouraged a universalist view of Christianity, insisting that the new religion should not differentiate between Jews and Greeks. There were no special provisions for "the chosen people." Paul's universalist approach to Christianity was probably in keeping with his Hellenistic education. He appears to have been aware of certain Stoic ideas that were extant in the Roman Empire. For example, he appeals to the Stoic conception of nature when he speaks of a natural law of conscience, inherent in every human being.

Paul was extremely influential in determining the way the story of Jesus was interpreted by the early Christians. He considered Jesus to be the Messiah predicted by the prophets of the Hebrew Bible. Jesus' appearance was a sign that a new age had arrived. It was Paul who interpreted Jesus as the Son of God the Father, Creator of the world. The Holy Spirit, the third person of the Trinity, conjoined the Christian community, on Paul's account, by imparting grace into the hearts of its members. Grace is a blessing of God which invigorates individuals' spiritual lives and assists them in their effort to live morally.

What must have seemed most persuasive and profound to many of Christianity's converts, however, was the Christian response to the old problem of guilt and the promise of a glorious afterlife for those who would be "saved" by God. Paul interpreted the crucifixion as an *atonement* for sins. (To "atone" is to "make up for.") Emphasis on the sinfulness of all descendants of Adam and the necessity of Christ's death to redeem it are teachings of Paul, which we know through his letters. Jesus probably did not present himself in these terms; at least, the portraits of his life in the four Gospels do not invoke this terminology. Paul also introduced the notion that God would decide who will be saved. According to

Paul's letters, Christ would eventually return "in glory" to judge humanity (both living and dead). Paul anticipated that this Second Coming of Christ would be relatively soon, as did most of his early Christian followers.

Were Christians still bound by the Law of Moses? Paul's universalism had considerable bearing on this question. As so often, the general question became heated because of a very particular issue. Circumcision was required by Jewish law, so some Christians insisted that Greeks should be circumcised if they wanted to become Christians. Others rejected this idea, considering the ritual unnecessary and cruel, especially for adults. Paul resolved that particular issue by declaring that circumcision was not required for Christians (no doubt evoking a sigh of relief from many male converts).

The implication of this decision was that the Mosaic law would not rule Christianity. Jesus' death and resurrection had both fulfilled and supplanted the Jewish law as the basis for religious life. The new faith was to be guided by love, according to Paul, not the legal restrictions of traditional Judaism. It would also encourage conversions, as opposed to endorsing separatism, like certain Jewish sects (notably the Pharisees). This tendency of Christianity to seek conversions, called *evangelism*, remains a distinct (if not unique) characteristic of the religion to this day.

Paul's judgment led to a significant number of overturned commandments, but, it is important to emphasize, the number of rejected doctrines does not signal an overall rejection of the Hebraic Law. All of the Ten Commandments remain intact and as binding for a Christian as for a Jew, including, of course, such commandments as "Thou shalt not kill," "Thou shalt not steal," and "Honor thy father and thy mother." What does change, however, are a great many of the restrictions that had been imposed by Jewish law, such as the *kosher* restrictions on diet and the injunction against "graven images." One purpose of the *kosher* restrictions was to keep the Hebrews together as a people and distinguish them from others, but the early Christians saw every reason to open up their religion to other people. The injunction against "graven images" had been based on the idea that God could not be pictured. But since Jesus Christ was God as man, there was no reason to consider all images as "graven" or blasphemous, and Christian art flourished accordingly.

Paul's decision regarding circumcision, which was supported by the first Christian Council, also marked a victory for the Hellenized Christian community. In undermining the importance of circumcision, this decision also accorded with the relatively important role for women in early Christianity, by comparison with other contemporary religions (including Judaism). Women's roles gradually declined, however, as the Church became a more organized movement. Paul himself, moreover, was far from a supporter of women's rights. He insisted on a woman's subordination to her husband. He also tended to speak of female sexuality as inferior, dangerous, and even evil. He encouraged sexual propriety, if not complete abstinence, among all Christians. Perhaps this was not so much because of a disdain for sexuality as to counter popular reports that some Christian celebrations of the Eucharist had degenerated into orgies.

Paul had based his decision regarding circumcision on the argument that the

Jewish law as such had been superseded by Christianity. Thus Paul made the new religion more accessible to the non-Jewish world, and the perspective of the non-Jewish, Hellenistic Christian community came to dominate Christianity. Christian beliefs and practices gradually became sufficiently distinct from Jewish beliefs and practices so that Christianity came to be considered a religion in its own right.

Neoplatonism and Christianity

Greek thought had considerable influence on later Christian thought. Christian awareness of Greek thought, however, was mediated by a movement of later interpreters of Plato called *Neoplatonism*. In addition to its impact on Christianity, Neoplatonism also had significant influence on Islamic thought, as we shall see.

The most influential Neoplatonist thinker was Plotinus (204–270). Plotinus emphasized the religious currents in Plato's thought, facilitating a later conflation of Platonic metaphysics with Christian theology. For example, he interpreted the Platonic form of the Good as a kind of person, inviting later interpretation of the Good as the Christian God. The Good, according to Plotinus, was the Supreme Mind, an indivisible unity that created the world. As an intelligence, this Supreme Mind was engaged in contemplation of itself, and Creation emerged as a kind of overflow from its thinking. Creation, in other words, emanated, or issued from, God's thinking. Plotinus's theory, therefore, is often described as a theory of *emanations*.

In contrast to Plato, who denigrated the material world as a lesser reality (comparing it to the shadows in a cave), Plotinus saw the material world as itself spiritual, the thought of a fully spiritual mind. Plotinus did, however, believe that the emanations constituted a hierarchy and that one order of Being emerged out of another. Spirit, the highest form of Being, emerges directly from the Divine Mind. Spirit illuminates Plato's Forms, the objects of the Divine Mind's contemplation. Soul proceeds from Spirit and guides life in the world by reaching beyond itself, ensouling matter. Matter is merely the lowest of the emanations.

The appeal of the doctrine of emanations may be less than evident in the twentieth century. In the first centuries of Christianity, however, the theory had tremendous appeal because it served several important philosophical and religious functions. Plato had divided the divine realm from the material realm without providing much of an account of their relationship. (His claim was that ordinary objects "participated" in the Forms.) The theory of emanations tries to explain how the two realms are related. From a strictly materialist standpoint (that is, the position that matter is the fundamental basis of whatever is real), this emanation theory might not seem like much of an account of the nature of things. But if one adopts the spiritual outlook presumed by Plotinus, his explanation is not only appealing but even edifying, insofar as it does not try to remove the "mystery" from an account of the world.

The theory of emanations also resolved the problem that the Pythagoreans had raised: "If unity is prior to everything, how does multiplicity ever come into being?" In the same way, one might ask, "How did the World of Becoming emerge from Being?" In the context of monotheistic doctrines about God as Creator, this question easily takes on religious significance: If God is conceived as the eternal and perfect unity, why does He create a temporal world that is distinct from Him?

Plotinus claims that Creation, the world coming into existence, is an essential aspect of the Divine Mind, the One (God) thinking Itself. Like an artist, the One is impelled to create, to express itself, by virtue of its own nature. Creator and creation, however, are not sharply distinguished in Plotinus's account. Furthermore, the levels of Being overlap and interpenetrate one another. The human soul already has its archetype on a higher level, and spiritual discipline enables a person to develop spiritual intuition. This is a harmonious merger of the mind with higher levels of being. The ultimate aim for the soul, accordingly, is mystical union with the One (God), who becomes fully present to the human soul. Plotinus envisioned this optimal relationship between human beings and the One (God) as involving the whole person, joined to the One not only through knowledge but through love.

Despite its extreme abstraction, Plotinus's philosophy conveys a simple and remarkably positive spiritual message. The human soul is already in some sense divine and even the material world of everyday life is spiritual. There is no evil in the world, and therefore there is no "problem" of evil either. At worst, we encounter an absence of good, a lack that can, through human devotion, be corrected.

St. Augustine and the Inner Life of Spirit

St. Augustine (354–430 C.E.) eventually bequeathed Plotinus's message that evil was only the absence of good to generations of Christians; but for much of his life, he found the problem of evil a devastating quandary. Augustine was born about sixty miles from the city of Hippo in North Africa (on the coast of what is now Algeria). His mother was a Christian; his father was not. Augustine later credited both his conversion and that of his father to her example. In his autobiography, entitled the *Confessions*, Augustine described his youth as a period of wanton sensuality which resulted in his fathering an illegitimate son. Motivated at least in part by despair over his own behavior, Augustine began seeking a solution to the problem of evil. Like Zarathustra, the Buddha, and Job, among many others, Augustine found himself searching for an explanation of the evil in the world—in particular, for the evils perpetrated, quite consciously, by human beings.

The first solution that attracted him was that of the Manichees, the followers of Mani (216–276 or 277 C.E.). Mani's sect was one of many *Gnostic* (the Greek term for "knowledge") schools, so named because they preached that redemption could be achieved through esoteric knowledge. Such knowledge was restricted to a small group or directly revealed to a sect's leader. Mani combined elements of Christianity and Zoroastrianism and attempted to appeal to both groups at once. His primary and best-known doctrine is that the world is a manifestation of a great battle between two equally powerful divine principles, one good and the other evil. During the course of their war, bits of the good god (the god of light) became mingled with bits of the evil god (the god of darkness).

It was incumbent on human beings to liberate the good bits from the material world. The secret knowledge (or *gnosis*) that had been revealed to Mani was how to liberate this goodness. Those who listened to Mani and thus learned to liberate the good were the elect, who would be redeemed. Those who considered them- selves elect pursued a life of asceticism and strict dietary practices, attempting to remove themselves from temptation. Mani was considered the Messiah by his followers, but he was considerably less respected by his many critics. Although Manichaeism strategically adopted elements of whatever culture it entered (ap- pearing as a variant of Zoroastrianism in Persia, for instance), it had the dubious distinction of being branded a heresy by three different religious orthodoxies— those of Zoroastrianism, Judaism, and Christianity.

Augustine found the Manichaean doctrine appealing as an explanation for hu- man evil. Evil existed, on this account, because bits of an evil deity had entered and come to dominate a human soul. The only way to protect oneself from this fate was to adopt the ascetic practices of the elect and to devote oneself to good behavior. Augustine soon became disillusioned with Manichaeism, however. He was less than impressed with the simplistic erudition of a Manichaean bishop to whom he put his searching religious questions. As a young man Augustine had a formidable, demanding intellect. He was not about to be satisfied with evasive answers regarding an already-obscure doctrine.

For several years, Augustine devoted his life to teaching and to pursuing his studies in Neoplatonism. He devoted considerable attention to the works of Plato and Plotinus. After he converted to Christianity at the age of thirty-three, he fully devoted himself to the task of philosophically integrating Christian doctrine with Platonic and Neoplatonic philosophy. From Plotinus Augustine accepted the view that true reality was spiritual and that all Being comes from God. Augustine read Plotinus's articulation of the levels of emanation in terms of the Christian doctrine of the Trinity. From Plato, he came to accept the view that a life of contemplation was the only way to knowledge and happiness, although he rejected the pagan framework within which Plato had developed this view. And with Christianity he embraced the view that the proper guide to living well was Scripture.

Perhaps Augustine's greatest single contribution to Western philosophy (and not only Christian thinking) was his emphasis on one's personal, inner life. The "I think, therefore I am" famously attributed to Descartes in fact appears in Augustine, twelve centuries earlier. It was Augustine, more than any other phi- losopher, who introduced and described in exquisite detail the "inner" or "sub- jective" experience of time. (The soul may be eternal, but it is in time that the soul is saved or lost.) The *Confessions* remains one of the boldest and most frank investigations of the self in Western literature. Ample concern for human reason can be found there, but the real attention is paid to the passions of the soul. These include love and faith, first of all, but also all of the urges, impulses, and vices (such as lust, pride, and "curiosity") that we all find in ourselves.

Augustine came to see the relationship between God and the human soul as the central concern of religion. Because the soul was created "in the image of God," self-knowledge became a means of coming to know God. It is thus with Augustine that we follow one of the most dramatic turns in philosophy, the "inward" turn (though we might note that a comparable turn appeared in Buddhism, many centuries before). Knowledge of the world, and of God in particular, is no longer conceived of solely as a matter of observation and reason but also as a matter of feeling as well. The early Greek philosophers may have talked on occasion about emotions, but they did not think of these as "inner experiences." The Jews and many early Christians talked about faith, treating faith as an attitude (a major step toward inwardness), but they did not conceive of what we would call "a rich inner life." Socrates did talk about the soul, but as he conceived of it, it was only the source of virtue, not the subject of profound experience.

With Augustine's *Confessions*, the personal, inner life of spirit starts to take center stage in Western thinking. The end, the goal of human existence, he tells us, is contemplation of God in awe and reverence. This and this alone, he insists, will make us happy. From this conception of the inner life will evolve a powerful new conception of Christianity. The Reformation would mark a further evolution of this emphasis on the inner life of spirit, and modern philosophy would also emphasize subjectivity and experience, culminating in Descartes and the philosophers who follow him. Indeed, the experiential or "inner" basis of knowledge would become something of a shared premise for generations of modern philosophers. One thousand five hundred years after Augustine, those German philosophers who called themselves "Romantic" would elevate such inner experiences to "the Absolute."[52]

In Augustine's vision of human knowledge, God is not only the Creator but also the active agent in the universe. God illuminates the human soul, sharing with it the ideas of the divine mind. Augustine embraces a Neoplatonic interpretation of Plato. The Forms (the ideas of the Divine Mind) are rendered intelligible to humans through God. "Participation" thus receives a more straightforward explanation than it had in Plato. God's illumination makes the immaterial Forms described by Plato directly evident to the soul. Because God is the source of both the faculty of reason and the truths known through it, Augustine argued, we can have confidence in human reason. He interpreted insights of the ancient Greeks as true products of reason, even though the Greeks did not have the further access to truth provided by Scripture.

Such revelation through Scripture is essential to a full understanding of the divine plan and our place within it, according to Augustine. Nevertheless, our experiences of the natural world can point us in the direction of religious truth. Augustine formulated a number of naturalistic grounds for acknowledging the existence of God. He appealed to the orderly design and beauty of creation, to the imperfection of created things (which implies a perfect creator) and to the movement of created things (which suggests an initiator of this movement). More persuasive than rational argument, however, was the hungry desire Augustine found in himself, a hunger for blessedness, which could only be satisfied by

Oneness with God. It is through such emotional experience, as well as by way of reason, that we recognize that our grasp of truth is partial. But from this sense of our own limitations we glean a sense of the permanent, eternal truth that is God.

Augustine thought of philosophy as an activity, involving the techniques of reason, and also as an approach to wisdom and the ultimate truths about life. With this dual conception of philosophy, he could allow himself the great luxury of pursuing abstract matters of logic and solving some of the paradoxes that Christian doctrine inevitably produced, but without believing that such activities were sufficient to satisfy his real quest, the discovery, articulation, defense, and practice of the ideal life of faith. At least one of these paradoxes was not at all academic or merely logical, however, and that was, once again, the problem of evil.

Augustine sought to show, first of all, that God did not cause evil to exist. Accepting Plotinus's doctrine that evil was only the absence of good, Augustine argued that God was therefore not the cause of evil. Evil was not a created thing, but the lack of something else. Evil was akin to disorder, which is the absence of order, but not an existing entity. A room can become disordered, but not because "disorder" enters the room. "Disorder" is merely a term for order disrupted. Similarly, evil was the disruption of the order God created, not one of God's creations itself.

In creating the world, God had constructed human beings and all other creatures perfectly, giving them natures that were designed for pursuing their natural and (in the case of human beings) supernatural ends. According to Augustine, his Greek philosophical predecessors had described the natural purposes of human beings quite aptly, but they had been deluded or unclear about their supernatural destinies. They had not realized that God had provided human beings with a nature that was geared to their supernatural aim—mystical union with Him in a state of blessedness.

While natural disasters that caused suffering might suggest otherwise, Augustine insisted that we simply could not see their ultimate significance in the entire plan that God had for His Creation. If we could conceive of that plan, we would see that God's Creation was entirely good. An essential part of the divine plan of the universe, however, was that God allowed human beings an intimate share in His own nature, by granting them the great blessing of *free will*. Unlike other aspects of Creation, which followed God's plan without fail, human beings were allowed to determine their own actions. The culminating perfection of God's creation was that He allowed human beings freely to choose to believe in Him and to join with Him in actualizing His plan. But because human beings have free choice, God cannot be said to have caused them to sin. The possibility of sin is a necessary feature of free will. Therefore, God *allows* humanly caused evil, but He was not and is not Himself the cause of it.

Genesis recounts the failure of human beings to choose the good consistently. Adam and Eve's original sin brought about the Fall of all humanity into an inferior state of being. One aspect of this inferior state was the tendency, bequeathed to Adam and Eve's descendants, to succumb to temptation and "corruption," particularly with respect to the body. This exacerbated the tendency of human beings to cause evil in the world. But Augustine insists, nevertheless, that "the corruption of the body, which weighs down the soul, is not the cause but the penalty of the first sin. . . . It was the sinful soul which made the flesh corruptible." Temptation is a consequence of human sin, human choice, not its original cause.

Augustine considered the counterargument that God's foreknowledge nevertheless makes God responsible for sin. It might be argued, for example, that since God is all-powerful and He foresees human sins, He is responsible for them, for He could prevent them. If God did not foresee sin, He would not be all-knowing—but then He would not be God, at least on the Christian conception. Augustine concluded that God does foresee human sin. Indeed, since God is not bound by time, He sees all of time in a timeless glance. Therefore, He can see all of the wrong choices that human beings have ever made or will ever make (and are making right now). Nevertheless, God's knowledge of these free choices does not imply that God engineered these choices. God *knows* the whole story of human history, but He is not a puppeteer who forces it to unfold as it does.

Far from causing human beings to sin, God gave human beings the ability to overcome sin, even in humanity's fallen state. In this condition, human beings cannot rely on their own nature to direct them to God. One of the effects of sin is to warp the tendencies that are basic to our nature, much as careless driving warps a car's alignment. God, however, freely gave *grace* to those who would accept it, where grace is divine guidance. Augustine did not think that everyone would accept grace, and the fact that some people do and others do not leads him to the conclusion that many people would fail to receive grace and the salvation that comes with it. Later on, this view would be formulated as the harsh Calvinist doctrine that some people are *predestined* for salvation and some are predestined for damnation, regardless of what they do or believe.

Augustine, however, also emphasized the protective power of God's grace, which directed believers away from temptation to the path that would lead them to their supernatural destiny. The greatest danger and temptation, Augustine insisted, was our very human insistence on self-determination, and, despite his emphasis on human free will, Augustine argues that the only antidote is a passionate but passive acceptance of God. It is human beings who choose evil, but as often through ignorance and arrogance as through malice. Against his contemporaries who urged active effort to secure salvation, Augustine insisted that the optimal human attitude is faith, which is available to everyone. Far from being the source of evil, God provided the means for human beings to overcome it.

The First Great Split Within Christianity

Ever since St. Peter established in Jerusalem what became known as the Catholic ("universal") Church in the first century C.E., Christianity has tried to think of itself as a unified religion. But when Christianity spread across the Mediterranean and up into Europe in its first few centuries, it had to adjust itself to many diverse practices and local styles. It began as a cult (or as a number of cults) and over the years the differences between different Christian cultures, different factions, and different philosophies started to become more pronounced. During the first millennium of the Christian era, Christianity became increasingly differentiated between the Latin world and the Greek world, a division that eventually culminated in separate churches. This separation is known as the Great Schism of 1054 C.E. This date, however, is somewhat arbitrary. The break that developed occurred gradually from the eleventh through the thirteenth centuries, and the roots of the separation go back much earlier.

Throughout the first three centuries of its existence, Christianity was an illegal religion in the Roman Empire, and Christians were often persecuted. The emperor Constantine legalized Christianity in 313 C.E. and later became a convert himself. In return, the leaders of the church elevated Constantine to a position equal to that of the apostles, and he was given authority to summon ecumenical councils, which were entitled to resolve disputes on Christian doctrine. At the time that Constantine adopted Christianity, the church was organized under three patriarchates—those of Rome, Alexandria, and Antioch—each governed by a bishop. The Roman patriarchate was the most influential, both because Rome was the imperial capital and because it could boast that both Peter and Paul had preached and been martyred there.

Constantine, however, added a new complication to the relationship among the patriarchates by declaring the city of Byzantium (later, called Constantinople; currently, Istanbul) the capital of the Eastern Roman Empire in 330 C.E. He proclaimed Constantinople "a new Rome," and he raised the bishop of Byzantium to the status of patriarch, with a domain that extended into areas previously governed by the bishops of Rome and Antioch. Subsequent ecumenical councils granted yet more status to the patriarchate of Constantinople, and the relative importance of the patriarch and the pope, the bishop of Rome, became an increasingly contentious issue.

The resulting political tensions led to the break between the Eastern and Western churches. The break was facilitated by deep cultural differences. Christianity developed quite differently in the East than in the West, and these differences became pronounced as the church became more organized. Education was widely disseminated in the Eastern empire, and both the laity and the clergy engaged enthusiastically in theological debate. Differences of opinion on religious matters were tolerated, and orthodox belief was never formulated as specifically or as dogmatically as in the West. Indeed, the clergy was not viewed as uniquely authoritative in doctrinal matters, and church leaders were understood to be fallible. One's beliefs were considered less important in the Eastern church than one's participation in the liturgy, which incorporated many artistic forms and involved the whole congregation. Nevertheless, dogma was held in highest esteem, and metaphysical speculation was elaborate.

The church in the West, by contrast, had very different—and challenging— circumstances. From the beginning, it faced competition from a variety of religions and sects. In consequence, strong emphasis was placed on correct belief, legalistically understood. Theological speculation was not encouraged nor much tolerated. The collapse of the western Roman Empire under invasions from the north in 472 resulted in the clergy's assuming political prominence. The church was the only institution that survived, and its leaders conducted negotiations with the invaders and administered local government.

After the fall of Rome, the only formal education was that organized by the church, almost exclusively for the purpose of training the clergy. The clergy also had the unique right to perform the Western liturgy. Lay participation was minimal. In time, most of the laity no longer understood the Latin language in which the Western liturgy was conducted. Accordingly, the Western church was run by an elite clergy who were also involved in temporal politics. The church itself became more and more hierarchical under the leadership of the pope, who came to be understood as the supreme, infallible authority on Christian doctrine.

Speaking different languages and embracing such different worldviews, the Eastern and Western churches became very different institutions. The two cities that were the centers of these respective Christian cultures also became increasingly different. Constantinople became the Christian world's wealthiest and most civilized city, while Rome was devastated by war and invasion.

Doctrinal and philosophical differences were not the primary cause of the eventual split, but they served as the occasion for political battles among church leaders over who had legitimate religious authority in doctrinal matters. The *Nicene Creed*, for example, was intended to be the official statement of Christian doctrine by an ecumenical council in 325. The original creed stated that the Holy Spirit "proceeds from the Father," but the Western church amended this to say that the Holy Spirit "proceeds from the Father and the Son." The expression "Filioque"—"and the Son"—became a point of great contention between the Eastern and Western churches.

The Western church contended that this was an innocuous statement of a doctrine that the fathers of the church had long believed and had not explicitly stated because they had presupposed it. The Eastern church, by contrast, claimed that this addition upset the delicate balance of the three Persons of the Trinity. The Eastern church made sense of the notion of three Persons in One God by claiming that all properties of God applied to God as a unity, except for those characteristics that specifically differentiated the roles of the three Persons. Thus, the eternity of God applied to all three Persons, who were equally eternal. The Spirit's proceeding from the Father, in the view of the Eastern church, was part of the characterization of the Father's unique role as the fundamental causal principle. If the Son also had this role, however, the role no longer served to differentiate the three Persons; nor did it apply to the union of all three Persons. The Western doctrine, then, was at least an indication of confusion, if not a heretical denial either of God's unity or of the three distinct Persons in the Trinity.

The Western church, by contrast, considered the *Filioque* to be an assertion of God's unity, not a threat to it. Several Western theologians, including Augustine, had described the Holy Spirit as forging the union of the Father and the Son. The Western church, therefore, contended that the role of the Spirit was precisely what was indicated by the amended, "We believe in the Holy Spirit . . . who proceeds from the Father and the Son." Doctrinally, therefore, the two sides were at loggerheads, each contending that its side was asserting the unity of God, as opposed to the other side's more dubious formulation.

Issues of authority were also central to the conflict between the Eastern and Western churches. The Western church accepted the authority of the ecumenical councils, but it contended that this authority was conferred by the pope. Thus, since the Nicene Creed had become the central statement of Christian doctrine by virtue of authority that the pope had extended to the council, the pope also had authority to amend the creed. No further approval by a council was necessary. The Eastern church, however, contended that the ecumenical council was the only unquestionable theological authority, and since the Nicene Creed had emerged from such a council, it could not be altered except by another ecumenical council. Western churches or the pope had no authority to change the creed or introduce such additions to it. It is not entirely clear to what extent this debate was motivated by the nuances of a metaphysical doctrine and to what extent the doctrinal dispute was merely an occasion for politics, but the political consequences were obvious.

The Eastern church was also not as willing as the Western church to accept the theological speculation of Augustine, who was one of the sources the latter used to support the idea that the Spirit proceeded from the Son as well as from the Father. Augustine was considered a central father of the church in the West. The East, while not disputing his importance, had not been nearly as influenced by Augustine's theological inferences. In this respect as in others, lack of communication and mutual awareness of each other's practices and central spokespeople was a major source of conflict.

So, too, differences in liturgical practice caused controversies between the West and the East concerning the type of bread used in the Eucharist, the practice of fasting on Saturdays, and the legitimacy of men who were already married becoming priests. Such details became fuel for a series of accusations that were made in a number of rather intemperate letters exchanged by the patriarch who was head of the Byzantine Church and a well-placed Western cardinal. A bull (an official proclamation) of excommunication was sent from Rome to the patriarch and some other high clerics in Constantinople. The result was public rioting, which the Eastern emperor attempted to control by ordering the offensive bull burned. Although the excommunication of the patriarch did not directly involve either the status of the papacy or that of most members of the church of Constantinople, bitterness and misunderstanding inflamed both sides. The patriarch encouraged the rumor that the whole Eastern church had been excommunicated, and the two churches went their separate ways. The grand image of Christian unity had been shattered.

The Rise of Islam

Meanwhile, a new religion was sweeping through the domains of both Eastern and Western Christianity. Muhammad (ca. 570–632 C.E.), once a merchant of Mecca, is the central prophet and founder of Islam. The term "Islam" derives from *salaam,* meaning "peace and surrender." It refers to the peace that comes from surrender to God. When Muhammad was in his fortieo, he went into the mountains for a religious retreat and experienced a revelation. He was commanded "to recite" by the angel Gabriel, and the "recitations" that he uttered have come to be considered divine revelation by Muslims. The *Qur'an* is a transcription of these revelations. The words of the Qur'an are considered so holy that even the letters on the page are sacred. Accordingly, translations of the Qur'an from Arabic are essentially inadequate, treated as "interpretation" only; and all prayer is in Arabic.

Before Islam, the religions of the Arabic world involved the worship of many spirits, called *jinn*. Allah was but one of many gods worshiped in Mecca. But then Muhammad taught the worship of Allah as the only God, whom he identified as the same God worshiped by Christians and Jews. He also accepted the religious importance of both the Jewish prophets and Jesus, as do his followers. Muslims, however, believe that Muhammad himself was the last and greatest prophet, whose mission was to restore true monotheism, proclaim God's mercy, and unify the diverse Arabic families into a single nation, conjoined by a common faith.

The Arabs were considered the "chosen people" by the Qur'an, which traces their origin to the same Abraham the Jewish people claim as their ancestor. Nevertheless, Islam was open to all those who worshiped the same God—to Christians and Jews as well as Arabs. Consequently controversies arose over how this universal appeal should be balanced against the specific conception of Islam as a religion of the Arabs. These controversies paralleled those in early Christianity about whether that movement should be understood as a Jewish sect or a universalistic creed that embraced non-Jews on equal terms.

The appeal of Islam lay in its simplicity and in the fact that it pervaded one's everyday life. The main requirement of Islam is a single affirmation. The believer must affirm, at least once during his life, "There is no God but God [Allah], and Muhammad is his prophet." This requirement is the first of the *Five Pillars of Islam,* the basic obligations of the believer. The other four are: constant prayer (interpreted by orthodox Muslims as praying five times a day while facing Mecca); giving alms (interpreted both as making an annual donation of a certain percentage of one's property to the poor, as well as responding generously to evident situations of need); the observance of Ramadan (a month of the lunar calendar during which the devout Muslim may not eat or drink during daylight); and a pilgrimage to Mecca once during one's lifetime (if one is physically and financially able).

Philosophically, a powerful notion of social and economic *justice* underlies the teachings of Islam, as evidenced by the third pillar, with its emphasis on charity. A good deal of Islamic theological speculation begins with the axiom that God is perfectly just. Justice, however, has two complementary meanings. One is compassion, exemplified by charity. The other is retribution. A person who does wrong must be punished, as a person who does right should be rewarded.

The Islamic conception of *jihad* (or holy war) is also understood in terms of justice, insofar as it is considered to be resistance to wanton displays of evil. War is legitimated, according to Islam, only when it is either defensive or a corrective to evil that has been done. The notion of *jihad* also extends to inner life, and this "struggle on behalf of God" includes the believer's inner struggles in the effort to bring greater religious awareness to his or her life and society. An assurance of God's justice is the key to the Islamic solution to the problem of evil. People are responsible for their behavior, and God is just in punishing wrongdoers because human beings have free will. Moreover, Muslims believe that individuals have immortal souls that go to heaven or hell after death, so crimes that are not punished and virtues that are not rewarded in life will justly be dealt with nevertheless.

God's role as *Creator* is also important in Islamic thought. Creation is the direct result of an act of God's will. Islam diverges from the Platonic outlook, which sees the material world as inferior to a more real, higher plane. Islam considers the material world to be both real and good. Huston Smith (in his *Religions of Man*) suggests that the strong tradition of science in Islam is a direct reflection of this belief in the value of the natural world.

Muhammad moved with his following to Medina in the year 622 C.E., and there they began a religious community called the *umma*. This event is called the *hijrah*, and the Islamic calendar dates the year of its occurrence as year 1. Scripture was given primary authority, and the prophet's sayings (called the *hadith*) were given considerable weight. But who should have more authority in interpreting Scripture—the individual or the umma? This question fueled an early controversy and was complicated by the fact that the leadership of the umma was in dispute almost from the time of Muhammad's death. Some, for instance, believed that leadership should pass by heredity from one family member to another. Others, stressing the universality of Islam, argued against this. Some of the most severe sectarian differences in contemporary Islam (for example, between Sunni and Shi'ite Muslims) can be traced to these disputes.

A more philosophical aspect of that issue concerned the status of the Qur'an in comparison with the status of God. The Christian teaching, based on the Gospel of St. John, contends that Christ is "the Word [*logos*] of God" and that he is co-eternal with the Father. Islamic theologians differed among themselves as to whether the Qur'an, as the Word of God, should similarly be considered co-eternal with God. Some emphasized God's Oneness and denied the notion of different Persons within God (the Christian conception). They distinguished God and the Qur'an: the Qur'an, existing within the natural world, was part of God's creation (even if it helped one to know God's eternal properties), they claimed. The opposing view held that the Qur'an's meaning is *one* with God's essence. The Qur'an's meaning is uncreated and eternal, according to this view, although the words printed on paper were created, in an obvious sense.

The Islamic worldview is fundamentally egalitarian. But a doctrine of universal equality makes the question of interpretation and interpretive authority critical. Does everyone understand the Qur'an equally? One prominent view in certain sects of Islam is that the Qur'an has several layers of meaning. The *exoteric* level is the literal meaning that is evident to all readers and accessible through reason and common sense. Beyond this, a deeper *esoteric* level is only available to those who are properly trained and initiated. Those who believe in multiple levels of meaning must therefore accept the authority of particularly saintly individuals concerning the deeper meanings of the Qur'an.

The Shi'ite sect, for instance, believes in multiple levels of meaning, and they believe that the Qur'an's ultimate meaning is subtle. They accept as authorities on the esoteric level of the Qur'an those who are known as *imams*. The imams are believed to be saints who continue Muhammad's work, thus granting each new generation direct contact with the "light" of the Prophet. The imams represent a hereditary line. The reigning imam indicates which of his progeny should succeed him. The Shi'ite sect itself is divided, however, on the number of imams, whether they are infallible, and whether they are higher authorities than the *caliph*, or highest political ruler. Some Shi'ites also believe that the last of the imams is hidden, in a state of suspension, and that he will reappear as the Messiah, bringing about judgment and justice as well as the ultimate interpretation of the meaning of the Qur'an.

Most Muslims are adherents of Sunni Islam, which takes its name from the word *Sunnah*, which means "the path of tradition" and refers to the practices of the Prophet. These, they believe, ensure the unity of the Muslim community, and Sunni Muslims, accordingly, are resistant to nontraditional forms of devotion (which have been more common among the Shi'ites). Sunni Muslims do not believe that any particular individual is a religious successor or continuer of Muhammad's work, and they accept the caliph as the central religious authority. They also tend to be suspect of elaborately subtle readings of the Qur'an. While the Shi'ites turn to the imam to resolve questions of Islamic law, the Sunnis accept the consensus of the community as an interpretive authority, although in practice the Sunni community turns to its legal scholars to offer the interpretations which come to be accepted by consensus.

The difference that initiated the split between the Sunni and the Shi'ite traditions was a dispute about the succession of caliphs. The Shi'ites contend that Muhammad's cousin and son-in-law 'Ali was the legitimate successor to the Prophet's authority. In fact, 'Ali was at first passed over for the caliphate, and when he finally became caliph, many refused to accept his authority. 'Ali was murdered, and one of his enemies declared himself caliph of Damascus and central authority. Led by 'Ali's son Husain, the supporters of 'Ali's cause challenged the second caliph of Damascus and were slaughtered in 680 in the massacre of Karbala. The Sunni Muslim tradition accepts as legitimate the caliphate of Damascus, which ruled for nearly a century. The Shi'ites, however, defend the claim of 'Ali's descendants. They commemorate the bloody massacre of Karbala in an annual reenactment, ensuring that the horror of this event, in which Muhammad's only grandsons were among the victims, will never be forgotten, either intellectually or emotionally.

Sufism, a prominent mystical tradition within Islam, also contends that the Qur'an has multiple levels of meaning. But Sufis do not believe that access to the esoteric levels is restricted to holy men and their disciples. They believe that *divine grace* renders the esoteric levels of meaning available to anyone. Sufi mystical practice, accordingly, cultivates various stages of self-perfection in the quest to reach the ideal condition of complete absorption in God. Obedience to Islamic law is the basic stage of spiritual practice. The next stage involves renunciation of the things of the world, the willful acceptance of poverty, and the suppression of desire. The third stage, that of *gnosis*, involves the elimination of one's ego. In this stage, a Sufi experiences moments of ecstasy in which he or she becomes one with God and knows the full truth. Such moments are the ultimate aim of Sufi practice.

The Sufis describe their entire spiritual quest in terms of love. They believe that God created the world from love, an overflow of His own being. The union with God that the Sufi seeks is also motivated by love. Indeed, human love and relationships ultimately aim at union with God (much like "Platonic love," as it came to be formulated in Renaissance Europe). Sufi poetry frequently takes the longing of the soul for this experience of union as its central theme, and this longing is often expressed in erotic terms.

Mysticism

The Islamic tradition is not alone in having a mystical school. Other traditions also believe in the transformation of consciousness and special experiences to gain access to the divine.

The Hindu practice of yoga, for example, is a discipline in which the practitioner employs techniques for gaining control over the mind and the body, with the ultimate aim of union with the Godhead. Many Buddhists, similarly, employ disciplined meditation as a means of transcending the illusory constraints of the mind's usual outlook. Judaism and Christianity, too, have long histories of mystical interpreters, who insist that true insight results from gaining access to higher levels of reality, usually by means of discipline and initiation. (We shall discuss the Jewish mystical tradition momentarily.) The Christian tradition includes, for example, the organized esotericism of the early Gnostic sects, whose members believed that insight depends on initiation into secret knowledge, and also the personal experiences and accounts of such individuals as the Spanish mystic Teresa of Avila (1515–1582), who was eventually canonized by the Catholic Church. Teresa documented her mystical experiences in her autobiography, *Life*. (She claims to have had a "conversion" experience in her late teens when she read Augustine's *Confessions*.) Employing vivid, often erotic imagery, her accounts resemble those of the Sufis. Teresa also described various stages of mystical experience by using the image of rooms in a mansion in *The Interior Castle*.

Most mystical traditions stand well within the scope of orthodoxy and some (such as the Jewish Hassidic community, the Hassidim) are religiously quite conservative. Nevertheless, the fact that mysticism depends on individual efforts and experiences creates a philosophical problem—and sometimes a practical one—for the authorities within organized religions. How do the private religiosity and written accounts of mystics relate to orthodox religious doctrine? If the two seem to conflict, is any philosophical resolution available? The political resolution to this problem has all too often been the charge of heresy, if not more aggressive persecution of the mystic. Being a mystic can be dangerous business, especially if one is at all a public figure. Al-Hallaj, an Islamic mystic, was assassinated in 922 C.E. for exclaiming "I am God" while at the peak of a religious experience. Although he earlier insisted that this expressed his experience of union with God, his remark sounded like blasphemy to his contemporaries.

Mystics frequently have difficulties expressing themselves insofar as they want to describe their mystical experiences. Because such experience is out of the ordinary, everyday language, with its mundane categories, is ill equipped for specifying what mystical experience involves. Mystics, therefore, usually resort to indirect means of description, employing metaphors, exaggerations, and paradoxical statements in their efforts to suggest what mystical experience is like. Often, when mystics have run afoul of religious authorities, the problem has begun when authorities have given literal or ordinary interpretations to statements that mystics have made with extraordinary intent.

Meister Eckhart (ca. 1260–1327?), a German Dominican, faced charges of heresy and had twenty-eight of his statements condemned by the pope (fortunately after his death and with due acknowledgment of Eckhart's various retractions). The problem was precisely that his statements sounded, from an ordinary point of view, like denials of orthodox doctrines. Eckhart claimed at times that creation was not at all distinct from God, suggesting to some that he was a *pantheist* (someone who believes that God is identical with the natural world). In other statements, Eckhart emphasized the distinction between God and creation; but as so often, the complaints against him focused on statements taken out of context. Eckhart also claimed that God created the world in the "now" of God's eternal existence, a claim that sounded to some as though he considered creation coeternal with God, a claim that would counter orthodox teaching. Similarly, Eckhart claimed that the intelligence of the soul was uncreated (although he eventually retracted this statement, claiming that the intelligence was not created in itself, but came into being with the soul).

Perhaps the religious establishment was most alarmed by Eckhart's description of mystical experience in a fashion that resembles al-Hallaj's outburst: "We are wholly transformed and changed into God." Eckhart went on to compare this change to transubstantiation, the bread becoming Christ's body during the Mass. (Again, Eckhart backed down under pressure.) Consistently, Eckhart's efforts to describe the state of union with God (whom he characterizes as most basically intelligence) struck church leaders as a denial of doctrine—hardly Eckhart's intent.

Persia and the Peripatetic Tradition

We have mentioned two approaches within Islam to the meaning of the Qur'an, one appealing to religious authorities, the other to mystical experience. A third group of Islamic theologians defend the centrality of *reason* in interpreting the Qur'an. The role of reason is problematic in Islamic theology much as in Jewish and Christian theological debate. Some Muslims questioned the appropriateness of using human reason in attempting to understand Allah, who surpasses our human faculties. Others considered the application of reason to religious problems completely proper, since reason itself is a gift from God. Still others contended, like Philo, that reason and revelation were both important, although revelation should be preferred to reason when the two conflicted. Debates on the role of reason were particularly important to the *Peripatetic tradition* of Islamic thinkers—a tradition whose influence extended beyond Islam to the rest of the West as well.

As the Arabs invaded the Persian and Byzantine empires, they imposed their language and religion on the peoples they conquered. The influence, however, worked in both directions. The Arabs encountered Greek, Jewish, and Christian traditions of philosophical discourse, and they set about developing a similar tradition of their own. Islam became centered in Baghdad, and Arabic became the reigning scholarly language. During the period of approximately 750 to 900 C.E., many Greek works were translated into Arabic, including certain works and parts of works by Plato, Aristotle, and Plotinus. Drawing on these works, Arabic scholars developed their own philosophical vocabulary. Certain terms were directly transposed from the Greek, including *falsafah*, a transposition of the Greek *philosophia*.

Like Aristotle, Arabic philosophers tried to systematize all knowledge, including what they learned from the Greek tradition. First on the philosophical agenda of the young Arabic tradition was to establish the role of reason in ascertaining the truth, particularly by comparison with revelation. A tradition of philosophers who sought to bring the teachings of the Greek philosophers to bear on these issues came to be known as the Peripatetic tradition because of their strong reliance on Aristotle, whose followers were called "peripatetics" after his habit of walking while lecturing. Several of the Peripatetics were also strongly influenced by Plotinus, however, with the result that their interpretations of Aristotle were often elaborated in terms of emanations.

The Persian philosopher al-Kindi (ca. 800–866) is an example. Following Aristotle, he considered the purpose of philosophy to be the discovery of the true nature of things through *causal* accounts. Naturalistic accounts sought the truth about nature, while "first philosophy," or metaphysics, was concerned with the higher, divine realm. God, according to al-Kindi, was the only true agent. The agency of human action was secondary and metaphorical. Al-Kindi also emphasized God's will more than God's intelligence as the power that caused creation to exist. God created the world, al-Kindi reasoned, and he accordingly rejected Plotinus's notion that the universe, with God, was eternal. Yet al-Kindi did accept Plotinus's notion that creation consisted of a series of emanations, each intelligent, proceeding from the Divine Unity.

Al-Kindi's acceptance of the Neoplatonic theory of emanations had significant impact on his conception of the human mind. He drew on this theory to interpret Aristotle's suggestion that the possibility of knowledge depends on a self-starting, active intellect. Al-Kindi interpreted the productive or "active" intellect as a higher Intelligence, on which the human mind depended in order to come to know. This active Intelligence was distinct from each particular human soul; nevertheless, it was active in all of them. In effect, this Intelligence was the author of the entirety of human thought. This view, which was accepted by the other Peripatetic thinkers, resembles that of Augustine, who believed that knowledge cannot be achieved through the mind's own resources alone—that it depends on God's illumination as well.

Like certain theologians in the Christian tradition, al-Kindi believed that God's divine nature made it impossible for human beings to fully understand Him. Thus, al-Kindi's descriptions of God are primarily expressed in negative terms, like Philo's *via negativa*. In most respects, however, al-Kindi's religious beliefs conformed to those of orthodoxy, and he was willing to allow that reason has its limits. He was not disturbed by the idea of miracles, for example, but accepted these on faith. Like the Stoics, he had a deep respect for *fate*.

By contrast, the Persian philosopher al-Razi (865–ca. 925), known as "Rhazes" in the Latin world, was a contrarian within the Arabic tradition. Al-Razi considered philosophy a whole way of life, embracing both knowledge and behavior. At times, he described the philosophical life as "godlike." In any case, philosophy was for him not merely a hobby, a pastime, a series of puzzles to be solved while the rest of life went on. He defended his very personal views about philosophy, appropriately, in an autobiographical work, *The Philosophical Life*.

Al-Razi did not particularly admire Aristotle but instead considered himself a disciple of Plato. He was convinced that reason is the ultimate means of determining truth and, if reason conflicted with revelation, revelation should be abandoned. This view, along with his contention that the average person was capable of ascertaining the truth, flew in the face of orthodox Islamic teaching, which considered the prophets to have special insight. Al-Razi further disputed al-Kindi's conception of creation, arguing that matter was eternal. In his view, the world was created by God, but God had not created the world from nothing. He rather gave shape to matter that was already there.

Al-Farabi (ca. 878–ca. 950) had a Turkish background, and he was far more conventional—and Aristotelian—than al-Razi. Most of his works took the form of commentaries on Aristotle, but in philosophical concern they transcended mere commentary. Al-Farabi sought to make Plato and Aristotle compatible and to make both of their teachings relevant to his own tradition. His most important original philosophical contribution, for example, concerned Aristotle's notions of "essence" and "existence." Using these two Aristotelian concepts, al-Farabi distinguished between the essence (or fundamental structure) of necessary being (that which could not be nonexistent) and that of contingent being (that which depended on causes and might have been otherwise). The existence of a necessary being was implicit in its essence. Reason alone, therefore, could ascertain the existence of a necessary being.

Like al-Razi, al-Farabi believed that reason was the primary access that human beings had to the truth. But al-Farabi defended prophecy as also important, and he criticized al-Razi for minimizing its significance. The ideal ruler of any society, al-Farabi contended, should be someone to whom God had given His revelations. Like the Sufis, he believed that full awareness of God's revelation depended on cultivated and heightened spirituality.

Al-Farabi also attacked al-Razi for believing that the matter of the world had preexisted Creation. Al-Farabi accepted al-Kindi's Neoplatonist view of Creation. He believed that all of Creation emanated from God, the First Cause, and that the human mind came to know this Creation by virtue of the illumination provided by a higher, external Intelligence. Although the lower emanations were less perfect than the higher ones, lower emanations mirrored the higher emanations, and, ultimately, all mirrored the perfection of God.

Ibn Sina, known in the Latin world as "Avicenna" (980–1037), was the Peripatetic philosopher with the largest influence on Western philosophers. He was renowned as a scholar in other fields as well, and his compendium on medicine was the most influential work in that field until the Renaissance. Drawing primarily on the works of Aristotle and al-Farabi, Ibn Sina's philosophy pursued the traditional problem of the nature of God's relationship to human beings. Ibn Sina, like al-Farabi, utilized Aristotle's distinction between a thing's essence and its existence, observing that in most cases, these two concepts are distinguishable. In other words, one can have an idea of a thing's basic structure without necessarily knowing whether it exists. Some essences may be well known to us (such as those of Mickey Mouse and Santa Claus) without our necessarily believing that an existing being (a *real* Mickey Mouse or a *real* Santa Claus) corresponds to them.

In the case of God, however, existence is part of God's essence. Because God is a perfect unity, existence cannot be a property that is added to His being—it is simply part of God's being. This being the case, God is a necessary being. All other beings, by contrast, are contingent, and they owe their existence to something outside themselves, ultimately, to God. This argument was later formulated in various ways in the West by Anselm and Thomas Aquinas, among others.

Following al-Farabi (and, ultimately, Plato and Plotinus as well as Aristotle), Ibn Sina argued that God created the world through emanation. Ibn Sina believed that God was Pure Thought, and that creation resulted from God's thinking, his fundamental activity. God's intellect emanated a First Intelligence, which emanated another, and so on. Like his predecessors, Ibn Sina contended that the emanations from God's Intellect formed a hierarchy, with our world on the lowest level. This vision presented God as transcendent and distant from the world of everyday human concerns. Nevertheless, Ibn Sina believed that human beings and all of God's creatures were drawn by love to God, on whom their existence depended. Among Ibn Sina's writings are mystical and esoteric treatises that expressed this theme of the creature's love of the Creator.

Although the theory of emanations derives originally from Neoplatonism, Ibn Sina abandoned certain features of the Neoplatonic view. For instance, he did not consider matter to be a pale emanation of spiritual reality; instead, he took it to be the eternal foundation of things, much as Aristotle had understood it. As a devout Muslim, Ibn Sina accepted orthodox teaching, although he sought to translate more popular conceptions of religious truths into philosophical terms. Ibn Sina's conception of Creation, however, was naturalistic. Thus, he did not think that God rules through providential or miraculous intervention but by virtue of the necessary order of nature that he has created. Because the world operated according to necessary laws, however, free will did not, could not, exist. Human actions were not free. Ibn Sina did contend, nevertheless, that the human soul is immortal.

Ibn Rushd, known as "Averroës" by the Latin world (1126–1198), came from the Islamic community that had developed in Spain after the invasion by the Muslims (in the early eighth century). Like Ibn Sina, Ibn Rushd was renowned in many areas of learning, including medicine and law. Although he was prosperous most of his life, he died in exile, having been attacked as unorthodox. Much of Ibn Rushd's philosophical writing took the form of commentaries on Aristotle, although many of these involve critiques of his predecessors' interpretations and the development of his own philosophical views. He tremendously admired Aristotle, even commenting, "I consider that that man was a rule and exemplar which nature devised to show the final perfection of man."[53]

Ibn Rushd aimed to extricate Aristotle's philosophy from the trappings of Neoplatonist interpretations. Ibn Rushd attacked the view, for instance, that Creation emanated from the Divine One. He believed that Creation was eternal. Moreover, God was not distant, on his account, but instead was actively involved in the world and knowledgeable about His particular creatures. By rejecting the Neoplatonic scheme, Ibn Rushd gave a reading of Aristotle that was more naturalistic than that of any of his Peripatetic predecessors.

Like Ibn Sina, however, Ibn Rushd accepted the traditional Islamic doctrine of the immortality of the soul. He believed, however, that at death a person's soul joined the universal Active Intelligence. (The Neoplatonic notion of a universal Active Intelligence remained part of his theory, despite his rejection of the Neoplatonists' central notion, the theory of emanations.) Immortality was thus not the survival of the individual soul as such. Ibn Rushd similarly rejected the idea of free will.

Ibn Rushd defended not only reason but disputation in scriptural matters, arguing that the Qur'an itself encouraged intellectual speculation. He believed that reason was compatible with revelation, although he did not himself seek to reconcile the two. Instead, Ibn Rushd contended that truth exists in various degrees. The Qur'an offered truth to all kinds of individuals, but it provided truth to different temperaments in different ways. The literal word might be sufficient for ordinary individuals, but educated people also require persuasive argument. Extremely intelligent people need rational demonstration as well. This position has been called the "double truth" doctrine.

Ibn Rushd used the double truth doctrine in his attack on the Persian al-Ghazali (1058–1111), who had developed a rigorous philosophical attack on philosophy as such and attempted to defend more mystical ways of knowing. Ibn Rushd allowed that philosophical discourse was not appropriate for everyone, but he insisted that esoteric truths should be conveyed only to those who were appropriately initiated. Al-Ghazali erred, he argued, in thinking that profound philosophical truths could simply be presented or understood through experience in an uneducated, uncritical public format.

Diaspora, Dialectic, and Mysticism in Judaism

From the time of the destruction of the first Temple in Jerusalem and the exile of many of the Jews of Israel, a considerable segment of the Jewish population has lived outside Palestine. This number grew considerably after the second destruction of the Temple. The Diaspora ("dispersion") separated the Jews by great distances. They were nevertheless united by their adherence to a common law.

The critical basis of the Jewish religion is the centrality of Scripture as a means of ascertaining religious truth and the appropriate way of living. The Hebrew Bible is the fundamental Jewish scripture. The Mishnah, edited in approximately 200 B.C.E. from the long oral tradition of interpretation of Jewish law, is composed of rabbinical reflections on the Bible. The Mishnah and many centuries of reflection on the Mishnah comprise the Talmud (meaning "teaching" or "study"), which is devoted to biblical interpretation and practical applications of Scripture. Two versions, one completed in Palestine in the fourth century C.E., and another completed in Babylon at the end of the fifth century, exist. It is the latter, however, that has been accepted by traditional Jews as the basic document establishing Jewish law and ritual. The Talmud also contains moral lessons, parables, and stories, which present the teachings of Jewish ethics in a less legalistic manner.

As philosophy, the most inspiring aspect of the Talmud is the nature of the work itself. Unlike many religious treatises or scriptures, it is not a single authoritative commentary or interpretation. Nor is it the least bit impersonal; it bears the indelible "fingerprints" of past readers. The Talmud is an exemplary instance of the technique the ancient Greeks called "dialectic" or conversation. Each and every interpretation or comment is commented on in turn, so that a copy of the Talmud looks somewhat like a textbook with marginal comments by many generations of students. Although God's law is absolute, its interpretations are always open to challenge and revision. In this sense, the Talmud perhaps represents the ideal example of cooperative dialectical philosophy—a philosophy which builds on itself and keeps going and developing from a single common foundation.

As a legal document, however, the Talmud represents a closed system, built upon rabbinical applications of scriptural teachings to legal problems at hand and extrapolations from these. Hence, trends in the more secular traditions of philosophical thought have had little influence on Talmudic scholarship. The Talmud became the central focus of Jewish scholarship for centuries. Beginning around the third century, this frequently took the form of Midrash, which consists of methodical interpretations of Scripture in an effort to uncover its more subtle meanings and implications. Such interpretations were common through late into the Middle Ages.

Neither the Bible nor the Mishnah nor the Talmud, however, are primarily works in what would later be known as *theology*. In Judaism, even the name of God is sacred and not to be spoken. It was hardly considered appropriate, therefore, to pursue probing questions about the intimate nature of God and His ways.

Such questions started to be raised when Jewish history and Greek philosophy were conjoined. Philo, as we have seen, was concerned to demonstrate the compatibility between the rationality enjoined by Greek thought and the truths of the Jewish religion. But such speculations were largely motivated by Jewish contact with foreign beliefs, not by concerns that were inherent to the Jewish system itself. On the whole, Jewish thought has been concerned with the application of the Torah to life in the changing circumstances of the Jewish people.

Like other religious traditions, Judaism developed a mystical strain. Jewish mysticism stresses the importance of esoteric teachings that can, or should, only be taught to certain qualified individuals. A presupposition of Jewish mysticism— as of Christian and Islamic mysticism as well—is that Scripture can be understood on a number of levels, with certain higher levels of interpretation accessible only to those who are properly trained and initiated. Jewish mystics frequently concern themselves with "inner teachings" available within Scripture.

They also make use of the cabbala (or kabbalah), which comprises the mystical tradition of texts that began to appear during the Middle Ages. The term "cabbala" literally means "tradition." For a long time, the Zohar (written in the thirteenth century) was the chief work of the cabbala, and it remains central to certain Jewish communities today (such as the Hassidim). Literally, the title means "The Book of Splendor," and it refers to God's splendor, evident in all things. The Zohar emphasizes the images of rebirth, exile, and redemption, treating Jewish history as symbolic of general human and cosmic processes.

Cabbalistic thought developed an interpretation of the Torah in terms of a theory of ten emanations (called *sefiroth*). God is conceived in this interpretation as the ultimate source of all that exists. Nothing can be said about God as the source of being, but God manifests Himself in emanations, divine attributes, whose dynamics and interconnections are reflected in Creation.

Life is a revelation of God's being, and also one with God, like the emanations. Much of cabbalistic thought is concerned with articulating the precise relationships between the emanations and the created world and its features. In particular, cabbalists believe that activity on one level has an impact on the others. The belief that the whole of reality is intimately connected also leads cabbalists to interpret events on the earthly plane as having supernatural significance. Human events are examined for their inner significance; and Creation is "read," like Scripture, as a source of inner meaning.

Cabbalistic thought is particularly concerned with divine language, which is intimately linked to divine energy. Divine language appears to human beings in the words and letters of the Hebrew Bible. That is the means by which Scripture possesses multiple levels of meaning. In addition to the literal level, Scripture can be read in terms of hidden levels, in which the words and letters carry with them concentrations of energy, filled with meanings that are not fully translatable. Cabbalists are concerned with these subtle levels of meaning encoded in the words of Scripture. In the course of interpreting scriptural language, they developed a complex numerology in which the words were conceived in numerical terms (based on the numerical uses of the consonants of the Hebrew alphabet). Words of the same numerical "weight" were understood as standing in significant relationships to one another, and meditation on the words of the Torah would reveal secret meanings and, ultimately, the "inexhaustible divine light."

The name of God is associated with the most intense concentration of power. In traditional Judaism, in which God's name could not even be spoken, it could be indirectly indicated as "the Tetragrammaton" (the four letters of the Hebrew word for God, transliterated as YHWH). Some cabbalists, however, describe the whole Torah as a complex statement of the name of God, and they understood "the name of God" as comprising the whole divine law that orders existence.

Because the Torah represents the divine law, it is taken by cabbalists to be one with God, and thus, in some sense, eternal as God is. Thus the debates over the status of the Qur'an in Islam have their counterpart in Jewish theology as well. The Torah is considered to be a living organism, not just an ancient book. It is akin to the body in which the living God is revealed. It is therefore described as "the Tree of Life," which is also understood by some cabbalists to be the entire complex of emanations that manifest God.

Such mystical traditions have flourished in relatively segregated Jewish enclaves. The Hassidic movement in eastern Europe, initiated by Israel ben Aliezer (called "Besht," ca. 1700–1760), for example, thrived in the Jewish ghetto. Indeed, the movement's emphasis on the inner meaning of external events and the presence of God in all things may have been a source of solace in the context of its adherents' grim political circumstances. But some Jewish thinkers throughout the Diaspora have been interested in forging syntheses of their religious faith and the more secular philosophical traditions they encountered.

Historically, the foremost of these is Moses Maimonides (1135–1204). Maimonides was a Spanish-born Jew who was forced to flee Cordova at age thirteen. He eventually settled in Egypt, where he was a physician as well as a rabbi. One of Maimonides' great accomplishments was to organize and systematize the Mishnah, the rabbinical reflections on the Hebrew Scripture that had developed over the centuries. He is sometimes considered to be one of the Peripatetics.

Because Arabic was the medieval language of scholarship, even some scholars outside the Islamic tradition wrote their philosophical works in Arabic, and Maimonides was among them. Like most of his era's Arab and Persian philosophers, Maimonides took Aristotle's philosophy as his foundation, and Aristotle's influence is evident in Maimonides' most famous work, *Guide for the Perplexed*. In this work Maimonides attempts to reconcile religion with reason. He contended that philosophy should be subordinate to revelation, but that reason could, nevertheless, be used to defend certain truths made known through revelation.

In particular, Maimonides contended that knowledge of science should not lead to the abandonment of religion. One of his especially interesting arguments is that God's creation of the world "from nothing" is compatible with the world's having always existed, as Aristotle held. Maimonides argues that the idea of God creating the world at some point in time is a projection from our time-bound circumstances. God's being is not bound by the timeline that conditions our experience. Hence, it makes sense to consider God's Creation as being part of his eternal nature, to think of God as always having been the Creator, who created the universe from nothing but IIis own power. This notion bears some resemblance to the Neoplatonic picture, according to which the world is created through emanations that emerge directly and necessarily from God's own nature.

Maimonides also accepted the current Arabic–Neoplatonic conception of an Active Intellect that renders knowledge possible to human beings, whose personal intellects are only passive. Like Ibn Rushd, Maimonides denied the *personal* immortality of the soul but believed that the Active Intellect, which was transpersonal, was immortal. Every gain in human knowledge becomes part of our common Intellect, and so, even if we ourselves (as individuals) do not survive death, our knowledge lives on in humanity.

Unlike some of his Arabic predecessors, Maimonides insisted that human beings had free will. As part of the Jewish tradition, he was particularly interested in and adamant about ethics. Moral goodness was the most important human aspiration, and, consequently, the ultimate aim of philosophy, according to Maimonides. A century later, Thomas Aquinas would find much in Maimonides' work that was compatible with Christian teaching, and he would adopt many of Maimonides' ideas into his own theological system.

Efforts such as Maimonides' attempt to reconcile the Jewish faith with the non-Jewish philosophical tradition represent one approach to a basic question that has concerned Jews throughout the period of the Diaspora: How should Jews relate to the non-Jewish cultures of their neighbors? Orthodox Jews answer this question by insisting on strict adherence to traditional rules and rituals, not only in connection with holidays and the Sabbath, but also in conducting the details of their daily lives. Conservative Jews in the modern era allow for more flexible application of Jewish law to modern circumstances; but they stress the importance of observing rituals and of maintaining a genuinely Jewish tradition.

In the last few centuries, reform Judaism has developed as a third approach to this question. Reform Judaism is largely assimilationist, rejecting most external practices of the tradition and adopting the secular lifestyle of surrounding society. More conservative Jewish groups tend to see Reform Judaism as scarcely Jewish at all; but reform Jews tend to see their approach as a way for Jews who still associate themselves with their heritage to assume roles in the larger society that were often barred to them in the past.

Thinking God: Anselm, Abelard, Aquinas, and Scholasticism

Let us return, however, to the medieval era, this time to consider the Christian thought of the period. Just as the "Peripatetic School" most often refers to the Islamic philosophical tradition of the Middle Ages, *Scholasticism* is the general term used to refer to the medieval thought practiced in the Christian West between approximately 1050 and 1350. More specifically, it refers to the method of philosophical speculation that prevailed in the Western "schools" of the time, a method that was grounded in Aristotle's logic and utilized dialectic in its inquiries. The typical format of Scholastic writings, evident in most of the philosophical works of the period, involved a series of questions, followed in each case by argumentation and a conclusion. Besides sharing a basic method, the Scholastics shared a commitment to the fundamental premises of the Catholic faith and a belief that human reason could be utilized to extend the truths learned in revelation. They were influenced in their view of reason by Augustine's belief that the same God who was revealed through Scripture had given human beings the faculty of reason, which enabled them to come to know the truth.

The most noteworthy figure of the early Scholastic period was St. Anselm (1033–1109). Anselm acknowledged Augustine as a source, although he did not share Augustine's enthusiasm for the Platonic Forms or Neoplatonic emanations. Anselm's philosophical enterprise was to explore the mysteries of faith. He had absolute confidence in the truth of Christian teachings on God, the Trinity, the Incarnation, the Resurrection, and free will. Nevertheless, he utilized reason to come to know them more fully. His motto was "Faith seeking to understand." He was also convinced that unless one accepted the mysteries of faith, one could not come to understand. One of his most famous axioms was *Credo ut intelligam*— "I believe in order to understand."

Accordingly, Anselm approached his subject matter with great feeling as well as intelligence. As a Scholastic, Anselm utilized dialectic and vigorous debate in his inquiries. He was convinced that at least some truths asserted by revelation could also be demonstrated by logically rigorous argumentation. Reason could also establish the plausibility and even the inevitability of those truths less susceptible to such demonstration. Anselm's most famous argument is (what Kant later called) the *ontological proof* for the existence of God. An "ontological" proof proceeds by showing that the very concept of something entails its existence. (Ibn Sina also used this type of proof, as we have seen.) Although Anselm's proof is traditionally considered one of the "ways" in which one might defend God's existence, Anselm did not for a moment intend his proof as a means of persuading nonbelievers. He only insisted that it made the nature of God clearer to those who already had faith.

In his ontological proof, Anselm argues that the very definition of God implies His existence. God, according to Anselm, is "that than which none greater can be conceived." Even those who do not believe in God understand that this is what is meant by "God." God is by definition the most perfect conceivable being. What follows from this is that God, so understood, must exist. If God were a mere possibility, a glorious idea without a referent, God would not be the most perfect being that could be conceived. One could conceive of a still more perfect being, namely, one that shared all the perfections of the idea, but also existed. Once one accepts the conception of God as the most perfect conceivable being, one is logically committed to the existence of God as well.

Peter Abelard (1079–1144?) was the outstanding logician of the Scholastic period. He was a flamboyant and not especially humble master of dialectic, and his unorthodox applications of logic to theology caused him to be condemned twice by the church. He insisted that the Greeks were already close to Christianity in their metaphysics, and, like several of his Christian forebears, Abelard argued that sin was more a matter of evil intention than of action that happens to conflict with God's law. By so emphasizing intention, Abelard placed choice and free will, rather than legalistic principles, at the center of ethics.

To history, however, Abelard is probably best known as the beloved of his student Héloïse. Soon after the already celebrated scholar was hired to tutor the young woman, the two fell in love. Héloïse tried to persuade him that they should not marry because of his illustrious career teaching theology. When they did marry, secretly, Héloïse's uncle and guardian, who had originally hired Abelard, sent thugs after him, supposedly to avenge her virtue. They castrated Abelard, who afterward persuaded his wife to join a convent when he took monastic vows. The letters exchanged between them constitute one of the most moving collections of love correspondence in the history of erotic love.

As a philosopher, however, Abelard was primarily interested in logic, or, more accurately, in what we now would call the philosophy of language. He believed, as do many philosophers today, that most theological and philosophical confusions are the result of confusions about language, about the meanings of words. His philosophical reputation is attached to his *doctrine of names*, or *nominalism*. He argued, first of all, that words are just names, *signifiers*. Words point things out or "signify" them. (The things indicated are their "signifieds.") But what sorts of words are names?—for not all words in fact designate entities. Abelard noted, in particular, the much-debated "problem of universals," which dated back to Plato and Aristotle and concerned the words that refer to classes (that is, open-ended groups or types of individuals—for example, "cats"), properties (which are universal in that any number of different objects can share the same property—for example, being red), and ideal types (for example, "triangle"). The question generally was whether such words refer in fact to real entities, namely, the essence of being a cat, the color red, or the perfect triangle (the Platonic Form of a triangle).

Some logicians, called *realists*, insisted that there were such peculiar entities. Others, called *conceptualists*, insisted that universals exist only in the mind. Abelard, by contrast, takes the radical view that nothing exists except individuals. He denies the existence of universals and rejects the view of those realists who claim that things have essences that make them the things that they are. There is no Platonic Form or essence of *cat*, only numerous cats. There is no color *red*, only innumerable red things. There is no Platonic Form *triangle*, only triangles.

Abelard further contended that a thing is what it is because of *all* of its properties. A thing's properties cannot be divided between essential and accidental properties, as Aristotle contended, and no particular property is more essential to its being than any other. Resemblances among things may be practically useful, Abelard admits, but such resemblances are not the consequence of their common participation in a Form or universal category. Words trick us into thinking in terms of universals, but universals are not real. They are only the constructions that we postulate when we use language.

Abelard applied this sharp distinction between words and realities to his interpretation of Scripture. He suggested that apparent conflicts among religious authorities are likely to be resolved by seeing if they used the same words in different ways. Abelard was the first to use the term "theology" in the modern sense to refer to the rational investigation of the mysteries of religion. (Before Abelard, "theology" referred to a distinctively mystical approach to religion.) Entering into what had now become a millennium-old argument, Abelard defended the application of reason to revelation, contending that faith was only opinion if not defended by reason. Since he believed that reason provided insight into religious truth, he insisted that the ancient Greeks went admirably far in the direction of Christian teaching, even glimpsing to some extent the nature of the Trinity.

Thomas Aquinas (Thomas of Aquino, 1225–1274) is the culminating figure of Scholasticism. A Dominican priest, he is considered by the Catholic Church to be one of its most important Doctors of the Church. His most significant and influential philosophical works are the multivolume *Summa Contra Gentiles* (A Summary Against the Gentiles) and his (incomplete) *Summa Theologica* (A Summary of Theology). The *Summa Theologica* is a systematic presentation of theology, written for novices in the clergy, but it is also the definitive summation of Catholic philosophy. The target of *Summa Contra Gentiles* was the naturalistic tendency he discerned in certain Arabic philosophers. However, in a sense, his work conceded several premises to the naturalists. Thomas aimed to show that Christian faith was grounded in reason and that the law inherent in nature is rational.

Thomas was the student of Albert the Great, who had attempted to make the thought of the Greeks, Arabs, and Jews available to his contemporaries. Thomas extended this effort. He was a great synthesizer and drew from the works of many thinkers, including Maimonides and Ibn Sina. He was concerned to show that reason and philosophical investigation were compatible with Christian faith. He contended that reason and revelation each had its own realm. Reason was an appropriate instrument for learning the truth about the natural world. Revelation, however, concerned the supernatural world, and the natural world was not the whole of reality. The true place of the natural world could only be known by reference to the supernatural.

Thomas was particularly influenced by Aristotle, whose significance he so took for granted (along with so many of his contemporaries) that he referred to him simply as "the Philosopher." Aristotle's works on logic had been available in Latin translation for some time, but some theologians and papal authorities were opposed to his more recently translated metaphysical and natural philosophical works. In particular, they objected to Aristotle's views that the world was eternal and that its continuing existence was independent of God. More generally, they considered his perspective inappropriately naturalistic, for Aristotle's "God" had been conceived as an abstract natural phenomenon (the Prime Mover) instead of a personal, spiritual being. Aristotle's differences with Plato were also seen as theologically suspect, since medieval Christians had long considered Plato as having "looked forward" in a number of ways to Christian ideas.

The distinction between the realms of reason and of revelation allowed Thomas to specify a distinct place for Aristotle's philosophy in a Christian worldview. Aristotle's philosophy was concerned only with reason and the natural world. Thomas believed that within that sphere, Aristotle's philosophy articulated the

truth adequately. One impact of Thomas's endorsement of Aristotelian philosophy was that he made room within Christian thought for a relatively high regard
for the natural world and human knowledge about it. This contrasted with the
more Platonic cast of earlier Christian thought, which emphasized the unreality
of the natural world in comparison with the real and heavenly world of the
Forms.

Thomas not only presented the natural world as real and knowable; he also
considered it to be a reflection of the Law of God. God had given the creatures
of his Creation particular natures, and Creation involved the interrelation of the
various natures of things in a particular order. God ordained the laws of nature
by virtue of his own divine law. In recognizing the intelligible structure of the
world of everyday experience through reason, therefore, human beings gain insight into the mind of God as well. Thomas's account was a major boost for the
study of science when science was still wholly on the defensive.

Seeing the work of God's law throughout the natural world, Thomas claimed
that the whole of metaphysics (concerned with all that exists) is directed toward
knowledge of God. Thomas believed that reason would be led in this direction
simply by contemplating the natural world. Thomas famously provided his own
proofs for the existence of God based on reason's analysis of contingent beings
(beings, in other words, that depend on something other than themselves to exist
or behave as they do). In general, his arguments take the form of a *cosmological
proof*, an inference from factual existence to ultimate explanation. For example,
the motion of contingent things is causally dependent on other things that moved
them. Believing, with Aristotle, that an infinite regress is unintelligible, Thomas
was convinced that this realization would lead the mind to seek a first mover.
This Prime Mover that the mind concludes must exist is God, according to
Thomas. In each of his five proofs of God's existence (also called his "five ways"),
Thomas makes a similar move, concluding that the contingent being of things in
the natural world depends on something that transcends them, namely, God.

In that reason directs the human mind toward the supernatural, the spheres
of reason and revelation are not absolutely distinct in Thomas's system. Indeed,
he believed that we come to know spiritual reality through its manifestation in
the material world. Nevertheless, he emphasized the limitations of reason as a
mode of insight into the divine realm. Thinking is imagistic, and the images the
mind produces are derived from sense experience of the world. Thus, when we
try to imagine God, we do so falsely, in terms of temporal and spatial images
that are utterly inappropriate. Philosophy can help theology, but, again, mainly
by helping us to understand what God is not, rather than what He is. Revelation
is necessary for human beings to have an adequate sense of the supernatural, a
vision of God in heaven. Grace helps to direct the individual's will toward this
goal, of which the intellect has only a dim awareness.

Regarding science and everyday reason, Thomas was an *empiricist* in the sense
that he thought the natural world was known to human beings primarily through
sense perception.[54] Thomas denied the position that ideas were innate, but, at
the same time, he denied that sense perception involved mental passivity. One
of his chief differences with Augustine and with Ibn Sina concerned their view

that the mind was a passive recipient of ideas and forms that are provided externally by divine illumination.[55] Thomas contended that the human mind itself was active. God did not offer the mind external illumination. Instead, God had given the mind an internal principle of activity, a *nature*. In this respect, the mind was like the rest of Creation. God had given a nature to every kind of thing He had made, its own kind of natural agency. Thus, the mind was not passive, but active, according to God-given principles.

The notion of active natures facilitated many of the moves in Thomas's philosophy. Human knowledge, for example, is possible by means of the nature of the human mind, which actively analyzes the images presented by the senses and seeks to determine their natures, or essences. So, too, human morality is neither a simple matter of freedom nor a natural determinism. Instead, it depends on the particular God-given nature of human beings. Morality depends primarily not on the vicissitudes of human calculation, feeling, and desire but on the *natural law*, the moral principles instilled in us and discoverable through reason.

Late Scholasticism: Duns Scotus and William of Ockham

The fourteenth century saw a good deal of controversy and, perhaps, the early signs of the social disintegration that was to become so obvious in centuries to follow. Perhaps what best captures the fate of late Scholasticism, however, is its intensifying emphasis on language and logic, together with what has been seen as an increasing skepticism about the certainties of natural reason, so confidently summarized by Aquinas. The arguments are often dense and the reliability of the texts is often problematic, with many difficult explorations into logic and an almost obsessive attention to the arguments of predecessors and opponents. However, what comes through clearly in late Scholasticism is a bewildering new complexity in religious thought, with new, worrisome obstacles to what, in Augustine and Aquinas, had been presented as the cooperation of reason and faith. Accordingly, it is sometimes said that the long-standing marriage of philosophy and religion began to come apart during this time, although one might better view it as slow separation rather than abrupt divorce.

Duns Scotus (1266?–1308) and William of Ockham (ca. 1285–1349?), both British Franciscans (Scottish and English, respectively), were central figures in late Scholasticism, and both had their disagreements with the Dominican Thomas Aquinas. Yet, with him, they also sought to accommodate Christianity and Aristotle. Scotus, the more conservative of the two, continued the tradition of "proofs" for God's existence, arguing, à la Anselm, from the idea of the infinite perfection of God to God's existence. But for Scotus it was extremely important that this famous argument *not* be construed as a mere matter of language or definition. Departing from Aquinas, Scotus rejected the smooth connection between natural reason and knowledge of the divine. Into the confident language of the earlier scholastics, Scotus cast the more modern insistence on *evidence*, the foundational basis for belief.

The details of Scotus's subtle metaphysical and linguistic analyses are far beyond the scope of this book. In fact, it is by way of Scotus, in particular, that the term "Scholasticism" came to suggest labyrinthine academic subtlety and became the butt of humor for the early moderns, who were impatient with such logical niceties. But, in brief, the debate that involved Scotus parallels the debate that has been going on since (and before) Plato about the existence of properties, types, Forms, and "universals" apart from the existence of the particular things instantiating them. Scotus rejected Aquinas's notion that the individual identity of a particular thing depends merely on its "matter," while it shares its form with infinitely many other things of the same kind. According to Scotus, the individual identity of a thing is also part of its form. Scotus distinguished between what he called a thing's "common nature" (its "quiddity" or "whatness") and its "individualizing difference."

In addition to the ancient question of One and Many, more modern questions about identity and differences received one of their first important airings in the meanderings of Scotus. Like his Persian counterparts, he utilized the distinction between essence and existence to develop a systematic account of the relationship between God and the human mind. It was not enough to accept the one truth, the existence of God, according to Scotus. Reason demanded the understanding of a hierarchy of truths, beginning with first principles and their consequences.

But Scotus was by no means wholly committed to the "reason" side of the perennial faith and reason debate. The most dramatic conclusion that he drew from his complex thinking was the need for a renewed emphasis on faith. Indeed, he emphatically insisted that human virtue was to be measured not by wisdom but by love. Like Augustine before him (and Descartes to follow), he was intrigued by the working of the mind and its passions, by our sense of self and self-knowledge. Accordingly, Scotus was particularly absorbed by the nature of the will and, especially, the will of God.

All too often in philosophy, theories that emphasize the importance of the will ("voluntarism") overstate the distance between will and reason and thus tend toward irrationalism. Scotus, however, while distinguishing the will from reason, also distinguishes it from the appetites and desires. Our actions are not wholly determined by our intellects, but neither are they wholly determined by our appetites and desires. This is sometimes called Scotus's "anti-intellectualism," but it should not be taken as an attack on reason. Similarly, Scotus's emphasis on God's will as opposed to His intellect should be understood as a rejection of Thomas's very Aristotelian thesis that through pure thought God creates the world. Scotus emphasized the love of God rather than knowledge. Scotus questioned the primacy of knowledge, and in this he might appear to be part of a growing skeptical movement in Scholasticism. He himself was not a skeptic, however. In fact, he regularly attacked skepticism in religious matters.

Scotus is often understood to be a realist (in the sense we have discussed, in contrast to Abelard's nominalism) who believed that the human mind apprehends genuine essences ("quiddities"), universals, by way of particulars. (In fact, his position was considerably more subtle.) William of Ockham, however, was closer to nominalism. He was an antirealist who did not accept the existence of universals as such, and, like Abelard, he refused to infer a multiplicity of strange objects (such as essences and universals) from the multiplicity of words in the language. "Plurality is not to be posited without necessity," he claimed. In particular there is no need to accept the existence of universals common to particulars but yet distinct from them. There are only particulars, individual things. (The "scholastic" nature of this debate did not dampen the enthusiasm of its advocates. Bertrand Russell once asked, somewhat mirthfully, "What if realism were true, but everyone were a nominalist, or vice versa—would there be any difference whatever in the world?" The excitement these debates generated in medieval Christian thought can be understood in terms of the religious implications of these disputes. Nevertheless, Russell, an atheist, joined in.)

Ockham was a rather radical empiricist, and he clearly anticipated later British empiricism, which was heavily indebted to him. Ockham largely dismantled the philosophy of Thomas, and he was sometimes called (although he did not call himself) the first of the "moderns" (see Part III, p. 175). He abandoned teleology and the Aristotelian concept of a "final cause." He is still famous for his principle of parsimony (simplicity), known as Ockham's Razor. Simply stated, this is his insistence that one should not prefer a more complicated explanation when a simpler one will do. For Ockham less is more.

Like Scotus, Ockham was also concerned with the nature of the will, God's will in particular. Like Scotus, he emphasized God's will rather than God's intellect, and he insisted that God could do anything, however miraculous (so long as it was not logically contradictory). He thus defended the thesis that God's power is absolute, although the laws of nature are set, since God *could have* willed the world to be other than it is. Thus natural law is contingent (in the way things actually are) but God's will was and is completely free. This very abstract conception has serious implications for human morals, insofar as morals are based on "natural" law. Nature (including our natures) could have been different; therefore, nature is not the ultimate basis of our moral obligation. Divine law, rather than human nature (as in Aristotle), constitutes our absolute obligation.

Ockham's Razor would ultimately come to shave many a philosophical beard. But in the twists and turns that immediately followed the decline of Scholasticism and the demand for a good deal more relevance, Ockham's principle was hardly followed, however important it might become in modern science.

In Search of Essences: The Alchemists

One virtue of late Scholasticism was the attempt to synthesize very different traditions. A very different attempt at synthesis was *alchemy*, the study and exploitation of supposed correlations between human and more cosmic levels of reality, developed in a wide range of cultures. The ultimate goal of alchemy was to transform the human condition, perhaps by achieving immortality or entrance to a higher spiritual plane, or, at least, by improving one's material well-being.

In ancient China, since the fourth century B.C.E., for example, sages and wise men had sought to achieve immortality by the use of drugs. The textual evidence in India suggests that alchemy was associated with mystical aspirations (as it came to be among later Western practitioners as well).[56] Arab and Hellenic alchemists were especially interested in making gold out of baser materials and, unfortunately, it was this limited goal that is usually associated with alchemy.

Even on the level of the merely practical, alchemy provided one of the impulses if not the basis upon which chemistry developed. Indeed (as in the case of astrology and astronomy) there never was a clear distinction between the two, and alchemy motivated a considerable number of important chemical and pharmacological discoveries. Among the by-products of alchemists' experimentation with materials we now call "chemicals" were "spirits," distillations intended to purify a person's essence. The alchemists' intentions may not have been realized, but their welcome practical result was the *eau de vie* ("water of life") that we now consume as "cocktails."

In the West, the alchemical tradition traces its roots to an Arabic text called the "Emerald Tablet," attributed to Hermes Trismegistus.[57] ("Trismegistus" means "three times great.") This text begins with an affirmation of correspondences between levels of reality: "As it is above, so it is below." The terminology of alchemical texts encourages symbolic as well as literal interpretations. Making gold is described as "the great work"; a substance that would initiate a rapid transformation is called "the philosopher's stone." Although religious authorities in the Christian religion eventually came to see alchemy as a threat, the church itself assisted the growth of the alchemical tradition in the West by devoting monastic labor to the transcription of alchemical texts. Indeed, Thomas's teacher, Albert the Great, took alchemy quite seriously, as did scientists Giordano Bruno (1548–1600) and Isaac Newton.

One of the most important alchemists and synthesizers in the Western tradition, Marsilio Ficino (1433–1499), was a Florentine priest. Ficino translated the work attributed to Hermes Trismegistus as well as some of Plato's works into Latin, and he developed a worldview that synthesized ideas from both, as well as from Plotinus. Ficino conjoined the Neoplatonist vision of creation as emanating from God with an alchemical cosmology of the universe as a hierarchy of levels that can influence one another. Accordingly, Ficino took astrology quite seriously. Ficino located human beings at the center of the cosmic hierarchy, and he defended this as a basis for the humanist view that the human being has a special, even cosmic, dignity.

Ficino modeled his conception of the ideal life on ideas from Plato, especially from Socrates' speech in the *Symposium*. Our goal is to ascend to higher levels of truth, he claims, and ultimately to a vision of God. Contemplation is the means to achieve this goal; at the same time, contemplation assures a proper moral perspective. As Plato had taught, contemplation initially directs itself to what is most beautiful. Love is the natural response to beauty. God loves the world, which he created as beautiful; and God's creatures are also moved by love when they encounter beauty. In particular, love of other human beings can help our ascent, for when we respond with love to the goodness and beauty of another human being, it is ultimately God that we are loving. Ficino's theory of friendship, or *Platonic love*, suggests that we experience communion with God through communion with another person. Even the most mundane level of human relationship, accordingly, reflects the ultimate relationship.

Ficino placed special emphasis on art's role in provoking the human soul's ascension to higher levels of beauty. In Ficino's view, art does not distract us from higher reality, as Plato had thought. Instead, it helps us to recognize formal features of the things around us, which is already a step toward a higher level of truth. Ficino's emphasis on the Neoplatonists' allegorical reading of the ancient texts had a strong influence on Renaissance artists.

Johann Faust (ca. 1480–ca.1540) is a more dubious figure in the history of alchemy. His name is forever associated with the story of the German magician who sold his soul to the devil in return for knowledge and power. Whether the historical figure actually made such a pact is unknown, but he supposedly practiced sorcery, astrology, and sodomy as well as alchemy. He became famous for a book, published many years after his death, that was nonetheless attributed to him. The bawdy *Faustbuch* (1587) told tales about wise men and magicians of the Middle Ages, and it included the story of a devil named Mephistopheles. Christopher Marlowe, Johann Wolfgang von Goethe, Hector Berlioz, Franz Liszt, and Thomas Mann are among those who have utilized the legend of Faust and his pact with the devil in artistic works. The pessimistic historian Oswald Spengler (1880–1936) has also suggested that the Faust story captures the historical essence of the modern West, which he sees in "decline" just because of its willingness to sacrifice virtually any other value in its quest for knowledge and power.

Paracelsus (Philippus Aureolus Theophrastus Bombast von Hohenheim) (1493–1541) was primarily interested in medicine. He wandered for ten years, getting an education from Arabic and European masters of practical alchemy. He put what he learned to work in his medical theorizing. One of Paracelsus's most controversial contentions was that nature would "naturally" heal on its own (a theme that reappears in several of our contemporary homeopathic movements). Paracelsus's interest in alchemy stemmed from his conviction that nature was filled with forces that could be utilized to benefit humanity, if only humanity could figure out how to tap them. Paracelsus attacked the view that disease was punishment for sin. Disease was itself "natural," he claimed, and he promoted the use of chemistry (with its own natural forces) in healing.

Paracelsus's opposition to the many medical techniques that he thought interfered with natural healing made him unpopular with the elitist medical establishment, as did his public notice inviting the entire community to attend his university lectures on medicine. His medical skill also aroused considerable envy, probably exacerbated by his high self-esteem. (He gave himself the name "Paracelsus," which means "superior to Celsus," the renowned Roman physician of the first century C.E.) Paracelsus wrote an influential work on surgery, *The Great Surgery Book* (1536), and developed the best clinical description of syphilis and the most effective mode for treating it until the twentieth century. Paracelsus was often compared to his contemporary, Martin Luther, and feared as an "insurrectionist." The religious authorities were on their guard, monitoring his activities. He died under suspicious circumstances; but his influence survived him, if not in philosophy then in the development of pharmacy.

Philosophical Syntheses Outside the West

The aspiration to synthesize several traditions was not unique to the West during this period. The neo-Confucian movement in China, which spanned several centuries, sought to assimilate certain aspects of Taoist and Buddhist thought into Confucianism. The most prominent figure of this movement, Chu Hsi (1130–1200), lived only a century before Thomas. Chu Hsi integrated the Confucian concern for social harmony with a Taoist attention to nature and a Buddhist concern for enlightenment. Nevertheless, Chu Hsi was fundamentally Confucian. His conception of enlightenment was that of the Confucian sage, whose spirituality was developed and practiced within the context of human society, not in isolation from it in the manner of Taoists and some Buddhists. (Chu Hsi criticized the Buddhists for conflating the mind and nature and making nature seem "empty" as a consequence.)

The Taoist influence is evident in Chu Hsi's organic vision of nature, in which all things are interconnected. Each thing and every human being has its own nature—its *li*, common to all things of its type—and also its particular vital, physical aspect—its *ch'i*. (Li and ch'i depend on each other, although they are logically distinct. Chu Hsi would not endorse Plato's view that our souls are only contingently in our bodies.) At the same time, the Supreme Ultimate (the *t'ai chi*), which includes every li, exists in all things. (Contemporary philosopher Fung Yu-Lan has compared the t'ai chi, as Chu Hsi understands it, to Plato's Form of the Good.) The t'ai chi is the basis upon which all things are related to each other; ultimately all things share in the same principle.

The t'ai chi is also the basis upon which human beings can obtain enlightenment. Our physical natures obscure the t'ai chi within us; but the goal of enlightenment is insight into the t'ai chi. Chu Hsi considers this recognition to be the essence of *jen*, of being humane. Evil comes about when one is motivated by selfish desire, but insight into the t'ai chi overcomes such selfishness. One becomes more compassionate, and thus more ethical, because one grasps one's unity with all other beings and things.

On Chu Hsi's view, the truly happy person is the sage, who is comfortable and finds value in every circumstance because every situation allows equally for recognition of the t'ai chi. Personal cultivation toward this end is achieved by means of attentiveness and reflection upon "things at hand." By reflecting on those things and events we see around us, we gain insight into their nature, their li. Cultivating ourselves in this manner is a gradual process. Nevertheless, this cultivation is the precondition for the eventual attainment of enlightenment and sagehood. (Chu Hsi emphasizes gradual development as opposed to the "sudden illumination" emphasized by certain other neo-Confucianists. Nevertheless, he contends that the process of gradual cultivation paves the way for the moment in which one crosses the threshold to expanded insight into the whole, the Supreme Ultimate.)

Meanwhile, in twelfth-century Persia, al-Suhrawardi was developing his own synthesis of traditions, in this case of Islam, Neoplatonism, and Zoroastrianism. Al-Suhrawardi taught "the Wisdom of Illumination," which equated degrees of being with degrees of light: all of being exists on a continuum of light, in al-Suhrawardi's vision of the chain of emanations. Every higher light subsumes all lesser lights, and every lesser light is drawn by love to the higher lights. God is the supreme light, who gives light to all other beings, and every other being is drawn by love to God, the Creator.

Around the same time the Zen school was effecting a new era in the synthesis of traditional Japanese religion and Buddhism. *Zen* was introduced into Japan from China. Buddhism had become the national religion of Japan in the eighth century, but in practice it coexisted with the indigenous polytheistic religion, Shinto ("the Way of the Gods"). This amalgamation was facilitated by Buddhist efforts to transform Shinto deities (who include descendants from the original divine ancestors of the Japanese imperial family, the spirits of great historical individuals, the ancestors of clans, nature spirits, spirits of particular places, and forces of nature) into incarnations of the Buddha, or bodhisattvas. Zen arrived from China (where it was known as Ch'an Buddhism) just as the samurai warrior class was becoming prominent in the developing feudal society of Japan (during the Kamakura period, 1192–1333).

The relative simplicity of Zen appealed to the samurai. Zen differed from the earlier form of Buddhism practiced in Japan, which had emphasized scholarship, good works, and ascetic practices. Zen deemphasized these and taught that anyone could attain enlightenment (*satori*, in Japanese). All that was necessary was to break down usual patterns of everyday, logical thinking. Zen urges meditation as a means to this end. One traditional technique is the use of a *koan*, which may be a word or a question, usually a puzzling one, such as the conundrum, "What is the sound of one hand clapping?" Usual habits of thought are so little equipped to deal with such a question that they are subverted by the process of meditating on it.

A sense of the innovation that Zen represented can be gained by comparing its simplicity and universality with the aestheticism and elitism evident in the writing of Sei Shōnagon (966 or 967–1013) a few centuries earlier. Shōnagon's diary, or *Pillow Book*, is one of the most significant works in Japanese literature. During the last decade of the tenth century C.E., Shōnagon was a lady-in-waiting to the empress. The Heian dynasty, of which the empress was a part, is particularly noteworthy for its aesthetic refinement. Shōnagon's diary is a desultory record of her impressions of daily events, her generalizations about them (often in the form of principles about appropriate behavior), and various aesthetic categorizations (such as "things that have lost their power," "things that arouse a fond memory of the past," "squalid things," and "elegant things").

The Shinto religion's emphasis on the rhythms of nature and beautiful ritual are evident in Shōnagon's diary, which describes the celebration of a number of Shinto festivals.[58] While not by any means a systematic work of philosophy, the *Pillow Book of Sei Shōnagon* reflects a philosophical vision that values beauty and reflection upon it, as well as a political elitism that exalts the imperial family and disdains members of the lower social classes, as well as those she considers intellectually inferior. (One might also see in the *Pillow Book* a protofeminist attitude toward men, to whom Shonagon clearly felt equal and with whom she even felt competitive.)

Perhaps the greatest of the early Zen Buddhists was Dōgen (1200–1253), who insisted on Zen as a philosophical discipline. He is considered the founder of the Soto school. Convinced that the body and mind are a unity, Dōgen promoted a specific posture for meditation called *zazen* (literally, seated meditation). The purpose of this practice is to enter a state of mind that is prereflective or "without thinking," as Dōgen describes it. By emptying one's mind of all its usual categorization and conceptualizations, one becomes receptive to the Buddhist insight that nothing is what it is "in itself." Things are what they are only in the context of their relationships to everything else. When one gains this insight, according to Dōgen, one sees the "nothingness" (or *sunyata*) of every particular thing. Everything is "empty" in this sense. All that exists is "the Buddha-nature," and everything within this nature shares in the Buddha's "enlightened" condition.

What differentiates the various schools of Zen are their divergent methods for awakening the insight that lies dormant in every individual. By contrast with the Soto school's emphasis on the quieting of the mind through seated meditation, for example, the Rinzai school emphasizes "lightening" intuitions and meditation while in the middle of one's everyday activities. Although they emphasize tranquility and spontaneity to different degrees, their shared goal is the state of enlightenment, which emerges only when the categories of everyday thought have been silenced.

The process of religious synthesis has a philosophical significance larger than the merger of ideas and perspectives. As religions merge and cope with one another on the plane of beliefs and rituals, people are encouraged to deal with one another with increased understanding and tolerance. Indeed, while one might well bemoan the loss of "pure" and "original" religious ideas in the amalgamation of newer and more broadly based religious perspectives, one will probably not complain about the consequent lessening of conflict and sectarian hatred that might result. But the direction of religious philosophy was by no means set on a synthetic course, in the direction of mutual understanding. On the contrary, the West, at least, was about to experience its most significant religious schism— far more explosive than "the Great Schism"—since ancient times.

The Reformation: Luther and His Progeny

The schism between the Eastern and Western Christian churches was probably motivated more by political and cultural tensions than by philosophical disagreement. The same is not the case for the later, more traumatic division within Christianity called the *Protestant Reformation*. The significance of the Reformation depends largely on the perspective of the observer. Some still see it as an unfortunate family quarrel, an unnecessary disruption of religious unity, a misunderstanding or a protest that got out of hand. Others might see it as the inevitable self-destruction of an institution that got too big, too powerful, too greedy and had too much *hubris*. Most Protestants view the Reformation as a movement devoted to moral reform within Christianity. It reflects other significant philosophical and social movements of the time, notably *humanism* (which rejected the extreme supernaturalism of the medieval worldview) and *nationalism* (which also played a role in defining and solidifying large religious groups within cultural and historical parameters).

The Reformation began when Martin Luther (1483–1546), an Augustinian friar, nailed ninety-five "theses" on the door of the church at Wittenberg on October 31, 1517. This gesture began an escalating series of skirmishes between Luther and the ecclesiastical authorities. He was ordered to recant views that were deemed heretical, and he repeatedly refused. Eventually, he was excommunicated, but once he was outside the Roman Catholic Church, he proceeded to form a new Christian church based on the principles he had been defending.

One of Luther's most immediate philosophical concerns was that perennial problem of the Western tradition, the problem of sin and redemption. Ever since St. Paul, one of the most appealing features of Christianity had been the forgiveness of sins. However, it was not obvious how the individual could be certain that his or her sins were forgiven. Luther was convinced that the Catholic Church had become so corrupt that it was now manipulating believers' doubts and fears by *selling* forgiveness, by way of what were called *indulgences*. Luther's ninety-five theses were particularly aimed against this practice.

Indulgences were dispensations from the consequences of sin which the church granted to particular individuals, sometimes for performing certain prayers or rituals but, quite often, for giving money to the priests. Indulgences, according to the church, would expedite a person's entrance to heaven, for they annulled one's sins. (The alternative even for a relatively good individual was to spend some period after death being punished for sin in Purgatory, a condition that was finite, unlike Hell, but hardly a desirable layover.) Indulgences could also be used to cancel the sins of deceased relatives. The practice of giving indulgences had degenerated into extortion, enriching the clergy and supporting ever more ambitious building projects. People feared for their own salvation and that of their loved ones, and that fear turned out to be a handsome source of funds indeed. Luther saw the practice as corrupt and doctrinally unsound. The very idea of indulgences presupposed that human actions (whether the recitation of certain prayers or the giving of alms) could have an impact on one's salvation. In Luther's view, this idea was tantamount to the claim that one could bribe God or buy salvation.

Drawing on Augustinian philosophy, Luther emphasized the sinful nature of humanity. Left to their own devices, human beings would not, in their fallen state, choose the good. Human beings are inherently torn, divided between the desires of the flesh and the aspirations of the spirit, according to Luther. Moreover, as sinners, they are absolutely deserving of damnation. God's justice should commit them to hell. In comparison with medieval Catholic theology, Luther placed even greater emphasis on the seriousness of sin and on God's sovereign right to punish sin. Christ had assumed human form in order to take humanity's sinfulness upon himself, according to Luther, and the death of Christ was the punishment for that accumulated sinfulness.

The medieval world had treated God as the Supreme Being, emphasizing His eternal status as the absolute substance. Many of the Scholastics had stressed God's divine intelligence and the intelligent design of the natural world. Luther, by contrast (like medieval thinkers Duns Scotus and William of Ockham), emphasized God's *will*. God, for Luther, is a fundamentally willful being. Accordingly, Luther reintroduces the Old Testament emphasis on the wrath of God. Humans are also willful, and a person is a single, willful unity, according to Luther. Nevertheless, the person has two aspects: material "flesh," our mortal, natural aspect, and "spirit," which transcended nature and was created in God's image. We experience our transcendence; but as flesh we also want to express our own wills and resist God's will. Luther sees sin as willful denial of our own finitude, expressed as misguided self-love, exerted in defiance of God's will. Sin amounts to a kind of corrupting self-idolatry.

The internal war of flesh and spirit described by Luther culminates in *despair*. The Law of God, Luther insists, is not so much a guideline as a "hammer" and "anvil" that smashes the pride of the sinner, solidifying that despair. Despair is only a means, however. When the sinner has collapsed in despair, God is able to effect redemption within. *Grace* comes just at this moment of despair— "deeper than No, and above it, the deep, mysterious Yes." Thus, despite God's wrath, His love emerges and dominates, and he freely chooses to forgive human beings and to give them grace. When one is reconciled with God by virtue of God's forgiveness, one is in a state of grace.

Luther's account of salvation, like his attack on the practice of indulgences, had clear implications for the role of human actions and for efforts to achieve salvation: human effort and "good works" had *no* role in salvation. Luther denied the medieval view that human merit had anything to do with God's forgiveness. One could not "earn" salvation. According to Luther, human beings should attend solely to *faith*. "Faith alone avails" and "faith makes blessed" are among the most basic maxims of Lutheran thought.

Although Luther denied that good works were either necessary or sufficient to ensure salvation, he expected Christians to perform them. Moral behavior and charitable action would follow inevitably from faith. Moral behavior did not secure one's relationship with God, but the relationship with God that was forged in faith ensured that one would behave morally. Luther believed that God directly effected the soul in faith, providing a person with the strength to overcome sin and to live a moral life. Christians had an obligation to love and serve others. The fulfillment of that obligation was not a condition of salvation but rather a sign of·an individual's salvation. In loving others, Luther contended, a Christian displayed love of God. The "love of neighbor" mentioned in the New Testament was particularly significant, for one's neighbor was God's representative in this world. In the person of faith, love and service of one's neighbors would overflow "from the heart," spontaneously, not from the ulterior desire to be saved.

In making his claim that faith alone justifies salvation, Luther was not merely rejecting the practices of those who sold indulgences. He rejected a whole mystical tradition (both in Christianity and in Islam) in which spiritual practice would bring the individual into union with God. Luther considered the gulf between God and humanity to be absolute. Union with God was an inappropriate goal for human beings. What was possible was personal fellowship or communion with God. But this could not be achieved by human initiative. It was God who must initiate the relationship.

Luther was also opposing Scholasticism, with its emphasis on rational argument about religious matters. He was no fan of Aristotle, and he was particularly skeptical of Thomas Aquinas's rationalism. In the fallen state of humanity, he argued, all human faculties were corrupted, including reason. Luther believed that reason was often hubristic, attempting to explain to itself truths of faith which are beyond reason's capacity to penetrate. Rational defenses of faith are not true religion. Genuine faith requires experience, not demonstration. This experience, moreover, was available to everyone.

Luther's insistence that faith alone was essential to salvation also amounted to a denial of the Catholic doctrine of the *sacraments*. The sacraments were rituals, performed by the mediation of a priest or a bishop, believed to have the power to impart grace to their recipients. Catholic doctrine not only held that the sacraments were an effective means for receiving grace; it also contended that the sacraments were essential to salvation. Luther denied both features of the Catholic doctrine. He denied that one could automatically receive grace by virtue of a ritual alone; he insisted that the receiver needed to have the correct inner disposition to receive grace. Here, again, the emphasis on the "inner," so evident in Augustine, comes to the forefront of religious philosophy. Although Luther accepted the sacraments' value for expressing and reinforcing faith, he also denied that they were necessary for salvation. Faith alone was required.

Similarly, Luther rejected yet another feature of the Catholic doctrine of sacraments, the priest's role in confession. Catholicism took the priest to be the essential intermediary between God and the individual. In confession, for example, the priest was taken to be God's emissary, capable of absolving the sins that the individual believer confessed. Luther rejected the idea that the priest was God's emissary and could dispense or withhold salvation. The status of an individual's soul was between that person and God; a priest had nothing to do with it. Luther thus rejected all sacraments except baptism and the Eucharist, though he sometimes seemed to favor some role for confession.

Those with faith, according to Luther, are blessed with the assurance that they stand in the right relationship to God and the conviction that God will save them, despite their sinfulness. According to Catholic doctrine, the assumption that one would be saved was the sin of presumptuousness; but Luther believed that the faithful could and should trust in God's mercy. However, he did not think that the Christian should be smug or proud; instead, he or she should maintain a continuous attitude of humility and repentance. Luther also believed that only God fully knew a person's motives. A Christian could not, therefore, trust in his or her own virtue. Instead, he or she should be vigilant in trying to maintain a good relationship with God. That meant less concern with external rituals, less dependence on priests and the church, less emphasis on the sacraments, less attention to externals. In contrast with the relatively ornate churches and vestments of Roman Catholicism, Luther called for sparse conditions of worship.

Luther emphasized the universal availability of salvation when he urged a demotion of the clergy from the ecclesiastical hierarchy that had crystallized in Catholicism. He denied both the necessity and the authority of such a hierarchy. Both the pope and ecumenical councils could be wrong about religious matters, and the individual did not need the clergy in order to understand the Word of God. Every Christian who helps another to become reconciled with God is acting as a successor to the Apostles, according to Luther, and only the Scriptures, not the clergy, were ultimate authorities on religious questions. It is the Christian community, not the church as an institution, that helps to nurture each individual's relationship with God.

Luther rejected the notion that "the religious life" of the priesthood, the convent, or the monastery was a "higher" form of religious life than that of the laity. He also denied the Catholic view that marriage was a distraction from religion. He denounced the Catholic insistence on celibacy for the clergy; he himself got married (to a former nun). He defended the "callings" of all Christians and importantly urged Christians to respect the variety of ways that God calls individuals to live.

Unlike Luther, the French reformer John Calvin (1509–1564) emphasized the importance of an institutional church and a system of theology. He became a significant force in the Reformation around 1530. By that time, the Reformation's split with Catholicism had resulted in a proliferation of new doctrines and, with the new emphasis on the "inner," some wild individualism. In response to this religious and philosophical anarchy, Calvin considered it necessary to build an institution of Protestantism that provided some clear basis for distinguishing religious truth from heresy. Calvin's great work *The Institutes of the Christian Religion* devotes considerable attention to the organization of the Christian church, and he presents the church as the means of salvation ordained by God.

Calvin went even further than Luther in emphasizing human sinfulness. Human beings were so corrupted by original sin, he argued, that even newborn babies are deserving of damnation. Indeed, Calvin characterized human beings as absolutely insignificant except as vehicles for illustrating God's grace in action. God, according to Calvin, is all-powerful, and He governs the world with absolute necessity.

Calvin's belief in the centrality of God's will had implications for his understanding of salvation and his own harsh answer to the problem of evil. Even though sinners resisted God's will, according to Calvin, they did not act apart from His will. In a sense, therefore, God willed their sinfulness. Calvin articulated this paradoxical relationship of God to sin in his doctrine of *predestination*. In accounting for why some, but not others, hear the word of God, Calvin argued that God had elected and predestined those who would be saved and those who would be damned for all eternity. But even that relatively small percentage of human beings who would be saved, being sinners, do not *deserve* salvation. God simply chose to forgive them. His forgiveness was a gift to *the elect* that he had planned from eternity.

Calvin considered the true vocation of all human beings to be knowledge of God. He was more sympathetic to the rational argumentation and the methods of the Scholastics than Luther was, and his doctrine of predestination was itself the consequence of reasoning about the implications of God's sovereignty. But Calvin considered the Scholastics' efforts to reason about the nature of God inappropriate. God's nature is too far removed from us for us to understand it. What can and should concern us is His relationship to us, and this relationship is made evident in the Bible. Knowledge of God, therefore, results from knowing and obeying what is said in Scripture. The Bible remains the sole ground of authority on all religious matters. Calvin rejected subtle and allegorical interpretations and insisted on taking the word of God at face value.

Although the Bible was the central means by which God redeemed the elect, Calvin stressed the importance of the church as a vehicle for God's grace. Luther had denied that the Christian community strictly required the church as its visible body, although he came to see the value of some organization as a means of propagating the Gospel. Calvin, by contrast, saw the church as the visible body of Christ (a view which Catholics also accepted, but with a different church in mind). Once again, the relationship between institution and symbol became a critical philosophical question within religion.

In many respects, Calvin described the function of the church in terms familiar from Catholic theology. However, he considered election the crucial basis of membership in the church. Thus, whatever role the clergy might play in assisting spirituality, the clergy could not see whether those to whom they ministered were genuinely members of the church, for they could not determine with certainty who was and who was not elect. Indeed, the individuals themselves could not see clearly whether they were elect.

Calvin did not consider this to be a problem. He believed, with Luther, that the Christian who is redeemed should have a sense of assurance. One could feel assured of one's election if one had fellowship with Christ, experienced as an inner calling to faith. Following Augustine, Calvin contended that one should not concern oneself with judging others, but attend to one's own spiritual faith and well-being. Nevertheless, it is admittedly difficult to know that one is elected, and so people inevitably tend to compare themselves with one another.

Max Weber has argued that this doctrine of election resulted in the development of "the Protestant work ethic." From the Calvinist's point of view, the only external evidence that one might be saved was one's behavior. Thus, despite the Protestant deemphasis of human efforts and good works, many Protestants became nearly obsessed with work and effort, since these now came to be seen as signs of blessedness. According to Weber, modern capitalism was the fruit of these labors.

Calvin insisted on the subordination of more local Christian communities to the larger church. In effect, he visualized a new universal church to replace that of Catholicism. Nevertheless, Christianity continued to be fragmented and divided. In England, Henry VIII renounced the Church of Rome and declared himself the head of the Church of England, a gesture of national (and personal) sovereignty in matters of religion. A further break was made in Britain by the Puritans, who demanded moral reform within Christianity and considered the Church of England too similar to Catholicism, with too many of the same expressions of moral laxity. Other sects dissented from the newly developing Protestant churches. The Anabaptists, Quakers, and Mennonites formed alternative sects that reemphasized the personal character of religious experience. The Anabaptists also rejected the practice of infant baptism (common to Catholics, Lutherans, and Calvinists) on the grounds that it was unscriptural and impersonal. Other groups rejected the practice of espousing a state religion and emphasized the religious freedom of the local congregation. "Pentecostal" and other "spiritual" groups organized worship around the premise that the inner light of the Holy Spirit could work within the individual soul.

The Counter-Reformation, Erasmus, and More

With the Reformation, the Catholic Church was under attack and undermined. In the future, it would have less power and less significance. Needless to say, the pope and his cardinals did not sit back and watch the dismantling of their church as merely horrified spectators. They fought back with a vengeance.

Before the Reformation, the church had already begun an aggressive campaign against heresy, most notably in the trials of the Spanish Inquisition. Only a few years after Luther's initial rebellion, the church sponsored the formation of the Society of Jesus by Ignatius Loyola. Insisting on the undiminished powers of reason in matters of religion, the "Jesuits" produced generations of well-trained and sometimes powerful philosophical minds. In Spain, Francisco Suárez (1548–1617) wrote a thorough and systematic compendium of Scholastic metaphysics, which also included discussions of Jewish, Islamic, and Renaissance thinkers. For the most part, Suárez adhered to the philosophical views of Thomas Aquinas, but he developed original views as well. In particular, he joined the medieval thinkers who emphasized the role of will in the foundation of law. Although he agreed with Aquinas that natural law coincides with the dictates of reason, Suárez stressed the importance of God's authority in all matters. Human reason, again, had to be put in its place.

Philosophically, the Counter-Reformation resulted in a continuation of Scholasticism, but now it had an activist mentality and a combative edge. Disputation and argument became more central to philosophy than at any time since the Sophists, and with much more at stake. Wars between Catholics and Protestants would rip Europe apart for the next six generations, and the emergence of modern philosophy as an extremely aggressive, largely confrontational discipline might well be traced back to those bitter years.

Between the extremities of the Reformation and the Counter-Reformation, it is all too easy to lose sight of the many quite reasonable philosophers who were caught up in the chaos but nevertheless refused to become parties to the follies and brutality of the times. Two of them deserve special mention, not only as brilliant thinkers but as among the very best examples—comparable to Socrates himself—of what a philosopher can and ideally should be.

The first is the Dutch humanist Desiderius Erasmus (1466?–1536), a devout but outspoken reformer who locked horns with the church but nevertheless refused to join the Reformation. Erasmus insisted that the Scriptures be made accessible to ordinary people (and therefore should be translated into ordinary language), and was himself one of the first serious biblical scholars, opening the way for generations who could explore the making of the Bible in elaborate detail. Erasmus was also a witty social critic, a free spirit, who earned himself both powerful enemies and perpetual admirers by skewering the pretentious and the pretensions of his times.

The second is his good friend Sir Thomas More (1478–1535), who served as chancellor of England under the infamous Henry VIII. Because he rejected the King's wish to break away from the church in Rome in order to get a divorce and marry his sweetheart of the moment, Sir Thomas was beheaded. However, he also left behind an admirable model of what a philosopher, a seeker after wisdom, should be.

Erasmus was one of many excellent scholars who nevertheless disliked the tedium of Scholasticism. He was, above all, a humanist, a defender of the *spirit* of the church and, when need be, a harsh critic of its practices. Like Martin Luther, he criticized the selling of indulgences and other unseemly commercial practices of the clergy. He rejected the papal claim to infallibility, and, early in Luther's career, Erasmus highly praised his reformist zeal. Unlike Luther, however, he had no desire to risk another schism. By 1524 he had turned on Luther and the two exchanged some vitriolic correspondence. Erasmus rejected the harsh Protestant doctrine of predestination, and unlike Luther, who defended the interpretive abilities of the common person, he was no particular friend of untutored innocence.

A priest himself, Erasmus vehemently criticized the ignorance of his fellow clergy. Although anti-Scholastic, he was nevertheless an enthusiastic scholar. He prepared the first Greek edition of the New Testament and a new Latin translation, which would become the basis for almost all New Testament scholarship to follow. But despite his rejection of Luther and the Reformation and his adamance about maintaining the unity of the church, Erasmus was blamed by many Catholics for "laying the egg" hatched by Luther.

A man of the world, Erasmus traveled widely, spending time in Oxford, Cambridge, and London as well as Paris, Freiburg, and Torino. His humanism was not a doctrine so much as it was part of his character, the result of his own modest upbringing as an illegitimate child and his extensive experience in many of the main cities in Europe. His most enduring and beloved work contains a biting, loving irony that manifests his humor and his humanism. It bears the accurately self-descriptive title *In Praise of Folly* (1549). He reportedly wrote it in a week. It became one of the most popular philosophical works of the late Middle Ages.

The book is, in his words, "biting satire," but it is nevertheless written with great compassion and humor. *Folly* is written by a narrator named "Folly," and self-praise is, predictably, one of the pervading objects of humor. Erasmus also has it in for "foolosophers," the rich, the powerful, the pope, doctors, gamblers, saints, writers, warmongers, theologians, Christians, and many others besides. He criticizes the Stoics for the attempt to expunge emotions from noble life, rendering the adherent of their doctrine a "marble statue of a man." He lampoons

Plato's republic as similarly unlivable, and Socrates himself comes in for Aristophanic caricature. Philosopher-kings, Erasmus assures us, undoubtedly make the *worst* rulers. Erasmus does not spare himself, and he and his fellow "Greekophiles" come in for similar abuse.

The point of *Folly*, easily lost in the fun, the satire, and the (prudently) unnamed targets of abuse is both to defend and to put limits on the virtue of wisdom. Only God has wisdom, he suggests, and in this, he explicitly agrees with Socrates. But there is so much of worth in human life—indeed, human life itself—that is not due to wisdom but to foolishness. Who would get married, have children, enter politics, fall in love, or become a philosopher if he or she actually possessed the wisdom to foresee the consequences and the implications? Quoting Sophocles with approval, he defends the very antiphilosophical position that "the happiest life is to know nothing at all." Erasmus's work, nevertheless, is philosophy at its best—moving, funny, profound, and exemplary of that special Socratic combination of freedom, humility, integrity, and humor.

Sir Thomas More was, like Erasmus, a deeply religious but highly independent man and thinker who famously put his personal beliefs and his integrity before both his secular loyalties and, it turned out, his self-interest. Despite his religiosity, he was raised in and participated in the business of a successful commercial family and had an admirable political career as well. Like Erasmus, More was a humanist as well as a devout Catholic, and he was appalled by the widespread abuses in the name of the church. But in England, he faced a problem quite different from those that were ripping apart the Continent. Whatever one might think of Luther and his Reformation, there can be little doubt that the palpable reasons for the attack on the church were sincerely religious and spiritual. Henry VIII's desire to break with the church, however, was not based on religion and spirituality at all. Henry wanted to divorce his wife Catherine and marry Anne Boleyn, and More, upon whose wisdom and advice Henry had long relied, refused to accept the king's plan. Despite Henry's threats and a brief (and, More claimed, quite enjoyable) imprisonment, More refused to give in, and Henry had him executed. Erasmus, who had stayed with More in London (and written *In Praise of Folly* there), called him "a man for all seasons," the title in our own century of a famous play (and later an Academy Award–winning movie) about More's life. More was canonized in 1935.

More's classic work is *Utopia* (1515), which, like Plato's *Republic*, provides a detailed blueprint for an ideal society. (More coined the term *utopia*, which is a pun meaning both "no place" *(u-topia)* and the good place *(eu-topia)*. Strikingly, the utopia More had in mind was a pagan, communist society, governed by reason. Like so many social philosophers to come, More sharply contrasts the life of reason with sheer egoism, which he traces back to the originally flawed nature of human beings. In the context of *Utopia*, More considers such still topical questions as women's rights, euthanasia and abortion, marriage and divorce.

With Erasmus, More campaigned to unify Christianity and open Christian scholarship to the wisdom of the Greek classics. But more generally, and perhaps more important, they jointly gave a human face to the often violent religious differences of the new modern world. Within the next two centuries, religion would lose its commanding central role in the life of Europe. In the transition to the more secular humanism of the modern age, there would be no more inspiring examples than Erasmus and More.

After Aristotle: Bacon, Hobbes, Machiavelli, and the Renaissance

The Reformation and Counter-Reformation emerged on an intellectual scene that had already been transformed by the Renaissance and its emphasis on the individual. The Renaissance, or "rebirth," was not as much a time of "starting over," as some of its more aggressive advocates have suggested, but it certainly was a time of rejuvenation, enthusiasm, and experimentation. In particular, that era rediscovered, or at any rate placed a new emphasis on, the classics, the literature of the ancient Greeks and Romans. The watchword of the Renaissance was "humanism," a conception of the dignity of the individual which had been developing since the twelfth century. Eighteenth-century French historian Jules Michelet commented that the Renaissance was distinguished by "the discovery of the world, and the discovery of man." This emphasis on rebirth and discovery, however, suggests a dismissal of the entire millennium that preceded the Renaissance, and one can rightly ask whether the new excitement about old books and letters really justifies the denigration of the medieval epoch (which was starting to be called the Dark Ages).

In historical context, however, one can understand the exhilaration that accompanied the passing of a plague (the Black Death) that had destroyed a third of the population of Europe and the end of the Hundred Years' War between England and France, which had destroyed so many as well. Renaissance humanism can be seen as a recoil and a relief from those awful years. Feudalism had all but collapsed and a new mercantilism and sense of exploration dominated Europe. A new secular ideal of a sophisticated and cultured urban class was coming into prominence. Humanism was not, however, contrary to the accusations of some evangelical polemicists both then and today, essentially secular or godless. In many ways, the Renaissance remained medieval and sometimes mystical, and it is important to remember that the new emphasis on the dignity of the individual was born and nourished within the embrace of Christianity and the Judeo-Christian tradition.

There is no single line separating medieval from modern times, and the Renaissance does not fall neatly into either period. Textbooks draw a convenient line at the year 1500, but the Renaissance transition spread from the mid-fourteenth century to at least 1600, and one could engage in a truly fruitless debate about how to classify the philosophical figures in this period. The Renaissance was first of all a literary and artistic movement. Its most valued products were the "humanities," those disciplines that came to be expected of every educated citizen.

However, the humanities also included a new respect for science, fueled by developments in technology and mathematics. Accordingly, the Renaissance might also be defined in terms of its most spectacular scientific revolution, the Copernican view that the sun and not the earth is the center of our universe. The pursuit of scientific knowledge, which had long had a lowly and clearly secondary relationship to the larger dogma of theology, now began its quick rise to ascendancy, coupled with a protracted and sometimes brutal antagonism with the church. In 1600, Giordano Bruno was burnt at the stake for heresy and, soon after, Galileo was forced to recant his Copernican view (a position not officially accepted by the Catholic Church until 1992!).

It would be a mistake to exaggerate the ongoing conflict between science and religion, however. As Nature was considered to be God's "handiwork" (a conception inherited from the ancient Hebrews and recently defended by Thomas Aquinas), science was seen as a mode of revelation, a way of appreciating God's wonders. For the most part, the church was perfectly happy to tolerate science so long as it did not conflict with doctrinal teaching, and science in any case had not yet developed a purely mechanistic, godless vision of the universe, despite the rediscovery of (and a certain amount of enthusiasm for) Lucretius.

The Renaissance was indeed a return to the classics and classical philosophy, but it nevertheless presented itself as a full-scale attack on the most illustrious of the ancients, the great philosopher Aristotle. Aristotle was both a central concern and the most problematic figure for the Renaissance. On the one hand, there can be no doubt that the entire temperament of the Renaissance "recovery of philosophy," as well as its essential vocabulary and vision, was thoroughly Aristotelian. On the other hand, the "pagan" Aristotle had all but disappeared, and most of what remained was embedded in the dogmas of Scholasticism, thoroughly integrated into the teaching of the church by way of St. Thomas Aquinas and into Islam through Ibn Rushd. Some perceptive individuals distinguished between the genuine and the scholastic Aristotle, but the general reaction of Renaissance thinkers was decidedly *against* Aristotle. Predictably, this response was coupled with a dramatic rediscovery and defense of Plato, who was now widely translated into popular Latin editions.

In science, Aristotle had ruled almost every discipline—physics, cosmology, biology, and psychology, to name a few—for fifteen hundred years. Theories and hypotheses that had seemed like common sense in the fourth century B.C.E. still held sway, in many cases untested, into the fifteenth and sixteenth centuries. Galileo's simple but famous experiment of dropping two differently sized rocks off of the Tower of Pisa, to test their respective speed of acceleration (which turned out to be the same, contrary to Aristotle's prediction), seemed to summarize the unappreciative disdain with which the new scientists considered Aristotle. "Common sense," as it was long ago defined and settled by Aristotle, was no longer to be simply accepted. For example, Aristotle believed (as did most of his contemporaries) in what later came to be called the *Ptolemaic* view of the universe, with the earth as the center and the heavens above. That commonsense belief, above all, had come into serious question, and, ironically, the Renaissance, the forum for emerging humanism, was founded in part on the shocking revelation that human beings and the planet they occupied were no longer the center of the cosmos.

Aristotle had also dominated politics, and Aristotle's celebration of the gradually disappearing Greek city-state remained an ideal long after such societies were practical or possible. (Aristotle's defense of slavery, unfortunately, was still pervasively accepted.) On the positive side, however, the centerpiece of Aristotle's politics—as well as those of Socrates and Plato—was an insistence that the primary purpose of the state, of government and authority, was the cultivation of moral human beings. Politics and virtue, statesmanship and ethics, went hand in hand. It is one of the less celebrated and more shocking features of the Renaissance that this noble view would be rejected. Politics came to be viewed as a compromise at best, if not outright "dirty dealing." It represented the worst in human nature.

In short, insofar as the Renaissance was a rebirth, it often involved not so much a rejection of the church or Christianity as a rejection of Aristotle. Of Aristotle's most illustrious Renaissance critics, we will only mention three: Francis Bacon (1561–1626), Thomas Hobbes (1588–1679), and, almost a century before them, Niccolò Machiavelli (1469–1527). All three can be seen as antagonists of Aristotle, although all three owe him an enormous (if unacknowledged) debt as well. Bacon is usually recognized as the founder of the modern scientific tradition, which means, in particular, that he broke with Aristotle and insisted that we "start over" with a purely empirical, experimental method. Hobbes has twofold significance, first as a friend and colleague of Bacon, another trailblazer for the New Science and a thoroughgoing critic of Aristotle's teleological view of the universe and, second, as one of the most influential architects of modern political theory and a harsh antagonist of Aristotle's view of "natural" human sociability.

Finally, we should at least mention the famous name of Machiavelli, who in the midst of the chaos and corruption of Renaissance Italy set the stage for modern politics. The unmistakable subtext of his infamous treatise *The Prince* is that there is nothing moral about politics. In his *Art of War* he treated war as a normal feature of relations between states, demanding continuous preparation and strategy, not mere response to a sudden emergency in which untrained troops must be hurriedly gathered for the occasion. Indeed, the break signaled by Machiavelli and Hobbes with Aristotle's equation of politics and ethics may ultimately be more momentous than the scientific rebellion initiated by Bacon.

Francis Bacon was not himself a scientist—that is, he is not known for his theories or discoveries in the way that Copernicus, Galileo, Kepler, and Newton are known. He rather theorized *about* science, and about knowledge in general. In particular, he developed the experimental method that would have so much influence on Galileo. It was Bacon who formulated what became the textbook version of the "scientific method," which involves careful observation and controlled, methodical experiment. The scientific method provided a fresh start on all of the questions supposedly answered by the ancients.

But Bacon, like Aristotle, still tended to trust reason over experience, and his continuing attack on Aristotle's influence (that is, on the uncritical acceptance of his fifteen-hundred-year-old theories) should not obscure the extent to which Bacon is Aristotle's indirect descendant, not his nemesis. Against the dogmas of the past, Bacon attempted to justify the pursuit of knowledge "for its own sake." This should not be misunderstood, as it so often is today, as a defense of inquiry without regard for consequences. Bacon insisted on precisely the opposite, namely, that knowledge is *useful*. Indeed, he famously proclaimed, *"Knowledge is power!"* He also defended science as the ultimate dominion of humanity over nature, as promised in Genesis, and as the study of God's works, which was just as legitimate a source of revelation as the study of his Word.

Bacon gave an egalitarian status to science by insisting that anyone, using the right methods, could discover the truth. Science was not the exclusive realm of geniuses. This would become a political claim of no small importance. But this is not to say that Bacon simply defended "common sense." One of the most powerful aspects of his philosophy is the critique of various "idols" of human nature which block or distort proper scientific inquiry. Among these are various prejudices and false notions which we are taught by our elders and do not question. There is a natural inertia or conservatism to human belief, making it difficult to give up an established, comfortable, but false, belief. Wishful thinking too often eclipses careful perception and "true experience." There is also the danger that our senses are not always trustworthy, a view Bacon shared with the ancients as well as his successor Descartes. Last but not least, Bacon attacked the belief in Aristotelian "final causes"—purposive or teleological explanations. Nature does not act as it does because objects and events have purposes but because they have (material or "efficient") causes and obey natural "forms" or laws. The attack on Aristotelian final causes was probably the most damaging and enduring aspect of Bacon's sometimes-unfair attack on Aristotle.

As a metaphysician, not a scientist, Thomas Hobbes developed a purely materialist and mechanistic model of the world—the world as mere "matter in motion." It was perhaps the most depersonalized, colorless portrait of the universe since Democritus and the ancient atomists, but such radical moves always have their counterweight. Hobbes may have believed in a mechanical universe, but it was not a godless one. He spent half his career (and virtually half of his most famous book, *Leviathan*) defending a cosmology that did not exclude theology.

Hobbes is best known, however, for his harsh vision of human life in the "state of nature," that is, "before" the formation of society. Selfishness was the reigning principle, he tells us in the early pages of *Leviathan*. Justice was unknown. Life, accordingly, was "a war of all against all," and consequently it was typically "nasty, brutish and short." In this mutually dangerous and combative context, men and women got together and formed a "social compact [contract]" for their mutual safety and advantage. They gave over some of their modest power to the "sovereign," the king who would rule over them, not by divine right but by common agreement. And with this agreement, humanity would further be protected by the idea of justice. Justice itself was the product of contractual society and not its presupposition.

Debate has persisted about whether Hobbes intended his state-of-nature model as a literal hypothesis or rather as a thought-experiment to introduce a radically new vision of society. It is generally agreed that only the latter makes much sense. Hobbes himself suggested in some of his later works that human nature is by no means so foul as his state-of-nature story suggests. The future of political philosophy would, however, be ruled by the idea of a social contract (a Scholastic idea that can be traced back even to the Greeks). Locke and Rousseau, even Immanuel Kant, would defend variations of this idea, and it would, of course, become the dominant political idea—in the form of "constitutions"—as a result of the revolutions of the following century.

Before the "Discovery": Africa and the Americas

As Europe tore itself apart in factional and sectarian conflict, as great nations emerged in more or less continuous war with one another, the Europeans turned outward to a "new" world, anxious to explore and exploit the resources of these apparently unlimited lands. They were also concerned to convert the natives of this new world, whom they considered to have been deprived of the Word, despite an evidently rich tradition of religions and a number of truly spectacular cities and civilizations, easily comparable to the wonders of ancient Egypt.

By a less than happy coincidence, it was just when Spain was initiating the Inquisition that Columbus "discovered" America in 1492. Soon Spanish priests joined the conquistadors in their attempt to capture the souls as well as the booty of these fabulous "new" empires. While French Catholics and the French Protestants (or "Huguenots") were murdering each other, French explorers and missionaries were sailing down the St. Lawrence River, around the coast of China, and down through the South Pacific. Similarly, the Spanish, the Portuguese, the Dutch, and some of the Scandinavians were making exploratory journeys. When the English church split from Rome and then proceeded to further fragment into dozens of separate sects, virtually all of them began to proselytize and send missionaries around the world.

The international competition for converts and new sources of trade and resources quickly became global. The Spanish and Portuguese colonized Central and South America. The English established settlements in Virginia and Massachusetts. The Dutch grabbed a few pieces of the Caribbean and the several hundred islands of Indonesia. The French took eastern Canada and Louisiana. Virtually all of them made their way to China and down the east coast of Africa.

In Africa, colonialism took a particularly vicious turn. Slavery had diminished in Europe with the rise of Christianity and, just as important, with the establishment of feudal society. As long as serfs were bound to the manor, slaves were unnecessary. But with the end of serfdom and, later, with the Industrial Revolution and the colonization of extensive plantations in the West Indies, the demand for slavery increased.[59] With this in mind, Columbus sent back five hundred Indians from America. (Queen Isabella, much to her credit, returned them to their homes.) Africa, however, became the primary source of slaves. A systematic slave trade was established by the beginning of the sixteenth century, first of all by England and Portugal. There is evidence that there had already been some slave trading within Africa, as there seems to have been throughout the world since ancient times. But the new colonial system turned slavery into an industry (rather than a by-product of war), and kidnaped African natives became that continent's single most valuable resource.

Colonialism was not a new phenomenon, of course. The ancient Phoenicians had colonized the Mediterranean and much of north Africa, the Greeks had colonized Asia minor and, under Alexander, had attempted to colonize half of Asia. The Romans invented the notion of "imperialism," and the Roman Empire had expanded the dominion of Roman culture and institutions throughout much of the known world, from the barbarian British Isles to the strife-torn land of Palestine. But the new colonialism and imperialism of the sixteenth and seventeenth centuries had seemingly endless room to explore and expand.

The main aim of this "age of discovery" was trade, but one should certainly not discount the spirit of adventure, religious zeal, and national pride in the reckoning. Everywhere the Europeans went, they spread not only their religion but their cultures and their systems of government as well. (They also carried with them some lethal diseases.) What gets lost in the standard celebration of "discovery" and conquest is the essential fact that these newly "discovered" lands were already populated by millions of people, many of whom had established great civilizations. The confrontation with people who had never been part of European culture and religion, in the midst of Europe's own ongoing turmoil, prompted at least some reflection which countered colonial imperialist attitudes. The French philosopher Michel de Montaigne scandalized a generation in France by suggesting that, in contrast to the rich, corrupt, and unhappy Christians of Europe, there were whole and happy civilizations overseas, in the newly discovered Americas. True, the inhabitants of those lands were "cannibals," Montaigne admitted, but they managed to live good lives without European luxuries, treacheries, or even, he pointed out, the teachings of the Bible.

For centuries to come, the discovery of new societies, notably the discovery of the Polynesian islands of the South Pacific, would prompt many such philosophical speculations. The idea of happy, "innocent" tribal societies living in harmony with nature had obvious appeal for the war-torn Europeans, and the wildly popular rumors of sexual freedom (not to mention cannibalism and the like) sparked the imaginations of an increasingly repressed Christian continent. Very few Europeans had any adequate knowledge of life across the oceans, of course, and much of what was suggested in philosophy and numerous popular publications was sheer fantasy. But the truth was that there were whole civilizations that had existed for centuries before the Europeans ever knew of their existence, across the Atlantic, south of the Sahara, and throughout the Pacific as well.

What were these civilizations like? The ancient Greeks and Romans already knew a great deal about Egypt and western Asia, and parts of northern Africa had been involved in the development of the three major religious traditions in the West, as our discussions of the Exodus, Philo, Augustine, and the Arabs have suggested. To be sure, the reports of Herodotus, Thucydides, and later historians are not always trustworthy, and neither the Hebrew Bible nor the Gospels contain consistent or accurate reports of those traditions. But through various literary accounts and other written descriptions, scholars have pieced together a more or less plausible picture about what life was like and what people believed in the civilizations of Asia and northern Africa.

The problem for historians of most of the cultures of Africa and the Americas, by contrast, is that we have few such written documents, if any. In some cases, they were destroyed, often along with the civilizations themselves. For example, the Aztecs of Mexico, who apparently gained ascendancy in the Yucatan after the disintegration of the previous civilization of the Toltecs, around 1100 C.E., had a thriving school of philosophers called *tlamatinime* ("knowers of things"). But all we have left are fragments of their teachings, largely because their Spanish conquerors deliberately burned most of the pictorial books in which Aztec history was recorded.

More problematic still are those many cultures whose literary traditions were entirely oral. When the cultures either died out or were overwhelmed by colonial conquerors, these traditions usually died out as well. (We might wonder: if Homer's great oral works the *Iliad* and the *Odyssey* had never been written down, but still depended on the memorization and transmission of their substantial texts from generation to generation, would we have ever heard of them?) The supposition that cultures that lack a written tradition therefore lack a literary and a philosophical tradition is utterly without justification. But we have no way of knowing, in a great many cases, just what those traditions were like.

What remains by way of folktales and legends may or may not be an accurate reflection of such cultures before the catastrophic invasions of a few hundred years ago. How those tales were embellished with philosophical reflection, commentary, and criticism, as we find in the Jewish, Greek, and Indian traditions, for example, is even less available to us. But we can be reasonably sure that most of the thousands of tribes and civilizations that populated Africa and the Americas did have distinctive views about the world and its origins, about themselves and their place in nature and among other people.

The lack of a written record also produces another troublesome problem for the scholar and the philosophical historian, and that is how to date and corroborate the history of a culture. A written record, even an inaccurate one, invites speculation and calculation, if not from one source then from others. For example, the historical information in the Old Testament concerning Abraham and Moses is by itself not very helpful to the historian; but with some cross-referencing to Sumerian, Babylonian, and Egyptian histories, a reasonably accurate chronology is possible. The historical existence of Thales, to take another familiar example, can be ascertained, despite the absence of any writings by him, through the writings of other philosophers and historians. But in the absence of any literature, it is difficult to tell even how long a civilization has been in existence, a problem that philosophers and historians sometimes gloss over by calling such cultures "ahistorical."

The history of philosophy, like history in general, tends to reflect change, and where there is no record of change, there is no evidence of history. How long had Aztec civilization existed before the Spaniards under Hernando Cortés entered the capital city of Tenochtitlán in 1519? How ancient are the abandoned ancient cities of the central African rain forest? How long had the Navaho, the

Hopi, the Ojibwa, the Apache, the Seminole, the Iroquois, and the hundreds of other American Indian tribes resided in the "new" world that was invaded during the westward expansion of the European colonies and later the United States? We do know that North America was populated thousands of years ago; and although the claim that the human species originated in Africa rather than Asia has not yet been settled, it is quite clear that Africa was populated top to bottom tens of thousands of years ago. The fact that these African and American cultures seem to lack a history reflects the lack of written records and the likelihood that stability, and not change, defines their history, at least until the colonial invasions.[60] That this should seem to be a detracting feature of a society could only be defended by a culture whose philosophy is obsessed with the notion of change, whether progress or tragedy, and is willing and ready to believe the worst of others.

What we do know about these various world cultures is, nevertheless, increasingly rich and fascinating. We will only indicate this growing awareness with a few general points here. With regard to Africa, of course, there are hundreds of different cultures, indeed, hundreds of different languages, but a good deal of precolonial African philosophy can be characterized by means of the twin notions of *tribalism* and a special sense of *identity with nature*.

Tribalism establishes an individual's identity and significance as a person only in the context of his or her family and community. This idea sounds striking, and worth mentioning, to those of us in the contemporary West who have thrown off such familial and communitarian sensibilities in favor of a radical individualism. But for those who live such a philosophy (and this would include the Confucian culture of China as well as the many tribal societies of the Americas and the South Pacific), the isolated individual, not defined by the concrete presence and intangible ties of kinship, would be understood as effectively dead.

Traditional African tribes tend to see personhood as something achieved over time by means of becoming a part of one's community. To become a person is an achievement. Birth and death do not mark the person's beginning and end. A newly born baby is not yet a person, while a deceased person who lives in the memory of his or her descendants is a person still, despite physical death. Initiation rites are crucial to achieving full membership in most tribal communities, and thus to becoming a full person. Similarly, throughout the individual's life span, rites and ceremonies keep the individual's life in rhythm with that of the community.

Even the very notion of time is bound up with tribal identity. John Murungi points out, for instance, that the Ameru tribe considers the beginning of time to be the origin of the tribe, which they mythologically describe as the time when the tribe migrated to their current home from captivity in Mbwaa by crossing a body of water. The beginning of time is the point of the crossing. Murungi also observes that African tribes typically consider the origin of each tribe to be independent. They do not attempt to integrate the stories of the various tribes into a comprehensive history; instead, they concern themselves with their own tribe's saga.

The Western conception of an individual, atomic soul for each person is alien to the thinking of most traditional Africans. In some tribes, such as the Yoruba (now mostly in Nigeria) and the Lugbara (now mostly in Uganda), the communal basis for personhood is reflected in a conception of the human being as composed of multiple spiritual elements, all of which are essential to the person's life. In the Yoruba tribe, moreover, ancestors' souls can return in their descendants, sometimes over and over again. So far are the Yoruba from believing in an isolated individual soul that they believe that even immediate descendants may be reincarnations of souls of their mothers or fathers, even while the latter are still living.

In light of this sense of identity, members of African tribes typically emphasize the worship of ancestors, who are considered living inhabitants of the spirit world, capable of assisting their living descendants. This practice, too, may seem "primitive" to modern individualists. But perhaps the proper line of questioning goes the other way: how much has a society lost when it no longer feels intimacy and immediacy with its past? Tribalism has its downside as well, needless to say—in particular the tendency to intertribal wars that still plague Africa today (and many other parts of the world where ethnicity is considered basic to personal identity). But given the internecine religious wars that were wracking Europe during the colonial period, who would be in a (morally superior) position to criticize the brutalities of others?

As for the African attitude toward nature (and this would apply to many of the tribes of North America and the South Pacific, too), we need only point out that for thousands of years many have accepted a philosophical perspective that we in the West are just now beginning to appreciate. On this view, human beings have not been placed here on earth to "have dominion" over all other creatures and things, as promised in Genesis and reiterated by Frances Bacon. True, Western religions also emphasize that human beings were appointed stewards of the earth, but as cities and populations grew, social need eclipsed ecological sensitivity. Today, a combination of romanticized tribal values and practical necessity has led us to recognize that we are a part of the earth; we are dependent on it and it is dependent on us. We have ecological responsibilities, and the world around us ("nature") is not just a resource or a source of fascination.

African tribal societies typically embrace *animism*, the belief that entities throughout nature are endowed with souls, often thought to be souls of ancestors who are no longer individually remembered. Nature, for most traditional Africans, is full of living forces. Spirits dwell within it, and human beings can interact with them to some extent, utilizing these spirits' powers or driving them elsewhere. Spirits are considered powerful, however, since they are more directly in contact with the divine than are human beings. They can appear to people and affect them, both benevolently and maliciously. The African conviction that human beings are intimately connected to nature is part and parcel of the traditional belief that nature is essentially spiritual.

American Indian tribes similarly emphasize humanity's dependence on nature. Nature, on their view, is an interconnected field in which every entity had its own energy, which interacted with the energy of every other thing. In many tribes, these interconnections are thought to involve extensive causal connections among apparently distant actions and events. Recent philosophers have noted the parallels between the ecological worldviews of native American Indians and the rising ecological consciousness that many contemporary thinkers see as the only perspective on nature that might divert us from a course of self-destruction.

Interestingly, hunting tribes among the American Indians acknowledged the debt that they had toward the creatures that provided their food. On their view, killing other creatures is not our right but a necessity which we should satisfy with a mixture of gratitude and reverence. Saying prayers and thanking one's quarry may strike most supermarket shoppers as a bit odd, but the consciousness of the fact that another creature has been killed for one's benefit might better be seen as a minimal gesture of humanity (in the sense of "being humane.") The Hebrew kosher laws *(Kashrut)* are similarly best considered as an expression of the reverence and gratitude that are considered obligatory if one kills an animal.[61] The gesture of prayer in thanksgiving to the animal one has hunted also reflects another feature common to most American Indian traditions, namely, the tendency to see everyday life as sacred.

In developing ecological worldviews in which nature is infused with sacred powers, the perspective of the natives of Central and South America resembles that of their neighbors to the north. The southern societies in precolonial times had complex and sophisticated systems of belief that invite comparison with the ancient civilizations of the West, and their destruction is one of the great tragedies of human history. The Europeans viewed the great civilizations of the Mayas, the Incas, and the Aztecs as representatives of the devil and made little attempt to understand them. In fact (as had been the case in Europe as well until recently), these ancient Americans had developed systematic cosmologies and a scientific worldview that were not separate from their religious beliefs. (The Maya, for example, had developed a mathematics employing the concept of zero as early as the first century C.E.) The philosophy of these American civilizations was neither esoteric nor abstract in the sense that had often defined Greek and European philosophy. It was not, in short, divorced from everyday life.

The core of Mesoamerican (that is, the area comprising Mexico and Central America) philosophy was a belief in three levels of time and reality—ordinary, mythical, and divine. This belief bears similarities to some of the Neoplatonist and Arabic images of emanations, but it was by no means as abstract. The mythic and divine levels of reality exerted tangible influences on the ordinary plane of human experience, and they did so at predictable times. This belief motivated detailed attention to the construction of calendars and to astronomical observation. The balance between the different orders of reality was sufficiently fragile so that human beings had to assume responsibility for maintaining the cosmic order.

Philosophically, the Mayas and the Aztecs believed in the systematic unity of the cosmos and the corelativity of opposites (a view that resembles certain beliefs of some of the pre-Socratics). Like the ancient Hindus, they believed in unified male–female divinities and saw life and death as a continuing cycle, not a beginning and an end. Like tribes farther north in America, the Mesoamericans took their responsibilities *to* the earth very seriously. They believed that the continued existence of the universe itself depended on human actions and rituals, and, in particular, on the willingness of humans to sacrifice themselves.

These beliefs, taken together, indicate the logic behind the best known and most horrifying of ancient Aztec rituals—bloody human sacrifice on an enormous scale. Similarly, the Mayan kings and queens regularly pierced themselves and lost enough blood to cause them to have religious visions. They understood such relatively modest sacrifice as repayment to the gods, who had sacrificed themselves to create the world. For the Aztecs, the sacrifice was far less modest, involving wholesale killing of the best youths of their society along with captured enemies. It has been suggested that one of the reasons the warrior Aztecs lost so quickly to the Spanish invaders was that, in desperation, they sacrificed so many of their best young warriors to the gods who had seemingly turned against them.

As Thales and the ancient Babylonians had thought that the world was essentially made of water, the Mayas and the Aztecs believed that it was essentially made of blood, understood as the fundamental life force. Inga Clendinnen, in her brilliant study *Aztecs,* weaves the complex tale of bloody ritual sacrifice in such a way that we can see how it all fits together in a coherent and powerful philosophy, however disturbed we may be by the practices involved. (We might contrast—and compare—this horror of mass killing with flint knives of sometimes willing individuals for religious purposes with the contemporary horror of killing unseen citizens with long-range missiles for merely ideological or territorial motivations.)

Like the Aztecs and Mayas, the Incas of Latin America believed that sacrifice to the gods was necessary in order to ensure continued well-being on earth. The Incas were innovative, however, in learning to ensure that well-being through their own skills as well as by appeal to the gods. They developed agriculture and created a sense of collectivism among diverse cultures. They succeeded in organizing and maintaining a vast empire comprised of many ethnic groups. The secret of their success was teaching agricultural methods to those they conquered in return for an annual percentage of the resulting produce. The only other demand that the Incas placed on those they conquered was that the latter worship the sun god Inti as primary. The two demands worked well together. As the sun god, Inti was believed to be the source of sustenance for crops as well as the director of human destinies. The conquered cultures thus came to share the central belief as well as the essential skills of the Incas.

Much more could be said about the enormous variety of much-neglected philosophies in Africa and the Americas and the often subtle differences among them, but we make no pretense in this short space about attempting to write a truly global history of philosophy. What we do intend is to maintain a certain demographic humility. The philosophy and the techniques of analysis in which we were trained are but one small sample of the enormous varieties and styles of philosophy to be found in the world, and there are many kinds of wisdom other than our own.

The rest of our story moves into modern times, resuming with the movement of philosophy in Europe during the tumultuous and fast-changing years following the Reformation and the Counter-Reformation, the Renaissance, and the development of the "New Science." By the beginning of the modern age, the rapid growth of the increasingly cosmopolitan cities of Europe, with their global reach, their extensive colonies and their increasingly bloody national and international rivalries, required a new kind of philosophy, intensely self-questioning but endlessly arrogant as well.

Part III

✍

Between Science and Religion:
Modern Philosophy
and the Enlightenment

Science, Religion, and the Meaning of Modernism

The very word "modern"—which has a surprisingly long history—suggests the beginning of a battle, a bit of arrogance, a cry of rebellion, a gesture of rejection (even destruction) of what is past. The Greeks of Alcibiades' generation unabashedly called themselves "modern" in opposition to the older (more democratic) politicians who stood in their way. The Arabs of the Middle Ages declared themselves "modern" *(muta'akhirun)* in opposition to the ancients from whom they distinguished themselves. During the Renaissance, those who rediscovered the classics called themselves "modern" in opposition to those who were stuck in the Middle Ages. Toward the end of the Scholastic age, William of Ockham was called a "modern" because of his rejection of earlier Scholastic doctrines, and in the eighteenth century, many nationalists called themselves "modern" because of their revolutionary activities. Young romantics declared themselves emphatically "modern" in opposition to those who were still steeped in the classics. Until very, very recently, almost every new fashion, every new set of ideas, every new invention, every new appliance was promoted as "modern," meaning not only "the latest" but the most up-to-date, the best.

Today, modernists have been one-upped in the style of their own rhetoric by the "postmodernists," but that is a story yet to come. The point is that modern philosophy, the very name of it, comes across as a declaration of war. It is not merely descriptive, and it does not merely designate a "period." In particular, the title "modern philosophy" is an attack on and a rejection of the Middle (now declared Dark) Ages that occupied the preceding thousand years. It is an attack on the church that ruled those ages and dictated its ideas. It is an attack on the very notion of authority itself, which was, as we have seen, very much at issue during the centuries preceding.

For the sake of sheer simplicity and the convenience of high school history publishers, the modern period is generally said to begin around 1500, give or take a decade one way or the other. This is understandable. Less than a decade before that arbitrary date, Christopher Columbus had landed his ships in what came to be known as "the new world," altering not only the geography but the politics of the world forever. Only a decade after, Martin Luther would tack his ninety-five theses to the door of the church at Wittenberg and initiate the Reformation, which would cause several centuries of upheaval in Europe, change the nature of the Christian religion, and, eventually, change conceptions of human nature. With the Reformation would come not only the rejection of medieval philosophy but the establishment of the "Protestant ethic" and the beginnings of modern capitalism. As a result of the Renaissance, there had already been a revival of ancient philosophy. Now Plato and Aristotle, who had been so thoroughly absorbed and used by Augustine and Aquinas, among many others, were once again consigned to the libraries. Aristotle, in particular, was vilified by the new scientists, who saw in his authoritative teachings the enemy of free inquiry and the pursuit of knowledge. Modern Western philosophy, like ancient Greek philosophy, has often been said to begin with the downfall of the old cosmologies and the rise of a new sense of science.

In fact, there was no cosmic curtain that was raised abruptly above the stage of Europe and European philosophy on or around the year 1500. The changes we have sketched were gradual and long drawn out, from the late Middle Ages through the Renaissance and on into the eighteenth and nineteenth centuries. Humanism, for instance, which is often taken to be one of the hallmarks of modernism and the antithesis of Christianity, took form *within* Christian thinking in the twelfth century and displayed a continuous (if not always smooth) development until well into the eighteenth century. The supposedly definitive philosopher of the modern era, René Descartes, was steeped in medieval (Scholastic) philosophy, and one of the most avant-garde existentialists, Søren Kierkegaard (1813–1855), insisted that what he really wanted was to "go back into the monastery out of which Luther broke." Indeed, the prevalence of Christian images and metaphors even in the world of modern science is striking.

Modern philosophy might, as we noted, be said to begin with the rise of science, as in ancient Greek philosophy, but we saw that the success of Greek philosophy was by no means based on the rise of science alone, and it is not as if there had been no scientific thinking during the thousand years preceding the Renaissance. True, science had been secondary and subservient to theology, and all theories of nature had been required to justify themselves in the court of religion. In the sixteenth century, Copernicus began to persuade a great many people that the earth was not the center of the universe, but a century later Galileo was still censored by the church for advancing this teaching. From the fifteenth to the eighteenth centuries, confrontations between science and religion were regular occurrences. Yet this was only so in a small corner of the world, from England and Scandinavia to Germany and south to Italy. India, Africa, and China did not witness simultaneous booms in science, nor did eastern Europe (although Copernicus was Polish) or the great civilizations of Central America. The Middle East and China had already displayed their considerable prowess in science and technology. The Arabs had done so during that spectacular period of productivity following the quick success of Islam and the recognition of the Arab world as the new center of learning and innovation. But today, in these same societies, "modernity" has come to mean "the invasion of the West," a threat to their traditional cultures.

We should not overemphasize the triumphs of modern science in the history of modern philosophy, however attractive and self-congratulatory that may be from the point of view of science-minded philosophers in the twentieth century. There is no denying that the advances in science during the fifteenth to eighteenth centuries were an inspiration to the early philosophers of modern times— Bacon, Hobbes, and Descartes, to name just a few—but much more was going on in the world than science, and there were many more influences on the growth of philosophy. Not all of them were obviously philosophical. Among them was the widespread use of money, an abstract medium that encouraged speculation (not just of the philosophical variety). There was the consequent spread of commercialism, the growth of great cities, and the need for a new kind of social philosophy. Fear and loathing were also powerful motives for philosophizing. In addition to being the most exciting time in the history of science since Aristotle, the sixteenth and seventeenth centuries were among the bloodiest and cruelest, even after a thousand years of almost continuous religious war. Worst of all, perhaps, was the so-called Thirty Years' War, which lasted from 1618 until 1648 and whose casualties were comparable to those of the Black Death of the fourteenth century. Whatever else modern philosophy was supposed to be or do, and whatever it might have to do with science, it had first to say something about the terrible state of the world and the seemingly interminable religious quarreling, intolerance, and mayhem.[62]

So what is modern philosophy and what is modernism? At the risk of being extremely simple-minded, not to mention contentious, we can summarize a few basic features, granting that these admit of many exceptions and variations even within the small area of Europe to which they must be restricted. Science does have something to do with modernity, but more as effect than foundation or cause. Science is but one manifestation of a new emphasis on *objectivity*. With a burst of hope and confidence, the philosophers of the late Renaissance came to believe that genuine knowledge was accessible, valuable not only for its own sake but also as a political instrument. "Knowledge is power," claimed Francis Bacon, and knowledgeable modernists took him quite seriously.

The source of this objectivity, paradoxically enough, was to be found in one's own subjectivity. Thus the modern age was founded on an apparent contradiction: we come to know the world "outside" by looking "inside." But it is not hard to see the virtue in this twin emphasis on subjectivity and objectivity. By insisting on subjectivity, the new philosophers could ignore or deny the established authority of the church as well as divinely appointed political leaders. The new emphasis on subjectivity also opened the way to a remarkable egalitarianism: establishing the truth is now up to each and every one of us. But, at the same time, what we establish, using the proper methods of reason and experience, is true not just for ourselves but *of the world*, objectively, even absolutely.

Modern philosophy is born of this paradox, objectivity out of subjectivity, the arrogance of knowledge coupled with the seeming humility of critical self-examination. It is also not unrelated to the "discovery" and colonization of the "new world" as well as the conquest of the far eastern reaches of the old one. The subjectivity so celebrated was, without a doubt, a distinctively European subjectivity. The objectivity it claimed, however, was global. The story of modern philosophy, accordingly, is not to be told merely in terms of the rise of science, the apotheosis of reason, and the successful pursuit of knowledge. It is also a story of power and politics. From the bloody violence of the Thirty Years' War to the merely verbal violence of Nietzsche and the postmodernists, there is an epic tale to tell, and despite artful whitewashing by traditional historians of modern philosophy, it is not altogether a pretty one.

Montaigne: The First Modern Philosopher?

In tracing the origins of modern philosophy, we face the same sort of academic (but by no means therefore inconsequential) dilemma we faced in ascertaining "the first philosopher" in ancient times. This is no mere chronological query, to be settled by looking up a few dates and deciding who had which ideas before anyone else. Indeed, the question is, *which* ideas? How were they presented? In what context or forum? Did the ancient Babylonian astrologers count as philosophers, centuries before the Greeks? Did the poets Hesiod and Homer count as philosophers, centuries before Thales? Should the earliest Greek scientists count as the first philosophers? Even more so, one can debate the merits of beginning the story of modern philosophy with one figure or another. (Here we have the benefit, of course, of having their works readily available.) Should we give the nod to Martin Luther? He is rarely even a candidate. How about Columbus? (Not a chance.) What about Copernicus or Galileo?

However difficult it may have been to distinguish philosophy from science in some of the earliest Greek philosophers, there seems to be no such difficulty in modern times. Copernicus, Galileo, and Newton are scientists, not philosophers (despite the fact that Newton spent more than half of his life writing theology). Hobbes and Bacon were undeniably philosophers, but historians tend to agree that they are best placed in the Renaissance, not in modernity. There is almost universal agreement, however, about their exact contemporary, René Descartes

(1596–1650). He is, as almost everyone has tended to agree, "the father of modern philosophy."

It is certainly worth asking why. He raised the right questions, the questions that, in retrospect, those who were recognized as philosophers (and those who later became philosophy professors) felt obliged to answer. Descartes was the philosopher who most dramatically insisted on the simultaneous turn to subjectivity and the use of logic, "the method of mathematics," to argue his way to objectivity. It was a method adopted or at least dealt with by almost every philosopher ever since. He was the philosopher who spent much of his time meditating on his own methods, devising rules for reason, doubting and then proving the obvious. Cynics might say that such clever solipsism, doubting and then proving (or disproving) the obvious, has been the favorite pastime of almost every great philosopher. Indeed, so luminous has been the figure of Descartes in the retrospective study of science-minded modern philosophy that the original concerns and motives of modern philosophy have been all but eclipsed.[63] And so, at the risk of seeming simply scandalous, we are going to postpone our discussion of the great philosophical methodologist and turn our attention instead to an earlier figure who is often ignored by historians of philosophy altogether, namely Michel de Montaigne (1533–1592).

Montaigne was a moralist, not a scientist or a mathematician. He wrote "essays," not methodological treatises. He mused on the follies of men, not their knowledge. Like his Dutch predecessor Erasmus, Montaigne doubted whether human beings were capable of finding the truth or recognizing it if they did find it, just as they seemed to be incapable of understanding justice or, more important, acting justly. He was an heir to the Skeptics of old, dubious of the senses and reason as well. He placed his emphasis on the idea of nature, embedded in us as *character*, a view also endorsed by the ancients.

The purpose of philosophy and education in general was to illuminate and inspire our own spontaneous natures. Montaigne found the intellectual exercises of Scholasticism pointless at best, and probably damaging to character. Divine revelation, however, was certainly worth accepting, and so, too, crossing the bridge between God and the animals was our innocent animal nature. Human society, and especially philosophy, was just so much vanity. (Jean-Jacques Rousseau, not surprisingly, would be deeply moved by Montaigne.)

While on a trip across Europe in 1580, Montaigne confirmed his opinion that human customs and ideas were very different from place to place; they changed "relative" to their context and, presumably, their times. Although his travels were confined to Switzerland, Germany, and Italy, this limited exposure to "humanity" was more than sufficient to make the point. Thus, Montaigne was quite at odds with Descartes, who sought only absolute, invariant truths, those which did not, could not, differ from place to place or time to time. Montaigne was fascinated (though sometimes appalled) by human differences—by the contingency of human belief and behavior. Descartes was after necessity, eternity, in other words, the inhuman. One can easily picture poor Montaigne, playing Protagoras to Descartes's nimble Socrates.

Montaigne was a pessimist living in a philosophical world desperately trying

to be optimistic, high on the promise of science and mathematics and the un-
veiling of absolute truth. Knowledge is power, perhaps, but recognizing one's
lack of knowledge, as Socrates also knew, can be wisdom. The refusal to insist
on absolute knowledge, while perhaps humbling, can lead to another virtue, of
particular importance in troubled times. It is called *tolerance*. And it would remain in short supply throughout the modern era, cosmopolitan claims to the
contrary.

Montaigne pursued the ancient art of developing a philosophy of life. Unfortunately, that was not where the spirit of philosophy was heading. He was left
behind, one more literary genius in the annals of French culture who didn't make
it into the English-speaking history of philosophy. (One can only surmise, in the
spirit of revenge, how much of today's devastating attack on philosophy and
especially on Cartesianism by literary critics could be construed as "getting even"
for the neglect of Montaigne.)

Descartes and the New Science

The acknowledged father of modern Western philosophy was raised in the Scholastic, Jesuit tradition, an accomplished scientist and mathematician. The basic
themes of Descartes's philosophy have come to define much if not most of philosophy. These include his use of mathematics and geometry, his emphasis on
methodology, his linking philosophy with science, his doubts about "common
sense," his insistence on intellectual humility ("the method of doubt"), his search
for certainty, and his confidence that certainty could be found, if anywhere, in
the demonstrations of mathematics and geometry. He was, of course, a brilliant
mathematician, and it was he who actually linked mathematics and geometry into
a single discipline, analytic geometry, and in so doing made possible some of the
greatest advances in physics. But one can properly question his faith in the use
of mathematics in philosophy and the narrow paradigm of philosophy that he set
for centuries to follow.

In order to understand Descartes's philosophy, it is necessary to appreciate
three aspects of the context in which he was writing. First, there was his own
religious training and the still-authoritarian nature of the Catholic Church. However revolutionary Descartes may have been, his revolution was carried out within
that climate of religious authority. Second was the rise of what was called the
"New Science." When he was just a young boy, Descartes heard that Galileo
had discovered the moons of Jupiter using a remarkable new instrument, the
telescope. Such discoveries quite naturally raised all sorts of questions about the
nature of knowledge, about the reliability of appearances, about the extent to
which we are ignorant of the world, about the methods we use to examine and
extend our knowledge. The New Science raised old questions about the relative
dependability of reason versus the senses, and it raised new and exciting questions
about how much could now come to be known. Although we are not here concerned with Descartes's contribution to the sciences, the excitement surrounding
the New Science (and its potential for conflict with religious authority) must also

be viewed as part of the framework within which Descartes's meditations take place.

A third aspect of Descartes's context is often ignored. Despite the rather cool and methodological appearance of his writings, Descartes was deeply disturbed by the ongoing religious turmoil in Europe. Montaigne had recommended tolerance. Descartes instead recommends reason. The calm and convincing demonstrations of reason offered a welcome alternative to the belligerent and bloody religious disputes that were ripping nations apart.

Descartes's most important thesis is one that we today take almost for granted, although against the background of the authority of the church and his own scholastic training it is radical indeed. This is his emphasis on the importance of intellectual autonomy, our ability to think for ourselves. The thinking he has in mind, however, is dramatically opposed to what is usually considered common sense. Common sense, he sarcastically explains, "is of everything in the world the best distributed, for everyone believes that he is so well provided with it that even those who are the most difficult to satisfy in every other respect do not usually demand more of this than they have" (a line borrowed, we might note, from Montaigne).[64] Common sense is just that—common, and it is often nonsense. "It is not enough to have a good mind," Descartes writes. "[T]he main thing is to apply it well."

Descartes's philosophy accordingly begins with the demand that each of us establish for ourself the truth of what we believe, and this means to establish it with certainty, using the application of mathematics. To this end, he invents a radical method, the method of doubt, in which he considers all of his beliefs suspicious, suspended in what the early Skeptics would call an *epoche*, until they can be proven to be justified. Descartes reminds us that he has often been lied to or misinformed by other people, and so he insists on suspending his trust in the authority of others. He realizes that he has sometimes been fooled by his senses (for example, a stick looks bent when seen through water), so he insists that he will remain suspicious of all knowledge gained through his senses. In fact, he even suggests that, since he is sometimes convinced that he is undergoing some experience in a dream, he cannot be sure that he is not dreaming now. Could he be dreaming all of the time, lost in the recesses of his own mind and wrong about the fact that there is a world outside of him? Could *all* of his experience, in other words, be mistaken? Indeed, could he even be mistaken about the most basic, indisputable knowledge—for instance, the basic truths of arithmetic?

Descartes's seductively charming approach to these questions is provided in his most popular work (the standard introduction to philosophy for millions of students), his *Meditations on First Philosophy*. In the *Meditations* (1641), as in his earlier work entitled *Discourse on Method* (1637), Descartes's style is borrowed from Montaigne, and it imitates an intimate, amiable, personal conversation. Descartes invites us into his study, as Montaigne had invited us into his private thoughts. He then asks us, slowly and considerately, to share with him a series of doubts.

Yet if the style is borrowed from Montaigne, Descartes has the very opposite intent and comes to a dramatically different conclusion. Montaigne intends for us to examine ourselves, using him as a mirror, to appreciate our own ignorance and be humble and human about it. Descartes insists that we push our doubts to the extremes, to the point of absurdity, where they will rebound and give us indubitable truth. Montaigne takes us by the hand and shares his reflections. Descartes subjects us to the rigors of scholastic disputation, taking great pains to examine and defend his every move along the way. Montaigne emerges a skeptic. Descartes declares his victory over skepticism. He was not, he concludes, mistaken at all. Indeed, he never really even doubted.

In the *Meditations*, Descartes begins by asking us to sit with him by the fire in front of him, where he is seated in his dressing gown, in the comfort of his study. He quietly asks us to consider the fact that there are some "troubled" people who are so insane as to think that they are kings or that their heads are pumpkins made of glass. He then notes that, in his dreams, he occasionally has equally improbable thoughts, and quite often he has dreamt that he was in his study by the fire when in fact he was asleep and in bed. Could he be sleeping right now? How would he tell? Descartes then offers us some assurance. Even in a dream, some things remain certain. Notably, there are arithmetic and geometry. "Two plus two equals four" is just as certainly true in a dream as it is in waking life. Not everything can be doubted.

Suppose, Descartes then suggests, that God were to deceive him in such a way that he could never discover the truth. Or, since God is necessarily good and "the fountain of truth," let us suppose that there were an "evil genius" of sorts, "supremely powerful and supremely intelligent, who purposely always deceives me." This evil being enjoys placing all sorts of wrong and mistaken beliefs into our minds. Suppose, Descartes suggests, he is mistaken in his belief that he has a body, that there is an "external world," even that there is a God. How could he ever sort out what he knows from what he merely believes, what is true from what was false? It is from this barren starting point that Descartes proceeds to once again build up his confidence in his own knowledge, beginning with such basic knowledge as the fact that he is not now dreaming and that there really is a world "out there."

Descartes's demonstration of these basic truths begins with his use of the mathematical method, the method of *deduction*, in which every principle must be derived or "deduced" from prior principles which have already been established on the basis of other principles, or premises. Ultimately, all principles must be so derived from a fundamental set of definitions and axioms—that is, from principles that simply spell out the meanings of the terms employed or are so obviously true that they are "self-evident." The key to Descartes's grand deduction, then, will be some axiom which will serve as a premise and is beyond doubt. That axiom, it turns out, is his famous claim (as it is stated in the *Discourse*), "I think, therefore I am."

This claim may look like an argument (because of the "therefore") but it is really a revelation, the self-confirming realization that I cannot be fooled about the fact of my own existence.[65] If I am fooled by the evil genius, I must nevertheless exist in order to be fooled. If I doubt my own existence, I must never-theless exist in order to doubt, and so on. Once Descartes has his premise, his axiom, he then goes on to prove God's existence, in the mode of the Scholastics. ("It is impossible that the idea of God which is in us should not have God himself as its cause.")[66] God's existence, in turn, can be used to establish the existence of the external world. If he can be sure of the existence of God, who is no deceiver, Descartes can therefore be confident that whatever he conceives "clearly and distinctly" must be true. The evil genius is defeated.

A number of objections can be raised against these arguments, against the too-easy notion of "clear and distinct ideas," against the assumption that thinking requires a thinker, against the arguments for God's existence, against the quick confidence with which Descartes declares the evil genius defeated. One can also question whether Descartes has indeed doubted as vigorously and as thoroughly as he originally claimed. He did not seem to doubt his confidence in the meaning of the words he used or consider the possibility that his own language might mislead him. He did not doubt the rules of inference that he employed in carrying out his logical deduction. It can be argued that he did not doubt the reliability of reason as such, or, if he did, he nevertheless assumed the reliability of reason in order to prove the reliability of reason, the notorious "Cartesian Circle."[67]

Nevertheless, Descartes established the basic rule for philosophical investiga-tion, the demand for certainty and immunity from doubt. Reason itself must be validated and cannot be taken for granted. Thus, Descartes's notion of "clear and distinct ideas" is essential. A clear and distinct idea is one that cannot be thought without believing it to be true. In other words, it cannot be doubted. It is irresistible. Such ideas are to be found, most obviously, in the simple propo-sitions of mathematics and geometry: "Two plus two equal four." "The shortest distance between two points is a straight line." "A triangle has three sides." (We should note the visual metaphor in the notion of clearness and distinctness, as well as in "the natural light of reason.")

We can see that the idea of one's own existence is also a clear and distinct idea, and so is the idea of God. The question remains, however, could an evil deceiver trick a person into having or seeming to have a clear and distinct idea? In other words, could we be utterly sure of ourselves and still be wrong? In details, perhaps. We willfully assent to error. But could we be wrong about everything, even our natural inclination to assume that the evidence of our senses demands the assumption of a world out there? Here is a clear and distinct idea, that the world exists, which would seem beyond intelligible doubt.

Or could all of this be foolhardy? Could it be that the method of doubt is itself a mistake, a dead end that, once undertaken, cannot be escaped? Perhaps the very idea that we need a set of indubitable (undoubtable) premises, a "foun-dation" for knowledge, is unreasonable and impossible. Perhaps all knowledge is at best only probable, or reasonable, or workable, as Montaigne suggested. Per-haps there are no "foundations," only a multiplicity of interconnections, a web and not an edifice. One might argue, with Montaigne and the Skeptics, that our knowledge is never certain (except in rather trivial or special circumstances).[68]

Perhaps we should be warned: taking mathematics as a paradigm of knowledge carries with it great dangers, for Descartes and his followers as it had for the ancient Greeks.

What is so tremendously new and important about Descartes, however, is not so much his insistence on certainty but the approach he takes to ancient skeptical questions. Many of the arguments he employs were familiar in Scholastic philosophy—for example, both the "ontological proof" of Anselm and a version of the "cosmological" argument of Aquinas. But Descartes's emphasis on what has since been called "subjectivity"—one's own thought and experience are as authoritative as the established teachings and the authority of others, including the Bible—was a truly revolutionary move in philosophy. The conclusions were not exciting. Descartes ended up proving God's existence and maintaining his faith, and, needless to say, he was confident that he had established what—outside of a philosophy seminar—would seem obvious to anyone, namely, the existence of the world around him. But his emphasis on subjectivity, as well as his use of the mathematical method to prove what otherwise is usually simply taken for granted, would provide the basis for many of the main moves in philosophy for the next two hundred years.

Subjectivity is one of those notions that has been so often used in so many different ways in philosophy that it now presents us with more of a problem than an insight. But as it applies to Descartes, we might note that it includes several significant features. Principally, it puts a premium on interiority, introspection, the idea that the mind is an inner realm containing *thoughts* (which should be understood broadly as including anything "mental"—emotions, sensations, desires, and all sorts of ideas). This notion of interiority was not at all evident in the earliest Greek philosophers, but it became increasingly plausible with the Pythagorean and Socratic notion of the soul and early Christianity, culminating in Augustine. The realm of the "inner" was still rather restricted, however, and developed much further through the Middle Ages before Descartes—and has developed more since. Buddhism, of course, had developed this sense of interiority even before Pythagoras and Socrates. Among the basic aspects of the Buddhist Eightfold Path are right mindfulness and right meditation. Moreover, enlightenment occurs as a result of an "inner" transformation.

For Descartes, the notion of subjectivity became identified with the notion of interiority. Unfortunately, that meaning is not the only one. Subjectivity is *also* taken to refer to what is mere opinion, personal belief rather than objective knowledge. In this sense, of course, the notion can be traced back to the ancients. (Plato often distinguished between genuine knowledge and mere opinion, even if those opinions turned out to be true.) Third, subjectivity may also refer to personal experience (which may or may not be conceived as "in" the mind), which implies a certain perspective and its limitations. For Descartes, of course, the idea was to transcend that perspective and its limitations. Fourth, and rather innocently, subjectivity refers simply to a particular standpoint, what in literature would be called the "first-person standpoint." This might be considered simply a stylistic device (namely, writing a "meditation" rather than a treatise) but it variously gets entangled with the previous three meanings as well.

Finally, we might note a meaning of subjectivity that does *not* apply to Descartes, and that is the notion of subjectivity as emotional, affectionate, and therefore prejudiced, biased. To be sure, one could view such bias as one aspect of the "limitations" just noted, but there is very little in Descartes's account that gives any credit to the affects or even raises the question about the role of feelings (including, notably, religious faith) in knowledge.[69] Whatever else it may mean, however, Descartes's subjectivism is a powerful form of individualism and a defense of individual authority and autonomy.[70] The revolution may still be (and may necessarily be) incomplete, but in Descartes it receives its most important thrust forward. The authority of philosophy is now to be found not in the sages and not in the Scriptures but in the individual mind of the philosopher.

One of the secondary but obviously important questions that Descartes raises along the way concerns the sort of being referred to as "*I*" in the realization, "I think, therefore I am." When he examines his famous premise, Descartes finds himself compelled to distinguish between those aspects of the "I" that are indeed self-evident and beyond doubt and those that are not. He concludes that he is, so far as his proof is concerned, only a "thinking thing," a thinking substance, whose body (and whose attachment to "his" body) is a matter of possible doubt. This raises familiar questions concerning the ancient Aristotelian and Scholastic doctrine of substance. Is an individual human being a substance, that is, a complete being, or is a human being a coupling of substances?

Descartes answers this question with the problematic thesis that a person is in fact a coupling of two different substances, mind and body. Since a substance is defined as that which is completely self-contained, however, the question of how mind and body interact is perplexing. According to Descartes, one has a clear and distinct idea of his or her mind as a thinking thing and a clear and distinct idea of one's body as an "extended" or physical thing. But one does not merely inhabit one's body, Descartes insists, like a pilot in a ship. What, then, is the connection between the two? A thought is obviously a very different sort of thing than a physical object. And if one hypothesizes (as Descartes did) that thoughts have something to do with the brain, the connection between them, the notion that the brain somehow causes or is the basis of thoughts, becomes more and more mysterious. The thesis that the mind and the body are separate substances has come to be called "Cartesian dualism," and it continues to trouble philosophers to this day.[71]

We should not suppose, as is often charged, that Descartes made some sort of stupid mistake, arbitrarily marking off the mind from the body as different "substances" and then finding himself unclear about how to get them together again. The dualism of mind and body was the product of several centuries of intellectual development, the progress of science and the newfound respect for individual autonomy. Distinguishing the mind and the body provided a realm for science, concerned with the physical world, to proceed unhampered by religion or moral concerns associated with the peculiarities of the human mind, human freedom, the human ability to "transcend" physical reality, and so on. The distinction also provided a realm for religion and human freedom and responsibility that would not be threatened by science. If the world from Aristotle to Aquinas had been largely defined by a single set of "natural laws," whether provided by God or nature, the new modern world would have to juggle two sets of concerns, one for bodies, one for the mind (one for the facts, one for values). From Descartes to Sartre, getting these two together would not be nearly so important as keeping them safely apart.

Spinoza, Leibniz, Pascal, and Newton

Much of "modern" philosophy has become defined by Descartes's arguments in metaphysics and epistemology concerning the nature and existence of God, the notion of substance, the justification of knowledge. This focus on metaphysics and epistemology has also dominated more recent approaches to philosophy. Some of those same concerns engaged those philosophers who followed and reacted to Descartes and his philosophy—in particular the Dutchman Baruch Spinoza (1632–1677) and the German Gottfried Wilhelm von Leibniz (1646–1716). They both followed Descartes's pursuit of reason into the realm of imaginative metaphysics. Playing off of Descartes's Aristotelian notion of substance, Spinoza and Leibniz came to dramatically different conclusions about what the world was really like.

According to Spinoza, since substances are by their very nature completely self-contained, there can be one and only one substance. That substance is God. God is therefore one with the universe, and the distinction between creator and creation, "God" and "Nature," is illusory. (This position is *pantheism*). All individuals, including ourselves, are in fact modifications of the One Substance.[72] The essence of a substance is an attribute, but there are infinitely many attributes, among them what we know as mind and body.

According to Leibniz, however, the same premise—that substances are by their very nature completely self-contained—leads to the conclusion that the world consists of innumerable simple substances. These simple substances are called *monads,* each of which is self-contained and independent of all of the others. God, on this view, is the super-monad, the Creator of all monads. Every monad is like a little self or psyche. It perceives the world—including what would seem to be interactions with other monads—from its own peculiar perspective. No monad, however, actually interacts with any other. Indeed, Leibniz insists that monads must be "windowless." A monad's "perceptions" are not perceptions in the usual sense but rather internal states that correspond to the internal states of all of the other monads in a "preestablished harmony," established by God.

It is difficult to think of these metaphysical images in Spinoza and Leibniz without conjuring up cartoonlike caricatures of what are surely absurd visions of the world. Perhaps this is what happens when the technical problems of metaphysics are cut off from their source in real human concerns. But the truth is that Spinoza and Leibniz were passionate men who were deeply moved by very human problems. Their metaphysical fiddling with "substance" was a vehicle for exploring much more demanding and difficult questions, and if we are to understand them, we have to move beyond the narrow disputes set by Descartes to a larger vision of the new humanism.

As we expand our portrait of these philosophers and this period, we might wonder what happened to all the other philosophers—and there were many—who pursued the ancient philosophical queries about life but did not really care for the increasingly abstruse formulations of metaphysics. Take, for example, Spinoza's exact contemporary Blaise Pascal (1623–1662). Like Montaigne before him, he emphatically rejected the scholastic confidence in the intellect and insisted, "The heart has its reasons, which reason cannot know." Because he had no metaphysics, however, he is typically ignored as a philosopher, except, perhaps, for a single famous argument that appears as a puzzle rather than a heartfelt dilemma. Thus it has primarily attracted the attention of game theorists and theologians.

The argument is Pascal's "wager," according to which it is (infinitely) more rational to believe in God than not to, on the grounds that the "payoff" if he exists is so enormous and there is no loss if he does not. (However, if one does not believe and He does exist. . . .) There is considerable controversy about how seriously Pascal, who denigrated the role of reason in matters of belief, intended this argument, and it is certainly not representative of his philosophical approach or his faith.[73] Nevertheless, in his *Pensées* (Thoughts), his deeply personal religious thinking, and his groundbreaking scientific and mathematical explorations, Pascal stands out as one of the superlative intellects of the seventeenth century.

Pascal was a genius—first a child prodigy who published breathtaking mathematical studies as a teenager and then a visionary who invented a calculating machine, the forerunner of today's computers. He was a scientist of the first rank and a philosophical–religious writer without peer. In 1646, when Pascal was still in his early twenties, he became involved with the austere Port-Royal movement and the Jansenists, who felt greatly removed from the world. In 1654, a profound religious experience completed a conversion in which philosophy came out the loser. He firmly rejected Scholasticism and "learned" theology.

The *Pensées*, published after his death, reveal his deeply personal religious thinking and his rejection of the philosophical rationalism that defined his times. Although he wrote some of the most remarkable treatises on the foundations of mathematics, he recognized the importance of those very human topics more often ignored by philosophers (except, of course, for Erasmus, Montaigne, and other humanists of the time). He worried about boredom, vanity, and human suffering. He lampooned the attempt to prove the truth of feelings by rational argument (and this, perhaps, is the more profound interpretation of Pascal's famous "wager" in the *Pensées*).

Like Montaigne, he took personal revelation to be the basis of the most important insights. Philosophy, according to Pascal, thus becomes a distraction, and it is for this reason, in all likelihood, that philosophers have largely ignored his work or dismissed him as a "merely religious" thinker (and, of course, a brilliant scientist–mathematician). Nevertheless, Pascal was one of the most powerful (if neglected) philosophers of modern times, fully deserving of the title, despite his own reservations.

The blame for such slights, perhaps, belongs to the historians of philosophy, who, like most accountants, prefer neat and tidy outlines as opposed to the messiness of human relationships. And so, a history has been invented. Three philosophers, united by their faith in human reason and jointly concerned with the

difficulties involved in understanding the technical Aristotelian notion of substance, constitute a tradition, which has come to be called *rationalism*. Descartes,
Spinoza, and Leibniz are the Rationalists. Other philosophers fit this description,
but to include them would disturb the tidy trinity.

The tidiness proved all the more satisfying because the three rationalists could
be neatly matched up with three other philosophers, the so-called *empiricists*, John
Locke, Bishop George Berkeley, and David Hume. Simply stated, empiricism
held that all knowledge comes from experience. Other philosophers also fit this
description, but—again—neatness is destiny. Making the list even more attractive, one of the empiricists was from England, another from Ireland, the third
from Scotland, and so Locke, Berkeley, and Hume could be conveniently grouped
as the "British Empiricists." Furthermore, one of the rationalists was from
France, one from Holland, and one from Germany, so Descartes, Spinoza, and
Leibniz are conveniently collected as the "Continental Rationalists." It is hard
to say how much damage this accountant's dream has done to our understanding
of modern philosophy. It not only oversimplifies the complex geography of ideas
in the seventeenth and early eighteenth centuries but makes it appear as if these
philosophers are only responding to one another along a few limited dimensions
of technical philosophical thinking. It encourages omitting altogether such edifying humanists as Montaigne, Pascal, and Rousseau, among many others.

We will get to the empiricists later on, and one of the first things we will
notice is that the distinction between rationalism and empiricism is of dubious
value, at best. But first, let us return to Spinoza and Leibniz. The picture that
emerges of these two brilliant human beings when we see them as more than
metaphysicians of substance is quite different from the one presented in most
philosophical commentaries.

Spinoza was a Jewish, freethinking individual whose skepticism did not appeal
to his orthodox brethren. He was excommunicated and, in effect, exiled from his
community. He spent most of his unhappy life in seclusion, earning a meager
living as a lens grinder. (Inhaling the glass dust eventually killed him.) Spinoza's
main work is called *Ethics*, a title that has often confused readers who have opened
the book expecting a philosophy of life and found instead a tangle of barbed
prose dressed up like an extended geometrical treatise, complete with axioms,
theorems, corollaries, and lots of "Q.E.D.".s.[74]

Appearances, however, can be deceiving. Descartes introduced his logical demonstrations in the cozy context of a meditation, inviting the reader into his study
and his thoughts, but Descartes's philosophy is anything but intimate and personally revealing. Spinoza, on the other hand, disguises his personal anguish and
his proposed philosophical solution in the most formal and formidable deductive
style. The book is, in keeping with its title, a philosophy of life, a heartfelt
proposal for a better way to live, a solution to loneliness and isolation, an answer
to the suffering and frustration of life. It is, in historical perspective, another in
a long line of Stoic texts, very much in the tradition of Chrysippus, Epictetus,
and Marcus Aurelius.

To be sure, Spinoza was attempting to carry out the Cartesian method in his
seemingly inappropriate use of the geometrical–mathematical method, and the

first two (of five) books of the *Ethics* are indeed attempts to establish the singular conclusion that there is and can be but one substance with infinitely many attributes. True, in a purely technical sense, this solves the troublesome mind–body problem (since mind and body are no longer different substances but just different aspects of one and the same substance). Spinoza's claims about substance, however, have much more important implications that cannot be understood in terms of metaphysical technicalities alone.

The first of these is that, in Spinoza's vision, there is no ultimate distinction between different individuals. We are all part of the same single substance, which is also God. That means that our sense of isolation from and opposition to one another is an illusion, and it also means that our sense of distance from God is mistaken, too. This edifying vision would become a powerful picture by the turn of the nineteenth century, when Christian philosophers would also try to overcome what they called "alienation" between people and peoples and the alienating conception of a transcendent God, a God "beyond" us. (Mystics, dating back to the earliest days of philosophy, have often claimed such a vision for themselves as well, though usually without the logical apparatus.)[75] Furthermore, since the One substance has always existed and will always exist, our own immortality is assured.

Spinoza makes generous use of Aristotle's notion of cause and the special notion, which Aristotle applied to God, of the "cause of itself" or *causa sui*. The Scholastics had employed this notion in the cosmological proof, and Spinoza predictably reproduces a version of that proof (and a version of the ontological proof as well). Yet Spinoza has something else in mind, and that is a defense of the thesis generally known as *determinism*. Determinism is the claim that, from a given cause, the effect follows necessarily. And yet, Spinoza's determinism is not particularly concerned with science but rather with what we would probably consider more akin to *fate*. On Spinoza's view, whatever happens to us happens necessarily. Given that the universe is God, we can therefore be confident that whatever happens to us happens *for a reason*.

This viewpoint is edifying, to be sure, but it is just the beginning. The stage is set for Spinoza's ethical prescription. He recommends seeing ourselves as One with God and other people and seeing our lives as determined by necessity. Spinoza attempts to prove these claims mathematically, yet he believes that the details of life count as much as the philosophical outlook that we adopt. Those details of life can best be summarized as matters of *emotion*.

The last three books, comprising more than half of the *Ethics,* are accordingly devoted to the study of the emotions. Many commentators simply skip them, since they do not add to the metaphysical framework established by the end of the second book. But if we are reading Spinoza as an extremely philosophical human being and not merely as a technical metaphysical wizard, his discussion of emotion is essential to his philosophy of life.

The early Stoics also paid careful attention to the emotions. They said that they were judgments, but faulty judgments, based on a flawed understanding of ourselves and the world. We can easily appreciate how Spinoza would readily agree with this. An emotion, he writes, is "a confused idea" through which the mind affirms its powers, affecting our desires via our bodies. We want what we cannot have, or we want what we already have (but do not know we have). Spinoza's vision teaches us that it is pointless to want that which we are not determined to have, and that much of what we want—union with other people, oneness with God—we already have. Most of our emotions are thoughts based on desires, typically bodily desires, and insofar as we are the slaves of our emotions and desires, we are passive and not in control of ourselves. But the "control" implied here is ultimately the control of one's attitudes, and the proper attitude is acceptance or resignation.

Unlike the ancient Stoics, however, Spinoza does not reject the emotions in general in favor of *apatheia* or apathy. Quite to the contrary, he assures us that the emotion that comes with an attitude of acceptance is *bliss,* and it is a far preferable emotion than any other, including the fleeting feeling of satisfaction of bodily desires. The feeling of power we gain, the feeling of control we get over ourselves, lies not in rebellion but in this philosophical vision, which Spinoza also calls the intellectual love of God.

Critics may well point out that this formulation of "God = Nature" is hardly orthodox theism, and, indeed, Spinoza's work was banned and he was branded an atheist for most of the next century and a half. Critics may also argue that choosing to accept Spinoza's vision is, if his determinism is true, not a choice at all. One necessarily agrees—or one does not. To dwell on these questions, however, is to miss the vision and the beauty of Spinoza altogether. Forget about the metaphysics of "substance." Spinoza brings us together with God and each other.

Leibniz was also worried about life and how to live, but in contrast to Spinoza's lonely life he was what we would call in this day and age a jet-setter. Leibniz knew everyone—the princes of Europe, all the great geniuses. (He even met Spinoza.) He invented the calculus (which was simultaneously discovered by Newton). He was a scientist, a lawyer, a historian, a statesman, an academic, a logician, a linguist, and a theologian. (His one published work, during his lifetime, was a book on theology.)

Philosophy was for Leibniz a continuing hobby, and he was involved in philosophical discussion and correspondence throughout his life. Whether out of prudence or indifference, he published very little, and much of what he published has been misunderstood. From a philosophical point of view, Leibniz has mainly been considered a logician and a metaphysician. What is more moving is Leibniz's optimistic outlook on the world, an outlook that must be viewed in the context of the horrible wars and religious disputes that racked Europe in the seventeenth century.

Leibniz famously suggested the development of a universal language, a universal logic in which all problems could be resolved by bloodless, rational calculation. He defended as the basic principle of his philosophy what he called the "Principle of Sufficient Reason," which, as in Spinoza, gave him reason to assert that nothing happens without a reason. Since all reasons are God's reasons and God determines the universe (by creating the monads and their perceptions), we can feel confident that these reasons are *good* reasons—in fact, the very best reasons.

This is one of Leibniz's best-known theses, but perhaps it is best known because it was brutally ridiculed by Voltaire in *Candide*. It claims that, given His infinite number of choices among different possible worlds, God would only choose the best of them, *the best of all possible worlds*. Leibniz's logic may be debatable but the vision is unassailably edifying. In times of turmoil, it is always a relief to believe that there is some reason behind whatever happens. And here is another classic answer to the ancient problem of evil. What we see as evil is due only to our limited vision, our failure to understand the sum total of the possibilities. If it is hard for us to appreciate Leibniz's hopeful belief at the end of our own particularly cynical century, that does not mean that we should not appreciate its power for those who did believe it, or reduce their visions to mere logical puzzles.

No account of early modern philosophy would even get started if it did not include at least some mention of the greatest physicist of the time—many people would call him the greatest scientist ever—Sir Isaac Newton (1643–1727). Newton's physics is beyond the scope of this book, and so is the theology with which he occupied himself for the last several decades of his life. But Newton's impact on science and his example to the world were so much a part of the eighteenth century that no account of philosophy is possible without appreciation of his importance. Furthermore, the tension that so troubled Newton, between his material and mechanical physical theory of the world and his pious, spiritual Christianity, was a tension that was now starting to preoccupy all of Europe as well.

Until the late seventeenth century, science had been an occasional annoyance to the religious authorities, but there was little sense that it would ever constitute an overwhelming threat to religion. The threats to religion had (supposedly) come from within, as one religious faction battled another over some small point of theology (and, often, some significant piece of land or political advantage as well). Science had come into its own, however, and it was no longer the source of mere annoyance and contradiction. The scientific worldview stood head to head against the established religious worldview, no longer David against Goliath. In many sensitive, inquisitive personalities, the apparent conflict between the two was becoming unbearable. Newton was one of those personalities.

Scientific debate overflowed the boundaries of science and poured into the larger world of philosophy. One such debate involved two no less distinguished figures than Newton and Leibniz, and the topic was nothing less than the very nature of space and time. Newton's physical theories, which concerned the movement of bodies and their effects on one another, presupposed a set stage on which these various movements and interactions would occur. That stage was space, and space was considered to be an infinite, empty void, in which various objects, from planets to pebbles, would take their places. Time was an endless and beginningless stretch that extended from the infinite past to the infinite future. Various events would take place now and then, according to whatever standard of temporal measurement one wished to apply.

Leibniz would have none of this. Space was nothing in itself, nor was time. These claims would follow from his metaphysics: monads as spiritual entities are not located in space, and time is internal, not external, to the monads' perceptions. Quite apart from Leibniz's metaphysics, however, the idea of "absolute" space invited the nonsensical question, "Where is space?" So, too, one could ask, "When does time begin?" or, if time has no beginning (or end), one could ask "In what dimension of time does time go back (or forward) forever?" With an eye to the Principle of Sufficient Reason, one could ask, "Why would God have created the universe here, rather than somewhere else?" All such questions are nonsense, according to Leibniz, but they are the sort of nonsense that reveals some deep conceptual problem. For Leibniz, space and time were strictly "relative," relative to bodies, relative to events, respectively. Space is coexistence, time is order of succession. What these claims would mean, in terms of the nature of knowledge as well as the very nature of the universe, would emerge dramatically toward the end of the century, in the philosophy of Immanuel Kant.

The Enlightenment, Colonialism, and the Eclipse of the Orient

With the rise of science and its emerging victory over the authority of the church, Europe entered into a celebration of a new faith, faith in reason. The so-called *Enlightenment* emerged first in England, following fast on the scientific achievements of Isaac Newton and the swift and relatively bloodless political changes of the "Glorious Revolution" at the very end of the seventeenth century. It then moved into France, carried by young intellectuals like Voltaire who had visited England, and it culminated in the French Revolution of 1789. Then it spread south and east to Spain, Italy, and Germany, where it ran into considerable opposition from the church and more traditional ways of thinking.

The Enlightenment as such was not antireligious—in fact, some of its most prominent participants were religious men (and women). But, following Descartes and the new science, the Enlightenment philosophers put great trust in their own ability to reason, in their own experience and their own intellectual autonomy, and this was bound to result in some opposition to the church and its more authoritarian teachings (which the Enlightenment philosophers called "superstitions"). In place of the sectarian battles that had bloodied the past several centuries, the Enlightenment philosophers insisted on being "cosmopolitan," citizens of the world, ignoring national boundaries, rejecting sectarian affiliation. Their truths would be universal truths, not imposed on others but to be discovered independently by them.

Quite a few of the French philosophers, in particular, were atheists, materialists who saw no place in the rational order of things for an authoritarian God. What all of the Enlightenment philosophers did agree about and believe in, however, was reason. Through reason, they believed, they would not only tap the basic secrets of nature through science but would also establish a living paradise on earth, a society in which there would be no more misery, no more injustice:

> How consoling for the philosopher who laments the errors, the crimes, the injustices which still pollute the earth and of which he is often the victim, is this view of the human race, emancipated from its shackles, released from the empire of fate and from

that of the enemies of its progress, advancing with a firm and sure step along the path of truth, virtue and happiness![76]

There was a dark side to this new optimism and prosperity. The riches and affluence that made the Enlightenment possible came from the toil of others. Not unlike the aristocracy of Aristotle's Greece, the elite members of European culture built their position on the backs of slaves. Even John Locke, the great defender of natural rights, owned slaves.

The European invasion of Africa began around 1415 when the Portuguese sought spices and gold on the African continent. They brought missionaries with them, bent on converting new souls to Christianity. By the late fifteenth century, however, the Portuguese were seizing Africans to sell as slaves. By the early sixteenth century, the Portuguese had conquered the trade routes to Asia that had previously been run by Africans, Asians, and traders from the Middle East.

Other groups soon followed the Portuguese and invaded non-European lands that they considered "unowned" and therefore ripe for the taking. The Spanish demurred from defying a papal bull that gave Portugal exclusive rights to the spice trade with lands to the east, but they sought the same markets by heading west, beginning with the expedition of Christopher Columbus. Although Columbus did not reach his intended Asian destination, the Spanish were not deterred from pursuing the new sources of wealth they found. They discovered gold and silver in the Americas in the early 1500s, and this motivated their conquest of the Aztecs and the Mayas. Missionaries came in the wake of the Spanish *conquistadors*, urging the victims to abandon their cultures in favor of Christianity. Little time elapsed between the "discovery" and exploration of these foreign lands and the rationalization of conquest as an effort to save these "heathen" souls.

Although the primary interest of the first colonizers was to siphon precious metals and raw materials from their new American "colonies," steady supplies of these goods depended on the development of mining and agricultural facilities in the New World. Dissatisfied with the work they were able to coerce from their American captives, the colonialists provided a new market for African slaves. The English, Dutch, and French all eventually joined the Spanish and Portuguese in seeking wealth by means of conquest and the establishment of colonies. By the late sixteenth century, the European superpowers, eager to displace each other in dominating their colonial ventures, had begun a series of proto–world wars that would span three centuries.

By the 1660s the Dutch controlled the Asian spice trade, and they were central players in the gold, silver, and slave trade. Throughout the eighteenth century, the British and the French colonized North America, making increasing inroads into Native American territories and expanding the market for African slaves. The French also invaded northern Africa and India in the eighteenth century, although the British dislodged them from India in the 1760s. The British lost their American colonies in the American Revolution later in the century, but they continued their expansion, eventually declaring Australia, New Zealand and a large number of Pacific islands British colonies as well.

Meanwhile, those parts of the world that were not subjected to colonial exploitation—for example, China, Japan, and the Middle East—prudently sealed themselves off from the West. They thereby became more "mysterious," "inscrutable." They were romanticized; they became symbols of exotic wisdom, sensuality, spirituality. Thus began the phenomenon that Edward Said has called "orientalism."[77] Montesquieu's *Persian Letters* (1689–1755) convey something of this attitude toward foreign lands. But, like so many romances, this romantic attitude would eventually turn vicious, depicting the Other not as infinitely more spiritual but as infinitely less so. This attitude would become a hallmark of the supposed "universalism" of the West. Here, for example, is Hegel, in his *Philosophy of History* (which appeared in the 1820s) inaccurately describing Chinese society: "Its distinguishing feature is, that everything which belongs to spirit—unconstrained morality, in practice and theory, heart, inward religion, science and art properly so-called—is alien to it. . . . While *we* obey, because what we are required to do is confirmed by an *internal* sanction, there the law is regarded as inherently and absolutely valid without a sense of the want of this subjective connection."

The "eclipse" of the Orient, of course, was not that at all, any more than an eclipse of the moon is, in fact, the disappearance of the moon. The Middle East and much of Asia were just positioned in such a way that those in Europe could no longer see them, nor did they care to. The security of their own prejudices was at stake. "Cosmopolitan" would continue to mean the unity and universality of humanity, but only on European terms.

Locke, Hume, and Empiricism

In England and the world of philosophy, John Locke (1632–1704) reacted critically to Descartes's uncritical confidence in reason. He suggested that, instead of abstract reason and speculation, we should place our confidence in experience, in our ability to learn and know about the world through our senses. (It was Locke's philosophy, in particular, that young Voltaire had carried back with him to Paris.) With Locke, the enduring tradition of British *empiricism* begins, jettisoning the long-standing suspicion of the senses that had persisted in the West since before Plato. Locke suggested that "all knowledge comes from the senses," and in this he was soon followed by the Irish bishop George Berkeley and the Scottish philosopher David Hume.

Locke was a physician, a practical man who had too little time for "the obscure terms" and tedious arguments of the Scholastic tradition. He was also a political man. By 1683 he had become so involved in British politics that he was forced into exile in Holland, where he befriended William and Mary of Orange, who would soon take over the throne in England (after the "bloodless" revolution of 1688). He subsequently wrote two of the most influential treatises on government since Plato's *Republic*. Unlike Plato's republic, however, Locke's new political world would be defined by the relatively recent notion of *human rights*—in particular, the right to private property.

Locke's empiricism is founded on a single, all-purpose principle: *All knowledge begins with experience.* This, he claimed, was a matter of "common sense," as opposed to the obscurity of the Scholastics and the complex schemes of the rationalists (Descartes, Spinoza, and Leibniz). Nevertheless, Locke assumed the central Cartesian metaphor, the distinction between the mind and the body, and he accordingly held that knowledge is concerned, first of all, with the examination of the mind. We inspect (or "introspect") our ideas, and we thereby infer the way the world is. As opposed to the rationalists, who assumed a rather rich and complex structure of the mind, Locke to the contrary assumed that the mind was a "blank tablet," which would be written on by experience throughout one's life. The rationalists argued for a fair number of inborn or "innate" ideas. By contrast, Locke suggested that the mind is more like an empty closet, which is illuminated only by the light that enters from the outside.

Experience gives us *sensations,* Locke argued, and from these sensations our *understanding* allows us to derive various new and more complex ideas. From sensations and our reflection on the ways our minds operate on sensations, all of our knowledge is derived. Locke compromised his empiricism, however, in at least two critical ways. First, he yielded to the metaphysicians he attacked in accepting the idea that we find it necessary to talk about things-in-themselves, apart from our experience of them. In this, Locke accepted the old Aristotelian notion of *substance.* One might think that Locke, according to his own method, should have concluded that all that we are ever aware of—and all that we can ever know—are the sensible properties or "qualities" of things. The thing "behind" the properties is never sensed, never experienced. But this would leave us with a problem: it would seem that we do not know things at all, only clusters of sensation that we suppose to be the properties of some thing. Locke's conclusion is that we *infer* the existence of the thing-itself, the substance, because we cannot imagine the notion of properties existing without their being properties of something.

Locke made a second compromise in his empiricism when he distinguished between two different kinds of properties or qualities: those which we perceive as inherent in an object itself, such as its shape or mass, and those which we perceive *in ourselves*—that is, in the effects that a thing has on us. An example of the latter would be color.

Locke was a pioneer in the psychology of perception, and he was one of those who made significant advances in our understanding of the apparatus of vision and the effects of light on the eyes. Accordingly, he concluded that what the light does is stimulate the eyes and the mind in certain ways, and we then "see" colors.

These *secondary* qualities (as opposed to the primary qualities of shape and mass) should be said to be "in us" rather than "out there," in the world. If one took Locke's arguments seriously, however, one might conclude that they should apply to all qualities, even to the notion of substance itself, insofar as any such concept could be justified. Everything that we experience, one might argue, is in the mind, in us, and there is neither a need nor a justification for talking about the world "out there."

Bishop George Berkeley (1685–1753) drew precisely this uncomfortable conclusion from Locke's own insistence on a purely empirical method. Berkeley was quite happy to suppose that there was no substantial world apart from the world in our minds. The world was indeed composed of ideas—a position subsequently known as *idealism*. As an authority of the church, Berkeley saw in this view a way of placing God at the core of his philosophy. We might also note how closely in spirit, if not in "method," his vision of a God-centered world, surrounded by infinitely many finite minds, resembles the "monadology" of Leibniz.

Locke was also a religious man, but in his philosophy of knowledge he had rather pulled God out of a hat, so to speak—for where in our experience is there justification for any such grand belief about the world beyond our senses? In order to defend his belief in God, Locke falls back on traditional Scholastic arguments—for instance, on the argument that nothing comes from nothing, and since we exist, we can be certain of the existence of God, our Creator. Berkeley, however, sees a different way to establish God's existence, one which he shares with Leibniz but which is also compatible with strict empiricist principles.

If there were no "external" world to serve as cause of our sensations, where would our sensations and our ideas about the world come from? It is God who must provide them, Berkeley argues. "To be is to be perceived," he insists, but everything that exists must therefore be perceived, all the time, by God. (It was regarding Berkeley's philosophy that some wit formulated the old gambit, "If a tree falls in the forest . . ."

Perhaps what is most remarkable is the fact that Berkeley's philosophy, which denies the material existence of the world, held onto the Lockean claim to be merely a matter of "common sense." (How often, in philosophy, would the appeal to common sense end up in nonsense.) The English Doctor Johnson thought that Berkeley's idealism was hardly common sense at all, and kicking a stone he commented to a friend, "Thus I refute him." This was, of course, no refutation, but a tangle of common sense and philosophical nonsense was becoming once again intolerable. What was starting to become obvious were the very uncomfortable consequences of the split between mind and experience, on the one hand, and the body and the physical world on the other.

David Hume (1711–1776) brought these consequences fully into the open. Hume's philosophy was a thoroughgoing *skepticism*, the likes of which had not been seen since the ancients. Indeed, Hume considered himself something of a pagan, and he achieved quite a reputation for himself in that regard, both in Paris, where he was acknowledged as the *bon vivant* of the Enlightenment, and in Edinburgh, where he was denied a university position because of his atheism. Whereas most of his colleagues had wholly grown up in the crisscrossing worlds of the new science and old-time religion, Hume had steeped himself in the classics as a young man. He aspired to emulate Isaac Newton by developing a complete theory of the mind, but behind the scientific façade was a more mischievous ambition.

Hume was one of the most brilliant of the Enlightenment enthusiasts, but he also recognized that reason—understood both as scientific method and as rationality more broadly conceived—had overstepped its reach. There is much, he saw, that reason cannot do—assurances it cannot deliver, proofs it cannot produce.

Hume's skepticism was, paradoxically, the clearest example of solid, self-scrutinizing Enlightenment thinking. His conclusion was that even the best thinking cannot do what the Enlightenment thinkers thought it could do.

As a self-styled pagan, Hume tended to naturalism, to the idea that what reason could not do, nature would do for us anyway. If reason cannot guarantee us knowledge, nature nevertheless provides us with the good sense to make our way in the world. If reason cannot guarantee morals, our human natures nevertheless supply us with adequate sentiments to behave reasonably toward one another. And if reason cannot justify the belief in God and the religious prejudices that go along with it, then so much the worse for religion. If the learned tomes of Scholasticism do not succeed in providing sound arguments or good evidence for such beliefs, then "commit them to the flames," pronounced Hume, infuriating the theologians. Luckily, he did not prescribe the same harsh treatment for other unprovable beliefs, such as our belief in the existence of the world and our belief in the importance of morals.

Hume's skepticism is based on a number of doctrines that had emerged from the debate about knowledge that now had gone on for a century. First of all, Hume was an avowed empiricist. All knowledge, he repeated, must come from experience. Second, he accepted the dualism of mind and body, the distinction between experience and the world to which it refers. Third, he accepted the exclusive distinction between two acceptable kinds of argument, those that were based on the facts of the matter and those of a purely deductive nature. Hume condemned the arguments for religion because they failed to succeed as either of these.

Our most basic beliefs, however, the very presuppositions of knowledge, also fail to pass the same two-part test. Can our belief in the "external" world (and the causal "cement" that holds that world together) be established by way of experience? No, because it is at least conceivable, as Descartes had argued a century ago, that we might simply be dreaming. Closer to home, it was at least conceivable, as Berkeley had argued only a few years before, that the world is nothing but the world of our ideas. Could, then, our belief in the "external" world (and causality) be established by way of deduction? If so, from what premises, without simply begging the question?

Hume concludes that the most basic beliefs, upon which all of our knowledge is founded, cannot be established by reason. Similarly, in the realm of morals, Hume applies his skeptical eye and concludes, "It is not against reason that I should prefer the destruction of half the world to the pricking of my little finger." Reason cannot justify or motivate us to behave. Nevertheless, our emotions can and do so. Each of us is born with a natural capacity for *sympathy* and a natural concern for *utility*, with which we construct, among other things, our ideas about justice and society.

Similarly, with respect to aesthetic values, we have a natural capacity to respond emotionally to beauty. "There is no disputing over taste," insisted Hume, but nevertheless he argued that the best artwork is that which stands the test of time and inspires "durable admiration," stirring aesthetic sentiments in observers beyond the period that produced it. We notice here, as in Hume's politics, a certain conservatism, an appeal to tradition in place of his lost Enlightenment appeal to reason. Reason, after all, has its limits. In its place, Hume (like Aristotle) defends the importance of individual character—a good upbringing, cultivation of the virtues, a respect for traditions. Reason may have its limits, but our sentiments and our natural common sense, cultivated through our social traditions, have power and virtue that have too long been neglected in the overly scientific atmosphere of modern philosophy.

The empiricists, with their emphasis on experience, are best remembered in the schematized version that has come down to us from the nineteenth century. They are opposed to the "rationalists," and to the rationalists' confidence that reason will provide us with certainly true, nontrivial knowledge of the world. The rationalists believed that there were "innate" ideas (that is, ideas that are literally "born into" us). The empiricists deny the existence of any such ideas.[78]

But what is most curious about this debate, which is often said to define modern Western philosophy and most "modern philosophy" courses, is how utterly restricted it seems, given the unlimited scope of philosophy as well as the larger enthusiasms of the Enlightenment and the times. Moreover, even the most limited exposure to science (especially the science of the fifteenth and sixteenth centuries) makes it obvious that virtually every scientific hypothesis requires knowledge of *both* mathematics and the facts, so why go to so much trouble to defend the importance of one of these against the other? (Bacon, in particular, had stressed both the empirical and the mathematical aspects of scientific learning.)

On the one hand, the battle between rationalism and empiricism seems like a family quarrel, with two closely related senses of reason (reason as reasoning and reason as confirmation through experience) pitted against one another over the question of innate ideas. But on the other hand, no one doubted that the mind was born with certain capacities or "faculties" already prepared to gain knowledge and experience. The real question was only *what* particular capacities were inborn, and this would certainly depend on a good deal of experimentation and observation, not the abstract arguments of philosophers.[79]

The real force of the dispute, however, was not concerned merely with the issue of innate ideas and the method by which certain foundational beliefs could be justified. By focusing their attention on this particular issue, the rationalists and empiricists together managed to eclipse unthinking dogma and superstition, which by contrast were deemed ridiculous. They gave themselves the opening to attack archaic political and economic structures that impeded progress and encouraged intolerance. They were arguing for universal human capacities of reason, whether empiricist or rationalist in flavor, which would combat the provincial prejudices and mutual hostilities that had killed so many millions and still divided Europe and Europeans against one another. Modern philosophy was not an extended debate about ontology, epistemology, and metaphysics. It was a defense of humanism and reasonableness, a plea for lively conversation instead of deadly massacres.

Irrationality was their true target. The Enlightenment was not about the nature of knowledge so much as it was a defense of knowledge and inquiry. "Dare to know!" wrote Immanuel Kant, the most illustrious German champion of the Enlightenment. The debate between reason and experience was a strategic technical distraction within the bounds of this cosmopolitan movement.

The debates carried on by the philosophers regarding the nature of society and human rights, in particular, were anything but academic. Locke's two treatises on government established the language of basic rights, including freedom of expression, religious tolerance, and freedom to own private property, which would become the focal point of two revolutions, first in the British colonies, then in France. Locke's theory of *natural* rights is especially powerful because, instead of making ownership, mutual tolerance, and freedom the product of prior agreement between people, a "social contract," these rights *precede* all such agreements. A person has the right to a piece of property, for example, because he (or she) "mixes his labor with it." The purpose of contractual agreements, including a constitution and laws of property, is to guarantee those rights. But the rights themselves belong to us by nature. They are "inalienable." They cannot even be given (or sold) away. (Despite such principles, Locke nevertheless owned slaves, as we mentioned. He thus set the standard for a common form of philosophical hypocrisy that would become more evident in the next century, in the new United States.)

The idea that a person was entitled to property, not by law or custom but by "natural right," provided the solid foundation for what would later come to be called *capitalism*, although it might be well worth noting that Locke by no means defended excess and unlimited acquisition. The Protestant revolution had already provided the "work ethic" that legitimized a worldly emphasis on success. A number of philosophers, not only Locke but Hobbes and later Hume, Rousseau, and Kant defended the conception of society as a "social contract," further destroying traditional authority (such as "the divine right" of rulers) and supporting the new emphasis on individual will and self-rule. The new-found wealth of the new world provided the fuel for one of the greatest economic revolutions in history. Like all revolutions, it was both stimulated and spurred on by philosophical ideas.

Adam Smith, the Moral Sentiments, and the Protestant Ethic

The new commercialism had been changing the face of Europe since the Renaissance, but it had not yet been defined. The old feudal order was long gone, with its self-enclosed systems of obligation and exchange, and the new commercial society, an increasingly open society, depended upon money as a medium of exchange in a way that would greatly alter not only economics but the very nature of society. As international trade became the source of considerable wealth, the great nation-states turned more and more to the newly respectable "middle class" of bankers and merchants. With more wealth in the treasury, the kings and queens of England, France, Holland, and Spain could afford more ships, more arms, more exploration, more colonies, which in turn would mean more wealth and more power.

Even the church, long hostile to commerce in general and "usury" (profitable money-lending) in particular, shifted its ground and accepted—and with the Calvinist reformation, encouraged—the new commercial consciousness. But this nation-based system of trade, called *mercantilism*, was itself only a stage in the development of the new economic order. Not only nations but individuals would become enormously wealthy through manufacturing and trade. The new economic order, which was already in full swing with the industrial revolution in England, needed a proper philosophy.

Calvin and Locke, in particular, had stimulated the thinking which was essential to the new business world, but profits were still widely viewed (as they are still viewed today in post–Soviet Russia) as immoral products of pure self-interest. In order for the new attitudes toward money, wealth, and commercial property to be legitimated, economic self-interest would also need a new defense. As long as the wealth of a nation was defined by the money in the royal treasury, the aspirations of the individual would remain on the defensive. And so long as commerce was still defined by a guildlike mentality, assuring quality but also minimizing competition, both individual initiative and industrial cooperation would be hampered.

Adam Smith (1723–1790) was David Hume's best friend and closest colleague, and it is perhaps revealing that he paid little or no attention to the themes that would come to constitute the definitive "Hume": his fascination with problems of knowledge and his skepticism; his Newtonian ambitions to develop a general theory of the mind; and his narrow focus on the logical and the empirical (which would later develop into the dismissive philosophy of "logical positivism"). What Smith shared with Hume was his love of history and literature and a conservative concern for the nature of what we would now call "liberal" society, with its definitive (if controversial) institution of "private property." Most of all, Smith shared with his friend Hume a deep sense of the ultimate importance of ethics and human nature. Nevertheless, he is best known, and in some corporate cathedrals still worshiped, as the father of the free-enterprise system. In 1776 Smith published his "bible" of capitalism, *Inquiry into the Nature and Causes of the Wealth of Nations*. It was the beginning of modern economics and what we might call the philosophy of the free-market system.

In *Wealth of Nations* Smith first redefined the meaning of the phrase "wealth of nations." It does not refer to the amount of money in the king's treasury. It refers to the prosperity of the nation as a whole, the well-being of its citizens. Moreover, self-interest can be defended in the following ingenious way. Suppose a society needs a new kind of implement, say, a tool to fix a common problem with some other newly invented and already popular commodity. In the face of such demand, inventors and manufacturers will fall over themselves to get an appropriate product on the market. They will be motivated not by altruism but by self-interest. The first one to do so makes an enormous amount of money and also makes an important contribution to society.

But, now, suppose there are several such products on the market, some better than others, some cheaper than others. Consumers, looking out for their own self-interest, will tend to buy the best product for the price, thus enriching those who can produce better quality for less and, in effect, driving out of the market those who lack either quality or efficiency. Or, better, forcing them to improve both their quality and their efficiency. On the whole, everyone is better off. Thus the law of *supply and demand* assures that, with time, the best and cheapest products will earn the richest reward, and the overall interests of both consumer and manufacturer will be optimized. It was a simple idea, an elegant and a radical idea. Self-interest could serve the public good.

This did not mean that self-interest should now be considered a virtue, however, and there is nothing in Adam Smith that would support the "greed is good" mentality of the 1980s. Still, one can easily imagine what a breath of fresh air the citizens of the late eighteenth century must have experienced when they were told, after two millennia of carping about the evils of money and the sins of avarice, that self-interest had its benefits, not just for one but for all.

The keys to this "magic of the market" were the consumer, who through his or her "sovereign" commercial demands drove the whole system; and the new specialization of labor, which allowed great efficiency by splitting the production of goods into separate steps and coordinating the work force accordingly. What was necessary for the system to work was that government, which had hitherto controlled or regulated virtually every major commercial transaction, should not interfere. "*Laissez faire*" (leave us alone) was the language of the day. It also meant that the guilds and guildlike corporations would no longer monopolize industry. Enterprise would now be "free."

On the basis of *Wealth of Nations*, Smith has been widely cited (mainly by those who have not read him) as the classic defender of commercial individualism, of the power and virtue of sheer selfishness, of the joys of profit-seeking and the wonders of commercial business society. The truth is that Smith, years before he wrote *Wealth of Nations*, wrote another book, an account of human nature in terms of the moral sentiments. Smith was concerned, as was Hume, with the gentler human *feelings*, with the motives that moved men and women and allowed them to live together in society. He took as his starting point the Aristotelian ideal that what is most essential to ethics is the development of character and the cultivation of those social sentiments that allow us to live together harmoniously.

In his book *The Theory of the Moral Sentiments* Smith writes,

How selfish so ever man may be supposed, there are evidently some principles in his nature, which interest him in the fortune of others, and render their happiness necessary to him, though he derives nothing from it except the pleasure of seeing it. Of this kind is pity or compassion, the emotion which we feel for the misery of others. . . . The greatest ruffian, the most hardened violator of the laws of society, is not altogether without it.

Smith and Hume thus attacked the "selfishness" theories of Hobbes and others and argued for the naturalness of the exemplary moral sentiment, *sympathy*. In common parlance, sympathy means "feeling sorry for" someone. Smith uses the term rather as "agreement of emotion," or what we would call "empathy." Sympathy so conceived is thus not actually a sentiment but rather a vehicle for understanding other people's sentiments, "a fellow-feeling with any passion whatever." It is an act of imagination by which one can appreciate the feelings of another person by "putting oneself in his place." Thus, despite the booming thesis of *Wealth of Nations*, people are not essentially selfish or self-interested but instead are essentially social creatures who act on behalf of others as well. A decent capitalist system would only be possible in the context of such a society.

Several years earlier, Hume had developed a theory of sympathy and justice, which greatly influenced Smith. Hume defended sympathy as a universal sentiment that is sufficiently powerful to overcome self-interest, at least in a great many cases. Indeed, Hume takes sympathy to be a form of benevolence, a feeling for one's fellow citizens and a concern for their well-being. But, according to Hume as well as Smith, sympathy is too often countered and overwhelmed by selfishness and, for this reason, a further sense of *justice* is required. Smith takes this sense of justice to be a natural revulsion at harming one's fellows. Hume takes it to be an "artificial" virtue which is constructed by reason for our mutual well-being. Nevertheless, it is a mutually advantageous conventional "scheme" that is so beneficial that it becomes inseparably associated with the moral sentiments. What could be more basic to these sentiments than our sense of the general good for everyone, "a feeling for the happiness of mankind and a resentment of their misery"?

Voltaire, Rousseau, and Revolution

The two most famous and influential philosophers of the French Enlightenment—and two of the most important events in the eighteenth century—are often left out of the standard accounts of Western philosophy. This omission is telling. The American and French revolutions (in 1776 and 1789, respectively) were both momentous and tortuous spectacles, and both were, in part at least, revolutions of ideas, upheavals provoked not only by bad government but by ideas of justice and injustice, ideas about the nature of society and about human nature, too.

Rousseau and Voltaire were both self-styled philosophers of the Enlightenment, but neither had any patience for metaphysics and epistemology. They confined their attention to less abstract and more practical matters such as politics and education. Consequently, they had enormous influence on their tumultuous times.

Voltaire (1694–1778) admired the English Enlightenment and Locke's political philosophy in particular. He imported both back to France, using them to attack both the French government and the Catholic Church. This elegant self-styled *philosophe* did not write what most philosophers consider to be philosophy, preferring to express himself in polemical essays, political commentary and criticism, and stories of an imaginative variety.

Above all, Voltaire defended reason and individual autonomy and delighted in pricking the hot-air balloons of metaphysics and theology in his day. In this he set the stage for Hume, many years his junior, and he set in motion the middle-class (or, more accurately, *bourgeois*) demands for reform, which would set the stage for revolution in France.

Jean-Jacques Rousseau (1712–1778) was a more subtle and complex thinker who, unlike his older contemporary, did not shy away from grand theories of human nature and society. His early essays, in which he challenged the alleged benefits of "civilization" and defended the life of contentment in an affluent and very un-Hobbesian state of nature, made him famous and began to shake up the staid and self-satisfied aristocracy of Europe. In such books as *Emile* and *The Social Contract* he elaborated his theory of human nature as "basically good" and his conception of human society, in which we do not band together out of mutual insecurity (as Hobbes had suggested) but rather realize together our "higher" moral natures. The state of nature was not, as Hobbes had said, "nasty, brutish and short." Presocietal human beings, Rousseau assures us, were essentially happy and content, "indifferent" if not sympathetic to others. Children should be educated "naturally," he argued, in order to develop this higher sense of morals on the basis of their natural dispositions, in their own way and at their own pace. They should not be straitjacketed into the often "unnatural" mores of society. As "citizens" and as participants in the "General Will" of society, we are free to impose the law on ourselves and, even in the context of society, remain independent, as we once were in nature. But if someone were to refuse to participate, Rousseau ominously suggests, it might be necessary to "force him to be free."

Happy as it may have been, the state of nature was no place to cultivate and exercise the human virtues. Accordingly, Rousseau finds no contradiction in his attempt to retain both our natural sense of independence and our mutual commitment to make and to obey the laws of society. Nevertheless, our original entry into society was itself neither willful nor happy. From our independence and contentment in the state of nature, humanity took a fall. A catastrophe took place, which was the beginning of society as we know it and the beginning of our unhappiness. Someone fenced off a piece of property and declared, "This is mine!" No greater crime has ever been committed in the history of humanity, according to Rousseau. From the establishment of private property came the whole litany of inequalities and injustices that have ruled human life.

In this condemnation of private property, Rousseau could not be more opposed to Locke, and in the battle for the minds of Europe and America, the two would often appear in confrontation. In America, already a land of lawyers, farmers, and businessmen, it was clear that Locke would win out. In France, at least for a short time, Rousseau would hold his own. But in both revolutions the Enlightenment assumption was the reality and importance of natural rights and independence. In society we can enjoy these rights and independence, but without necessarily sacrificing the blessings of nature by way of the social contract.

The social contract is not, of course, an actual historical event. It is a philosophical fiction, a metaphor, a certain way of looking at society as a voluntary collection of agreeable individuals. The terms of the social contract, accordingly, define the ideal society as one in which we willingly impose the law on ourselves. We are self-governing and, as in the state of nature, we remain free and independent. Thus the central Western ideal of individual autonomy is rendered compatible with the legitimacy of the state, and the ideal of the natural goodness of humanity replaces the age-old notion of "original" human sin. Then came the American and French Revolutions.

In America, Thomas Jefferson (1743–1826) took up a number of European concepts, in particular from Locke and from the Scottish Enlightenment. As the primary author of the American Declaration of Independence, he happily included the idea of self-evident truths (self-evident, that is, to those who were in a position to see them); the moral-sentiment theorists' emphasis on fellow feeling and the development of character; and the idea of natural human rights, including the rights to life, liberty, private property, and "the pursuit of happiness." With Jefferson, the new invention of the political philosophers, "the people," becomes central to politics. Self-reliance becomes the primary civic virtue, and it becomes the responsibility of government to make sure that everyone has sufficient education and property to allow the development of a self-reliant civic character. Education thus becomes not a privilege but an individual right and a political necessity. Religious freedom is no longer just a matter of mutual toleration but also a matter of rights and social tranquility. Government is no longer a matter of divine privilege or mere might but of popular legitimacy.

The Declaration of Independence was not only a justification of revolt against English colonial rule. It was also a spectacularly well crafted endorsement of Enlightenment principles. The revolution was not only a rejection of "taxation without representation"—Americans have not shown much love of taxation even with representation. It was a vision of an entirely new form of government, one which, as a later American president would with equal eloquence sum it up, is "of the people, by the people and for the people."

The Constitution and the Bill of Rights, which were drawn up after the War of Independence, constituted perhaps the first genuine instance of a social contract—not a fiction, not a metaphor, but an actual agreement, arduously negotiated and actually signed by "the people" or their representatives. The Constitution actually "set up" a government and the rules for distribution of power. The Bill of Rights, consisting of the first ten amendments to the Constitution, explicitly forbade the (federal) government from interfering in the lives of the citizens. The ideas may not have been new, but their implementation was indeed a novelty and a new model for the world.

Was the American War of Independence a "revolution"? In the sense that revolutions literally turn things up-side down, no, it was not. It was the comparatively untraumatic booting out of a government already far removed and somewhat indifferent to their troublesome new world holdings. England was embroiled in a hundred-year war with its neighbors, and the American theater was but one concern among many. The American War of Independence, accordingly, was but a scene in an international war, as the French, the Dutch, and the Spanish took advantage of this added irritation in the far-flung British Empire.

There was no drastic shift of power. The men who made the revolution were already leaders beforehand and remained the established government after the revolution as well. One could live in the American colonies in the midst of the seven-year war and pay it little attention—and many did. For a good many American businessmen, farmers and households, the difference between colonial rule, rebellion, and independence was just a matter of detail.

In France, by contrast, what began as a shift of power (from the aristocracy to the *bourgeoisie*, or "middle class") turned into a firestorm. Every aspect of life and every part of the country was profoundly affected, torn apart, threatened, and seduced with promises. Conservatives around the world were horrified. The creation of a National Assembly, representing all classes, including the "third estate,"[80] promised to introduce cooperation and harmony in place of bitter class divisions, but it would soon fail.

The revolution began with a Declaration of Rights, including the right to life and the right to resist oppression. Thomas Jefferson, visiting Paris as the American ambassador, predicted a gradual improvement in the monarchy and the establishment of a truly representative government.

The third estate, however, was itself an unwieldy amalgam of classes, the new, increasingly prosperous and powerful bourgeoisie, the workers, the farmers, the small shop owners, those urban peasants called *sans-culottes*, as well as the perennially poor, the perpetually unemployed, and assorted street riffraff and criminals. It was not long after its first easy successes and the largely symbolic attack on a hardly used ancient prison called the Bastille that cracks in this coalition became painfully apparent.

By 1792, the revolution had taken a violent turn. Representatives of "the people" fomented local uprisings and led the country into a bloodbath. Maximilien Robespierre and Jean-Paul Marat, devoted followers of Rousseau, pushed to implement their mentor's notion of a "General Will" on a populace that seemed primarily set on historical revenge. The king and then the queen were executed by guillotine. Then followed "The Terror," which would eventually claim the lives of its own Rousseauian architects.

In England, Thomas Carlyle wrote that the extreme violence of the French Revolution did not come to an end "until all the fuel was done." When it was done, the country lay in ruins. The monarchy was all but dead. Much of the old aristocracy had fled the country. In 1795 France was on the verge of anarchy within and invasion by its neighbors when appeared a young Corsican colonel named Napoleon Bonaparte. By 1800, the Enlightenment and its ideals were about to begin another new chapter.

Immanuel Kant: Saving Science

Back in Germany, the Enlightenment (or *Aufklärung*) was greeted with some suspicion, and the French Revolution was viewed (from a safe distance) with horror. The Enlightenment was rightly viewed less as a universal or cosmopolitan philosophy than a projection of the reigning ideas in London and Paris, a bit of intellectual imperialism. The Revolution in Paris was not viewed as the triumph of philosophy but rather as the eruption of chaos. It would still be more than a decade before the fruits of the revolution would seriously affect the Germans.

Nevertheless, the scattered and disunited German states had a right to be defensive. Their language and their culture had too long been treated as barbarian and second-rate. The arts were mainly imported. Local talents were often ignored. Even the king of Prussia spoke mainly in French! In Germany the new ideals born of science and universal rationality played, in general, a secondary role.

Still, the Enlightenment did have its philosophical champions in Germany. Leibniz, for instance, was not only an active proponent but a spectacular example of the new Enlightenment spirit. He was steeped in the new science, a pioneer of the new mathematics and the new rationality, a cosmopolitan of the highest order. But then, he spent much of his time traveling throughout Europe and carrying on an enormous amount of correspondence with scholars in every country.

The ultimate philosophical champion of the Enlightenment within Germany was Immanuel Kant (1724–1804), a student of a student of Leibniz (named Christian Wolff) as well as an enthusiastic follower of Newton's physics and Rousseau's radical new theories of society and education. Unlike most of his countrymen, he was also an enthusiastic supporter of the French Revolution, albeit from a very safe distance in East Prussia, even during the terrible years of the Reign of Terror. But what got him most deeply involved in the Enlightenment project was a different revolution, one that began with his encounter with David Hume's skepticism.

Hume's skepticism awakened Kant from his "dogmatic slumbers," that is, his uncritical acceptance of Leibnizian metaphysics. Kant, among many other things, would answer Hume's troublesome skepticism and, accordingly, save the Enlightenment from its own ceaseless questioning.

However, Kant also recognized the limits as well as the power of reason, and his culminating work in philosophy consisted of three great "Critiques" of reason and judgment. From one rather limited perspective, we might say that Kant provides what can be seen as the culmination and synthesis of both rationalism and empiricism, at the same time rejecting the underlying idea that our knowledge of the true world is either inferred from experience or discovered by way of reason. So construed, Kant would be a figure of limited philosophical interest, another intellectual technician concerned only with the furious debates of his fellow philosophers.

Kant's genius was devoted to far larger questions, to the great ideas he summarized as "God, Freedom, and Immortality." Put more historically, Kant marked the definitive juncture of the confrontation of religion and science, a conflict that had been growing more acute ever since the Middle Ages.

The Enlightenment had more than its fair share of atheists, including Hume, who would dismiss religion as childish superstition. Voltaire had once boasted,

"I'm tired of hearing about twelve men who made Christianity. I would like to show that one can destroy it." There was the Frenchman Baron d'Holbach, who proclaimed that the world consists of matter only, like early Democritus, leaving little room for God. But Kant was a devout Christian, a Pietist Lutheran, and his faith was unshakable. He was also a firm believer in the new physics of Isaac Newton. How could these two be reconciled?

Newton himself, of course, spent the last decades of his life trying to answer much the same question, but for Kant, the answer became obvious. One must "limit knowledge to make room for faith," he declared, much in line with the already well established Cartesian move to separate the realm of science from the realm of faith and freedom. He confessed, "Two things fill me with awe, the starry skies above and the moral law within." Kant's basic move in philosophy was to separate the starry skies and the moral law and search for reason in (and beyond) both of them.

Nevertheless, neither science nor religion is limited *within* its own separate sphere. The basic principles of science—which Hume had questioned with his skepticism—would be shown to be "universal and necessary," known a priori. The existence of the external world, complete with causal relationships and the explanatory apparatus of science, could be shown to be known beyond doubt. At the same time, the realm of God and the immortality of the human soul, together with human freedom and moral obligation, would not be compromised by science. Causality and the substantial world of science had their place, as *phenomena* in the world of our experience. But God, freedom, and immortality—morality too—had their place as well, their own "intelligible" world, a world quite independent of experience but, nevertheless, equally ruled by reason.

Reason, the watchword of the Enlightenment, would in fact be the primary player in Kant's supremely rational philosophy. Science would be demonstrated, against the efforts of Hume, to be rationally justified. Morality would be shown to consist of universally obligatory moral laws. Even faith, so often taken to be the epitome of irrationality (or, at least, beyond reason) would be defended as rational, justifiable belief.

Kant's strategy, first of all, was to distinguish the realm of experience from that which transcended experience, what was usually called "metaphysics." The problems of metaphysics seemed unresolvable, he suggested, because the limits of knowledge are the limits of experience, and metaphysical problems by their very nature transcend experience. Some of these questions, notably those all-important questions concerning God, freedom, and immortality, could be answered, he insisted, but not as matters of knowledge. They are matters of reason, but *practical* reason, "postulates of morality." They are not like the truths of science. (We will return to these in a moment.)

Once he had thus distinguished the world of experience, the world of knowledge, from the questions of metaphysics which transcend experience, Kant could then go on to explore the nature of these two realms. In science, he would prove the necessary existence of the external world, complete with causal relationships and the explanatory apparatus of science. In morality, he would establish the universal obligations of the moral law, or what he calls "the categorical imperative," and its postulates, human freedom and the basic beliefs of any rational religion.

The problems of knowledge and the foundations of science are addressed in what many philosophers take to be the greatest single book in philosophy, Kant's magnificent *Critique of Pure Reason*, first published 1781. Within the realm of phenomena and the world as we know it, experience presupposes *sensibility* (or "intuition") and *understanding*, that "faculty" which orders and organizes our sensations with the help of the *imagination* so that they become an experience *of* something.

According to Kant, we "constitute" the objects of our experience out of our intuitions, locating these objects in space and time and in causal relationships with other objects. Without the concepts of the understanding, Kant famously suggests, our intuitions would be blind. But without sensations, he says, our concepts would be empty. Experience is always the application of the understanding to sensations, and the world as we know it is the result.

Some of our concepts, however, are not derived from experience (that is, "empirical") but rather *precede* experience. They are *a priori*. They are part of the built-in structure, or, if you prefer, the basic rules of the human mind. These are called "categories." The category of substance, for example, is the rule governing every human experience that requires that sensations be organized in such a way that we experience material objects.

Here is Kant's answer to Locke and, more generally, his answer to both the rationalists and the empiricists. Substance is not inferred from properties. It is the principle of organization according to which we experience a thing and its properties to begin with. To his squabbling colleagues, Kant suggests this synthesis of their claims: all of our knowledge begins with experience (and is based on sensations), but the basic categories of our experience are not learned from experience but instead are brought to experience, as a priori organizing principles.

Here, too, is Kant's response to Hume's skepticism. The external world is not inferred from our experience but (as a basic category of our thinking and perceiving) is essential to the constitution of our experience. Causality, another category, is also not derived or inferred from our experience but imposed, as another of the basic rules of perception.

Not all of the most basic or a priori structures of the mind are concepts or categories. There are also a priori "forms of intuition," certain dimensions that every experience must have. In particular, these are the dimensions of space and time. We cannot have any experience that is not within the bounds of three-dimensional space and irreversible one-dimensional time. Here Kant answers Leibniz and Newton on the question of absolute versus relative space. Space is "absolute" if by that you mean that it is an inescapable framework for all and any experience and as real as the world itself. It is "relative," however, if by that you mean that it is ultimately the product of our own subjectivity, our way of viewing the world, rather than a property of the world in itself.

The discovery of space and time as a priori forms of intuition allows Kant to make an even more radical suggestion concerning the nature of mathematics, those disciplines whose necessity had so impressed the Greeks and which modern philosophers had more or less taken for granted as consisting of "truths of reason." The propositions of mathematics and geometry, according to Kant, are necessarily true because they are, in effect, formal descriptions of the a priori structures of time and space, respectively.

Kant's new "idealism" was, needless to say, an extremely radical view of our knowledge of the world.[81] Without going quite so far as to say that we actually create our world (a thesis which some of the Romantic post-Kantians would happily endorse), Kant is suggesting that we do not in any sense have to infer or prove the nature of the world "outside of" us. We impose the basic rules of organization, the fundamental nature of that world, and so the skeptical idea (or even the purely philosophical doubt) that the world might not resemble our experience of it no longer makes any sense. We can be mistaken about details, of course. We misperceive, misinterpret, miscalculate, misunderstand, but about the basic principles, those Descartes had methodically but unsuccessfully doubted and which Hume insisted lie beyond the powers of reason, we cannot be mistaken.

But if we organize or "constitute" our world, could we not do so as we please? Could we not choose to perceive a world with four or five or any number of dimensions of space? Could we not reverse time? Could we not choose to see the world as Leibnizian monads or insubstantial Berkelean ideas? The answer, according to Kant, is a flat "no!" We do not choose the sensations that form the basic material of our experiences, nor can we choose any alternative to three-dimensional space and irreversible one-dimensional time. Nor could there be different sets of categories, different ways of organizing, interpreting, or "constituting" our experience. The categories that form the basic structures or rules of the mind are universal and necessary. There are no options, no alternatives. To prove this Kant offers us a formidable "Transcendental Deduction of the Categories," showing not only that the categories are necessary for every experience but that there could not be any alternative view of the world. It is a remarkable combination of radical rethinking and conservative support of our common sense and scientific view of the world.

Nevertheless, the argument cannot stop here. What about God, who has thus far remained quietly to the side of Kant's argument? God does not know the world through sensations, and certainly He is not bounded by the finite rules of the understanding. God knows the world immediately (that is, not mediated through the senses and through concepts). He knows it as it is *in itself*, not as phenomenon and according to the limited rules of our experience. Furthermore, this idea of the world-in-itself still survives as a limiting concept in our own thinking. If, after all, we can talk so confidently about the world as constituted in our experience, it at least makes sense—indeed it seems inescapable—to ask, "What could the world be like apart from the peculiarities of our experience?"

Moreover, given that we do not choose our own sensations, which are given to us (thus "data," or "given"), what causes these sensations in us? Is it the objects themselves (as Locke had argued)? Is it God (as Berkeley and Leibniz had argued)? But notice that the notion of causality is inappropriate here. As one of the categories, it rules all relationships *within* our experience. Between our experience and the world in itself, that is, outside of our experience, it does not apply. Nevertheless, the nagging question, "What about the world as it is in itself?" remains.

There is also the question of Kant's conception of the self. He denies that the world is outside of our experience, but he also denies that the objects of the world are *in* our experience—that is, "in us." They are, by their very nature as objects, outside of the self. What, then, is the self? The self is, first of all, an activity, or an enormous set of activities, imposing the categories on sensations received and coming to understand the world. This self is not a thing, a "soul," or even a "mind" but rather the *transcendental ego,* and its operations are inherent and recognizable in every experience whatsoever, although it is itself never experienced.[82] It is what Descartes recognized, but then misconceived, as the "thinking thing" that he took to be himself.

There is also that more ordinary conception of oneself as a person, however, as an embodied, emotional intelligence that has features, friends, a history, a culture, a context. This is what Kant calls the *empirical* self. It is known, like anything else in the world, through experience. But in addition to the transcendental and empirical selves there is also what we might awkwardly call "the self-in-itself." This is the self that acts as an agent, the self that deliberates and acts, the self that is moral or immoral, responsible or irresponsible, the self that lives at the heart of the practical world.

It is important to see that Kant's notion of the world in itself (and the self-in-itself) is not just an afterthought, a dangling question in his otherwise-coherent philosophy (as some of his successors took it to be). It serves an all-important function. If science and knowledge are limited to (but unrestricted within) the phenomenal world, then outside the phenomenal world, that is, in the world as it is in itself, there is room for freedom and an infinite place for God. These are the topics addressed in Kant's second critique, *The Critique of Practical Reason,* and linking the first two is a third, the *Critique of Judgment.*

Kant's Moral Philosophy and the Third Critique

Kant granted to common sense that the world and our selves had a reality in addition to what we experience. He described this reality as "noumenal," in contrast to the "phenomenal world," the world as we experience it. He also called the reality that is beyond our experience "the thing-in-itself," reminding us, with his use of the singular, that we are so far from directly encountering it that we cannot analyze it into components. By formulating this distinction between the noumenal and the phenomenal worlds, Kant establishes the absolute boundary of our knowledge. We can know only the world of our experience. We can have no knowledge of whatever is outside the realm of our experience, of reality as it exists "in itself."

Yet we have already seen that Kant does allude to the reality outside our experience. Why does he not consider this to be a contradiction? To answer this question, we must return to the issue that led Kant to distinguish the empirical self and another practical or "intelligible" self and their "two worlds." That issue is the question of how we can be morally free in a world in which we are subject to the lawlike regularities of nature.

This issue had become increasingly pressing over the prior few centuries. More and more, science seemed capable of predicting and controlling events within the natural world. This development led many to wonder whether the same control could be possible with regard to human behavior. After all, human beings were part of the natural world. Could people also be controlled, like so many of the new machines? To avoid this specter of *determinism,* Descartes and his predecessors had sharply distinguished the self from nature. Some of the Enlightenment philosophers, however, enthusiastically embraced determinism, embracing the analogy "man the machine."

Kant himself intensified this concern about determinism when he claimed that the world of our experience is necessarily and universally structured by causality. Since human behavior occurs within the phenomenal world, it would seem to be subject to causality as well. But if human behavior is caused, then it would seem to be determined—and thus not free. If we do not exercise freedom in our behavior, however, we do not seem to be responsible for our actions or capable of moral choices.

Kant addresses this issue in his second critique, the *Critique of Practical Reason.* He contends that we are both part of the phenomenal world and capable of free moral choice. He resolves the apparent incompatibility of these claims by contending that we have both noumenal and phenomenal existence. As part of the natural world—as empirical self—each of us is subject to causal influences. These influences manifest themselves in the form of desires, moods, felt needs, and emotions, which Kant collectively calls "inclinations." Inclinations "naturally" lead to actions. If a person desires food (since some time has elapsed since his last meal) and desirable food is put before him, he will feel inclined to eat it.

Not all actions are motivated by the inclinations, however. People have the capacity to *will.* They have "will power," and this will is *free.* It is not part of the phenomenal world. Every person has a noumenal existence, an intelligible self, that is not determined by phenomenal causes. The intelligible self is able to resist inclinations. Thus, we can choose not to eat food even when we desire it— for example, if the food in question is on someone else's plate, is thought to be poisoned, or is presented as temptation in the middle of a hunger strike.

Because of our noumenal existence, we are not passive pawns of natural forces. We are able to regulate our behavior in accordance with our own law, the law that our reason constructs for itself, *the moral law.* According to Kant, we demonstrate our freedom precisely when we act in accordance with this moral law. We are unfree, on the other hand, when we simply follow the causal dictates of nature.

Kant is convinced that, because we all have the same faculty of reason within us, we will reach the same conclusions regarding morality. In general, reason tells us that we should resist inclination when we cannot endorse the same type of behavior on the part of others in similar circumstances. Thus, we should not take food off another person's plate unless we are willing to consider this an acceptable principle of behavior for everyone. A moral principle is one that allows this form of impersonal universalization. Furthermore, morality requires that we respect the rationality in others, their essential *humanity*, or what we sometimes call their *dignity*. In other words, morality, like knowledge, has an a priori aspect, a set of considerations that precedes any particular circumstances.

Kant formulates the basis of the moral law in what he memorably calls "the categorical imperative," a singular command that applies across the entire range of human behavior. (In fact, he postulates a number of such formulations, but he contends that these are ultimately equivalent, dictating the same moral conclusions.) The categorical imperative, according to the best-known formulation, asserts that *one should only act on a maxim* (or principle) *that one can will to be universal law.*

Another of Kant's formulations of the categorical imperative summarizes the moral law as follows: *One ought always act so as to treat humanity, in oneself or in another, as an end in itself, and not as a mere means.* In other words, it is always wrong to use another person as a mere instrument to reach one's own objectives. To do so is to "use" a person and so show disrespect for that individual's dignity, dignity derived from the fact that he or she is capable of acting freely in accordance with the dictates of reason and morality.

Kant's ethical theory, with its emphasis on human freedom, does not explain morality in religious terms. In fact, Kant was adamant in his insistence that morality must provide its own justification and not depend on religious sources or sanctions. Thus, although Kant himself was quite religious, his moral theory is compatible with a secular or atheistic perspective. Yet, Kant wanted to establish room for faith along with freedom. So how does religious faith fit into Kant's moral theory?

One may not need faith to recognize the moral law, according to Kant, but faith is necessary for our rational motivation to obey the moral law nevertheless. It is what Kant's hero Rousseau had called "a moral vision of the world." Without faith, our experiences of injustice are bound to discourage us away from morality. We see evildoers who seem happy, while very moral people suffer. In order to persist in our commitment to morality, we need to believe that, ultimately, moral behavior converges with happiness. And it is not enough that this be "wishful thinking." Like morality itself, it must be a rational belief.

These considerations lead us to "postulate" the existence of God, the immortality of the human soul, and an afterlife. This allows us to believe that moral goodness and happiness ultimately belong together, not as a "reward" but as a rational necessity. Although we can have no *knowledge* of these "postulates of practical reason," since they pertain to the world outside of our experience, practical reason, which dictates the moral law, nonetheless requires these notions. Although these beliefs do not count as knowledge, they are nonetheless rational. Reason, not knowledge, points us in the direction of religious faith.

Kant pursued the relationship between our mental faculties and the natural world, but in an entirely different way, in his third critique, the *Critique of Judgment.* There he considers the nature of aesthetic experience, especially our experience of the *beautiful.* He considers the apparent conflict between two commonly held views about aesthetic taste. On the one hand, there seems to be no way to adjudicate disputes about taste, which seems to be purely "subjective." On the other hand, we generally expect others to agree with our judgments of taste; someone who claims that something is beautiful expects others to see it as beautiful as well.

Kant reconciles the tension between the two by claiming that the experience of beauty is *universally subjective.* As a person's experience, it is a subjective experience, occasioned by the "free play" of the imagination and the understanding. In the pursuit of knowledge, imagination integrates the data of sensation into unified objects, while understanding interprets these objects in terms of its concepts. Understanding allows us not only to see something but also to recognize it as the kind of thing it is. In aesthetic experience, however, imagination and understanding collaborate, not to the usual end of assigning a definite classification to an object, but by "playing" with the object, bringing various facets into temporary focus. This activity is inherently enjoyable, and it is also profound. It is not, like most of our other activities, undertaken with any further purpose in mind, but rather simply for its own sake. We are justified in assuming that our aesthetic experiences of beauty have a universal aspect because anyone can use his or her cognitive faculties in this way.

Kant considers other modes of aesthetic experience besides the appreciation of beauty. In particular, he analyzes the *sublime,* the aesthetic appeal of objects that are too massive or too dynamic to be fully comprehensible to the human faculties—the innumerable stars on a very dark night or a close-up view of Niagara Falls. Our enjoyment in these cases, Kant claims, is based on our recognition that reason is only able to master such recalcitrant "objects" by conceiving of infinity or totality—even though our imaginations are inadequate to encompass the spectacle. We gain a further sense of our dignity as rational beings in this way, while at the same time experiencing our relative insignificance in the natural scheme of things. Thus, we are "overwhelmed" by a magnificent seascape, which reminds us of an infinity we cannot comprehend.

Beauty, Kant tells us, is ultimately a "symbol of morality." In assuming the necessary stance to engage in "free play," we must be "disinterested." In other words, we must ignore any practical motives or inclinations that we have and instead contemplate the object without being distracted by our desires. (One should not be tempted to eat the fruits depicted in a still-life painting.) In a sense, therefore, the stance that we take toward the beautiful object is similar to that which we take toward other human beings when we are properly respectful of their dignity.

The beautiful is also the symbol of the moral in a larger sense. It encourages us to believe that nature and we ourselves are part of an even larger design. This sense of order in a beautiful object is not translatable into a formula or a recipe (which is why Kant insists that *genius* is essential to artistic creativity). This notion of a larger design, the belief in a *teleology*[83] in which every aspect of the phenomenal world has its place in a larger purpose, draws our thoughts toward a supersensible reality. Ultimately, Kant believes that the orderliness of nature and the harmony of nature with our faculties guide us toward an even more profound religious perspective, a sense of the world not limited to knowledge and freedom or even to faith, in the ordinary sense of the term. It is a sense of cosmic harmony, perhaps not reminiscent of Aristotle and his Christian interpreters but looking forward to some of the most dramatic philosophical visions of the nineteenth century.

The Discovery of History: Hegel

G. W. F. Hegel (1770–1831) was nineteen years old when the French Revolution began, just across the border and not far from his home in Stuttgart. Like many young men in Germany, he had followed the Enlightenment and the events in France with a cautious enthusiasm. The world was changing. The world was becoming "modern." In 1806, as Hegel was just beginning his philosophical ascendancy and completing his first book, Napoleon was at the height of his powers, promising (or threatening, depending on your point of view) to unify Europe and initiate a new era of internationalism. In fact, Napoleon's greatest battle took place by the town of Jena, in which Hegel was then teaching. Hegel actually saw Napoleon after his victory, "world history on horseback," he would later write.

Philosophically, Hegel greatly admired and emulated Kant, but the significance of his philosophy went far beyond the academic battles that were then being fought in Kant's wake. Hegel summarized the trauma and euphoria of his age. He announced the birth of a new world, which was now manifesting itself in philosophy as well as in international politics. Now that the *Weltgeist*, or "World Spirit," was about to enter into this new era, philosophy, too, was about to achieve its final goal, the all-embracing comprehension of history and humanity.

It is often said that Hegel added a new dimension to the enterprise of philosophy, namely, its history. To be sure, other philosophers had generously or critically referred to their predecessors, but the idea of a true history of philosophy, that is, the idea of philosophy as a progression, as an organic enterprise, that was an exciting idea whose time had come. Hegel's philosophy was a self-conscious attempt to transcend the various distinctions and warring camps that had defined philosophy for the past two and a half millennia. All such distinctions must be seen in the larger context of World Spirit, Hegel insisted—as local scuffles and disagreements rather than as definitive contrasts. Secularism and monotheism, science and spirit, reason and passion, individual and community— all find their place, as concepts that may be useful in certain contexts and may conflict in certain instructive ways.

The conclusion of Hegel's philosophy, although sometimes stated in the arrogant language of "the absolute," simultaneously suggests a kind of grand philosophical humility, the awareness that we are all part of something much greater than ourselves. Our individual contributions to knowledge and the truth can never be definitive but will always be partial, "mediated," and one-sided.

The philosophers that followed Kant in Germany collectively called themselves "idealists," indicating first of all that they were loyal to Kant and, second, that they shared his view that the world was constituted by us and regulated by reason. But exactly what Kant's thesis was, concerning the constitution of the world, and how that fit into his overall view of philosophy, that was a matter of ongoing and sometimes bitter dispute. In the final years of the eighteenth century, while Kant was still alive and very active, dozens of young philosophers fought to be his true successor. Foremost among them were Johann Fichte (1762–1814) and Hegel's college friend Friedrich Schelling (1775–1854). Each would make a name for himself in the shadow of Kant, trying to "complete Kant's system."

The idea of a "system" comes from Kant, who aspired to provide a unified and all-encompassing "science" of philosophy. According to Fichte and Schelling and several other philosophers who greatly admired Kant, he had not succeeded. He left us rather with a fragmentary philosophy which, however stunning, failed to show the unity of human experience. In particular, Kant left a gaping abyss between his conception of knowledge and his theory of morals, and so left the human mind as if cleft in two.

Moreover, Kant's conception of the thing-in-itself, while in fact central to his philosophy, was greeted by these post-Kantians as an oversight, a mistake, a flaw that threatened to undermine the whole critical enterprise. For example, the idea that there could even be an intelligible conception of things as they are in themselves and not as phenomena—that is, as experienced by us—left room for the skeptic to dig in his or her wedge with the challenge, "How can we know that we really know anything at all?" In his philosophy, therefore, Hegel would argue against the very intelligibility of skepticism, against the intelligibility of any conception of the thing-in-itself as distinct from things as we know them, and against the bifurcation of human experience into incommensurable separate realms.

Fichte made a reputation for himself as a radical, an incautious sympathizer of the French Revolution and, later, he was accused of being an atheist (which he fiercely denied), causing a considerable scandal. Later still he would become one of the first great spokesmen for German nationalism. Philosophically, however, he set out to reconcile what seemed to be the warring factions of Kant's philosophy and synthesize them into a unified system.

Kant objected, predictably, that his philosophy was already complete and unified and he did not need any help from these young enthusiasts. But Fichte took the very science-minded philosophy of the first *Critique* and the moral philosophy of the second and declared, in effect, that one must *choose*. The scientific worldview, which Fichte considered vulgar and "dogmatic," was not the choice he recommended. The moral point of view, or what he enthusiastically recommended as "idealism," was by far the better choice. "The kind of philosophy one chooses," Fichte moralized, "depends on the kind of man one is."

Borrowing freely from the first *Critique*, Fichte argued that we constitute the world as a moral stage, on which we then display our valor and our virtues. The world is indeed the product of our categories, but it is a mistake to think that these categories are essentially concerned first and foremost with knowledge. They are primarily concerned with action, with our freedom, and we "posit" the world in order to prove ourselves within it.

It was, without doubt, a dramatic interpretation of Kant. Kant, of course, utterly rejected it. Young Schelling admired it but recognized its limitations. In particular, Fichte's philosophy left out not only science but also nature. It was all action, no substance. And so Schelling developed his own philosophy to "complete" that of Kant, emphasizing the importance of nature and, in particular, the various concepts through which we constitute and understand nature.

Schelling, like Fichte, pushed Kant's notion of "constitution"—and in fact his entire philosophy—much further than the old idealist would be willing to go. For Schelling (as for Fichte), there is a sense in which we actually *create* our world, but, to make this both more plausible and more complicated, it is not as if we do this as individuals. Rather, all of us together, as a unified "will" or "spirit," create the world. Schelling cautiously identified this unified Creator with God. (The Romantic philosophers loved this suggestion and took on Schelling as their philosophical champion.)

The idea of "completing Kant's system" dominated philosophy at the turn of the new century. Hegel's first professional article—published in a journal he edited with Schelling—was a comparison of the systems of Fichte and Schelling in the light of the Kantian philosophy. As a young man, Hegel was educated in a seminary but seemed to have no religious inspiration. His earliest philosophical essays were somewhat misshapen, blasphemous attacks on Christianity, including a piece entitled "The Life of Jesus," which went out of its way to make Jesus into an ordinary human being, an eccentric moralist who, in his Sermon on the Mount, espoused Kant's categorical imperative.

Unfortunately, young Hegel seemed to have little philosophical talent either. His friend Schelling was world-famous before Hegel seriously set pen to paper, and Hegel's best ideas were directly borrowed from another college friend, the poet Friedrich Hölderlin. Indeed, it is still sometimes suggested that Hegel's philosophy is ultimately the translation of Hölderlin's spiritual poetry into the cumbersome language of German philosophy.

Hegel's earliest (unpublished) essays, in addition to being blasphemous, were surprisingly easy to read. The style was crisp, concrete, and ironic. There was a noteworthy absence of jargon and obscurity. There was no attempt, in other words, to imitate Kant and the new academic style. But it seemed that the way to philosophical success was to imitate Kant—not his genius, or even his ideas, but his ponderous, sometimes tortured, style. Around 1800 Hegel decided that he, too, would like to reenter university life, and so he adopted the obfuscating style for which he has since become famous. With Kant, philosophy had become resolutely an academic discipline. (It has never recovered.)

In 1807 Hegel published his first—many would say his greatest—book, *The Phenomenology of Spirit*. It represents a magnificent conceptual odyssey that carries us from the most elementary to the most all-encompassing and complex conceptions of human consciousness. Its stated purpose is to reach the truth— the "absolute" truth—but the term "absolute" does not mean "final and finished," nor does the term "truth" refer to "the facts." What Hegel is after is an all-encompassing vision, and this will include not only a variety of philosophical theories about the nature of knowledge but material from religion, ethics, art, and history as well.

The central concern of the *Phenomenology* is the nature of "Spirit" (or *Geist*), the cosmic soul that encompasses all of us and all of nature as well. Indeed, the only "absolute" in the conclusion of the *Phenomenology* is this sense of all-encompassing Spirit. It is not as if all disagreements are resolved, all disputes are settled, all questions are answered. It is rather that, no matter how difficult these disagreements, no matter how bitter these disputes, and no matter how unanswerable the questions, we are all in this together. Napoleon only aspired to unify the world. Hegel actually did it—in theory, of course; but nevertheless, the idea of an all-embracing consciousness is the first step toward achieving it.

The first part of the *Phenomenology* is concerned with the questions of knowledge that had so obsessed modern philosophy from Descartes to Kant. Hegel, in effect, says, "Enough of this." He accepts Kant's theory as a refutation of skepticism. He decries the exclusive focus on questions of knowledge to the neglect of other questions about human history, culture, art, ethics, religion, and happiness. He rejects, even in Kant, the atemporal treatment of knowledge (and everything else) and the timeless conception of the categories.

Knowledge, Hegel insists, *develops*. Like Aristotle, he takes biology and the organic as his paradigm, not physics and not mathematics. Consciousness, too, is not timeless, nor is it just the transcendental perspective from which or within which we gain knowledge of the world. Consciousness grows. It develops new concepts and categories. It finds itself torn between one "form of consciousness" and another, and it learns to reconcile them or, in any case, move beyond them. Consciousness and knowledge are dynamic. They are a *dialectic* (see Part I). They grow through confrontation and conflict, not by way of mere observation and understanding.

At the beginning of the *Phenomenology*, Hegel considers the "common sense" notion of knowledge that he calls "sense certainty." It is the theory—if it deserves to be called a theory—that we simply perceive things. It is the commonsense view that things are just there, to be seen, heard, touched. We know them through our senses, and of that we can be certain. Elevated to the level of a philosophical theory, we simply know, prior to any description or understanding, what it is that we experience. Our experience is immediate and *unmediated*.

Hegel demonstrates that such a conception of knowledge is hopelessly inadequate and needs to be supplanted by a more comprehensive and sophisticated conception (or "form of consciousness") which appreciates the fact that all of our knowledge is in fact mediated, that is, filtered through concepts and already determined in part by the senses. Thus in a few quick steps, Hegel brings us from "naive realism" through a number of theoretical variations in which we can recognize the major insights of Leibniz and some of the empiricists to the philosophy of Kant's first *Critique*, in which knowledge is demonstrated to be a mediated form of understanding.

But this is not enough. Knowledge by itself is inadequate. Suppose, Hegel suggests, we have different sets of competing categories. Or suppose, borrowing from one of Kant's central theses, we can nevertheless draw an intelligible distinction between the world as we know it and the world in itself. Suppose, Hegel mischievously suggests, that the real world, the world-in-itself, consisted of properties exactly opposed to the properties of the world of our experience, so black is white, good is evil, and so forth. How could we possibly make sense of such a suggestion? How can Kant defend a conception of action that wills in one world and actually changes things in another? The "two worlds" notion, Hegel therefore concludes, is reduced to nonsense.

Similarly, what about the possibility of two different phenomenal perspectives, two sets of categories, or two opposed theories—for instance, the Leibnizian and Newtonian pictures of the world? Hegel's response is very contemporary, and it can be read as an appeal to *practical* considerations. Kant's first *Critique* folds into the second, and questions of knowledge find themselves facing the interests of life and the dictates of desire. The choice between theories, he suggests, is practical and not based on theory alone.

It is here that consciousness develops into self-consciousness and the *Phenomenology* makes an abrupt turn to "self-certainty." Like the chapter on "sense certainty," this begins with a commonsense, cocksure conception of the self—in this case, Descartes's maxim, "I think, therefore I am." Hegel goes on to show that the Cartesian self is not certain at all. In modern terms, Hegel will go on to argue that the self is *socially constructed*, created by society in interpersonal interaction. As in the preceding chapters, Hegel brings us from a naive view to a more complex and sophisticated philosophical standpoint. In its confusions of desire, the self gets monumentally confused about itself, until despair can finally find its way to "absolute" self-affirmation.

The problem of selfhood provokes the best-known and single most dramatic chapter in the *Phenomenology*, the parable of "master and slave." Told in the most stark and minimalist terms, in the parable two "self-consciousnesses" confront one another and fight for mutual recognition. In a battle that is (almost) to the death, one wins, one loses. One becomes the master, the other the slave. Each gets recognition and thereby identifies himself through the eyes of the other.

Hegel tries to show us that, first, selfhood develops not through introspection but rather through mutual recognition. That is, the self is essentially *social*, not merely psychological or epistemological. Hegel is also concerned to show the nature of a certain kind of interpersonal relationship, presupposed by many philosophers (for example, Hobbes and Rousseau) in their hypotheses about the "state of nature." The common assumption is that human beings are first of all individuals and only later, by mutual agreement, members of society. Hegel thinks that this assumption is nonsense, because individuality begins to appear only *within* an interpersonal context. What people basically want and need is not only security and material comfort but *recognition*. Any other view of human nature will miss the essential complexity of human existence.

Throughout the *Phenomenology* Hegel displays inadequacies in one form of consciousness after another, guiding us from one view or attitude to another in an ongoing "dialectic." From the unhappy conclusion of the master/slave parable—it turns out that both the master and the slave are miserable—we are led through various philosophical strategies for coping with or evading the difficulties of life (Stoicism, Skepticism, asceticism, and certain forms of Christianity). When we finally get to "Spirit," which is the beginning of the (very long) culmination of the *Phenomenology*, we come to understand that not only do we mutually define ourselves through recognition and the roles that we play, but we identify ourselves, ideally, all together. We do this in our sense of ourselves as a moral community, and we do it in our conceptions of the world and ourselves through religion. Ultimately, we are all one "Spirit," and recognizing this all-important truth is the "absolute" end of Hegel's philosophy. Politically, we can understand the end of the dialectic as *freedom*, not just freedom from constraint but the freedom to be ourselves, as individuals but also as much more.

Nevertheless, the dialectic of the *Phenomenology* proceeds by way of conflict and confrontation. Periodically we hit a contradiction, and occasionally a dead end. Tragedy, for instance, exemplifies the impossible conflict when one form of consciousness contradicts another. Hegel's favorite example is Sophocles' play *Antigone*, in which Antigone's duty to bury her brother and obey the divine law of the family conflicts with the orders of her king and civil society not to do so. The conclusion of the play represents reconciliation and synthesis, but this hardly helps Antigone, who is already dead. The dialectic is bigger than mere individuals, and it will demand its victims.

An example of a dead end is the French Revolution, which Hegel uses as an illustration of how uncontrolled "negative" freedom ends only in self-destruction. It is in reaction to this excessive individuality that Hegel then turns to the more "communitarian" spiritual sensibility from which he will evolve his political philosophy.

Hegel intended his *Phenomenology* as the "introduction" to a larger system of philosophy. The *Phenomenology* was supposed to establish the standpoint of absolute knowledge from which the system itself, the "completion" of the work begun by Kant, could be formulated. Indeed, Hegel even promotes the new age he celebrates as "the end of history," that is, the end of the long development of universal self-recognition. That task occupied him for the rest of his career. The philosophical system to which the *Phenomenology* is an introduction continues in Hegel's *System of Logic*, which is not a logic in the formal, mathematical sense but rather a system of relations and "deductions" of basic philosophical concepts such as "being," "becoming," and "nothing" and a wide-ranging discussion of the role and interplay of concepts in knowledge.

In particular, Hegel focuses on that basic set of concepts or "categories" that Kant had defended as the a priori basis of all knowledge. Where Kant had defended a rigidly ordered, neatly defined set of such categories, Hegel is concerned to demonstrate the "fluidity" and mutually defining nature of such concepts. Concepts are always contextual. Their meaning depends on their contrasts and complements. And concepts are ultimately intelligible only on the basis of experience. Snatched out of context and merely formalized, they have no real meaning at all.

Despite its formidable appearance, Hegel's *System of Logic* in many ways supports commonsense notions of knowledge as contextually dependent and as an interdependent system of oppositions whose polarity is always subject to scrutiny. The sharp and problematic philosophical distinction between "subjective" and "objective," for example must be seen as a contextual and shifting set of oppositions. Indeed, the whole point of this work is ultimately to show the futility of that movement in modern philosophy that so insists on distinguishing merely subjective experience from objective reality and knowledge, a point which has been brought home in this century by virtually every work in contemporary physics.

Kant had gone a long way in showing how objective reality is constituted by way of subjectivity, but he had left the distinction intact. Hegel wants to show us, in one of the most difficult books of philosophy, to what extent we do experience objective reality, but we conceive of it in many different ways and these various ways can be contrasted, compared, and combined into a single, overall system of thought.

In his later years, when he was the most celebrated philosopher in Germany and professor at the great University of Berlin, Hegel expanded and completed his conception of this system in his lectures. He developed a philosophy of nature, following Schelling (who by now had become a bitter adversary). He simplified his logic and added to it a comprehensive history of philosophy, in effect inventing the subject as we know it today. Hegel further developed his "philosophy of Spirit," which now encompassed everything from psychology and the new science of anthropology (as "subjective spirit") to politics and religion ("objective" and "absolute" Spirit, respectively).

Perhaps Hegel's most important and most controversial contribution to the modern conception of society was his view of the individual as secondary to the state. His target is that whole history of social and political thought that stretches back to Hobbes and the Enlightenment, but his is not the totalitarian or authoritarian vision that it is sometimes said to be. Hegel should not be confused with certain later philosophers (for example, Lenin and Mussolini, who made bad work of this notion). Hegel's point was that our conception of the individual is the product of a very particular sort of society, which he called "civil society." (It is worth noting that Hegel was an enthusiastic reader of the British political economists, Adam Smith in particular.) His point was not that the individual doesn't count but rather that the significance of the individual is dependent on the social context in which he or she lives.

Hegel's politics went back to his earliest lectures in Jena at the turn of the century, when Napoleon was making his way across Europe and instigating revolutions in the fragmented German states. His politics and social theory were suggested in the *Phenomenology*, and they emerged in 1821 in his concise *Philosophy of Right*, written only six years after the fall of Napoleon and at the onset of that stable but oppressive period in European history often called "the Reaction." Needless to say, Hegel's views were affected by that turbulent history, but this was not only true of his later political views. His early *Phenomenology* was very much a book of liberation, an announcement of the "birth of a new world," a "Bacchanalian revel" anticipating the success of Napoleon's revolutions. The *Philosophy of Right*, by contrast, begins by describing the "gray" of philosophy and the post-twilight flight of the owl of Minerva (the Roman goddess of wisdom), suggesting that philosophy comes after the fact to merely describe what has already happened.

For all its insistence on fluidity and the dynamics of history and ideas, Hegel's final system becomes a staid, inert conception, inviting a new upheaval, a new and more dynamic dialectic, a new turning of ideas on their heads. Shortly after Hegel's sudden death in the cholera epidemic of 1831, a young group of revolution-minded Hegelians, led by Ludwig Feuerbach, turned to philosophy in Berlin. One of them was a young romantic poet named Karl Marx.

Philosophy and Poetry: Rationalism and Romanticism

At the turn of the nineteenth century, philosophy might have appeared to be preoccupied with a small number of gigantic questions, beginning with the possibilities of human knowledge and ending with the search and eventual seizure of "the Absolute." But within that thin if cosmic framework there were a number of lively disputes taking place, not only between (what Schopenhauer would call) "irritable philosophy professors" but among the most gifted poets and prophets of the age. They all wanted to be the *Dichter* of the new Germany. The German word *Dichter* refers to someone who is much more than a wordsmith, a modern-day troubadour, a rhythm-and-rhymer. He (or she) would also be wise, indeed, sagelike, the spokesperson for the spirit of the age. Thus competition arose, not only between the irritable philosophy professors but also between the philosophers and the poets, the spokesmen for reason and the Absolute and the expounders of the soul. Plato's ancient quarrel with the poets came alive again in Germany, except, this time, the philosophers were on the defensive. The poets were "modern" and aggressive, insisting that the truth be found neither by way of the deductions of reason nor through the inquiries of science but rather through pure inspiration, aided by individual genius.

Thus the hard-fought battle for the objectivity of reason was effectively compromised by the modern cults of passion and genius, the misshapen but enthusiastic movement we generally know as *Romanticism*. The Enlightenment never dominated Germany in the way that it pervaded both England and France. Instead, Kant's rationalist philosophy stood uneasily side by side with the mysticism of his virtual next-door neighbor, Johann Hamann. Insofar as the Germans looked westward for enlightenment, it was not Hume who awakened them but rather Rousseau, with his comforting fantasies of natural independence and benign sentimentality.

The emerging champion of the German spirit was not Kant but a *Dichter* named Johann Herder (1744–1803). He was also a philosopher (and we should take care not to fall into the trap of exaggerating the differences between philosophy and poetry). But he was a philosopher of a very different temperament. Kant and the Enlightenment claimed to be "cosmopolitan" and universal; even as a young man, Herder complained that such a philosophy made him feel "homeless." For him—and in part because of him—German culture and peculiarly German ideas had a right to their own special place on the world stage.

Unlike Kant and the Enlightenment champions of reason, Herder emphasized feeling and immediate experience, or *Gefühl*. It was through feeling that we were one with the world, through which we came to recognize our own "vital powers"; and it was through consciousness and, most important, through *language* that we reflectively ruptured that original unity in search of objectivity and knowledge.

This was not itself a bad thing, and, as so often, we should guard ourselves against overstating the differences between admittedly very different thinkers. Our ability to reflect and conceptualize and distinguish consciousness from the world made us, Herder insisted, the first of God's creatures to be "liberated." But the life of reflection was a limited life. The life of feeling, the *Sturm und Drang* (Storm and Stress) captured by poetry, was essential to being a whole person, at one with (and not just knowing about) the world.

Finally, unlike Kant and the Enlightenment, searching for universal and necessary timeless truths, Herder, decades before Hegel, believed in history. In this, he was the German incarnation of another neglected genius, an Italian named Giambattista Vico (1668–1744), who had died the year Herder was born. Both Herder and Vico went against the grain of virtually the whole of philosophy, which tended to ignore history and culture and treat the truth as a timeless, changeless reality.

Vico bitterly attacked Descartes, his rationalism, and his method of deduction. Like Herder, he appreciated the importance of the irrational in life, and he emphasized the role of religious faith and obedience, as opposed to philosophical reflection, as the essential ingredient in social life. Both Herder and Vico were early opponents of technology, or at any rate, they felt very uneasy about the new celebration of the machine. Like Rousseau, they challenged the general Enlightenment wisdom that praised science and technology for its improvement of human life.

Prompted by a youthful enthusiasm for the work of his countryman, Machiavelli, Vico recognized the sad but obvious fact that human life tended to be defined not by reason but by discord, by conflict, by change. Thus, Vico defended an evolutionary vision of history, stages of social growth much like the stages of growth of an individual. But like an individual, a society too can become corrupt, decadent, and die. Herder employed the same analogy but included a bit more German idealism. He, too, played rationality against history, but he also held out for a "higher unity." This became the definitive image of romanticism, unity out of discord and conflict, universality emerging out of particularity, God and the Absolute emanating from the complexity and confusion of everyday life.

Hegel's account of the triumph of reason positioned him halfway into the romantic camp. His was a "logic of passion," as one later Hegelian (the American philosopher Josiah Royce) would call it. It was not a "deduction" but a celebration of the vicissitudes of the human heart as well as the dialectic of ideas and different forms of consciousness, all leading tortuously to an ultimate rational unity.

Hegel refused to acknowledge his debt to and importance for the romantics, however. (Friedrich Schelling, his onetime friend turned rival, was clearly one of them.) He rejected both the Enlightenment and romanticism as "too limiting" and "too one-sided." But so, too, did many of the great minds of the era. If there is one truth that the advantage of retrospect allows us here, it is being able to comprehend the underlying similarities of German rationalism and romanticism: we see that their sibling rivalry itself is a mark of their jointly emerging modernism.

Both the rationalists and the romantics traced their ideas back to Kant, whose taste in poetry tended toward the limerick and whose taste in music could be satisfied by a Sunday afternoon military band concert. But the Kant who so excited the romantics was not the Kant who had been awakened by Hume and took on the challenge of defending the foundations of Newton's physics. Nor, in fact, was it the Kant who defended the categorical imperative and the universality of the moral law. It was rather the Kant of the third critique, *The Critique of Judgment*, concerned with aesthetic judgment and the purposefulness of the cosmos, that so intrigued them.

What captured the imagination and the *hubris* of the young romantic poets of Germany was Kant's apparent suggestion that the purpose of the world was to be found in art, not in science, and true inspiration was to be found not in methodical reason but in the spontaneous promptings of *genius*. "A genius goes beyond the rules," declared more than one enthusiastic young modernist poet. A lot of bad poetry was one of the inevitable, if less than tragic, consequences of this idea.

The unchallenged *Dichter* of the age was Johann Wolfgang von Goethe (1749–1832), who not only became the most influential spokesman for the age but still represents the German spirit and self-image at its finest. He also spread his creative sensibilities and his much-honored words of wisdom across the seeming abyss that separated two warring camps. In his early work, he often followed the classical ideals of reason, rigor, and clarity. He declared romanticism "sickly." But his later and greatest work, the play *Faust*, displayed all the earmarks of great romantic genius. Although he had read Kant, Goethe confessed that he had little patience for philosophy. Nevertheless, he read and was extremely impressed by Kant's third *Critique*, and Goethe's ideas had at least as much impact on the thinking of Germany as those of the great philosopher.

Goethe's best friend and literary equal, Friedrich Schiller (1759–1805), had not only read but mastered Kant, and like Hegel (his near-contemporary), he saw himself as "correcting" what he saw as the inadequacies of Kant's philosophy. In his *Letters on Aesthetic Education*, Schiller took very seriously both Kant's emphasis on the importance of morality and his celebration of beauty in the third *Critique* and argued that the way to moral character is not by way of the abstract rules of practical reason but rather by way of art and aesthetics. Schiller, like Goethe, remained above the debates concerning romanticism. Nevertheless, the two of them had a profound if confusing effect on the generation of philosophical poets who enlivened the first part of the new century. What the young romantics were lacking was a true romantic philosopher, someone who would follow Kant's genius but tailor the world to suit their cosmic and typically tragic sensibilities. It would not hurt, however, if he also had a wry sense of humor.

Romantic West Meets East: Schopenhauer

That philosopher was Arthur Schopenhauer (1788–1860). Schopenhauer is best known for his pessimism and his curmudgeonly style. His antipathy toward Hegel was so profound that he insisted on teaching courses in the same university at the same times that Hegel gave his lectures. Given Hegel's popularity, Schopenhauer's courses were little attended, and his teaching career came to a quick end. Fortunately, he was independently wealthy and thus able to devote himself to writing books in which he frequently alluded to "charlatanism," which, as he clearly explained in footnotes, meant Hegel.

What Schopenhauer most despised in Hegel was his optimism, his sense that humanity was improving. Schopenhauer, by contrast, thought that most people, most of the time, were completely deluded, and that this had not changed much since the human race began. A great admirer of Kant, he utilized Kant's distinction between the noumenal and the phenomenal realms to explain the source of human ignorance. As part of the natural world, we are motivated by our inclinations. We see ourselves as part of a causal system in which things causally relate to us, and so we busy ourselves in a multitude of practical projects, plans, and desires.

This phenomenal world, however, is a world of illusion, according to Schopenhauer. Insofar as we consider ourselves part of the world, we ignore the profound reality that underlies it, the noumenal reality, the thing-in-itself. So far, this account remains fairly close to Kant (although Kant would not agree that the phenomenal world is "illusory"). There is the world of experience and inclination, and then there is the world-in-itself, which is *Will*. For Kant, of course, the Will is essentially rational and presupposes freedom. As noumenal, however, it can neither be experienced nor known. Schopenhauer departs from Kant both in denying the rationality of the Will and in claiming that we can have experience of the thing-in-itself as Will.

For Schopenhauer, the Will is not peculiar to human agents, nor does each agent have his or her own Will. There is but One Will, and it underlies everything. Every being in the phenomenal world manifests the Will in its own way: as a natural force, as instinct or, in our case, as intellectually enlightened willing. In each case, the same inner reality is expressed, and in every case, there can be no satisfaction. Schopenhauer's Will is ultimately without purpose, and therefore it cannot be satisfied. An animal is born. It struggles to survive. It mates, reproduces, and dies. Its offspring do the same, and the cycle repeats itself generation after generation. What could be the point of all of this? And are we, as rational creatures, any different?

We do not usually think of ourselves as sharing the same pointless reality with the rest of the natural world. Our lives, we suppose, have meaning. We fancy that by our actions, our desires will be satisfied in a rational way. In fact, they never are. When any particular desire is satisfied, we move on to the next one, or become bored (and thereby dissatisfied) until we do. Our fundamental nature is willful. No change of situation, no temporary satisfaction will quench our endless thirst. Schopenhauer thus sees the willful nature of reality, a reality that has no point and cannot be satisfied, as the grounds for his well-known pessimism.

Following the Four Noble Truths of Buddhism, Schopenhauer contends that all of life is suffering. (Schopenhauer was perhaps the first great philosopher to import wholesale the ancient teachings of Asia.) Suffering is caused by desire, and we can alleviate suffering, as the Buddhists taught, by "putting an end to desire." The most common palliative for us, according to Schopenhauer, is aesthetic experience. Schopenhauer borrows Kant's aesthetic framework as well as his metaphysical framework and contends that aesthetic experience involves a stance of "disinterestedness." Although we are usually slaves to our desires, always laboring in some way to get what we imagine we want, we can forget our desires in aesthetic contemplation. It allows us a "Sabbath from the penal servitude of willing."

Schopenhauer believes that the artist of genius has talent precisely to the extent that he or she can assume this stance of disinterested contemplation and then communicate it to others. In aesthetic experience, both the beholder and the object are transformed—in a sense, removed from their normal roles as particulars within the causal nexus of the phenomenal world. The observer becomes "the universal subject of knowledge," completely divorced from ordinary personal concerns. The object, in turn, becomes an epiphany of a universal archetype, a "Platonic Idea," according to Schopenhauer.

Yet aesthetic experience is only a brief vacation from the delusion of egoistic hankering. Worst of all, our egoism produces the illusion that other people are separate and opposed beings, in competition for the satisfactions we crave. In fact, they are manifestations of the same fundamental reality that we are. We only imagine that they are detached from us, and therefore we imagine that we can further the aims of our own will at their expense. The result is that our desires lead us to harm each other. Ultimately, this amounts to harming ourselves. The person who wickedly exerts his will against others suffers too. (Schopenhauer suggests that the faces of wicked people reveal this inner suffering.) Nevertheless, so long as we are limited to the phenomenal perspective, all of us will continue to assert our will against others, adding to the overall suffering of human experience.

Schopenhauer returns to the insights of Buddhism in an effort to indicate an alternative route to salvation. If the only way to eliminate the suffering caused by desire is to eliminate desire, then the only successful way to escape the misery of the human condition is resignation, the complete abdication of desiring. Ethical insight, the realizations that all beings are part of the same unity and that one cannot gain any advantage at the expense of others, motivates resignation. Saints in particular cease *willing*, for they see that they can gain nothing through the satisfaction of desire. They adopt ascetic lifestyles, the life of self-denial, in which they undercut even their bodies' tendencies to will. From the standpoint of the phenomenal world, such individuals seem to have chosen a life of nothingness, but, from their perspective, they have chosen a life of "bliss." Buddhism had moved to Germany.

Critics are quick to point out that Schopenhauer, for all his talk, was far from an ascetic himself. Bertrand Russell delighted in the fact that Schopenhauer enjoyed good wine, epicurean dinners, and the company of women. Indeed, he was so personally willful, not to mention cantankerous, that in anger he once pushed an old woman down a flight of stairs and had to pay her compensation for the rest of her life. This, however, is an extreme case of an embarrassment we have met before. There is the philosopher and the philosophy. The relationship between the two is not always simple or flattering.

Schopenhauer initiated a new project in Western philosophy, the effort to engage seriously with non-Western philosophy in the hope that some synthesis might afford more wisdom than the Western tradition had found on its own. More immediately, Schopenhauer had tremendous influence on Western thinking. The romantics took his emphasis on art and aesthetic appreciation as a mode of salvation (albeit temporary) quite seriously, and in his old age Schopenhauer became the philosophical darling of the romantic movement. Nietzsche and Freud developed their philosophical and psychological perspectives on the Schopenhauerian premise that human beings are fundamentally willing beings, often in ignorance. Ludwig Wittgenstein would be deeply influenced by Schopenhauer's metaphysics when he tried to elaborate a "picture" theory of the world in his *Tractatus*.

Schopenhauer maintained the age-old role of the philosopher as a nonacademic critic of humanity, an imaginative if harsh visionary, a colorful eccentric. As he himself so vitriolically noted, he had deviated from the path of philosophy, the path now occupied by the post-Kantian "frauds" of German idealism. But in doing so he opened up the way for a new breed of philosopher, as irreverent and as iconoclastic as any before.

After Hegel: Kierkegaard, Feuerbach, and Marx

Schopenhauer was not Hegel's only philosophical antagonist. Søren Kierkegaard (1813–1855) was another. Kierkegaard was born and raised in Copenhagen, where the rationalist influence of Kant and Hegel absolutely dominated the Lutheran Church, which in turn dominated the whole of Danish life. Apart from a brief sojourn to Germany as a youth, Kierkegaard spent his entire life in Denmark, battling the rationalist influence of the two great German philosophers and devoting his life to his role as a Socratic gadfly in the otherwise bug-free and self-satisfied Lutheran bourgeoisie.

Against the rational and reasonable reconstructions of the concept of religious faith in Kant, Kierkegaard insisted that faith was by its very nature irrational, a passion and not a provable belief. Against Hegelian holism, which synthesized all of humanity, nature, and God into a single "Spirit," Kierkegaard insisted on the primacy of "the individual" and the profound "Otherness" of God. And against the worldly Lutherans, carrying out their business as usual and treating church as part of the weekly ritual, Kierkegaard preached a stark, passionate, solitudinous, and unworldly religion that, in temperament, at least, would "go back into the monastery out of which Luther broke." His task in life, a Socratic task, Kierkegaard insisted, was to redefine "what it meant to be a Christian."

In defining this new sense of Christianity, Kierkegaard gave a rather spectacular interpretation to the otherwise banal concept of "existence" and insisted on the importance of passion, free choice, and self-definition in opposition to the rationalist philosophies then popular in Copenhagen. Existence, according to Kierkegaard, is not just "being there" but living passionately, choosing one's own existence and committing oneself to a certain way of life. Here is the beginning of "existentialism," the "philosophy of existence." Such existence is rare, he says, for most people simply form part of an anonymous "public" in which conformity and "being reasonable" are the rule, passion and commitment the exceptions. In his *Concluding Unscientific Postscript*, he compares existence to riding a wild stallion and "so-called existence" to falling asleep in a hay wagon.

Kierkegaard's own chosen way of life was Christianity, which he distinguished with great irony and frequent sarcasm from the watered-down beliefs and social hand-holding of "Christendom." To be or become a Christian, according to Kierkegaard, it is necessary to passionately commit oneself, to make a "leap of faith" in the face of the "objective uncertainty" of religious claims. One cannot know or prove that there is a God; one must passionately choose to believe.

At the heart of Kierkegaard's philosophy is his emphasis on the Individual and his related notion of "subjective truth." The main targets of his attack included the Hegelian philosophy and the Lutheran Church of Denmark, both of which emphasized the importance of rationality and collective spirit. Against them, Kierkegaard urged attention to the individual human being and his or her particular life-defining decisions. Thus he criticized Hegel—with his long view of history and his all-encompassing concept of "Spirit"—as "an abstract thinker" who completely ignored "the existing, ethical individual."

Hegel had formulated a "dialectic" which defined the course of history and human thought and resolved the various tensions and conflicts therein, but Kierkegaard would emphasize the personal importance of concrete choices, such as whether or not one should get married—a decision which played a dramatic and continuing role in his own biography. Hegel had developed what Kierkegaard called a "both/and" philosophy in his dialectic, a philosophy of reconciliation and synthesis, but Kierkegaard would urge the unavoidability of an "either/or" philosophy, an "existential dialectic" that emphasized choices and personal responsibility rather than overall rationality.

The notion of "subjective truth" was polemically formulated in opposition to the idea that all such choices have a rational or "objective" resolution. In choosing the religious life, for example, Kierkegaard insists that there are no ultimately rational reasons for doing so, only subjective motives, a sense of personal necessity and passionate commitment. Similarly, choosing to be ethical—which is to say, choosing to act according to the principles of practical reason—is itself a choice which is not rational. The notion of subjective truth does not mean, as it may seem to mean, a truth that is true "for me." It is rather resolution in the face of the objectively unknown—for example, the existence of God or Kant's concern for the ultimate commensuration of virtue and happiness—for which, Kierkegaard argues, there can be no adequate argument or evidence.

Kierkegaard's emphasis on passionate faith, on devotion instead of rationality, on the individual instead of what he rather unflatteringly called "the Christian mob," represented not only a profound reaction against the modernization of religion but an equally profound and forward-looking insistence on the ultimate importance of feeling, the unavoidability of uncertainty and the place of irrational but passionate and always individual choice in life. His dramatic "leap of faith" applied as well to the conduct of life in general. One was not automatically or naturally moral or bound by the moral law, even if the moral law were, as Kant insisted, "the dictate of practical reason." One had to choose the ethical way of life, another "leap of faith," and, again, this choice was by no means rationally justified or guaranteed. The deliberations of reason took place *within* the realm of morality, not prior to the choice of the ethical way of life.

One could, of course, choose a life of pleasure, of desire and its satisfactions, of art and its edification, but this "aesthetic" life was not, as most philosophers had assumed, a natural state of affairs. It, too, was a choice, albeit a dangerous choice, Kierkegaard warned. Having leapt into such a life for a rather licentious but extremely unhappy year as a youth (along with his good friend, the writer Hans Christian Andersen), Kierkegaard dutifully described the guilt and depravity that can come of such a choice. Even the most successful Don Juan could become jaded and desperate. (Mozart's opera *Don Giovanni* was Kierkegaard's favorite piece of music.) Despite its evident attractions, the aesthetic life had its perils, its built-in dissatisfactions, the danger of becoming "jaded." Indeed, so did the ethical life, for the more morally sensitive and dutiful a person tried to be, the more despairing he or she would inevitably become, given the unjust and generally immoral behavior of humanity in general.

What would be the answer to this double threat of disappointment and despair? Well, first of all, it is important to emphasize that, according to Kierkegaard, neither of these choices, of the ethical life or the aesthetic life, is wrong. As the first existentialist, Kierkegaard should be read as neither approving nor condemning but rather as insisting: "Here are your choices. You take the consequences." All that the philosopher can do is describe, persuade, cajole, perhaps "seduce" the reader. He or she is in no position to declare that a way of life is right or wrong, rational or irrational. (In reaction to Kant and Hegel, Kierkegaard perversely insisted that he was not a philosopher at all but rather "a kind of poet.")

There is a third choice, however, that transcends the disappointments and the ultimate despair of both the aesthetic life and ethical life. That life, of course, is the religious life, by which Kierkegaard seems to mean only his own rather special conception of Christianity. It is the ultimate leap of faith, for contrary to the assurances of so many philosophers and theologians, there is no proof, there is no possible knowledge of God. One believes, or one does not believe. But if one chooses to believe, what one believes is that one is continually, intimately, overwhelmingly in the presence of an all-powerful, all-knowing, *personal* being. More important than *what* is believed is *how* it is believed—namely, passionately, with "fear and trembling." Against the calm deliberations of so much of the history of philosophy, in opposition to the celebration of reason and rationality, Kierkegaard celebrates *angst* and the passions, the unknown "leap," the irrationality of life.

Back in Germany, philosophy was beginning to take another violent turn, as so often, heading back in exactly the opposite direction or, in the favorite metaphor of the time, turning itself once again upside-down. Against the sometimes-crass materialism of the Enlightenment in France and England, German philosophers had become, virtually all of them, idealists or romantics of one kind or another. While the Hobbesians and Newtonians and the French physicists talked about matter in motion, the Germans insisted on spirituality. (Of course, most of the French and English philosophers, including Newton and Hobbes, insisted on the importance of spirituality and religion, too, but such vulgarization of "the other side" is and has always been the nature of these philosophical rivalries.)

By the middle of the (nineteenth) century, there seemed to be no alternative to idealism in philosophy. The world was constituted by ideas, and whether it was thereby an illusion (as in Schopenhauer) or transcendentally objective (as in Kant) or even absolute (as in Hegel), crude materialism was dismissed or ridiculed as another example of British and French vulgarity and spiritual poverty.

Into this German philosophical world marched an iconoclast named Ludwig Feuerbach, who had first made his scandalous reputation with a book that was harshly critical of Christianity. Feuerbach's down-to-earth materialism can be summarized in his famous line (and infamous pun), "*Der Mensch ist was er isst.*" (You are what you eat.) So much for the idealistic constitution of the world. What a philosopher eats for dinner, and, more generally, how one physically copes with the world, defines one's life. The ideas merely follow.

After Hegel's death in 1831, his philosophy, coupled with the radical new materialism of Feuerbach, provided inspiration for a new generation of politically rebellious students who saw in a Feuerbachian interpretation of Hegel's "dialectic" a way of understanding history and political conflict. The most famous of these young materialist Hegelians was Karl Marx (1818–1883), who began his career as a romantic poet and a polemical journalist but then turned to converting Hegel's dialectic of ideas into a theory about the power of economics. In place of Hegel's World Spirit there were the forces of production. In place of ideas in confrontation there were competing socioeconomic classes.

History has always been filled with class conflict, Marx tells us, the "haves" against the "have-nots." This was true in the master–slave relationships of the ancient world and of the manor lords and their serfs in feudal times. In the modern industrial age, it has become a conflict between the owners or "entrepreneurs" and their workers, between the *bourgeoisie* and the *proletariat*. But just as Hegel had shown how a way of thinking or a way of life can fail because of its own internal contradictions, Marx argued that the capitalist way of life, which pits a few wealthy industrialists against a mass of exploited subsistence workers, will collapse of its own internal contradictions. Ultimately, Marx predicts, this will result in a "classless society" in which work and its rewards will be equitably shared, no one will be exploited, and no one will suffer the deprivations of poverty.

Marx's utopian vision would eventually become one of the most powerful ideologies in the world, even surviving the worldwide collapse of communism in the 1990s. Whatever one may think of the Marxist dream compared to the free-enterprise system defended by Adam Smith (and one should not underestimate the extent to which the two are sometimes in agreement—for example, concerning the intrinsic worth of human labor and in their shared contempt for monopolists), the worldly world of economics and a more dynamic conception of materialism had clearly found their way back into philosophy.

Mill, Darwin, and Nietzsche: Consumerism, Energy, and Evolution

Napoleon lost the battle at Waterloo in 1815 and went into lifelong exile. Hegel's youthful optimism similarly collapsed in the busy but reactionary years spanning the middle of the nineteenth century. Indeed, the years from 1815 until midcentury are often dubbed by historians as the "Reaction," and it was in the repressive atmosphere of that period that Hegel's philosophy turned more cautious and conservative, that Kierkegaard's rebellion against the tedium of the "present age" began, and that Marx and his comrades gathered steam for their assault on the political–economic structures of that age. In the middle of the century, there were a number of mostly futile revolutions that swept across Europe, but the revolutions that were really to make a difference were taking place in a quieter, less obviously disruptive way.

In England, the Industrial Revolution was already spanning a new century. Commerce was booming and consumerism, hitherto a minor force in the world of economics, was changing the world. The new emphasis on personal satisfaction naturally suggested a new philosophy, a philosophy in which the maximization of personal happiness would become the ultimate end. That philosophy was called *utilitarianism*, and although it had its roots in the previous century (at the beginning of the Industrial Revolution), it really hit its stride in the philosophy of its most eloquent spokesman, John Stuart Mill (1806–1873).

David Hume had been something of a utilitarian. (In any case, he insisted that all ethics had its basis in "utility.") Jeremy Bentham (1748–1832) had given the movement its first full and official statement as well as its name, and John Stuart Mill's father, James Mill (1773–1836) had been one of its more enthusiastic advocates. But it was John Stuart Mill who gave utilitarianism its most brilliant defense, its most appealing presentation, its definitive formulation.

Bentham had argued that the essential principle of utility was to maximize pleasure and minimize pain, and he proposed a serious reform of, among other things, the English penal system on this basis. (A criminal should be punished just to the extent that the amount of pain or suffering is more than the rewards of the crime. The sole purpose of punishment, according to this theory, is the deterrence of crime, not "getting even.")

What Mill adds to this rather crude quantitative theory is the question of the *quality* of pleasure, thus emphasizing the importance of poetry and philosophy despite the fact that, in terms of sheer hedonism, mud-wrestling and bowling may give far greater pleasure to those who have not been exposed to more subtle enjoyments. But utilitarianism captured the mentality of the consumer revolution perfectly. With little resistance it spread into France and, of course, to America, where it would find its warmest welcome. In Germany, it was still considered extremely vulgar, but, then, the industrial revolution in Germany had hardly begun. (One of Nietzsche's most cutting lines: "Man does not live for pleasure. Only the Englishman does.")

In conjunction with his utilitarianism and his early elaboration of the virtues of "free enterprise" philosophy, Mill also defended a powerful theory of individual rights. His view is a classic statement of what is traditionally called "liberalism,"[84] a position which he clearly inherited from John Locke. Mill later moved closer to socialism, but throughout his career he was an ardent champion of individual liberty. The only reason to limit any person's freedom, he argued, was to protect the freedom of someone else. Especially important was freedom of speech. Mill, like so many philosophers throughout history, believed that the truth would only emerge through open discussion and argument. No one can be so sure of his or her opinion that censorship of another is justified, and the possibility that the censored view might in fact be correct is a further reason to condemn censorship in any form. Individual freedom, however, can be further justified by appeal to the value of individuality and self-realization. Without freedom, a person cannot realize his or her talents and happiness. (Later in life, when he had pulled back from his early free-market enthusiasm, Mill argued that economic security was an equally essential condition of freedom.)

Mill's philosophy was also revolutionary or, rather, a more radical continuation of an older British revolution in the theory of knowledge. He renovated British empiricism (although he did not call it that), partly in reaction, as in his ethics, to the overwhelming influence of German idealism. Indeed, his insistence that all knowledge comes from experience was so thoroughgoing that he even insisted that mathematics, far from being a priori (as Kant had argued) or existing in an eternal realm of ideas (as Plato had suggested), was also a matter of experience, a very high-level set of generalizations and abstractions from our experience of counting, our experiences of shapes, and so on.

Mill's empiricism was timely in terms of renewed impetus in science. Psychology, which had always been an aspect of philosophy (insofar as it was distinguished at all) was now making dramatic strides toward becoming an "empirical science." Sociology and anthropology were becoming established as social sciences. Physics had made several great leaps forward (so much so that, by the end of the century, some prominent physicists would declare that all of the problems of physics were or soon would be solved).

What was thought of as "physics," however, was undergoing a dramatic change, with more astounding implications for the future than anyone (except, perhaps, Jules Verne and H. G. Wells) could imagine. That change was the deemphasis of the traditional notion of matter, which had defined "materialism" since the Greeks, and a new emphasis on *energy* (for example, the discovery and quantification of electromagnetic and gravitational fields), which opened up new possibilities not only in physics but in all other areas of knowledge as well.

The bold new empiricism had its most astounding impact in a field that had long been short on theory although rich in observational data—biology. Of course, ever since Aristotle (and, for practical reasons, well before) people had been collecting, noting, and distinguishing the various properties, interactions, and differences between the seemingly endless number of species of animals and plants. There were perennial disputes over taxonomy ("Is a whale a fish?") and, of course, the continuing discovery of strange, new, and remarkable specimens. But, as a science, biology remained largely descriptive, not theoretical.

Why there were so many species and *how* they managed to fit so well into their environment were occasionally pursued by unusually speculative naturalists or theologians, but for most people, the traditional answer provided in Genesis, "Because God created them that way," seemed quite sufficient. But in the middle of the century, two naturalists (in hot competition), Alfred Russel Wallace (1823–1913) and Charles Darwin (1809–1882), proposed a theory that would change the very conception of nature, not to mention throw some biblical literalists into convulsions.

It was the theory of *evolution*, the idea that species randomly appeared upon the earth over tens or hundreds of millions of years. Depending on their adaptability to their environment, they survived and reproduced or they disappeared. The sticking point of the argument, of course, was the suggestion that human beings had also evolved. Some people were deeply offended that their great-grandparents turned out to be some sort of ape. Others found it blasphemous to suggest that chance and opportunity, not God, had created species. But even those who had no problem with the idea of human evolution, like Darwin himself, found themselves facing a momentous question. Could human beings still be evolving? If so, into what? Indeed, could we also be living just some brief, intermediary existence between the "lower" animals and some higher, mightier, or in any case more adaptive creature than ourselves?

It was toward the end of the century that such questions received their most shocking, provocative answers. The German philosopher Friedrich Nietzsche (1844–1900), wrote a flamboyant, fictional epic that purported to trace the educational exploits of a character named Zarathustra (intentionally named after the Persian prophet Zarathustra, or Zoroaster, who talked about the cosmic forces of good and evil). In *Thus Spake Zarathustra*, Nietzsche offered up the incredible suggestion that human beings were nothing but a bridge between the ape, on the one side, and the *Übermensch* (superman) on the other. The future of "human nature" was now called into question.

Alternatively, in the same work, Nietzsche teasingly introduced a character called "the last man," a frightening (or flattering, depending on your point of view) possibility for the "end" of evolution. The last man is the ultimate bourgeois, the satisfied utilitarian, the absolute couch potato. "We have found happiness," says the last man, and blinks in dull contentment. This, Nietzsche warns, is also one of our possibilities. We can continue to consume our comforts, minimize dangers, ignore the mysterious and unknown, and discourage creativity, until the world is so safe for us that we will become "ineradicable, like the dog-flea." Or, we might strive to become something more than "human-all-too-human" and aspire to the *Übermensch*. To understand what the *Übermensch* might be, however, we would have to reexamine the whole of Western history to see who we are and how we came to be what we have come to be.

In his insistence that we have to look back to history to appreciate what we are and what we can be, Nietzsche is reflecting not only Darwin but Hegel, Vico, and Herder. In tracing the evolution of Western thought, he looks back to early Christianity, to the ancient Greek philosopher Socrates, and even earlier to Homer and the pre-Socratic dramatists. Nietzsche was by training a classical philologist, and he saw the West's Greek heritage to be in conflict with its Judeo-Christian background. He utterly rejected the "synthesis" of the two that had developed throughout the history of Christianity.

Nietzsche was struck, for example, by the difference between the two traditions' approaches to human suffering. While the Judeo-Christian tradition sought the explanation of misfortune in sin (a kind of "blame the victim" approach, in Nietzsche's view), the ancient Greeks took profound suffering to be an indication of the fundamentally tragic nature of human life. Nietzsche's first book, *The Birth of Tragedy*, analyzed the art of Athenian tragedy as the product of the Greeks' deep and nonevasive thinking about the meaning of life in the face of extreme vulnerability. Tragedy, according to Nietzsche, grew from this unflinching recognition and the beautification, even the idealization, of the inevitability of human suffering.

In *The Birth of Tragedy*, Nietzsche speculated that the Greek view of tragedy reflected two different perspectives, which the Athenians associated with the gods Apollo and Dionysus. Dionysus, the god of wine, sexuality, and revelry, represents the dynamic flux of being, the acceptance of fate, the chaos of creativity. The individual is dispensable from this perspective, but the individual can find profound satisfaction in being part of the wild, unfolding rush of life. Indeed, from the Dionysian perspective, individual existence is just an illusion; our true reality is our participation in the life of the whole.

Apollo, the sun god, by contrast, reflects the Athenian fascination with beauty and order. From the Apollonian perspective, the individual's existence is undeniably real and human vulnerability is genuinely horrible. Yet the Apollonian perspective makes this reality appear beautiful and enables us to forget our vulnerability for a time and simply love our finite lives in the world.

The brilliance of Athenian tragedy, according to Nietzsche, was its simultaneous awakening of both perspectives in the observer. Although ostensibly reminding its audience of the senseless horrors of human existence, tragedy also provided the means to deal with them. Greek tragedy provided an experiential reinforcement of insights from Greek religion—that we can nonetheless marvel at beauty within life, and that our true existence is not our individual lives but our participation in the drama of life and history.

Nietzsche infinitely preferred this tragic resolution of the problem of evil to the Judeo-Christian resolution in terms of sin and salvation. He also preferred it to the reactive pessimism of his philosophical hero Schopenhauer and to that modern, scientific optimism which ignores the tragic and pretends that all problems that concern us are correctable through technology. Nietzsche applauded the ancient Greeks for their ethical outlook, which stressed the development of excellence and nobility in the face of fate, in contrast to what he saw as the gloomy Judeo-Christian obsession with sin and guilt.

Plato and Aristotle still displayed vestiges of that more ancient outlook, but they were already "decadent," according to Nietzsche. The Greeks he admired were the pre-Socratic playwrights and the warrior heroes they described. Socrates had defended the ideal of reason, according to Nietzsche, too vigorously, changing it into a "tyrant" over our natural impulses. Aristotle had defended the virtues, but they were only faintly related to those fatalistic virtues that one found, for example, in Homer's heroes.

Referring to those early Greeks, Nietzsche fantasized, "They knew how to live!" Insofar as they had a "morality," it was based on healthy self-assertion, not self-abasement and the renunciation of the instincts. In Nietzsche, more than any other philosopher, the new physics of energy enters into his thinking, not only in his spectacularly energetic writing style but in his very notion of human nature. Enough of the traditional emphasis on "peace of mind" and *apatheia*. Our ideals must be energetic ideals, creative ideals.

Like Schopenhauer, Nietzsche contends that human beings and other beings in nature are essentially willful, but Nietzsche goes further and suggests that we (and all of nature's creatures) are "will to power," driven by the desire to keep expanding our vitality and strength. Survival, Nietzsche adds, is secondary. Against Schopenhauer's pessimism about the meaning of life, Nietzsche insists that vitality is itself the meaning of life, and it is the affirmation of life that should be the conclusion of philosophy, not its rejection, not "resignation."

In contrast with the morality of the ancient Athenians, a morality of heroism and mastery, Christian morality has made the bland, mediocre person the moral exemplar. Worst of all, the Christian moral worldview has urged people to treat the afterlife as more important than this one. Instead of urging self-improvement in earthly terms, the Christian moral vision emphasizes abstaining from such "selfish" concerns. The person who does essentially nothing with his or her life but has avoided "sin" might merit heaven, on the Christian view, while a creative person may be deemed "immoral" for refusing to follow "the herd." This, Nietzsche protests, is backward, and it will lead (and has led) to the downfall of the human race.

According to Nietzsche, many if not most of the prohibitions of Judeo-Christian (and Kantian) ethics are "leveling" devices that favor the weak and mediocre and put more talented and stronger spirits at a disadvantage. Accordingly, Nietzsche defends a view "beyond good and evil," beyond our tendencies to pass moralistic judgments on our own and others' behavior, toward a more creative psychological and naturalistic perspective.

Nietzsche brought to an end what might be seen as a long progression of attempts to gain access to a transcendent world. He did this by denying, in the most vituperative terms, the very idea of such a world, a reality behind the appearances, a world that is other than—better than—this one. Nietzsche's attacks on the "otherworldly" had their most obvious target in the Judeo-Christian tradition, with the idea of an all-powerful benign deity behind the scenes. Accordingly, he called for the redirection of human energies back into the life of this world. As an antidote to the Christian worldview, which treats human life as a mere beeline to the afterlife and celebrates an "eternal" world outside time as more important to this one, Nietzsche advocates a revival of the ancient view of *eternal recurrence*, the view that time repeats itself cyclically. If one were to take this image of eternal recurrence seriously and imagine that one's life must be lived over and over again, in just the same way, the same joys, same pains, same successes, same failures, suddenly there is enormous weight on what otherwise might seem like a mere "moment." It is life, this life, that alone counts for anything.

Nietzsche's indictments reach beyond Christianity back to Plato, whom he also sees as a proponent of the view that another world is more important than this one. Indeed, Nietzsche's attacks are addressed at virtually the entire Western tradition in philosophy. He sometimes even rejected the very idea of "truth," suggesting that ideas we take to be true are just those beliefs, possibly false ones, that have proven to be useful. He also defended the notion of "perspectivism," the idea that all our "truths" are relative to our particular perspectives, which are historically and individually contingent, and which we cannot escape.

Against the philosophers and social thinkers of his day, Nietzsche urged a return to a primary emphasis on the vitality of the lives we live, not detached truth and a hypocritical, merely leveling morality. Philosophical thought, he insisted, should always be subordinate to our efforts to live well, never the other way around.

Early Philosophy in America

The "new world" was the subject of considerable philosophical speculation in Europe (now the "old world"). The great German poet Goethe summarized the fantasy in the line, " '[T]hou hast it better than our world, the old one." Kant had looked upon America with some enthusiasm. Hegel, who had declared the "end of history" in Europe and insisted (contrary to the ambitions of his most famous students) that philosophers should not try to predict the future, nevertheless predicted that the next stage of the World Spirit would be found across the Atlantic. But across the Atlantic, the spirit of American philosophy was still largely stuck in Europe. It is telling that one of the first thriving schools of philosophy in America was a group of Hegelians in St. Louis, Missouri, in the very heart of the country. At Harvard and elsewhere, Germany and Britain provided the dominant philosophical models. Even today, from New York to California, the latest philosophical fashions are often imported from France, while homegrown ideas are confined to academic journals.

The early colonists had more to worry about than the ultimate nature of reality. The first settlements were often endangered, and immediate practical reality was an unavoidable preoccupation. American philosophy, accordingly, was always defined by a no-nonsense, practical or "pragmatic" sensibility. In the nineteenth century, with the expansion of industry and the growth of cities in America, philosophers rebelled and celebrated the more sublime aspects of the country's natural beauty. In the twentieth century, by contrast, American philosophy would become almost wholly enamored with science. In Europe, over the past dozen centuries, one can readily trace several continuous philosophical themes, interweaving or in confrontation with one another. In America, philosophy never really defines itself, leaping rather from one enthusiasm to another.

The philosophical history of the new world (and, in particular, New England) began for the most part with religious squabbles and separatist movements. Many of the early settlers had left Europe in search of religious freedom and tolerance, but, as so often, once they found it, they became less than tolerant themselves. The early history of New England is the history of religious exclusions and exiles, not to mention the occasional trials for heresy and witchcraft. This religious fanaticism would have much to do with the new American temperament. The Catholic Church in Rome had already lasted more than fifteen hundred years. The half-life of certain New England churches seemed to be a matter of months.

One of the early motives for philosophizing in America was the desire to firmly establish and stabilize religious movements. The first work of American literature was an attempt to fortify Puritan doctrine. Michael Wigglesworth's "Day of Doom; or A Poetical Description of the Great and Last Judgment" (1662), a long poem in ballad style, sold eighteen hundred copies within the first year, indicating the American public's already obvious hunger for apocalyptic edification. The sermons of Jonathan Edwards (1703–1758), a New England Puritan minister, were similarly aimed at bolstering religious doctrines. Edwards was instrumental in recalling many colonists back to what he saw as the basic insight of Protestantism, that we are "born depraved" and can find salvation only in God's grace. According to Edwards, salvation first of all involved an *experience*, an immediate intuition of God's glory, a divine "light." A vision of the sovereign God would dispel all worries about God's actions, about His justice, and predestination.

Like most New England thinkers, Edwards relied upon the British tradition in his philosophical formulations. He believed that reason and experience would confirm Christian doctrine. Following John Locke in particular, Edwards held that God reveals Himself through nature, giving us knowledge by means of our senses. Even more importantly, however, God gives the faithful an additional sense, which provides the vision of God in glory, the "knowledge" that secures salvation.

Edwards helped inspire *the Great Awakening*, the religious revival that swept the American colonies from 1740 to 1742. The Great Awakening was distinctive for its manner of seeking conversion: the arousal of intense emotion. Edwards sought to bring his congregations "to their knees" through his sermons, although he himself was repulsed by the overly dramatic tactics of some of his fellow preachers and the bodily contortions and groans of their followers. (One significant consequence of the Great Awakening was the development of the Baptist movement in American Protestantism, which emphasized the experiential nature of conversion and the personal role of Jesus Christ in a Christian's life.)

Although religious philosophy dominated the early years of the colonies, the establishment of civil society provided a very different (and not always compatible) concern for political and social philosophy. The business of setting up a new country, establishing towns and eventually cities, creating elegant and pros-perous plantations and, in general, making money, allowed neither the leisure nor the inclination for reflection that had characterized the lives of the Greek, European, and various Eastern philosophers. Even when the cities and plantations were settled and the money was made, philosophical discipline still seemed to hold little appeal for the busy businessmen and the energetic farmers who were pushing into the "wilderness" and sowing the seeds of what later writers would call the great American empire. Nevertheless, there were a number of philo-sophically talented thinkers, mainly lawyers and businessmen. Among them were Thomas Jefferson (1743–1826), the main author of the Declaration of Indepen-dence, and Benjamin Franklin (1706–1790), who found in the revolutionary ideas of the Enlightenment an ideology (or, more accurately, a complex set of ideolo-gies) upon which to found a new nation.

And so the United States became the land of ideas. It became the first or, in any case, the best-known modern example of a nation founded on a constitution. By the mid-eighteenth century, the Enlightenment had taken firm hold along the American eastern states. In Philadelphia it was declared, "All men are created equal, and they are endowed by their Creator with certain inalienable rights, including life, liberty, and the pursuit of happiness" (not to mention the right to property). The premise of both the Declaration of Independence and the American Constitution was that governments were formed contractually, by the consent of the governed, and that they could also be replaced when they ceased to reflect the will of the people. By the end of the century, those principles had been put in practice. But what was most revolutionary and is still the focal point of the Lockean philosophy that defined the new nation was its powerful insistence on basic "inalienable" rights, defined and enforced in the amendments to the Constitution. No other society had so formally and finally guaranteed that the government would respect such individual rights as the freedom of speech, the freedom of religion, and basic judicial entitlements.

But political philosophy in America was never divorced from the celebration of emotion encouraged by the early religious thinkers. Consequently, political philosophy has perhaps never been so passionately (though not always rationally) argued as in America, where political fanaticism seems to have taken the place of the European wars of religion. Indeed, America has always been filled with articulate demagogues on virtually every subject, and almost all of them have transcendental pretensions. Nevertheless, the scholastic and epistemological disputes that defined so much of European philosophy held little attraction for these bold new ideologues of the new world. Thus, much of what had been called philosophy was largely ignored, and those who did still find fascination in the old scholastic and epistemological disputes moved into the ivory-tower enclaves of the universities. Thus, American philosophy would retain a secure, if secluded, home in the halls of academia, while on the outside anti-intellectualism and, with it, ignorance of philosophy became increasingly routine among the educated pub-lic.

Outside of the academy, however, there were and are some great and original American philosophers. Significantly, they usually did not see themselves as philosophers; nor have they been viewed this way in the history of a subject so rigidly defined by academic problems. Jonathan Edwards saw himself as a minister of God; Walt Whitman, the great American poet; various eccentrics and speakers for the oppressed, including women. There were also philosophical jottings by politicians; these included Presidents Thomas Jefferson and Abraham Lincoln and several distinguished also-rans, among them Alexander Hamilton and Eugene McCarthy.

The philosophical ideas of American politicians were virtually never of merely theoretical interest. The public philosophy was to be "practical," with some real influence on daily life and the politics of the day. Some of these ideas were to present enduring obstacles to the well-being of the new country. For example, colonial resentment against British taxation did not cease with the departure of the British. Some American philosophers developed an elaborate argument against taxation of any kind, and that was an argument that easily penetrated the public consciousness. Some of the new ideas were dangerous. One of the most pernicious of these practical ideas was the notion of "manifest destiny," a journalistic coinage that became popular with American politicians. Manifest destiny is the idea that the American continent, with its open spaces, was not only available to European colonial expansion but determined by fate. The doctrine served as a philosophical rationalization for the rape of the continent and the subjugation of its indigenous inhabitants.

In a nation still excusing itself on the grounds that it was "new," some of the greatest philosophers, not surprisingly, came from the oppressed minorities. We have lost a great deal of the rich oral traditions of Native American Indian philosophy, but we have an eloquent if underappreciated canon of African-American philosophy, registering articulate cries of protest and some deep thinking about human nature and the injustice of human relations and institutions from those who suffered most from the new American prosperity and who were not included in the grand Bill of Rights that protected other Americans.

Frederick Douglass (1817–1895) was a former slave who became the leading orator of the Abolitionist movement. He later became a crusader for the civil rights of former slaves and women. Douglass wrote his autobiography, *The Life and Times of Frederick Douglass* (1845; revised 1882), to allay the rumors that he spoke too eloquently to have been a slave. The book is one of the boldest, sharpest reflections of American life and its most despicable institution, slavery. Douglass's elegant oratory primed the moral sentiments that would (for many other, less noble reasons besides) erupt in the American Civil War of 1860–1865.

W. E. B. Du Bois (1868–1963) was cited by Henry James (a man who seems to have traveled around the world without ever noticing a black face) as the one author worth mentioning in the entire century.[85] Du Bois's famous work, *The Souls of Black Folk* (1903), analyzes the complex character of the American black's sense of identity. The African-American has a dual soul, Du Bois argues, one that is American and one that is black. Initially confident in the effectiveness of intellectual efforts to undermine racism, Du Bois came to believe that political activism was also necessary. He rejected the strategy of gradualism—the acceptance of discrimination for the time being, so long as the situation was improving—on the part of American blacks. Du Bois was an early spokesman for what was later called "black pride." He also defended a notion of Pan-Africanism, the view that those of African descent should see themselves as allies, united by a unique set of common political concerns.

Douglass and Du Bois together inspired the American civil rights movement. As practical politics, one would be hard pressed to think of a more important philosophical movement in the United States (except, perhaps, the women's movement, which was born of many of the same ideas and concerns). Following them, we can trace such later works as those of Martin Luther King, Jr. (1929–1968), who defended the idea of a fully integrated society, and in a very different mood, the writings of Malcolm X (1925–1965). But now we are getting ahead of our story, for despite the social and political pressures of the nineteenth century, politics was by no means the only focus of philosophy.

The environment, rather than European "nature," was a perennial subject of concern in the Americas since long before the arrival of the Europeans. Native American philosophy is through and through a philosophy of the world around us, its blessings and dangers, its marvels. Some of the more recently arrived Europeans also developed philosophies focused on nature as a source of spiritual sustenance rather than an invitation to European imperialism. As America became more industrialized and more urbanized, a romantic revival rejected comfort and consumerism in favor of a simpler life. And as American cities grow more and more populated and troubled, it is a fantasy that appears again and again in popular American thinking.

Henry David Thoreau (1817–1862) was but the most famous of a long line of self-styled ecological hermits. Thoreau famously took up residence on a rather luxurious and convenient parcel of land (belonging to his friend Emerson) by Walden Pond in Massachusetts. An anarchist without a regular profession, Thoreau praised the simple life of individual communion with nature over the citified lives of commercial venture that attracted so many of his contemporaries. He set the tone for what would become something of a national ideology (in competition with many others, of course)—namely, the rejection of city life and "civilization" and a retreat back to nature and the "natural."

Thoreau's distaste for the excesses of civilized society led him to advocate the tactic of pointed noncooperation with unjust laws and practices as a peaceful means of achieving important social reforms. His essay "Civil Disobedience" has had lasting impact; it inspired both Gandhi and King in their movements against imperialism and racial oppression.

Although he was an eccentric, Thoreau was self-consciously part of a larger philosophical movement, *New England transcendentalism,* which flourished from 1836 until 1860. The great New England "transcendentalists" were direct philosophical descendants of Kant and Hegel. (Emerson wrote his doctoral dissertation on Kant. Thoreau studied Hegel and admired Carlyle.) Transcendentalism conjoined ideas from the Enlightenment and European romanticism with progressive ideas for social reforms, especially the abolition of slavery and female suffrage. The transcendentalists were optimists, convinced of the inherent goodness of humanity and enthusiastic about its possibilities. They were also quasi-mystical in orientation, emphasizing humanity's union with nature and the importance of intuitive insight over logical reasoning.

Beside Thoreau, the most famous transcendentalist is Ralph Waldo Emerson (1803–1882). His essays are among the classics of American literature as well as essential influences on the American pragmatists. (He also had a profound effect on Nietzsche.) Emerson stressed the importance of Nature as a source of spiritual sustenance. Following Hegel, he also believed that humanity is linked by a collective "Oversoul" that gives intuitive moral guidance. Emerson popularized and encouraged *self-reliance* as the ultimate virtue. Confidence in the intuitive part of the self, in his view, was the best basis for gaining fulfillment in life.

Emerson began his career as a minister in the Unitarian Church (a Protestant sect with no formal creed, which emphasized the unity of religions). Emerson eventually resigned from the ministry, however, when he began to doubt the value of religious institutions as such. Organized religions, he concluded, were symptoms of human failure to attain more direct religious experience. Such experience was available, most notably, in the contemplation of nature. It was from his religious sensibilities that Emerson developed the philosophy of *secular humanism*, a philosophy sometimes reviled by contemporary evangelicals. But just as humanism had its origins within the context of the Christian church, secular humanism is based on a religious sensibility. It focuses on the well-being of humanity in this life, and it is opposed to sectarian approaches that are mainly concerned with salvation in the hereafter.

The transcendentalists were obviously influenced by the European romantics as well as the German idealists. But this intellectual dependency on Europe rightly bothered American intellectuals of the second century of American life. These Americans had rather self-consciously rejected much else that was distinctly European, and they generally took pride in their own originality and ingenuity. Thus the felt need for a genuine American philosophy.

A genuine American philosophy would have to be something quite different from the scholastic and metaphysical reflections of Europe. It would involve a uniquely American style of practical, hard-headed thinking—a reflection of the American experience. This philosophy developed in the antimetaphysical school of *pragmatism*. The movement included such luminaries as William James and John Dewey. Pragmatist philosophy grew out of the practical cast of mind that developed in America, demanded initially by the challenges the European settlers faced in their efforts to construct new lives on foreign soil. Accordingly, American pragmatism is inspired by the conviction that the ultimate test of a theory's worth is its practical *usefulness*. With pragmatism, unlike so much of traditional metaphysics, one could actually set out and *do something*, even change the world.

The practical approach of the pragmatists appealed (and continues to appeal) to the American psyche. It is, accordingly, an ideal transition from the European-dominated nineteenth century to what has often been called the "American century." As we make that turn, we might note that, despite the age-old bloodshed between the long-standing European nations, the new twentieth century began following a remarkable eighty-five years of relative peace and stability in Europe. This, of course, would soon change, and the philosophy of pragmatism would continue to nurture American optimism through an era of global wars and revolutions.

Pragmatism spans the years ending the nineteenth century into the twentieth. Thus, we will save most of its history for Part IV, where pragmatism mixes uneasily with the new, more scientific trends in European philosophy and psychology. Throughout most of the nineteenth century, however, America was still a philosophical backwater. It had its eloquent spokesmen—the poet Walt Whitman, for example, and Emerson in particular were much admired by some European philosophers, notably Nietzsche—but America had yet to produce a real philosophy of its own, and the momentous shifts in Western philosophy at the turn of the present century would, again, be found mainly in Europe.

Part IV

From Modernism to Postmodernism: The Twentieth Century

The Rejection of Idealism: A Century of Horrors

Nietzsche died in August 1900. Toward the end of his lucid years, he had made some dire prophecies about the new century. This new, awesome age would experience the awful realization of the "death of God," the agony of modern decadence and disbelief, the violent consequences of resentful herd morality, and the difficult truth that there is, after all, no "truth." Nietzsche predicted a desperate search for new gods or, failing that, *führers*. He predicted a similar search for new myths or, in their place, *ideologies*. He predicted wars such as the world had never seen. History, unfortunately, would soon prove him right.

The twentieth century might well be defined, from its own point of view, as the time of collapse of traditional truths and ultimate horrors. But, of course, almost every epoch has been described in much the same way. The religious wars of the seventeenth century were surely horrible. The collapse of the feudal world order and the various plagues of the late Middle Ages must have seemed like the end of the world. The Reformation certainly struck many Catholics as the end of stability and civilization, like the fall of Rome a millennium before. The advent of the industrial age, the success of capitalism, and the movements toward democracy and socialism must have struck many people in the mid-nineteenth century (as did kindred movements in Socrates' Greece) as the victory of chaos over order.

Nevertheless, there was a terrible violence to the two world wars of this century that—partly because of the global scope of the wars, partly because of new technology—was indeed unprecedented. The First World War involved tanks, airplanes, poison gas, and submarines, and the theater of war extended from Europe through Africa to east Asia. To make it all the more horrifying, frustrating, and futile, there were no great conquests, no definitive battles. It was a war in which tens of thousands of lives would be sacrificed for a few yards of muddy terrain. It was a war of attrition, a war of sheer destructiveness.

The Second World War altered the very concept of war with the introduction of the atom bomb. It extended the boundaries of the conflict to every island, every glacier, and every desert as well as to the heart of every city and town on the planet.

The relativism that emerged at the turn of the century, similarly, was far more sophisticated than anything that had been thought or taught before. It began to emerge in Nietzsche's polemical "perspectivism," but early in the new century it also manifested itself in other quarters, including the brilliant scientific writings of young Albert Einstein and his colleagues which ushered in a new age of physics. To be sure, one can find precedents for such thinking. The philosopher Leibniz had argued, against Newton, a version of the thesis that space and time were not absolute but matters of relation—"relative," in other words. Indeed, the Sophist Protagoras had argued, against Socrates, that "Man is the measure of all things," a relativist thesis. The degree of uncertainty and confusion at the turn of the century, however, combined with some very sophisticated arguments, turned relativism into a thesis to be dealt with, and not just as an awkward skeptical aside. It would become the central concern of the century. Idealism, the transcendental and sometimes even absolute confidence that had heralded the beginning of the last century, would not be found in this one.

Some of this uncertainty, confusion, and concern was straightforwardly political. The world had grown remarkably smaller. Communications and transportation had improved so much that the world, which only a few centuries before consisted of isolated civilizations hardly aware of each other's existence, now began to approach a global human menagerie, filled with often hostile nation-states and an already-overcrowded population. (World population in 1850: one billion; in 1900: a billion and a half; in 1990: over five billion. Estimated in the year 2000: over six billion; and in 2050: ???)

People needed more room to live (Lebensraum). They needed more resources, new markets. From a European perspective, the once seemingly endless expanse of new colonies and continents to be conquered and explored had been exhausted. The colonial powers fought one another for prized possessions in Africa, Asia, and the no longer "new" world. They argued jealously over small tracts of heavily industrialized and thus extremely valuable land in Europe, while China and Japan in the East nurtured new ambitions and displayed remarkable new capabilities around the Pacific.

Nevertheless, the age of empires was quickly drawing to a close. Nationalism was the ideology in the air, and with nationalism and the proliferation of small nations came an enormously confusing and perpetually shifting network of protective alliances. One of the most crowded and most tumultuous stages of nationalist competition and conflict was located in southeastern Europe in the area generally known as the Balkans. It would be there, in Sarajevo, that the first fatal shot would be fired in what was to become, though falsely titled, "The war to end all wars."

Frege, Russell, and Husserl: Arithmetic, Atomism, Phenomenology

Philosophy is never isolated or immune from its time and place, no matter how abstract it may be or however "eternal" or "untimely" it may declare itself. Philosophy can be prophetic, it can be nostalgic, it may simply act as a mirror, a reflection of a culture. But more often than not, it expresses in idealized and abstract terms the ideals and aspirations of society. Plato's republic was an idealized model of Athens, idealized, that is, according to a certain controversial political and philosophical vision. Most of medieval philosophy, no matter how "schoolish" or scholastic, was an unabashed expression of the faith of the era. The Enlightenment was first of all an expression of hope, of optimism, of faith in the rational ability of human beings to learn about the world and create a society that would assure peace and prosperity. The details of philosophy, the rigors of epistemology, imaginative metaphysics, all had to be understood within the embrace of the overwhelming confidence that had come of age in the Enlightenment. The philosophical idealism of the nineteenth century expressed a new global idealism as well. Even Nietzsche clearly saw himself as a harbinger of good things to come, despite his warnings.

Similarly, the often scholastic, sometimes tedious and very academic and technical European philosophy at the beginning of the twentieth century nevertheless is a product of its times and, perhaps, a symptom—a symptom of retreat, or, perhaps, a symptom of despair. None of this is immediately obvious in the work itself, however. Indeed, if one were to characterize the most important work of the early twentieth century both in Europe and in England, clarity and exuberance would seem to be its key features. It was bold and confident. It was rebellious to the point of being brash. It showed not a hint of despair or self-doubt. Indeed, it had very little to say about life at all.

The dominant topics were logic and mathematics. The major goal of the century was to find the "foundations" of arithmetic, the proof that such elementary equations as "two plus two equals four" were indeed true. Three of the major figures were Gottlob Frege (1848–1925), an extremely conservative German mathematician; Bertrand Russell (1872–1970), an extremely liberal English aristocrat, and Edmund Husserl (1859–1938), an extremely single-minded but also famously absentminded Czech–German mathematics professor.

The interest in pure logic had had a resurgence in the nineteenth century, although it had always been a topic of intense interest for a few unusually brilliant, formal-minded philosophers. Beginning (as did so many scholarly subjects) with Aristotle, logic had been a passion for some of the Stoics, for some of the most creative Arab philosophers, for Peter Abelard in twelfth-century Paris, for Duns Scotus and Ockham in fourteenth-century Britain, and for Leibniz and Kant in seventeenth- and eighteenth-century Germany, respectively. There were also alternative conceptions of logic—in ancient China, for example—and in the rich literature of Indian philosophy. Hegel also attempted to formulate a decidedly non-formal (perhaps even antiformal) logic, but in Western philosophy, at least, that was not the way logic was going.

In the nineteenth century, John Stuart Mill in England and several German philosophers and mathematicians, under the sway of the new emphasis on science *(Wissenschaft)*, began to develop purely formal techniques for the depiction of ordinary language in its most reduced and minimal logical form. The prototype of such techniques, of course, was mathematics, and the wedding of mathematics and logic was one of the definitive achievements of the century, comparable, perhaps, to Descartes's marriage of arithmetic and geometry three centuries before.

It was Frege, however, who most stimulated the renewed interest in logic and its relationship to arithmetic. And it was he who most moved logic beyond the study of the relationship between propositions ("propositional logic") that had dominated the field since Aristotle. Frege created the "quantificational" logic (concerned with the categories of "all," "some," "none") that is best known and used by philosophers today. Indeed, it is hard to imagine, in retrospect, how this seemingly simple innovation transformed and resurrected a nearly moribund subject. It has been said for better or worse, that just as Descartes started modern philosophy down the royal road of epistemology, so Frege steered contemporary philosophy down the royal road of logic.

The first part of that story can be quickly told. Young Bertrand Russell, reading Frege, was inspired to prove that the elementary propositions of arithmetic could be demonstrated by using logic alone. (It is said that his interest in doing so was first stimulated when he was a youth of eleven, when the rebellious young genius was told not to question the arithmetic tables but simply to memorize them.) He teamed up with an older mathematician of similar inclinations, Alfred North Whitehead (1861–1947). Russell and Whitehead produced the *Principles of Mathematics* in 1903 and the more formidable, three-volume classic *Principia Mathematica* (published in 1910–1913). The central obsession of Anglo-American philosophy was established, and to this day there are philosophers who consider only mathematical logic to be "real" philosophy.

Meanwhile, Edmund Husserl, under the influence of German empiricists whose orientation closely resembled that of John Stuart Mill, wrote his own *Philosophy of Arithmetic*. Quite unlike Russell and Whitehead, Husserl argued that the elementary propositions of arithmetic were not based on logic (or *a priori*), but were rather very abstract generalizations from experience, an argument very much like Mill's theory a few decades earlier. Frege reviewed Husserl's book and soundly refuted its central thesis. Husserl, in a most unusual move for a philosopher, completely changed his mind (quoting Goethe to the effect that one is never more opposed to a thesis than after one has rejected it as one's own). He then produced an elaborate set of *Logical Investigations*, published at the turn of the century, in which he, like Russell and Whitehead, argued that arithmetic was indeed an a priori science. There the similarity stops, however, for while Russell and Whitehead based their analysis on logic, Husserl was developing an entirely new method of philosophical inquiry into the nature of such necessary or a priori truths.

What does this have to do, one might ask, with philosophy? Well, the status and nature of mathematics are among the oldest topics of philosophical wonder, first of all, and it was through their admiration for mathematics that many of the earliest Greek philosophers (most notably Pythagoras) took up philosophy. The apparent indubitability of mathematical truths also presented a singularly difficult problem for those modern philosophers who divided up the world of knowledge between logical truths and empirical matters of fact.

Some (such as Locke, Leibniz, and Hume) took it to be self-evident that such truths were self-defining and a priori, but, then, how did this abstract network of propositions manage to relate so well to the world? A few bold individuals (such as J. S. Mill and the young Husserl) suggested the alternative, that the propositions of arithmetic were abstract generalizations from experience, but how, then, could one account for their seeming necessity? Kant had developed what was no doubt his most ingenious theory, explaining both applicability and necessity. Kant contended that mathematics was *both* basic to experience *and* a priori. The status of mathematics would remain a challenge for any all-embracing theory of knowledge, however, and the theory of knowledge had become basic to what many philosophers now considered to be philosophy.

The work that initiated Western philosophy in our century was far more sophisticated, far more complex, and far more technical than the work that had gone before. But, it was, nevertheless, not wholly indifferent to the more visceral philosophical questions concerning the meaning of life, the human condition, and the need for harmony and understanding in the world. Leibniz once suggested that the problems of life could be solved through a universal calculus, and young Russell, himself an enthusiastic fan of Leibniz, must have believed in or, at any rate, hoped for some similar solution.

At this point, however, it would be unwise to delve into the complexities of Frege's logic or the rather specialized topics that motivated *Principia Mathematica* and the *Logical Investigations*. Generally speaking, both works were addressing esoteric questions in a world filled with anxiety. In the first decade of the new century, Europe found itself near the end of an unprecedented century of peace, interrupted only by the brief but bitter Franco–Prussian War of 1870–1871, in which Germany became a major world power. German intellectuals (for example, the young Max Weber) were attacking the decadent aristocracy of eastern Europe, and some of the great cities, notably Vienna, were enjoying a great carnival of self-indulgence and self-loathing, lamenting the obvious fact that they had seen better days.

No cataclysmic changes were immediately in sight, however; and so in the quiet, secluded studies and offices of a Europe about to explode, some of the most ingenious intellectual work was going on. Einstein was constructing his theory of relativity and, despite his resistance, the first stages of quantum theory were under way. Russell and Whitehead were transforming the face of philosophy, while Schoenberg and Webern in Vienna and the Fauvists in France were revolutionizing the arts. Old empires sat on their territories, their dominions fragmented in fact into thousands of clusters, cults, and little worlds. Theirs was a social universe of Leibnizian monads in which nations large and small, families great and impoverished, gaggles of intellectuals and artists lived their separate lives.

In philosophy, even narrowly construed, the changes were going much faster and further than the specific accomplishments in logic and the philosophy of mathematics would suggest. The two primary architects of these changes, perhaps, were Russell and Husserl, although it would probably be a mistake to think that they did much more than get the new world of philosophy started. Both of them would, in fact, be soon surpassed by their own most brilliant students, who would take their work in very different directions. Their own contributions were significant, if not monumental, however. Both of them wrote an enormous amount. Russell published virtually every kind of philosophical work, newspaper editorials against war and bolshevism, treaties on love and marriage, attacks on Christianity and books on epistemology and metaphysics, at the remarkable rate of several thousand words a day. Husserl published slowly but thought and wrote feverishly, some fifty thousand pages, most of it still unpublished and unseen by anyone but a handful of devoted scholars.

Although they would not have known this (nor did they know of each other), Russell and Husserl shared a common nemesis (whom neither really understood). That nemesis was Hegel, who still had a powerful hold on philosophy both in England and on the Continent. However, Russell and Husserl reacted against quite different aspects of Hegel's philosophy. Russell rebelled against Hegel's idealism, the conviction that the world was made up (in some sense) of ideas and not good, solid, scientific matter. In a famous quote, Russell comments, "[G. E.] Moore took the lead in the rebellion, and I followed with a sense of emancipation. . . . We believed that the grass is green, and that the sun and stars would exist if no one was aware of them. The world which had been thin and logical now became rich and varied." Russell's philosophy, accordingly, was thoroughly scientific. Like his illustrious predecessor David Hume (and unlike his *logic* hero Leibniz), he was a good British empiricist. He was a scientist and a materialist.

Husserl, on the other hand, rebelled against Hegel's dialectical pluralism. Husserl did not see the world as a clash of conflicting visions except insofar as philosophers had failed to be properly scientific. Husserl, too, saw himself as a scientist. But he was also (with many qualifications) an idealist—that is, he believed that the world was constituted by consciousness. In this, he and Russell would disagree. Husserl never for a moment doubted the existence of the material world. (Neither did Hegel, of course.) Like Descartes and Kant before him, and in fact like Russell across the Channel, he simply insisted that consciousness is our access to the world, and all of our knowledge came through experience, properly understood.

For Russell, this claim was the basic thesis of classic empiricism. We have sensations, which are caused by the world. Reflecting on those sensations we can understand the world. What is particularly worth noting about Russell's theory, at least the theory that he defended during the years before the First World War, is its basic structure, so in temper with the times. Russell, like Hume before him, was an unabashed *atomist*. That is, he believed that simple bits of language—sentences (or, more properly, propositions)—referred to simple bits of experience—sensations—which were caused by simple bits of reality—facts. In his theory of knowledge as in his logic, Russell was very much a minimalist. He tried to reduce the complexity of the world and our experience of the world to its simplest "atomic" bits. Philosophy should proceed, according to the school he helped establish, by way of *analysis*, breaking up the bits and understanding how they fit together. (The British Hegelians, by way of contrast, were always insisting that everything is connected to everything else, and that parts could not be understood without reference to the whole.)

Our language, accordingly, would also have to be simplified, improved, *idealized*. We had to redo our grammar, in formal logic of course, to more accurately reflect the structure of the world. To take one famous and illuminating example, Russell wrote several essays analyzing the simple English article "the." The problem was that, as ordinarily used, the word "the" always seemed to indicate reference to something. But consider a use which had no such referent. Russell's example was, "The present king of France is bald." (There was in fact no current king of France.) Is the sentence therefore true or false? Clearly that is a question that cannot be properly answered with a "true" or a "false."

Where the word "the" does not refer, the problematic sentence must be analyzed in terms of its logical and not its ordinary grammatical form. The logical form shows it to be three atomic sentences, not one. ("There *is* a present king of France, *and* there is *only* one king of France, *and* he is bald.") Such ontological hardheadedness, combined with the dazzling tools of the new logic, would transform philosophy in England and America. Those logically demanding, minimalist tendencies still remain. Indeed, for many professional philosophers the only thing in the game that has dramatically changed is its location. Whereas once the primary playing field was in Cambridge (England), it has now moved to Cambridge (Massachusetts), Pittsburgh, Chicago, and Berkeley.

Russell was, throughout his life, a philosopher's philosopher, a paragon of intellectual integrity. He struggled with the problems of logic and epistemology, trying to perfect his ideal language, changing his mind every decade or so for the better part of a century. But the awful war had already made it impossible for him to live in what he now called "the thin and trivial" world of abstract ideas (or what his arch-nemesis, Hegelian F. H. Bradley, called "the unearthly ballet of bloodless categories"). During the war, he had spent several months in prison for his pacifism, and afterward he had been vilified by the nation whose

honor he had tried to defend. His writings on sex and marriage, although fairly
tame by today's standards, created a scandal, first in England and then in New
York, where he was denied a teaching position at the City University of New
York as a result of a humiliating public outcry.

By the 1940s Russell's ideas and his approach to philosophy were already
dated. (Despite its pretensions to timelessness, philosophy as practiced has always
been fickle and fashion conscious.) Russell turned his attention to other, more
worldly matters—to, for instance, the fact that he now found himself without
funds. He wrote his best-selling book on the history of philosophy in 1945, and
he produced a steady stream of controversial attacks on Christianity and organized religion in general, following on *Why I Am Not a Christian* in 1927. He
publicly defended what would later be called "free love," though in fact he was
an outspoken proponent of sexual responsibility. Nevertheless, his advocacy of
sex before marriage and his noncondemnatory attitude toward extramarital affairs
outraged a hypocritical public. He continued to be a vocal and eloquent opponent
of militarism, helped to found the antinuclear movement, and (with Jean-Paul
Sartre) established a "war crimes" tribunal that condemned the American military involvement in Vietnam.

Toward the end of his long life, he wrote an elegant and impassioned autobiography, conclusively documenting his political commitments, his love of philosophy, and what we might politely call his love of love. Curiously enough,
when Russell's philosophy became so thoroughly engaged in the world, his philosophical colleagues often deserted him. Most philosophers failed to confront
Russell's most pessimistic opinion that "the world is horrible." From a safe
distance, and especially after his death, they staunchly defended him, as Plato
defended Socrates, as a martyr for the truth and an enemy of nonsense. But they
generally preferred his logical minimalism, his healthy British skepticism. Perhaps that is why he is so often ignored today.

Husserl, on the other hand, was no minimalist. His philosophy overflowed
with new concepts, new distinctions, new ways of looking. Husserl was enthusiastic about logic, but he was unwilling to simply take logic, or any set of logical
axioms—no matter how obvious—at face value. Logic, like arithmetic, had to be
explained. In that sense he was more radical than Russell (at least if one appeals
to the etymological sense of "radical," which refers to the "roots"). He also saw
himself as a radical, even though, from another perspective, he was quite the
reactionary.

To begin with the latter, Husserl was firmly—some would even say dogmatically—opposed to the changes that seemed to have been taking place in philosophy. Not only Nietzsche but a number of other German philosophers suggested
that philosophy could not be reduced to a single perspective, that philosophy
could not come up with any single answer to its questions, that philosophy might
be *relative* to a people, or to our particular species, or even to individual psychology. Against any such relativism, Husserl insisted on philosophy as a singular, rigorous science.

Indeed, one of the main themes of his *Logical Investigations* was a protracted
argument against *psychologism*, the thesis that truth is dependent on the peculi-

arities of the human mind, that our philosophy is reducible to our psychology. In other words, it was an argument against the very thesis that he himself had argued in his first book on the philosophy of arithmetic.

But Husserl's philosophy was not at all negative. However incensed he may have become about relativism, his continuing effort was dedicated to developing a method for finding and guaranteeing the truth. That method was *phenomenology*. The word "phenomenon" comes directly from the Greek, meaning "appearance." Kant had used the same word to refer to the world of our experience. Husserl intends a similar meaning, except for the crucial fact that, for him, it does not imply a contrast between the appearance and some underlying reality, between the phenomenon and a "noumenon" or "thing-in-itself." That, according to Husserl, is where the trouble starts, when one supposes (even if only through the seemingly innocent process of philosophically doubting) that what one experiences is not, or might not be, the truth.

Husserl defines phenomenology as the scientific study of the essential structures of consciousness. By describing those structures, Husserl promises us, we can find certainty, which philosophy has always sought. To do that, Husserl describes a method—or rather, a series of continuously revised methods—for taking up a peculiarly phenomenological standpoint, "bracketing out" everything that is not essential, thereby understanding the basic rules or constitutive processes through which consciousness does its work of knowing the world.

The central doctrine of Husserl's phenomenology is the thesis that consciousness is *intentional*. That is, every act of consciousness is directed at some object or other, perhaps a material object, perhaps an "ideal" object—as in mathematics. Thus the phenomenologist can distinguish and describe the nature of the intentional *acts* of consciousness and the intentional *objects* of consciousness, which are defined through the *content* of consciousness. It is important to note that one can describe the content of consciousness and, accordingly, the object of consciousness without any particular commitment to the actuality or existence of that object. Thus, one can describe the content of a dream in much the same terms that one describes the view from a window or a scene from a novel.

What interests the phenomenologist are the contents of consciousness, not the things of the natural world as such. Thus, in *Ideas: General Introduction to Pure Phenomenology* (1931) Husserl distinguishes between the natural and the phenomenological standpoint. The former is our ordinary everyday viewpoint and the ordinary stance of the natural sciences, describing things and states of affairs. The latter is the special viewpoint achieved by the phenomenologist, as he or she focuses not on things but our consciousness of things. (This is sometimes confused by the fact that Husserl insists that the phenomenologist pay attention to "the things themselves," by which he means the phenomena, or our conscious ideas of things, not natural objects.)

The phenomenological standpoint is achieved through a series of phenomenological "reductions," which eliminate certain aspects of our experience from consideration. Husserl formulates several of these and their emphasis shifts throughout his career, but two of them deserve special mention. The first and best known is the *epoché* or "suspension" that he describes in *Ideas*, in which the phenomenologist "brackets" all questions of truth or reality and simply de-scribes the contents of consciousness. (The word is borrowed from both the early Skeptics and Descartes.) The second reduction (or set of reductions) eliminates the merely empirical content of consciousness and focuses instead on the essential features, the *meanings* of consciousness. Thus Husserl defends a notion of "intuition" that differs from and is more specialized than the ordinary notion of "experience." Some intuitions are *eidetic*, that is, they reveal necessary truths, not just the contingencies of the natural world. These are the essence of phenomenology.

In *Ideas*, Husserl defends a strong realist position—that is, the things that are perceived by consciousness are taken to be not merely objects of consciousness but the things themselves. A decade or so later, Husserl made a shift in his emphasis from the intentionality of the objects to the nature of consciousness. His phenomenology became increasingly and self-consciously Cartesian, as his philosophy moved to the study of the ego and its essential structures. In 1931 Husserl was invited to lecture at the Sorbonne in Paris, and on the basis of those lectures published his *Cartesian Meditations*. (*The Paris Lectures* were also published some years later.) He argues there that "the monadically concrete ego includes the whole of actual and potential conscious life" and "the phenomenology of this self-constitution coincides with phenomenology as a whole (including objects)." These statements suggest a very strong idealist tendency in his later philosophy. The ego is—or, at any rate, presents us with—the world.

Toward the end of his life, as National Socialism was tightening its grip on Germany and the world was once again preparing for war, Husserl underwent another, perhaps predictable, philosophical change, a shift toward the practical or what some might call the more "existential" dimension of human knowledge. Warning of a "crisis" in European civilization based on rampant relativism and irrationalism (an alarm that the logical positivists were raising about the same time in Vienna), Husserl published his *Crisis of European Philosophy* (1937). There the focus turned to the "lifeworld" and the nature of social existence, topics that had played little role in his earlier investigations of the philosophy of arithmetic and the nature of individual consciousness.

The relativism and "irrationalism" Husserl had railed against and for which his phenomenology had been formulated as the antidote were no longer intellectual conceits. They were active forces in society. Philosophy, he believed, could save the world. As we shall see, this was not an uncommon idea in the terrifying years of the 1930s, or, for that matter, throughout the history of modern German philosophy. These concerns would loom large for the phenomenologists that followed Husserl—in particular, for Martin Heidegger, who had already published his *Being and Time* a decade earlier, and for the Frenchman Jean-Paul Sartre, whose phenomenological work was just then developing.

One final comment before we move on: there is much made today of the contrast and supposed conflict between what is called "analytic" philosophy, on the one hand, and "Continental" philosophy on the other. One might note, to begin with, that the contrast is a false one. "Analysis" refers to a method (one largely inspired by Russell). "Continental" refers to a place—continental Europe.

Apart from the nitpicky fact that those who speak of "the Continent" usually mean only Germany and France, and the more interesting fact that "analytic philosophy" includes a fair number of contrasting and competing methodologies, it should be clear from this chapter that even the basic contrast is mistaken or misleading. "Analytic philosophy" is often defined in terms of its interest in logic and language, but, as we have seen, that interest itself emerges first in Germany (with Frege in particular) and is fully shared by Edmund Husserl, the founder of this century's "continental" movements.

Later we will find that one of the outstanding philosophers of the century, the definitive philosopher of the "analytic" tradition, Ludwig Wittgenstein, also came to England from Austria, without ever leaving his "continental" roots behind him. The truth is that, while there are many twisted and interwoven schools, methods, and styles of philosophy, they are rarely easily distinguished by so narrow a body of water as the English Channel or, for that matter, even an ocean. It is the movements between as well as within the various ways of philosophy (not only in Europe, England, and America but also around the world) that make up the history—and the future—of philosophy.

Zarathustra in the Trenches: The Limits of Rationality

In 1911 an extremely intense, brilliant, and wealthy young aristocrat from an old Viennese family showed up on Russell's doorstep in Cambridge. Ludwig Wittgenstein (1889–1951) was indisputably a genius, and it was not long before Russell admitted that he had taught the young logician everything he had to teach him. Wittgenstein mastered the new logic, adopted his teacher's minimalist and atomistic view of the world, and within a few years he transformed philosophy, although not at all as he had intended.

Having said "all that he had to say" (in a terse book of less than eighty pages) and fought in the trenches of the First World War, Wittgenstein left philosophy. He taught school, built a house for his sister, composed some music, and disappeared from the scene. But by 1929 he was back in Cambridge, rethinking all that he had done, struggling not only with the new logical forms of philosophy and the search for an ideal scientific language but with the whole history of human thought. He found himself struggling with the anguish and suffering that had concerned the Stoics and his own predecessors Schopenhauer and Nietzsche, even if such topics were virtually absent from the philosophical discussions he had inspired in Cambridge and elsewhere. He took up a professorship in philosophy at Cambridge, "an absurd profession." He decided, however, that this was "a living death," and so he dropped out of academia once again.

But we are getting ahead of our story. When Wittgenstein showed up in Cambridge in the second decade of the century, the Vienna he left behind was the crucible in which the new world was taking shape. Vienna displayed, more than anywhere else, the decadence of the old aristocracy, the anxieties of the middle class, the anger of a new generation of artists, writers, and critics. Wittgenstein himself personified that old aristocracy (although he gave away all of his fortune so that he would no longer be associated with it). He shared the anxieties of his era. (Three of his brothers had committed suicide, and he saw as clearly as anyone the collapse of the old moral order.) He belonged to the Viennese clique of artists, writers, and critics. Arnold Schoenberg was a family friend. The fearsome radical journalist Karl Kraus was an early associate, although by contrast Wittgenstein's own writing virtually writhes with irrepressible tension. In Vienna one could find many of the minor political intrigues that would soon explode into a world war. There one could also expose the pathologies that were undermining the well-being of Europe. Before we pursue the remarkable exploits of the unhappy genius Wittgenstein, we should perhaps examine the neuroses of his times, the pathologies that were undermining him as well as the rest of Europe.

In Vienna one could find the good doctor who was pursuing that diagnosis to its horrible conclusions, choosing the most sensitive subject he could find—himself. Sigmund Freud (1856–1939) is not usually considered a philosopher, which is surely philosophy's loss and shame. For better or worse, Freud's ideas established the framework for twentieth-century thinking about the mind, about human nature, about the human condition, and about the prospects for human happiness. His anti-Enlightenment idea that we often do not and cannot know what is going on in our own minds would become the premise—or at least the problem—for generations of philosophers and social thinkers. On the other hand, his very Enlightenment idea that the mind was ultimately a material entity (namely, the brain), analyzable in terms of neurology, energy circuits, and the language of physics still defines the science of psychology. So, too, the idea that everything can be explained, even the little "mistakes" and "slips of the tongue," even forgetting and dreaming, remains the underlying supposition of twentieth-century thought, both popular and sophisticated.

As always, one can find predecessors for these ideas. The "unconscious" was a topic of discussion for generations of German philosophers, including even the rationalists Leibniz and Kant. Some form of the idea that the mind and the brain are one had been defended by Spinoza and before him by generations of materialists ever since Democritus. The idea that everything can be explained is, in one sense, just another application of the Principle of Sufficient Reason, the a priori demand that every event have a cause. But Freud put this philosophy together with an unprecedented boldness at a time when the world was hungry for explanations. He coupled with his philosophy experiences with hypnosis, his Jewish upbringing, and his time in the clinics. Then he outraged the world by giving just the sort of explanation least wanted, that human conduct by its very nature is based on vile, murderous, incestuous motives. So much for the enlightened thesis that human beings are basically good. Sexual desire was everywhere, and everywhere repressed. Unhappiness was inevitable, and civilization itself was its cause.

As a physician, Freud's theorizing grew out of his practical efforts to treat his patients with nervous disorders. Discovering that some of his patients' problems grew out of previous traumatic experiences, often from their infancy, Freud developed a psychological theory based on an analysis of childhood development. Infants begin life with a desire for pleasure. Freud called this *the pleasure principle*. As an infant becomes aware that the external world does not always accommodate its desires, the infant recognizes the need to work with its environment if it is to get the pleasure it desires. This discovery demands the recognition of *the reality principle*, which often counters the pleasure principle in practice.

In the process of maturing, the child learns to subordinate the demands of the pleasure principle to the reality principle. One means by which the "psychic apparatus" is able to do this is by developing an internal mechanism of censorship, which pushes out of consciousness desires that are dangerous or inappropriate. Freud calls this process *repression*. In particular, repression affects many of our sexual desires, which by nature are often perverse.

Desires, when repressed, are forced into the "Unconscious," where they remain psychically active but not consciously evident. In the case of individuals with nervous disorders (*neuroses*), however, certain repressed desires and memories demand expression despite the fact that they are socially unacceptable. Since the censoring mechanism rejects these desires and memories, they are only partially felt or remembered, in distorted form, and this results in aberrant behavior and disturbing thoughts, impulses and, significantly, dreams. In dreams, we can often "see" what we refuse to see. On the other hand, a person who becomes hysterically blind is, according to Freud, literally trying not to "see" the repressed desire that is protruding into the realm of consciousness.

Neurotic symptoms express desires in a jumbled way, and the psychoanalyst's job is to decode the jumble, to find the source of a nervous problem by uncovering the repressed desire that motivates it. Freud developed a number of methods for doing this, for moving from the behavior to the underlying idea. One of these is his method for dream interpretation. Freud held that dreams present desires in a disguised form, the *manifest content*, and that one can decode a dream to discover its hidden message, or *latent content*. Neurotic symptoms, in his opinion, are similar to dreams, in that the overt behavior involved is a coded disguise for a consciously unacceptable desire. The philosophy of signs, as well as the philosophy of the mind, was in for a wholesale upheaval.

Freud was revolutionary in treating mental disorders as partial departures from normal development, not as radically different from what we call "mental health." With Freud the notion of "normalcy" began to get seriously thrown into question, and it is with Freud that the idea of "the psychopathology of everyday life" took hold. Everyone faces challenging hurdles in the course of development, according to Freud; some are just more fortunate than others in their efforts to surmount them.

For example, male children at the age of four or five confront a psychological challenge that Freud called the *Oedipus complex*. After years of being primarily attached to its mother, a child comes to see the father as a competitor for its mother's attention. Freud names this condition after Oedipus, the Greek tragic hero who (unknowingly) killed his father and married his mother. Further development depends on resolving this complex, abandoning the fixation on the mother and accepting the authority of the father. Some men are not able to fully achieve this resolution, and as a result, their adult lives are burdened by difficulties in forming love relationships with anyone besides their mothers or in deferring to authority.[86]

Freud's later works take on a decidedly dark cast. In *Civilization and Its Discontents* (1930), Freud argues that those who live within civilization can do so only by repressing desires and forgoing many instinctual gratifications. Unfortunately, the more civilized we become, the more we have to contain ourselves; and the more repressed we become, the more likely it is that we will become neurotic. Thus, the price of civilization is the sacrifice of happiness. Freud also argues, in *Beyond the Pleasure Principle* (1920), that besides the drive toward pleasure (and the related "life instincts," which are mostly sexual), human beings also have an urge toward death, a principle Freud calls *"Thanatos"* (Greek for "death").

Freud did not mean that we are all literally suicidal. The Thanatos principle is essentially a principle of energy conservation which seeks to minimize tension within any organism. But the result is that every organism aims at death, as the end to the life cycle, a morbid idea that inspired other German thinkers as well. Ultimately, Freud argues, our lives are guided by the cosmic principles of Love and Death. Death may end the individual life, but love sees that life continues in the species. Love, nevertheless, is hardly the romance that was so celebrated in Freud's Vienna. It is "lust, plus the ordeal of civility," in Freud's now famous cynical phrase.

Freud's theories have had their share of critics. One of the first was Freud's disciple, Carl G. Jung (1875–1961). Jung thought that Freud overemphasized the importance of sex as the basis of neurotic problems. He also argued that Freud placed too much emphasis on the importance of traumas within the individual's personal biography. Jung argued that at least much of unconscious life is directed by patterns, or *archetypes*, that are common to the species. One common cause of neurotic behavior, according to Jung, is the activation of an archetypal pattern—a typical way of handling a life situation—without the person's awareness. The individual, in such a situation, ignores the specifics of the situation and behaves "automatically," in a fashion that is inappropriate from the standpoint of consciousness. Jung also theorized about the ideal of mental health, which he described as "individuation," the mature and balanced standpoint in which one has learned to accept all of one's traits, the weaknesses as well as the strengths, and has integrated them into a way of life that is personally and uniquely fulfilling. (Jung had read a lot of Nietzsche.)

In Germany, another movement would complement the work of Freud and Wittgenstein in ways that are still not sufficiently appreciated. Max Weber (1864–1920) was a sociologist (indeed, he created the field now known as sociology), but he was also a goldmine of ideas, particularly concerning one of philosophy's favorite topics and postures, *rationality*. (Once again, the artificial separation of disciplines is philosophy's loss. How much of philosophy is the unacknowledged expression of certain social structures rather than the exposition of truth as such? And how much of sociology is covert philosophy?)

As a young man, Weber was a liberal advocate of German nationalism and imperialism. As an older, respected scholar, he courageously opposed both the imperialism of the war and the new right wing in Germany, and he denounced the potentially hateful ideas they represented. His enormous status in sociology had much to do with the rigorous methods he promoted, but his more influential contributions were in his analysis and, if we may use the more Freudian term, diagnosis of contemporary society.

Two theses are of particular interest to us here. The first is Weber's famous thesis that capitalism, and consequently the very structure of modern Western society, is the product of Protestantism. In his *Protestant Ethic and the Rise of Capitalism*, Weber argues that the harsh Christian philosophy of Calvinism, with its central thesis of predestination, condemned millions of people to unresolvable anxiety. People could not know with certainty whether they were part of the "elect" or not. And so one felt it necessary to "prove" one's worth in this life, working feverishly and living ascetically. Of course, no amount of success could possibly quash the anxiety that motivated such energetic entrepreneurship, but between effort and an ascetic existence, the result was a lot of money—that is, capital. Capital could be used to make more money in an unsuccessful attempt to lessen anxiety. The results were further effort, more money, and so on, leading to the ultimately unsatisfying decades of greed that have defined so much of our current experience.

It is not hard to couple this diagnostic thesis with Freud's view that civilization itself is responsible for our inevitable unhappiness, that the anxieties we experience because of our innermost but forbidden desires are part and parcel of our human nature. But Weber, unlike Freud, was not so easily caught in the trap of generalizing from his own experience and the structures of his own society. He saw that the structures that determine "the human condition" were not just the product of civilization but of particular civilizations, particular beliefs and desires.

Weber was thus led to an interest in the notion of rationality as such. Philosophers since ancient times had viewed rationality as a God-given gift, a peculiar, spectacular capacity that allowed human beings, alone among all of earth's creatures, to transcend their immediate experience and contemplate the distant future, explore the distant past, and get a glimpse of heaven, not to mention mathematics and the joys of philosophy. Philosophers have often challenged the reach of reason, for example, in the long-standing medieval debates between reason and faith in approaching God and in modern attempts (by Locke, Hume, and Kant, for example) to "critique" reason and set its limits. Weber, however, recognized that there are several different senses of "reason" and "rationality," and that much of what passed for rationality in contemporary life was in fact a valueless, merely "instrumental" form of thinking, devoid of human and spiritual sentiment.

In a word, what rationality had come to signify was *bureaucracy*. What was once a fair-minded governmental policy (invented by the Romans, perfected by Napoleon) had become a law unto itself, an emphasis on efficiency (no matter how inefficient a bureaucracy may be) in place of all of those values that in fact made life meaningful and worthwhile. Reason, as Weber's one-time mentor Nietzsche had said several decades before, had become a tyrant. It no longer recognized its own limits, and it no longer recognized the values that it was supposed to serve. By the end of his life, Weber had become something of a neo-Romantic. Drawing from Nietzsche, Weber analyzed the concept of "charisma," leadership by means of spiritual inspiration, although he took this in a more conventionally religious way than Nietzsche.

Now we turn back to Wittgenstein. Wittgenstein left Cambridge to serve in the Austrian army during the First World War, and he distinguished himself as a soldier and a leader. But he was distinctive in that, while most of the soldiers around him carried copies of Nietzsche's *Thus Spake Zarathustra* in their backpacks, he carried around his own philosophical manuscript as well, working on it when he could. Like Zarathustra, Wittgenstein's book descended upon warring humanity as a prophet might descend from the mountain, chastising them for their confusions and attempting to straighten out their misunderstandings once and for all. The book came to be called *Tractatus Logico-Philosophicus* (the *Tractatus* for short), and when his old teacher Russell finally arranged for its publication in 1921, it was recognized immediately as a philosophical classic.

The *Tractatus*, much like some of Nietzsche's books, is a pithy work of carefully ordered and numbered aphorisms. But unlike Nietzsche's always self-questioning works, this one is unashamedly assertive, even dogmatic. It is, or seemed to be, first and foremost a book on logic. It is, or, at least it seemed to be, an uncompromising defense of scientific rationality. The bulk of the book is a manifesto of classic logical atomism—that is, Russell's picture of minimalist simple sentences, which, according to Wittgenstein, "picture" minimalist simple facts. "The world is everything that is the case," he says. Much of the rest is an answer to the question of how sentences (or, more properly, propositions) picture the world.

But the most interesting parts of the book, from a philosophical point of view, have to do with what reason cannot do. Here the influence of Schopenhauer and Nietzsche, as well as several generations of German romanticism, are much in evidence. What reason tries to do but cannot do is investigate itself. It cannot set, or for that matter even describe, its own limits. It cannot even describe itself. ("I am not in my world. I am the boundary of my world.") Nor can one say what is beyond those limits. One cannot say the "unsayable." Outside of the limits of scientific rationality lie all of the problems of value, the pressing questions of ethics, the very nature of God and religion. The end of the *Tractatus* points in this direction: "Whereof one cannot speak, one must be silent." This is not a simple tautology but profound mysticism, silently pointing us toward a multitude of experiences that lie beyond the bounds of philosophy and beyond the limits of reason.

One of the effects of Wittgenstein's work was to inspire a philosophical movement in Vienna that would come to be called "logical positivism." The Viennese positivists took up certain central theses of the *Tractatus*, including not only the central arguments about logical form but also, more problematically, the final statements about what cannot be said. As the movement developed and worked its way over to England and America, it seemed increasingly to dismiss the most important aspects of philosophy and of life—ethics, aesthetics, and religion—as "meaningless." Philosophy, according to this desiccated view, was logic and logic alone. But what the positivists themselves were about cannot be so vulgarly summarized. (We shall say more about them later.) Wittgenstein, certainly, never accepted any such viewpoint. For him, ethics, aesthetics, and religion were *too important* to be captured by the logical language of science. But Wittgenstein left philosophy behind him, and when he came back to it a decade later, he had very different ideas.

The American Experience in Philosophy: Pragmatism

The American philosophical response to the conflicted twentieth century continued the antimetaphysical spirit of the last century, and the best example of that spirit was that uniquely American philosophy called *pragmatism*. The first two pragmatists were Charles Sanders Peirce (1839–1914) and William James (1842–1910), brother of novelist Henry James. Peirce had intended his pragmatism as a corrective to the clumsiness and equivocation he found in the scientific method of his day. James turned it into a philosophy. The hallmark of that philosophy was a renewed emphasis on *experience*, a "radical empiricism" that would make none of the compromises of the older empiricisms. It was James who coined the phrase "stream of experience." He also bridged the old and new worlds by establishing a fully American version of what in Europe was being coined "phenomenology" (the science of experience). He held a deep sympathy for Freud's ideas. (The two men met just before James's death.)

Harvard philosopher Charles Peirce was primarily a logician, and he is most famous for developing a theory of signs and their interrelations, which has relatively little to do with his pragmatism. He developed the theory of pragmatism as such primarily on the basis of his interest in science. Reflecting upon the naturalistic descriptions of biologists, Peirce was convinced that habit is the key to survival in virtually every animal species. (Thus, an early pragmatist obsession concerned neurology and the "reflex arc," matters that preoccupied both William James and John Dewey.)

Most animals get their habits through instincts, but human beings need to develop habits. In particular they need to acquire beliefs, which give them (preferably dependable) presuppositions for action. Accordingly, Peirce analyzed belief as one manifestation of habit in human beings. But beliefs, on Peirce's view, are provisional and contingent. They can and often must be changed, depending on circumstances. Indeed, circumstances and our own actions constantly force us to refine our beliefs. Belief is not a "once and always" matter and, apart from mathematics and logic, beliefs that are said to be "eternal" and amenable to a priori proof are almost surely of no real use. We constantly test the reliability of our beliefs, and we discard those that fail the test.

Peirce similarly argued that the terms of science only have meaning to the extent that they are connected to actual experiential reality. He defended theoretic constructs as legitimate postulates in science, so long as definitions focus on perceivable results ("operational definitions"). He firmly rejected the old-world style of nonempirical philosophical speculation, and he was joined in this belief by another member of the Harvard philosophy department, William James.

James was a scientist who lived and worked in what now is the border (too often a gap) between philosophy and psychology. He was one of the first Americans to become interested in the new science of neurology, and his two-volume *Psychology*, although obviously dated, is still considered one of the classics in the field. Over and above his scientific interests, however, James was primarily interested in the problems of everyday living. It was he who first popularized pragmatism and brought it out of the halls of Harvard and into the mainstream of American intellectual life. (Peirce, we might note, disdained James's popularization of the movement, and came to distinguish his own work by calling it "pragmaticism"—"a word so ugly no one else will ever use it.")

Our ideas are of use, James argued, only if they have "cash value," in other words, only if they are actually useful when we employ them in our practical projects. Good ideas are good for something. But, despite this practical emphasis, James did not dismiss the importance of religion or moral beliefs. Indeed, he considered religious experience an indispensable aspect of our experience. Religious experience was more important than religious doctrine. But James also acknowledged that moral and religious beliefs can have "cash value" if they help us to navigate and make sense of our lives. (The vulgarity of the metaphor was not lost on his European critics.)

It is in the context of the emphasis on experience that we can understand the enduring appeal of James in American philosophy, or rather, outside of philosophy, for he has more often been celebrated by historians, journalists, and literary critics than by philosophers. "Experience" seems to be just what twentieth-century America is all about, from the continuous invention of new media to "the experience industry" (not just entertainment but vicarious adventures and well-secured flirtations with danger of every sort). In philosophy, this emphasis on experience came down to the commonsense, practical insistence that if it doesn't make a difference in our experience, it cannot be significant no matter how rigorously argued or a priori persuasive.

Nowhere is this emphasis on experience more pronounced and more appealing than in religion, where the varieties of religious experience have come to define spiritual life. From the conservative charismatics and Southern Baptists to the gurus at Esalen Institute in Big Sur, California, religion is frequently identified in terms of personal, subjective experience, not sophisticated theological doctrine. James (who was a physician, after all) treated religion as a kind of a cure—for doubt, depression, insecurity—and he prescribed it as therapy, not dogma. The pragmatist doctrine also carried with it a message of *pluralism*, the legitimacy of different ways of experiencing and living in the world. It was a perfect philosophy for an increasingly multicultural society of ambitious, adventurous immigrants.

It is curious that one of James's most enthusiastic students was Kitarō Nishida (1870–1945), a Japanese philosopher who promulgated the Jamesian celebration of "pure experience" in his homeland. Not surprisingly, what Nishida meant by "pure experience" differed from the understanding of the pragmatists. Pure experience, as Nishida understands it, is akin to the ideal experience of Zen meditation, in which the nature and unity of all things are experienced immediately. Insisting that pure experience could not be grasped from a third-person point of view, Nishida took as the basis for his theory the experiencing subject's pre-reflective lived experience. Nishida's pure experience is prior to any division between subject and object; in it, one encounters both the self and objects simultaneously. In pure experience one transcends one's individuality and encounters (both intellectually and emotionally) something that is truly universal, the Ultimate Reality, in which self and universe are one.

Historically, it is understandable that although American pragmatism began in the antimetaphysical spirit of Peirce and James, the second generation of pragmatists was influenced by Hegel, the great German metaphysician. Defying the nihilistic tendencies of the era with the conviction that thought can master the most difficult situation, Josiah Royce (1855–1916), one of James's colleagues at Harvard, conjoined pragmatism with Hegelianism and defended the holistic notion of absolute truth. James had treated "truth" rather gingerly, sometimes suggesting that the word referred to the most useful theory, other times suggesting the more radical thesis that we *make* something true by using it effectively in a concrete context. Royce, on the other hand, claimed that all philosophers, even pragmatists, appealed to absolute truth, even when they denied it. The "Spirit" of modern philosophy, according to Royce, was irreducibly idealistic, incorporating both the Jamesian emphasis on experience and the dynamic, transcendental reach of the German idealists. Oddly enough, James's pragmatism and Nishida's Zen meet on the common ground of Hegel's "science of experience."

Many Americans tend to put little stock in the origins of a philosopher, perhaps on the grounds that Americans tend to be so mobile and rarely stay in one place. But one of Royce's distinctive contributions to philosophy stemmed from his California background and perspective. He expresses great enthusiasm for this background in a book about his native state that to this day is one of the best analyses of that strange mix of materialism, spirituality, sophistication, and vulgarity that defines the California psyche. Royce's twin emphasis on experience and on what he called "voluntarism" is particularly appropriate from this perspective. Royce's voluntarism is not at all akin to the voluntarism of the Will in Schopenhauer, with its emphasis on irrationality and pessimism. Rather, it is defined by that familiar California optimism, a vague yet overpowering sense of purposiveness, and an abstract Hegelian sense of "spiritual" identity in the larger community. Aptly, for one who was so appreciative of his background, one of Royce's most important but still unappreciated ideas in ethics is the central role of such virtues as *loyalty* in human life. It is a virtue that, sadly, has largely dropped out of American ethics, both in corporate and, more tragically, family life as well.

The central figure of twentieth-century pragmatism, and perhaps the definitive American philosopher, was John Dewey (1859–1952). Dewey was also influenced by the dynamic character of Hegel's vision, and as a young philosopher he was something of an evangelical Hegelian. Although he moved away from Hegel and turned on the abstract idealism that continued to be defended by Royce, Dewey built his entire philosophy on a concept of dynamic unity that he inherited from Hegel. He was, throughout his career, opposed to all of those exaggerated dualisms—between mind and body, between necessary and contingent propositions, between cause and effect, between secular and transcendent—which split up rather than clarify experience and, in his view, make philosophical progress impossible. He was an antireductionist, preferring rich theories and viewpoints to minimalist ones (such as those of the logical atomists). In addition, he always looked for a functional understanding—"How does this work?" "How does this fit in?"—rather than a static, abstract analysis.

In accordance with this all-embracing attitude, Dewey sought to direct pragmatism away from a one-dimensional emphasis on science and logic (as in Peirce) and an overly personal emphasis on subjective experience (as in James). Dewey was interested, in particular, in the application of philosophy to the abundance of increasingly evident and serious social problems facing the country. Characterizing himself, he would insist that he was, above all, the philosopher of democracy, and by no means simply a theoretician talking *about* democracy. The main aim of his philosophy was to make democracy work, and this was the goal of his theories of knowledge and education as well as his straightforward political and social theories. Dewey's engaged social concerns, which would become a broad-based social activism, marked the maturity of pragmatism. He not only preached but practiced social engagement, putting his indelible mark on several distinctively American institutions.

Dewey's brand of pragmatism, called *instrumentalism,* treats ideas as tools in our efforts to tackle practical problems. Dewey's emphasis, more than any of the other pragmatists, was on *practice,* on the actual ways in which we learn to do things by *doing* them. Thus his theory of education, often ridiculed for its "permissiveness," is first of all the view that children learn by doing, not by just listening or reading. Dewey has many harsh things to say about all of those philosophers, including to some extent his fellow pragmatist Royce, who limit their view of human knowledge to a mere "spectator" perspective, merely watching, perhaps comprehending, but not participating in the practice. Thus, in place of traditional philosophy of science, which emphasized the method and the results, Dewey expands his vision to explore the nature of inquiry and learning.

In Dewey's view, the quest for knowledge should not be viewed as an abstract search for "truth." Our search begins because of felt tensions, real discomfort, whether by way of a concrete practical problem or that more complex, obscure set of feelings we sometimes call "curiosity." Our situation presents the problems we should address. They do not appear from nowhere. Scholarly inquiry should always be focused on rectifying real problems and correcting genuine inadequacies. Science and ethics, on this view, have essentially the same goal—the improvement of experienced conditions. Experience, once again, is the key term of Dewey's pragmatic philosophy, understood not only as a dynamic but also as a practical concept. It is not just appreciation and understanding. Experience is problem-solving, participatory, and engaged.

Nevertheless, Dewey's pragmatism, which was lampooned by many Europeans, should not be thought of as a particularly vulgar American version of utilitarianism, concerned only with the "cash value" of experience (the phrase was used metaphorically by James). To underscore the point, Dewey published a groundbreaking book on the apparently *impractical* (and quite civilized) subject of art and aesthetics. *Art and Experience* applied the instrumentalist method to the viewing of art objects. Aesthetic experiences, Dewey argues, help us to structure our experiences in ways that we find meaningful. They reveal with unusual clarity the structure of *every* experience, the resolution of tensions into a satisfying unity.

Philosophers have often expressed an interest in education as part of the social process, but virtually no philosopher, except perhaps Plato and Rousseau, ever put so much emphasis on the subject as Dewey. As in all of his work, Dewey stresses the importance of a large and flexible viewpoint. He firmly rejected the rigid curriculum structure of his day, insisting that it presented an obstacle rather than inspiration to learning. He emphasized engagement, problem-solving, practice, and experience, the delightful experience of learning, most of all.

Dewey also rejected the idea that schools are or should be different in kind from the institutions of adult society. A school is, first of all, a place where children learn to become citizens in a democracy. School itself, therefore, should be a model of democracy. And although it may be a repository and a medium for the culture and traditions of the past, it must also look forward to a changing future. Properly understood, education is a lifelong pursuit, involving the whole of our efforts to structure our experience in meaningful ways. Again, one can compare Dewey's American optimism to the bitter cynicism and despair that was gripping Europe, both before and after the First World War. Europe was bemoaning its tragic destruction. America was looking forward to an exciting future.

George Santayana (1863–1952), a Spanish philosopher who spent most of his life in the United States, was a student of Josiah Royce. Like Dewey, he forged a philosophy that was a blend of Hegelianism and pragmatism, emphasizing experience. Like Dewey, too, he was antireductionist, anti-Cartesian in particular, and he rejected the static, reductionist models of philosophy that had been so prevalent, especially in the various forms of atomism and empiricism that were becoming so influential in Europe and America. Santayana particularly loathed the scholastic emphasis on methodology that was consuming so much of philosophy, both in Europe (for instance, in phenomenology) and in English and American "analytic" philosophy. He instead insisted on a far more personal and literary style. For Santayana, philosophy was an extremely human—humanistic—endeavor.

In one way, however, Santayana rebelled against the views of Dewey and his teacher Royce. He was hostile to democracy and the whole "can do" culture of America. He preferred the Mediterranean. Like many of the nineteenth-century Germans, he waxed nostalgic about the ancient Greeks. He became something of a patrician at Harvard, and when he found that he had received a substantial inheritance, he reputedly walked out of his class at Harvard and resigned on the spot.

Santayana's philosophy, like Royce's Hegelianism, put a premium on dynamic, or what they both called "transcendental," experience. But Santayana, like Royce, shifted his views from the idea that one could simply "intuit" reality, all at once, to the idea that some more systematic, rational process was required. But for Santayana, this "transcendental subjectivity" could never be wholly rational, and it was certainly not amenable to philosophical "proof." Rather, one had to ultimately have faith in one's natural sensibilities, one's "*animal faith*," and give up the self-undermining philosophical demand for demonstrable certainty. In one of his best books, *The Realm of Spirit*, Santayana writes:

> In the animal psyche the passions follow one another or battle for supremacy, and the distracted spirit runs helter-skelter among them, impressed by the sophistical arguments which each of them offers for itself; but if the psyche grows integrated and rational, its center, which is the organ of spirit, becomes dominant, and all those eloquent passions begin to be compared and judged, and their probable issue to be foreknown and discounted. The waves will not be stilled, but they will now beat against a rock. And with inner security comes a great inner clearness.

Santayana debunks metaphysical pretensions in favor of an enthusiastic (he would say "Castilian" or, more generally, Spanish) naturalism, but he nevertheless maintains an important place for religion. Religions impose mythic, or poetic, interpretations on nature, and while not literally true, they are essential in giving meaning to life. They help us to organize our experiences and see things in a moral perspective. Religion is by no means perfect, and as in the case of any other kind of knowledge, the search for certainty and "absolute knowledge" in religion is a serious error. Nevertheless, one's religious views are an essential part of one's identity, like the rest of one's culture, and should not be dismissed or demeaned in the name of progress or practicality. Thus, on some of the most important questions of philosophy, Santayana sharply departs from the views of his pragmatist colleagues.

Changing Reality: Philosophies of Process

After completing the *Principia Mathematica* with Russell, Alfred North Whitehead went off in a very different direction. Moving from England to Harvard, he also moved away from the hard-headed formal conception of philosophy that had been so well exemplified in the *Principia*. Indeed, he began to doubt, much as Wittgenstein had been doubting, the whole tenor of Western philosophy thus far. The purpose of philosophy, he would later insist, is to rationalize mysticism, to "express the infinity of the universe in terms of the limitations of language," and gain "direct insight into depths yet unspoken." This was clearly not the language or the sentiment of the philosopher-mathematician who had coauthored the *Principia* with Russell. (Russell later confessed he could not comprehend a word of Whitehead's new philosophy.)

According to Whitehead's new "process" philosophy, most of the models and metaphors employed by philosophers throughout most of the Western tradition have been of a single kind. They are static models, metaphors of eternity and timelessness. These models and metaphors are only reinforced by an interest in the logical foundations of mathematics, such as Whitehead had shared with Russell, or that more general fascination with the timeless truths of arithmetic and geometry that had captivated the earliest Greek philosophers. Western philosophy is based on such categories as "substance," "essence," and "objects." Its ideals are permanence and logical necessity.

But Whitehead saw an alternative metaphor, a countercurrent that courses through the history of Western philosophy as well. It is the metaphor of change, of progress, of process. One finds it in Heraclitus. One even finds it in Aristotle. One finds it in the modern world, in Hegel, then in Darwin, and in Nietzsche. (It is worth noting that the British "Hegelians," against whom Russell rebelled, had missed or ignored this particular dimension of Hegel's philosophy. Indeed, some of them took as Hegel's primary claim the very un-Hegelian idea that "time is unreal.")

In this century, the Italian philosopher Benedetto Croce defended a faithful Hegelianism, particularly in his later years. The most influential single figure in the development of this process view of reality, however, was the French philosopher Henri Bergson (1859–1941). Bergson's philosophy turned on the idea of *duration*, the reality of change. The point was not just that the properties of things change (blue things turn red, young things turn old), but rather that the stuff of life itself is change. Concepts, on the other hand, are static, one-sided. When we try to analyze anything, we therefore distort and deform it; we get one view but not another; we freeze the thing in time and fail to understand the thing's growth, its development, its life. Analysis is lifeless and at best proceeds by taking successive points of view. But it is, of necessity, always dissatisfied, for there are infinite angles, endless moments.

Bergson is, if indirectly, another adversary of Russell's logical atomism and his method of analysis. But unlike his English (and Austrian) counterparts, Bergson does not just modify the method of analysis and the proper philosophical conception of language. He insists that, in philosophy, we should reject both analysis and language altogether. Metaphysics, he tells us, is that discipline that dispenses with symbols. The metaphysician is thus in the awkward position of having to express the inexpressible. Moreover, Bergson rejects not only the idea of simple facts, simple things, simple sensations, but the very idea of facts, things, and sensations in philosophy. His basic ontology is an ontology of change, not the change of this thing or that property but change as such, change as the whole.

The alternative to analysis, according to Bergson, is to "seize from within," to grasp things as a whole by *intuition*. Here he leaves Hegel and instead joins with the romantics and their idea of the inexpressible, all-embracing intuition. Through intuition, we see things in their wholeness and in time. We see how they embody oppositions and justify opposing viewpoints. We get beyond the frozen moment and appreciate the life, the vital force of things. Nowhere is this intuition of life more immediate and more important than in our intuition of our selves as pure duration. We are "the continuous progress of the past which grows into the future, swelling as it advances." Our desires and actions are not momentary; they carry with them our entire past. (Our thoughts, by contrast, are more selective.) Through ourselves, we recognize the truth about the world. The world is duration. The world is evolution. "We extend ourselves infinitely, and we transcend ourselves." What we call "matter" is nothing but the repetition of experience. To ask *what* it is that changes, that develops, is to miss the point. Indeed, the whole aim of Bergson's philosophy is to get away from such questions, with their bias in favor of stasis and substance.

One of the more charming features of Bergson's philosophy, perhaps, is its uncompromising optimism. In this as well as its evolutionary enthusiasm, it bears some cautious comparison with the popular philosophy of his contemporary, Pierre Teilhard de Chardin (1881–1955). A Jesuit theologian, Chardin was concerned to demonstrate that acceptance of the theory of evolution and Christian belief were compatible. Chardin contended that humanity is evolving toward spiritual unity (a unity which he describes as Christ). In this ongoing process, the species continues the same process of evolution from which it evolved. In the later stages of evolution, according to Chardin, the striking transformations occur not so much in the physical appearance and physiology of the organism as in human consciousness.

Bergson's optimism is all the more striking given that its context is the anxiety- and terror-filled years before, during, and after the Great War. Indeed, in those terrible years, Bergson defends a philosophy of love and freedom as opposed to a Kantian morality of obligation and law, a religion of dynamic openness rather than one that is static and closed. This optimism seems to have stayed with him until the very end, when as a frail old man in 1941, he obstinately lined up with the other Jews of Paris to submit himself to the new Nazi order. (The Germans had excused him from doing so.)

Whitehead, unlike Bergson, retained his love of mathematics, his Platonism regarding "eternal objects," his keen interest in science, particularly the new physics. But his attack on traditional philosophy is very much the same. The categories of philosophy, he complains, are left over from seventeenth-century science. They focus on inactive material objects; conceptualize static, "duration-less" moments; distort our experience. They are "indifferent to time." Whitehead, like Bergson, insists that philosophy adopt a new set of categories. Instead of focusing on objects, it should focus on *events*, conceived of not as static instants (like a "snapshot") but rather as moments in a process of realization.[87] Instead of inanimate objects, Whitehead concentrates on the notion of an organism, "an event, coming into being through patterns." An organism is not a mechanism. It functions through time. Its aspects are "vibrant," not static. Whitehead introduces an old romantic category into twentieth-century philosophy, the category of *creativity*. It is not just that the philosopher should be creative, "speculative," imaginative. Nature itself is continuously creative, novel, imaginative. Accordingly, the philosopher has to invent not an ideal language but a perpetually new and changing language, a poetic language, to capture the evolving patterns of reality.

Unamuno, Croce, and Heidegger: The Tragic Sense of Life

The First World War had ended. In one sense, nothing had changed, but it was nevertheless a different world. Germany had lost a few treasured strips of territory (less than ten percent of its land) and America, which joined the Allies in 1917, had become a world power. But the Great War had not settled anything. The old alliances remained in place, shifting as whimsically as they had before. Europe was not reconciled with Germany. The antagonism between them would only grow more bitter and vengeful. The terms of the Treaty of Versailles (1919) were harsh beyond belief, blaming Germany for the war and demanding "compensation" of more than thirty billion dollars for all civilian casualties and losses.

The German economy was headed for ruin. The great empires were teetering, and a few of them had disintegrated. The most traumatic immediate change, however, was the awful philosophical realization that the Enlightenment was over. The idea of the "perfectibility of humanity," the notion of moral and spiritual progress, had been shattered by a war that had killed over 8.4 million people and laid waste to much of Europe. In the name of nationalism, in pursuit of profits, out of sheer vanity and pride, the civilized world had proved itself to be as irrational, as blind to its own basic values, as any imaginary hell or dystopia.

Germany had been destroyed as a great military power or, at any rate, so insisted the treaty. Germany was left with a tiny army and no munitions production capability. But as the more or less liberal Weimar Republic collapsed under the weight of financial burdens and the bitterness and resentment of the Germans, a new force was sweeping through Europe and getting an iron grip on those countries that had been hardest hit by the war. Under the banners of National Socialism and Fascism, Germany, Italy, and Austria remobilized. Adolf Hitler and Benito Mussolini began to impose a new and terrible philosophy on their people, who were not all unwilling victims.

Fascism was a philosophy of revenge and resentment that cloaked itself in the chauvinist rhetoric of recapturing lost greatness and grandeur. In 1935 Germany snatched back some of its lost territory and Italy made a grab for Ethiopia. The world, exhausted, stood back and did nothing. When Hitler invaded Czechoslovakia and then Poland in 1939, it was already much too late. The world was in the grip of a debilitating depression. The world was headed for another war.

The European philosophy that followed the First World War was, first and foremost, a philosophy of *resentment*. One could not read this directly from some of the texts of logical atomism or the new applications of the phenomenological method, but even the most abstract philosophies could not be oblivious to the fact that "the world is horrible," in Russell's phrase, and that it was getting no better. Russell himself complained that, while he enjoyed philosophy and logic as a refuge, it was no place for a man to live. The response of the "analytic" philosophers who had taken hold of Anglo-American universities was to belittle or ignore the topics they chose not to include. No longer did most of the philosophers of Oxford and Cambridge discourse eloquently on human nature, the meaning of life, on ethics, on beauty and political philosophy. Indeed, such topics were routinely dismissed either as nonsense or simply with a guffaw. Practical matters, such as the Great Depression and the horrors of the world, were excluded from the shallow, thin, formal concerns of logic and the analysis of language.

In France, meanwhile, philosophy was all but dead, kept alive only by the buoyant optimism of Bergson. By 1941 the French were utterly demoralized by a devastating defeat at the hands of the Germans. But outside of England and France, other philosophers were coping with their times in more direct and confrontational ways. To see this best, perhaps we should start at the edges of Europe, where philosophical fashion tended to be less dictatorial and political and economic conditions were even worse.

Miguel de Unamuno (1864–1936) was perhaps the greatest philosopher of Spain, and he took great pride in the fact that his philosophy was distinctively Spanish. In poetry and novels, as well as in philosophical essays and literary commentary, he wrote elegantly about the "tragic sense of life." He was concerned not with the new ambitions of the Northern philosophers but with the problems of coping with a life so filled with anxiety, brutality, and disappointment. He was one of those very individual voices, crying out passionately on the behalf of honesty and integrity, who can be properly counted among the "existentialists" (a movement of philosophers who were especially concerned with responsibility and the concrete circumstances of human beings).

Kierkegaard was Unamuno's philosophical hero. Unamuno bemoaned the failure of objective science and reason to answer life's questions and defended a version of subjective truth. What is important in life is passion and commitment, not reason and rationality. Reason inevitably leads to skepticism, and skepticism to despair. Faith, by contrast, offers its own guarantees, even if they are "only" subjective. "All or nothing," Unamuno would say. What a human being wants is immortality, nothing less. Reason and science tell us that is impossible. Faith satisfies that ultimate demand. And through faith, through passionate commitment, the anxiety of life can be channeled into a drive to live life to the fullest. One "philosophizes in order to live," not the other way around.

Unamuno lived his life to the fullest, and this often got him into trouble. He supported the Allies against Germany in the First World War and opposed the military dictatorship after the war, for which he ended up in exile. He returned a few years later and turned his outrage against Francisco Franco, the new Fascist dictator. He was put under house arrest and died a short time after. Meanwhile, the Spanish Civil War (1936–1939) had given the world a taste of what was to come. Germans and Italians, as well as defenders of the Spanish Republic worldwide, had taken part in what would be remembered as one of the most brutal and tragic conflicts in an already brutal century.

Benedetto Croce (1866–1952) was the greatest Italian philosopher since Vico. Italian philosophy, like Spanish philosophy, is often left out of historical accounts, at least those written in English, because Italy showed relatively little interest in the new technical movements that were taking over Cambridge and Heidelberg. Once the seat of the great Roman Empire, Italy had been fragmented for centuries. In fact, Italy had only been unified—more or less—in the late nineteenth century by the *risorgimento* (reorganization). This unification, like the unification of Germany some years earlier, required its prophets, its philosophers, its moral leaders. Croce was all of these. He was a spokesman for democracy, for integrity, for liberty and liberalism, in some of Italy's darkest hours.

Croce's philosophy was always political, but it manifested itself as a philosophy of Spirit. His philosophical mentor was Hegel, whom he often followed closely and on whom he commented at considerable length in *What Is Living and What Is Dead in the Philosophy of Hegel* (1907). Hegel's philosophy had followed the vicissitudes of Spirit through history, synthesizing and reconciling or in any case embracing conflicts. The central thesis was always spiritual growth, which embraced individual differences in an overall harmonious unity.

Croce's philosophy, like Hegel's, was through and through a philosophy of history and of culture, a study of the inner dynamics of time. In his early work, Croce defended a strict developmental scheme, much as Vico had done. But later, as Italy struggled for its self-identity and the world headed for war, he created a more flexible vision. History is undetermined, he now insisted. It exhibits spontaneity, unpredictability. It is the work of freedom and of free individuals. History creates structures rather than discovers them.

Like Hegel, Croce ultimately concludes that the history of humanity is the struggle for and the emergence of liberty. Accordingly, when Mussolini came to power, Croce was a courageous and outspoken anti-Fascist. After the fall of Mussolini, Croce became a national hero, Italy's moral teacher. He is a stunning fulfillment of Nietzsche's demand that the philosopher ultimately be an example. His is a fine example of philosophy at work in the world, comparable to Russell and Sartre and to John Dewey in America as well as all of those ancient philosophers who envisioned philosophy as a courageous love of wisdom rather than a convenient career move.

Martin Heidegger (1889–1976) was a student of Husserl, but unlike his teacher he was not primarily concerned with philosophical method or Husserl's rather bloodless inquiries concerning mathematics and the "formal sciences." He was a theology student before he became a phenomenologist, and his questions were existentialist questions, questions about how to live and how to live "authentically," that is, with integrity, in a complex and confusing world. To this end, Heidegger offers us a series of provocative but often-obscure suggestions.

Heidegger's philosophy is a monumental achievement, one of the most powerful and influential philosophies of the century. But as an example (the existentialist test we applied to Unamuno and Croce), it must be said that Heidegger does not pass with flying colors. Whereas both Unamuno and Croce denounced the Fascists and risked the consequences, Heidegger joined them. He became a member of the Nazi party in 1933, when he became rector of the University of Freiburg. He fired Jewish professors. He gave speeches praising Hitler and the Nazis' ideals. The following year, he resigned his position, but he never expressed regrets about National Socialism. He only complained that the Nazis had failed their own philosophy, which he continued to defend.

Heidegger's case raises difficult questions which we have not adequately confronted. Throughout this book, we have pressed the question, "How does the philosophy express the culture and the individual?" We have insisted that one cannot entirely uncouple the philosophy from the philosopher. Of course, this connection is always "more or less" relevant. One can state an idea, a thesis, or an entire system of ideas without saying much of anything about the person or persons who produced them. And óne can, like many philosophical biographers, describe the life of the philosopher in detail without providing very much at all about his or her philosophy. Nevertheless, the one affects the other in profound ways.

Critics of Heidegger have scrutinized his difficult texts and sometimes-obscure conclusions looking for evidence that his Nazi sympathies seeped into—or perhaps even motivated—his philosophy. Defenders of Heidegger, on the other hand, have insisted that the work stands alone, without taint, however harshly we may criticize the individual. We would say that these two extremes are both nonsense. Philosophy dictates a way of life, and a way of life dictates a philosophy. We should leave ample room to acknowledge hypocrisy and self-deception, of course, and we must also allow for some slippage between a person's ideals and deeds. Still, Heidegger emerges as a genuine problem, partly because it is by no means clear exactly what the philosophy has to do with the philosopher, Nazi or otherwise.

Heidegger's philosophy, like Wittgenstein's, falls into two parts. His early work as a phenomenologist, culminating in his great tome, *Being and Time* (published in 1928), suggests that Heidegger, too, deserves to be counted among the "existentialists." Like Kierkegaard, he investigates the meaning of authentic existence, the significance of our mortality, our place in the world and among other people as an individual. Heidegger's later work takes a different turn. Throughout his philosophizing, Heidegger insists, as did his teacher Husserl, on starting from scratch, "without presuppositions"; but he later comes to see his early work as still mired in the suppositions of traditional metaphysics.

Turning back to the work of the earliest Greek philosophers, before philosophy became contaminated by Plato and by metaphysics, by Descartes and by subjectivity, Heidegger tries to show us the way to a genuinely presuppositionless and holistic philosophy. Such a philosophy will involve a new openness, a new receptivity, a oneness with the world, which in more recognizable language turns out to be very much in line with the program of many radical or "deep" ecologists and, as Heidegger himself discovered, with several non-Western cultures, which had never been distracted by the dualisms and humanistic arrogance of his own philosophical tradition.

We will focus only on Heidegger's early "existentialist" philosophy. Two themes, in particular, define Heidegger's early work. First, Heidegger displays a profound anti-Cartesianism, an uncompromising holism that rejects any dualism regarding mind and body, the distinction between subject and object, and the linguistic separation of "consciousness," "experience," and "mind." Second, Heidegger's early philosophy is largely a search for authenticity, or what might better be described as "own-ness" *(Eigentlichkeit)*, which we can understand, with some explanation, as integrity. This search for authenticity will carry us into the now familiar but eternal questions about the nature of the self and the meaning of life, as well as Heidegger's somewhat morbid conception of "Being-unto-Death." It will also lead to Heidegger's celebration of tradition and "historicity," the importance of resolutely committing oneself to one's culture. This is one of the points at which some critics of Heidegger's political activity have found evidence of his philosophical predisposition to German chauvinism, if not directly to National Socialism.

Heidegger's anti-Cartesianism begins with a rejection of the language of "consciousness," "experience," and "mind." He is a phenomenologist, but being a phenomenologist, according to Heidegger, only means beginning from one's peculiar point of view. It does not require the metaphysical supposition that there is a mind in which ideas appear, or that there is such a thing or activity as consciousness, like a beam of light aiming itself at the world.

To assure the neutrality of this starting point, to ensure that we do not fall into the language of Descartes, which has now worked itself so thoroughly into our ordinary everyday language, Heidegger suggests a new term (the first of many). *Dasein* (literally, "being there") is the name of this being from whose perspective all of this is being described. Dasein is not a consciousness or a mind, nor is it a person. It is not distinguished from the world of which it is aware. It is inseparable from that world. (We might compare these claims to Wittgenstein's in the *Tractatus*: "I am not in my world. I am the boundaries of my world.") Dasein is, simply, "Being-in-the-World," which Heidegger insists is a "unitary phenomenon."

Moreover, our Being-in-the-World is not primarily a process of being conscious or knowing about the world, as is assumed in so much of modern philosophy. Science is a distant concern. The immediate paradigm is rather that of the craftsman, the image that so captivated the early Greek view of virtue as well. The craftsman "knows his stuff," to be sure. But he might not be able to explain it to you. He might not even know how to show it to you. What he can do— what he does do—is engage in his craft. He shows you that he knows how to do this and that. This knowing *how* is prior, Heidegger tells us, to knowing *that*.

In effect, our world is essentially one extended craft shop, in which we carry out various tasks and only sometimes—often when something goes wrong—stop to reflect on what we are doing and look at our tools as objects, as *things*. They are, first of all, just tools (or material) in the craft shop, and in that sense we take them for granted, relying on them without noticing them.

This primitive view of the world is the beginning from which we must understand the role of knowledge and the dangerous temptation to talk about "consciousness" and "experience," which distance us from our world. In fact, one of the central concepts in Heidegger's early philosophy is the concept of *mood*. It is in our moods, not the detached observational standpoint of knowledge, that we are "tuned in" to our world. (This is a pun in German: "mood"—but also "tuning"—is *Stimmung*; "to tune" is *bestimmen*.) Mood is also the starting point for understanding the nature of the self and who we are.

To begin with, the notion of *Dasein* does not allow for the dualism of mind and body or the distinction between subject and object. All such distinctions presuppose the language of "consciousness." Thus Heidegger defends an uncompromising holism in which the self cannot be, as it was for Descartes, "a thinking thing," distinct from any bodily existence. But, then, what is the self? It is, at first, merely the roles that other people cast for me, as their son, their daughter, their student, their sullen playmate, their clever friend. That self, the *Das Man* self, is a social construction. There is nothing authentic, nothing that is *my own*, about it. (*Das Man* is another of Heidegger's coinages. It derives from the colloquial idiom, "*Man ist . . .*"—that is, the anonymous "One is. . . .")

The authentic self, by contrast, is discovered in profound moments of unique self-recognition—notably, when one faces one's own death. It is not enough to acknowledge that "we are all going to die." That, according to Heidegger, is merely an objective truth and inauthentic. It is *one's own* death that matters here, and one's "own-ness" thus becomes "Being-unto-Death," facing up in full to one's own mortality. We saw a similar thesis in Unamuno, and in this sense, at least, Heidegger too acknowledges a "tragic sense of life." Unfortunately, he did not appreciate or acknowledge the tragedy of Germany in particular, and his not negligible role in it.

Max Scheler (1874–1928) was also a student of Husserl, but he, too, took phenomenology in a different and more obviously passionate direction. Scheler was an intense man whose considerable contribution to philosophy was the introduction of emotion into the overly formal Kantian conception of ethics that still ruled the Continent. In a book on "sympathy," he resurrected moral-sentiment theory and gave a central place in ethics to such emotions as love and hate. He argued that emotions have been understood by philosophers as merely "subjective" and argued for a "cognitive" view in which emotions could be construed as a source of knowledge. There is even, he argued, an *emotional a priori*, a universal and necessary status to the emotions that philosophers had neglected.

Scheler summed up the theme of the unfolding century between the wars in his book *Ressentiment*, in which he develops Nietzsche's accusation that modern morality is a "slave morality," a morality of *resentment*. But where Nietzsche blames Christianity, Scheler (a Catholic) exonerates his religion and shifts the blame instead to the bourgeoisie. (In the half century to follow, the bourgeoisie will be in for considerable abuse, especially in the more bourgeois capitals of Europe.)

Scheler's phenomenology, unlike Husserl's, was primarily concerned with *value* and, in particular, the source of values in *feelings*. What was becoming evident in phenomenology—and in European philosophy more generally—was a loosening up, a rejection of formality, an acceptance and an attempt to understand the more "irrational" aspects of human existence.

On this note, we might well end this section by moving into the far eastern reaches of Europe, where the world was also rapidly and monumentally changing. Russia had been racked by revolutions for the first two decades of the new century, culminating in the Bolshevik revolution of 1917. Vladimir Ilich ("Nicolai") Lenin, a second-rate philosopher but a first-rate revolutionary, transformed the still feudal state into the avant garde of Marxism (or Marxism–Leninism, as it came to be called). After Lenin's death, Joseph Stalin took over and ruled the country with a cruel, iron fist, murdering tens of millions of his own people, supposedly in the name of the socialist idea.

Such extremism in the name of philosophy was not new to Russia. If it seems as if we have slighted the Eastern Bear, it should be remembered that for the better part of the nineteenth century, and certainly long before the communists came to power, philosophy was outlawed in Russian universities as a subversive activity. Perhaps as a result rather than as the cause of this prohibition, philosophy in Russia has tended to be zealous and even subversive. The concept of *nihilism* (understood as an attack on all authority) was invented in Russia, and the term took root as an apt label for the new specter that was haunting Europe. (The term was popularized by Ivan Turgenev [1818–1883] in his novel *Fathers and Sons* [1862].)

On the other hand, Russian thought was not solely preoccupied with subversion. The two great Russian novelist-philosophers, Fyodor Dostoyevsky (1821–1881) and Count Leo Tolstoy (1828–1910), spun magnificent philosophical narratives of despair, spirituality, and love. Dostoyevsky despised the calculating utilitarianism and socialism that he saw (along with Catholicism) devouring Russia. In his *Notes from Underground* (1864), an existentialist classic, he presents us with a character who is so opposed to the philosophy of "seeking one's own advantage" that he will do anything out of spite, just to prove that freedom and dignity, not the mechanical pursuit of one's own welfare, are one's "most advantageous advantage."

In *The Brothers Karamazov* (1880), Dostoyevsky distills the philosophical tensions of modern Russia into the eccentric personalities of three brothers, their half-brother, and their father. One brother (Ivan), a Nietzschean atheist who declares that "without God, everything is permitted," literally drives himself mad trying to understand the implications of his atheism and attempting to come to terms with the seemingly inevitable injustice of the world. Meanwhile, his brothers Mitya and Alyosha serve as his foils, the first a vulgar and sometimes-violent egoist, the second a conscientiously naive, devoted young Christian. Similarly, in *The Idiot* (1869) Dostoyevsky attempted to create the image of a "perfectly good man" in the corrupt society of St. Petersburg. Needless to say, such a character does not fit in with his greedy and jaded social milieu.

If Dostoyevsky was primarily concerned with the intrinsic worth and dignity of the individual, Tolstoy was more concerned with the inequities and brutality of society. His religious leanings developed into a social ethics. Raised as a pampered aristocrat, he skewered the pomp and pretense of the Russian aristocracy in his novels. His heart went out to the peasants. A student of Schopenhauer, he recognized all too well the irrationality of their world, but he also shared Schopenhauer's insistence on the ultimate importance of compassion in ethics. Hegel's influence on Tolstoy is evident as well, especially in his great novel *War and Peace* (1869), where even Napoleon is depicted as nothing but a victim and a tool of a world spirit that has little interest in mere individuals.

The maelstrom that Tolstoy recreated in his epic, however, was only a preview of what was to come in the twentieth century. Following the violence of the revolution, Stalin started taking his terrible toll. And then, despite a tenuous peace agreement with Hitler, German troops from the West would once again march across the Russian steppes toward St. Petersburg (later called Leningrad and now St. Petersburg again). Russia, more than any other country in Europe, would come to illustrate the self-imposed tragic sense of life — what the Russian philosopher Nikolai Berdyayev (1874–1948) would call the "profound failure" of history.

Hitler, the Holocaust, Positivism, and Existentialism

The Second World War began in 1939 with Hitler's invasion of Poland, but the world had been readying itself for an epic confrontation for many years—in fact, since the Treaty of Versailles in 1919. Germany had been harshly punished and its economy wrecked. The Weimar Republic had collapsed and the fanatic Adolf Hitler began his meteoric rise to power in the early thirties, riding on a distractionist wave of anti-Semitism.

It is hard to say exactly when the Shoah, the Nazi's attempted extermination of the Jews of Europe, began. Jewish civil liberties were curtailed soon after Hitler came to power in 1933. The Jews were thoroughly ostracized by law by 1935, and their property was confiscated in 1938. On *Kristallnacht* (Night of Broken Glass) in November 1938, the Gestapo spurred riots that destroyed most of Germany's synagogues and began a full-scale reign of terror against the Jews that would last (and spread) for the better part of a decade. Austria and Italy willingly joined in the purge and, a few years later, so did occupied France.

The pope, who had the one voice that might have made a difference, said nothing. In fact, Catholics, gypsies, homosexuals, and other minorities shared the horrors of the concentration camp, the execution squad, and the gas chambers. Some have alleged that most of the leaders of the world and most of the people in the countries involved did not know about the mass murders, although little evidence supports this claim. President Roosevelt, whatever he may have thought or felt, did nothing until late 1941, when the Japanese provided an excuse for war by attacking Pearl Harbor in Hawaii. Whatever the world had seen before, including the horrors of the First World War, it had never seen, or at least had never seen so clearly and so close up, anything like this: the use of modern technology and managerial efficiency to systematically wipe out a people. With the war, the very existence of the oldest and greatest cultures of Europe was threatened.

In northern Europe, the rise of the Nazis and the rumbles of war stimulated two radical philosophical movements, one of them frontally attacking irrationality in all of its forms, the other embracing irrationality as the human condition. The first, best known as *logical positivism*, was loosely based on the early philosophy of Wittgenstein and traced itself back to Hume and the British empiricists. It prided itself on being hard-headed and scientific and on tolerating no nonsense. The other, *existentialism*, was drawn from Kierkegaard and Nietzsche, using Husserl's phenomenology as its method. Whatever their differences, both movements were based on brutal experience, the horrors of war, and irrationality on a mass scale. Both in fact endorsed an honest, unsentimental rationality, but they both theorized about the role of the irrational, particularly in ethics.

The logical positivists, insisting on scientific and logical rigor and rejecting the German romanticism they blamed for the horrors, pushed ethics to the side. Like

Wittgenstein at the end of the *Tractatus*, they seemed to insist that nothing intelligible could be said about such matters. Like Russell, they seemed to be satisfied with the idea that ethics is simply subjective, a matter of emotion, not of logic and rationality. But that left the status of ethics dubious or, at best, dangling. If philosophers were not in a position to address the sins of the world, then who would be? The logical positivists fought to keep the Enlightenment alive, despite its demise in the First World War. Instead, they brought about the virtual exclusion of ethics from philosophy.

Oddly enough, the existentialists, perhaps the most moralistic or in any case the most moralizing philosophy of the twentieth century, also seemed to be avoiding ethics. Nietzsche had insisted that Western morality is slave morality, and he wrote with delight (in his book *The Gay Science* [1882; revised 1887]) about dancing on morality's grave. Heidegger emphatically insisted that he was not offering any ethics, and he continued to speak with disdain about those who "fish in the false sea of values." Even Sartre, moralist par excellence, followed Heidegger in insisting that his existentialism was not an ethical philosophy, although he did promise that the "ontological phenomenological description" of his great tome *Being and Nothingness* (1943) would be followed up by an ethics. (Sartre's notebooks on ethics were in fact only published a few years ago.)

What the existentialists were rejecting was a certain "bourgeois" conception of morality, the kind of ethics that worries about keeping your hands clean, paying your debts, and avoiding scandal. The watchword of the existentialists' philosophy, *authenticity* (expressed in different ways by the various existentialists), was above all a call to integrity, a call for responsibility, even a call to heroism. Authenticity could hardly be calculated (or even described) according to traditional philosophical and scientific rationality. Thus the existentialists resorted to literature, to prophecy, to ponderous obfuscation, to pamphleteering, to any means necessary to wake up the world from its brutal and irresponsible behavior.

In Austria, where the threats against the Jews were perhaps the worst, a number of brilliant, mostly Jewish philosophers established the "Vienna Circle," a group of logical positivists. The Vienna Circle was, first of all, a response to irrationalism. Many of the early positivists were physicists and mathematicians as well as philosophers. Their bias was heavily toward the sciences, and their method, which they traced back to Hume and, more recently, to the logical atomism of Russell and Wittgenstein, heavily favored logic and science as paradigms of rationality. That method began with one rather harsh distinction between facts and values and a second, problematic but not so harsh distinction between logical and empirical truths. Logical truths, including the truths of mathematics, were all deductions from a small set of basic, virtually trivial axioms. (This had been demonstrated by Russell and Whitehead.) Empirical truths, on the other hand, were based on experience, experiment, and observation. Philosophers had no special vision, talent, or equipment for the discovery of such truths. Instead, the positivists saw their role in life as making the world safe for those who did. They tried to do this by defending rationality and logic.

The positivists' primary concern was to separate the meaningful hypotheses that science could and should consider from those that were meaningless, a waste of time, and only a source of unresolvable disagreement. They found their standard, their cutting instrument, in the notion of *verifiability*. A hypothesis—and this was quickly expanded to include any sentence whatever—was meaningful only insofar as it could be verified by the evidence. Thus, "There are twelve rabbits in this room" is meaningful (although it happens to be false). "There are twelve utterly undetectable angels in this room" is meaningless, neither true nor false, given the impossibility of identifying and counting undetectable angels.

The standard of verifiability soon required some logical tinkering. It became evident, for example, that some hypotheses (some sentences) might be verifiable "in principle" but were not currently verifiable in fact (for example, "There is life on some planets in other solar systems"). Some of the positivists also considered it a matter of some embarrassment that the verification principle itself did not seem to be prone to empirical verification. Nevertheless, the basic idea was clear enough and the temperament quite firm. There is more than enough nonsense in the world, claimed the positivists, and it is the job of philosophers, to the best of their abilities, to make sure that there is no more of it.

The positivists were not, as is sometimes thought, narrow-minded science fanatics and logic-choppers. They were, first of all, champions of sanity in a world going insane. Nevertheless, in their efforts to root out nonsense they also eliminated a good deal of what is most important in philosophy. Given that ethical utterances (or "value judgments") could not be scientifically verified, the ethics of the positivists became an unjustifiable subjectivism, or more precisely, a philosophy called *emotivism*. Emotivism, in its more sophisticated versions, was elaborated in terms of approval (and disapproval). "This is good" means, on the emotivists' reading, something like, "I approve of this. I want you to do so as well." On this view there is no evidence or argument for the goodness (or badness) of something. Ethical "argument" is merely a matter of persuasion. According to the more radical advocates of emotivism, for example, the late A. J. Ayer (1910–1989), ethical utterances really mean no more than "Boo!" and "Hooray!" Such utterances are literally "meaningless," however important they may be to the speaker and/or his audience. (Despite his emotivism, Ayer polished off his career with a work lionizing and celebrating the work and courage of the great French moralist Voltaire.)

Hitler entered Paris in 1941, and thus began the occupation of that once-proud city. We can now only imagine the humiliation, the fears, and the moral pressures of everyday existence for the citizens. Jews and subversives were being rounded up daily, and a few brave French were establishing a durable "resistance" to the Germans. Daily life raised the question, who would be brave enough to risk his or her life? And who would be so unprincipled, so treacherous, so cowardly as to collaborate with the occupying enemy?

In this wartime context existentialism reached its fullest form. We have mentioned existentialism several times in the text, and it might be best conceived as a philosophical movement that includes Kierkegaard, perhaps Nietzsche, Unamuno, and Heidegger. One might add Dostoyevsky and the Czech writer Franz Kafka. The movement is usually traced back as far as Kierkegaard, but some enthusiasts have on occasion taken it all the way back to Socrates. The term "existentialism" itself was coined by Jean-Paul Sartre (1905–1980) in the thick of the occupation and the war.

The expression "existence philosophy" had been used earlier by the psychiatrist Karl Jaspers (1883–1969), who also belonged to the tradition. Jaspers was the first to see that Kierkegaard and Nietzsche, two distinct and very different figures (a Christian fundamentalist and an atheist), were far more alike than they were like anyone else. He employed the special word, "existence," borrowed from Kierkegaard, to summarize the centrality of freedom (albeit freedom within given, objective limitations) that defined human existence. Jaspers himself was a scientist and a defender of scientific rationality and objectivity, but he opposed the one-dimensional focus of the positivists and insisted on a proper place for nonobjective (but not necessarily "subjective") insight into the nature of the human condition.

Sartre's philosophy is usually taken as the paradigmatic example of existentialist philosophy, and other figures are considered existentialists insofar as they resonate with certain Sartrian themes—his extreme individualism, his emphasis on freedom and responsibility, his insistence that we and not the world give meaning to our lives. But let us be very clear that the existentialists differ widely from one another. Given their emphasis on individualism, it is not surprising that many of them denied involvement in any "movement" at all. Kierkegaard was a devout Christian. Nietzsche was an atheist. Unamuno was a liberal Catholic. Jean-Paul Sartre was a Marxist, and Heidegger was a Nazi. Sartre enthusiastically insisted on the freedom of the will. Nietzsche denied it. Heidegger hardly talked about it at all.

Nevertheless, one would not go wrong in saying that existentialism represents a certain attitude particularly appropriate for modern (even postmodern) mass society. If we may generalize for just a moment, we might suggest that the existentialists share a concern for the individual and personal responsibility. They tend to be suspicious of or hostile to the submersion of the individual in larger public groups or forces. Thus Kierkegaard and Nietzsche both attacked "the herd," and Heidegger distinguished "authentic existence" from mere social existence. Sartre, in particular, emphasizes the importance of free individual choice, regardless of the power of other people to influence and coerce our desires, beliefs, and decisions. Here he follows Kierkegaard, especially, for whom passionate, personal choice and commitment are essential for true "existence."

Although Kierkegaard's work inspired an influential school of twentieth-century religious existentialists (including Paul Tillich, Martin Buber, Karl Barth, and Gabriel Marcel), the existentialist attitude is more often associated with atheistic thinkers to whom religious belief seems like an act of cowardice, or, as Albert Camus calls it, "philosophical suicide." Nietzsche's attack on Christianity and Christian morality is based on his accusation that religion provides crutches and weapons for the weak. Nietzsche's most famous image, in *Zarathustra*, introduces the exciting but obscure ideal of the *Übermensch*. If the ideal is obscure Nietzsche's aim is nevertheless clear—to encourage individual unique ness rather than mere mediocrity and conformity, a "this-worldly" attitude instead of a longing for a better, "other" world.

Twentieth-century existentialism was greatly influenced by phenomenology, which had been originated by Husserl and pursued into the existential realm by his student, Heidegger. The "ontological" problem for *Dasein* was to find out who one is and what to do with oneself or, as Nietzsche said, how to become what one is. Phenomenology, for Heidegger, became a method for "disclosing [one's] being." Following both Husserl and Heidegger, Sartre used the phenomenological method to defend his central thesis that humans are essentially free.

Retreating from Heidegger's attack on the Cartesian view of consciousness, Sartre argued that consciousness (described as "being-for-itself") is such that it is always free to choose (though not free not to choose) and free to "negate" (or reject) the given features of the world. One may be cowardly or shy, but such behavior is always a choice and one can always resolve to change. One may be born Jewish or black, French or crippled, but it is an open question what one will make of oneself, whether these will be made into handicaps or advantages, challenges to be overcome or excuses to do nothing. Sartre's philosophy would have a particular poignance in the midst of the horrors of war and occupation.

After the war, Sartre's younger colleague Maurice Merleau-Ponty (1908–1961) convinced him that he should modify his "absolute" insistence on freedom in his later works, although his insistence on freedom and responsibility remained. Merleau-Ponty went on to develop his own radical revision of the phenomenology of freedom and the essentially embodied nature of human consciousness. Albert Camus (1913–1960) borrowed from Heidegger the sense of being "abandoned" in the world, and he shared with Sartre the sense that the world does not give meaning to individuals. But whereas Sartre joined Heidegger in insisting that one must make meaning for oneself, Camus concluded that the world is "absurd," a term that has (wrongly) come to represent the whole of existentialist thinking.

Indeed, one of the persistent errors in the popular understanding of existentialism confuses its emphasis on the "meaninglessness" of the universe with an advocacy of despair or "existential *angst*." Even Camus insists that the Absurd is not license for despair, and Nietzsche encourages "cheerfulness." Kierkegaard writes of "glad tidings" and for both Heidegger and Sartre the much celebrated emotion of *angst* is essential to the human condition as a symptom of freedom and self-awareness, not as reason to despair. For Sartre, in particular, the heart of existentialism is not gloom or hopelessness but a renewed confidence in the significance of being human. We will return to his philosophy, and the philosophy of Camus, momentarily.

The notion of "authenticity" is not new. In various guises, it has been one of the central and certainly most influential concerns in philosophy. Socrates could easily be viewed as a philosopher concerned with the authenticity of the self— the genuineness of his thoughts and actions, "the good of his soul." He sought not mere opinions but knowledge, self-knowledge in particular, and prescribed not just right action but virtue, being "true to oneself." Augustine was concerned with the spiritual nature of the "true" self as opposed to the inauthentic demands of desire and the body. Jean-Jacques Rousseau was adamant about the essential goodness of the "natural" self in contrast to the "corruption" imposed by society.

Kierkegaard, as the first existentialist, insisted that the authentic self was the personally *chosen* self, as opposed to one's public or "herd" identity. This opposition of the genuine individual versus the public or "the herd" was taken up by Nietzsche, and both Kierkegaard and Nietzsche influenced Martin Heidegger, whose conception of own-ness came to dominate contemporary existentialist thought. Jean-Paul Sartre utilized what Theodor Adorno later called "the jargon of authenticity" in his conception of "bad faith"—self-deceptive attempts to dodge responsibility by making excuses for one's actions. This notion was clearly based on Heidegger's notion of inauthenticity. The positive notion of authenticity ("good faith") remained a problem for Sartre, however, and one of the continuing criticisms of existentialism is the obscurity and the seeming elusiveness of the ideal of authenticity. (Might this be a vestige of "original sin"?)

No Exit: The Existentialism of Camus, Sartre, and Beauvoir

Albert Camus was born and raised in wartorn Algeria, and although his best-known writings are not ostensibly political, the bitter experience of civil war informed everything he ever wrote. Just as the Second World War began, he published a novel entitled *The Stranger* (1942) and an essay called *The Myth of Sisyphus* (1942). With those two books, he became a spokesman for the new modern morality, the ability to confront life in the face of the "Absurd." Camus describes this as "the sensitivity of our times." It is important that the Absurd should be distinguished from the mere absurdities of everyday life. The Absurd is a metaphysical perspective, a sense of confrontation between ourselves and our demands for rationality and justice, on the one hand, and an "indifferent universe," on the other.

The titular figure of *The Myth of Sisyphus* is the classical Greek character who was condemned to spend all of eternity pushing a rock up a mountain, which would then roll back down of its own weight. This is the fate of all of us, Camus suggested. We expend all of our energy pushing our weight against futility and frustration. The absurdity of this existence is not made any less painful, one should note, by the fact that Sisyphus is immortal. The primary question of philosophy, accordingly, is presented by Camus as the question of whether life is worth living, or, differently put, whether we ought to commit suicide. His answer to the first is an enthusiastic yes, to the second, a moralistic no. Camus's Sisyphus, instructively, throws himself into his meaningless project, and thereby makes it meaningful. "One must consider Sisyphus happy," concludes Camus, and so, too, by acknowledging and throwing ourselves into the absurdity of our own lives, might we be.

The protagonist of *The Stranger*, by way of contrast, accepts the absurdity of life without much thinking about it. He makes no judgments, especially moral judgments. He accepts the most repulsive characters as his friends. He remains unmoved by the death of his mother and his own killing of a man. Facing execution for his crime, he without regret "opens his heart to the benign indifference of the universe." He, too, claims to be happy. But the novel ends on a sour, striking note. The condemned man, having been prodded into an awareness of the absurdity of life and his own human nature by the rigors of the trial and imprisonment, looks forward to being greeted by the crowd at his execution "with howls of loathing." So, too, Sisyphus accepts his futile fate, but he makes himself happy, in part, by "scorning" the gods. Is our acceptance of the Absurd therefore tinged with bitterness and resentment? Camus seems torn between acceptance and defiance.

Similar themes inform *The Plague* (1947) and *The Rebel* (1951). In *The Plague*, Camus's defiance takes on a social dimension as the citizens of an Algerian city collectively fight off a merciless epidemic and a claustrophobic quarantine (perhaps a metaphor for the Nazi occupation). In *The Rebel*, Camus goes back to his theme of "defiance" and suggests, in nonpolitical terms, that we resist not only the Absurd but all of those who murder and lie in the name of this or that ideology. (On this note, Sartre, a Marxist, ended his friendship with Camus.)

In Camus's final novel, *The Fall* (1956), a perverse character named Jean-Baptiste Clamence sums up the bitterness and despair rejected by earlier characters and by Camus himself in his essays. Clamence, like the character in *The Stranger*, refuses to judge people, but whereas Meursault (the "Stranger") was incapable of judgment, Clamence (who was once a lawyer) makes such incapacity a matter of philosophical principle, "for who among us is innocent?" "Judge not, that ye not be judged," is his motto, although his strategy (as an extremely seductive narrator) is to get us to judge ourselves. Such questions of guilt and innocence play a central role in Camus's philosophy from beginning to end. How can one be innocent in a world that is absurd? How can a person be sensitive and responsible in such a world?

An all-powerful notion of freedom and an uncompromising sense of personal responsibility lay at the heart of Jean-Paul Sartre's philosophy. In the oppressive conditions of the Nazi occupation and during the embattled years following the Second World War, Sartre insisted that everyone is responsible for what he or she does and for what he or she becomes or "makes of oneself," no matter what the conditions, even in war and in the face of death. Thirty years later, Sartre would insist (in an interview a few years before his death) that he never ceased to believe that "in the end one is always responsible for what is made of one," a slight revision of his earlier, brasher slogan, "Man makes himself."

As a student of Hegel and Marx—and as one afflicted by physical frailty and the tragedies of the war—Sartre had to be well aware of the many constraints and obstacles to human freedom. But as a Cartesian, he never deviated from Descartes's classical portrait of human consciousness as free and sharply distinct from the physical universe it inhabited. One is never free of one's "situation," Sartre tells us, but one is always free to "negate" that situation and to (try to) change it. To be human, to be conscious, is to be free to imagine, free to choose, and responsible for one's life.

In his early work, Sartre followed Edmund Husserl's phenomenology and established the groundwork for much of what was to follow. In particular, Sartre celebrates our remarkable freedom to imagine the world other than it is, and he denies that the self is "in" consciousness, much less identical to it. Our perceptions of the world, he argues, are always permeated by imagination, so we are always aware of options and alternatives. The self, Sartre suggests, is out there "in the world, like the self of another." It is an ongoing project in the world, not simply self-consciousness as such (as Descartes suggested with his "I think, therefore I am"). This preliminary defense of freedom and the separation of self and consciousness provide the framework for Sartre's greatest philosophical treatise, *Being and Nothingness* (1943).

Despite the strong influence of Heidegger on Sartre at the time, the structure of *Being and Nothingness* is unabashedly Cartesian (that is, akin to Descartes's philosophy). On the one hand, there is consciousness ("being-for-itself") and on the other, the existence of mere things ("being-in-itself"). Sartre describes consciousness as "nothing"—"not a thing"—and he affirms Husserl's notion of "intentionality"—the idea that consciousness is always directed at an object. Sartre avoids all talk of objects "in" consciousness and denies that consciousness is or could be part of the causal order. Consciousness is not a "thing"; it lies outside of the causal order of the world. Instead, it is "a wind blowing from nowhere towards the world." Through the nothingness of consciousness, negation comes into the world, enabling us to imagine the world as other than it is and, inescapably, to imagine ourselves other than we seem to be. Thus consciousness "always is what it is not, and is not what it is"—a playful paradox that refers to the fact that we are always in the process of "transcending" ourselves.

Sartre defines his ontology in terms of the opposition of being-in-itself and being-for-itself. In us as individuals this opposition is manifest in the tension between the fact that we always find ourselves in a particular situation defined by a body of facts that we may not have chosen—our "facticity"—and our ability to transcend that facticity, imagine, and choose—our transcendence. We may find ourselves confronting certain facts—poor health, a war, advancing age, or a Jewish pedigree in an anti-Semitic society—but it is always up to us what to make of these and how to respond to them. We may occupy a distinctive social role as a policeman or a waiter, but we are always something more; we always transcend such positions. When we try to pretend that we are identical to our roles or the captive of our situations, however, we are in "bad faith." It is bad faith to see ourselves as something fixed and settled, defined by a job or by "human nature." It is also bad faith to ignore the always restrictive facts and circumstances within which all choices must be made. We are always trying to define ourselves, but we are always an "open question," a self not yet made. Thus, Sartre tells us, we have a frustrated desire to "be God," to be both in-itself and for-itself, defined and free.

Sartre also defines a third ontological category that he calls "being-for-others." Our knowledge of others is not inferred—for example, by some argument by analogy—from the behavior of others. Our experience of other people is, first of all, the experience of *being looked at*, not spectatorship or curiosity. Someone "catches us in the act," and we define ourselves in their terms, identifying ourselves with the way we appear "for others." In his ironically titled *Saint Genet* (1953), Sartre describes the conversion of ten-year-old Jean Genet into a thief and pervert when he is caught in an act of theft by "the look" of another. So, too, we "catch" one another in the judgments we make, and these judgments become an inescapable ingredient in our sense of ourselves. They also lead to conflicts so basic that in his play *No Exit* (1943) Sartre has one of his characters utter the famous line, "Hell is other people."

In his *Critique of Dialectical Reason* (1958–1959), Sartre turned increasingly to politics and a defense of Marxism in accordance with existentialist principles. He rejected the materialist determinism of Marxism, but he contended that political solidarity (a notion lacking in *Being and Nothingness*) was the condition most conducive to authenticity. Not surprisingly, Sartre found the possibility of such solidarity in revolutionary engagement. In accordance with his revolutionary principles, Sartre turned down the Nobel Prize in 1964. (Camus had accepted one in 1960.)

Simone de Beauvoir (1908–1986) was a philosophical novelist who shared with Sartre this emphasis on freedom and responsibility for what one is and "what one makes of what is made of one." In her *Ethics of Ambiguity* (1947) she spelled out the ethical implications of Sartre's philosophy far more clearly than he had. Beauvoir advanced the important thesis (shared with Merleau-Ponty) that the "ambiguity" of situations always undermines the wishful thinking that demands "right" and "wrong" answers. Beauvoir was always fascinated by her society's oblivion or resistance to sensitive topics, and accordingly she was one of the most controversial authors of the age. Notably, she was appalled that her society, and virtually all societies, gave very little attention to the problems and inequities afflicting the female subset of humanity. Similarly, later in life, she attacked the unsympathetic insensitivity to the inevitability of aging, and she wrote two books on the topic, *A Very Easy Death* (1964) and *Old Age* (1970).

Beauvoir's most lasting contribution to philosophy and social thought was her revolutionary discussion of the one topic that had been decidedly ignored throughout most of the history of philosophy: what it meant to be a woman. In her book *The Second Sex* (1949), Beauvoir initiated one of the most energetic discussions in contemporary philosophy, on the significance of gender. The question of women in philosophy, however, was not yet part of the philosophical discussion, especially back in England (despite the presence of several very fine female philosophers).

From Ideal to Ordinary Language: From Cambridge to Oxford

One of the more provocative questions among Anglo-American philosophers in the last half of the century has been whether or how much Wittgenstein changed his mind between his "earlier" and his "later" work. He is not, to be sure, the only great philosopher to have turned and attacked his own earlier work. But his turnabout is one of the most spectacular on record. His turn was all the more dramatic, no doubt, because he was a charismatic, even mesmerizing, teacher, more of a guru than a professor. His students—and then the students of his students—emulated his intensity and (sometimes rather ludicrously) imitated his tortured mannerisms. According to those who sat at his feet, to be in Wittgenstein's presence was to be present at the painful birth of something most profound. The problem seems to be that no one, including Wittgenstein when he was still alive, could be sure exactly what it was.

Wittgenstein's philosophy after the *Tractatus* emerged slowly in his seminars, in his notebooks, and in his various "remarks," and eventually it came together, sort of, in a big, bold book of barely connected aphorisms, musings, anecdotes, and questions called *Philosophical Investigations*, which was published only after his death. It was concerned with a bewildering number of questions, many of them about language and its reference to the world. Wittgenstein had clearly rejected the "picture" theory of meaning. But he now concerned himself with the details of logical atomism, examining the nature of the knowing mind, its sensations, emotions, perceptions, experience. Given the pastiche format of the book, we cannot easily summarize its contents. Nevertheless, certain themes clearly emerge.

The first has to do with meaning, which in the *Tractatus* involved the correct logical form of sentences and their reference to or "picturing" of the world. In the *Philosophical Investigations*, meaning is use. In other words, the meaning of a sentence depends on how it is used *to do* something, and that something is by no means limited to the scientific description of the facts that made up the world. The meaning of a word depends on its use in a sentence, and we use sentences in conversations, to communicate, to question, to challenge, to make jokes, to ask for the butter, to talk about philosophy, to seduce, to argue, to declare, and to proclaim. Thus the fundamental unit of language is not the simple sentence (and the simple fact it pictures), but the larger *language game*, a "form of life" which may have any number of purposes and goals, many of them having little to do with the search for scientific truth.

The later Wittgenstein attacks not only the idea of atomic sentences (or propositions) but the idea of atomic facts as well. The world is not just "everything that is the case" but instead becomes defined in terms of our interests and our activities, our "language games." Nor do things have essences, as if things and their names are a natural pair. Indeed, taking the concept of a *game* as his illustration, Wittgenstein argues that there is no single definition of games, and no one thing that all games have in common. (Some games do not have goals or end points. Some games are played alone. Some games are played without rules or with rules made up as one goes along. Some games are not [and are not intended to be] fun. And so on.) Borrowing an expression from Plutarch, Wittgenstein tells us that there are only "family resemblances," similarities, and apparent grounds for comparisons, and what counts as a game—or as anything else—can be ultimately decided only in the particular context.

Second, whereas the *Tractatus* maintained a healthy respect—even reverence— for philosophy, the *Philosophical Investigations* threatened to turn philosophy into a kind of intellectual malady, for which, fortunately or unfortunately, only more philosophy seems to be the cure. Philosophy, writes Wittgenstein, is "language going on a holiday," language removed from its ordinary contexts and the "games" in which it normally functions. One recognizes here one of the most critical themes from the *Tractatus*, but no longer formulated in terms of what can or cannot be said. The important thing now, Wittgenstein tells us, is to look and see how language actually functions. Philosophy sets traps for us by allowing us to misuse the language, mistaking one application for another, thinking that because a certain question makes sense in one context or in one form of life, it must therefore make sense in another.

Third, Wittgenstein questions the very notion of "mental states," so central to all of Cartesianism and empiricism. Perhaps the best single (and most talked about) example in the *Philosophical Investigations* is his analysis of what it is that we are doing when we "report" a sensation. Consider an example, in which we tell someone that we just had a flash of pain. Or perhaps one in which we say (in a nonphilosophical context) "That is red," by which a good logical atomist like Russell would understand something along the lines of "I have a sensation of red." Wittgenstein challenges the very idea of reporting and referring to such sensations. This, in turn, raises the question, at least, of what sense it even makes to say that we "have" them. Wittgenstein's argument here is by no means clear, and many philosophers have reconstructed it with more or less nonsensical conclusions. In any case, it has come to be called the "private-language argument," and in its more modest versions it looks something like what follows.

To refer to something, anything, requires that the speaker have some "criteria" for identifying that thing and, consequently, being able to identify it again. Those criteria must, in turn, be part of a larger language game, and this means, among other things, that they must be publicly accessible. But sensations, by their very nature, are "private." They can be perceived (felt) by one and only one person. Therefore there is no way for language to refer to them, for there can be no public criteria for doing so.

One might ask if a person couldn't have his or her own "inner" criteria, something like a color chart (or a pain chart) to use for comparing this sensation with others. But how would one know whether one remembered the other sensations correctly? Indeed, how can one be sure—now—that one remembers that sensation of a moment ago correctly? Wittgenstein's argument has led many of his followers to the modest but problematic conclusion that we cannot refer to sensations by means of criteria, and therefore we cannot, strictly speaking, use language to refer to them at all.

But, of course, there are other criteria that we can use. We regularly ascribe to other people psychological states of all kinds, including the experiencing of various sensations. Those criteria include the circumstances ("I see that you have just stepped on a sharp carpet tack") and especially one's behavior ("I see that you are wincing, howling, and grabbing your foot"). So the ascription of sensations to people is not a matter of referring to something private but rather part of a way of talking in which their behavior, not their private inner life, is the basis of our knowledge.

From this one might draw a tempting but foolish conclusion—that there are not or cannot be any sensations at all. (If there were a private experience, it would be "a wheel that is no part of the mechanism," quips Wittgenstein.) Wittgenstein's "behaviorism" may sound plausible with regard to other people's sensations, but it is hardly intelligible "in one's own case." What does it mean, for example, when a person reports his or her own pain? Here, Wittgenstein comes down hard. These are not reports, he tells us; there is only further pain behavior (including the utterance, "I have a pain"). Pains and other sensations play no role in the language game.

What is exemplified here is not only a perplexing thesis about our knowledge of our own minds (a thesis that had come much into doubt with Freud as well), but also a profound thesis about the nature of language. On Russell's model (which the younger Wittgenstein had cautiously endorsed) a simple sentence corresponded with a simple sensation, and by putting such atomic sentences and atomic facts together we built ourselves a picture of the world. But according to the older Wittgenstein, there are no simple sentences, only whole conversations and forms of life; and if there are any simple sensations (or "sense-data," as they were vulgarly called), they cannot possibly be the building blocks of our knowledge.

Much more in Wittgenstein is worth exploring. But let us move on to look at his "influence." (How many philosophers have altered the face of philosophy not only once, but twice?) Soon after Wittgenstein left Cambridge, the philosophical center of the English-speaking world moved to Oxford. The *Philosophical Investigations* may not have been the text of the Oxford philosophers (most of whom preferred to think of themselves as good Aristotelians), but Wittgenstein's emphasis on ordinary language surely won the day. The dean of Oxford philosophers, J. L. Austin (1911–1960), summarized the new mentality in the title of his book *How to Do Things With Words*. Like Wittgenstein, he used the new analytical method and careful attention to ordinary usage to tear apart the logical atomist talk about sensations and sense-data (in a book cleverly entitled *Sense and Sensibilia*, punning on Jane Austen's *Sense and Sensibility*). Austin developed his own cult following, first in Oxford and then in America.

Meanwhile Austin's colleague Gilbert Ryle (1900–1976) launched a wholesale attack on the very idea of an "inner life" and the Cartesian idea of a mind distinct from the mechanical body, which Ryle lampoons as "the ghost in the machine." In the *Concept of Mind*, he variously undermined and ridiculed all talk of mental "twitches, itches and twangs" and argued that all such talk about the mind was essentially talk about various "dispositions to behave." Thus, to be angry is not to "feel" anything, much less to have an inner, private experience. Rather it is to be disposed to behave in any number of specific ways, depending on the circumstances. If you are mad at your congressman, you write an "angry" letter. If you are mad at your boss, you bitterly mumble around the water cooler. If you are mad at your cat, you throw it outside. But there is no *anger*. There is only behavior. To ascribe this behavior to an internal "occult" occurrence is to make a "category mistake," to mistake one kind of thing for another.

So much for "the mind." The battle was on. For at the same time that Austin and Ryle were making such pronouncements in England, the phenomenologists had gathered a full head of steam on the Continent. The presupposition of phenomenology, of course, was precisely the accessibility of experience. Until late midcentury, the two sides were rarely conjoined. In a famous and somewhat embarrassing exchange, the French phenomenologist Maurice Merleau-Ponty turned to Ryle at a conference and asked, "But are we not doing the same thing?" to which Ryle, with typical Oxonian sarcasm, bellowed, "I hope not!" And yet Ryle had, in fact, read and reviewed Husserl, and Merleau-Ponty had been steeped in the work of the behaviorists with whom Ryle has always (against his objections) been associated. Thus began a long and often hypocritical misunderstanding between two ill-defined academic camps, one that has not, unfortunately, been rectified to this day.

Both the "philosophy of language" and the "philosophy of mind," as they have come to be called, are flourishing enterprises in contemporary philosophy, but the terms of the debates have changed enormously. Perhaps the most dramatic influence on both disciplines (and they are rarely far apart) has been the proliferation of computers, and, consequently, computer models, computer metaphors, and computer language. The intellectual explosions that have taken place in these fields is far beyond the scope of this book. Let it simply be said, as a hopeful introduction to a very different kind of work, that the new cooperation between philosophers, linguists, computer scientists, neurologists, and psychologists promises a new kind of chapter in the future history of philosophy, one which, thankfully, harks back to older periods of history when philosophy was not nearly so narrowly conceived or hermetically professionalized.

But let us get back to our history, which is nevertheless not complete. In fact, some of the most important chapters follow, and they are important in part because we frankly do not know where they are going or where, how, or *if* they will end.

Women and Gender: The Feminization of Philosophy

Any attentive reader, many pages ago, must have asked a simple but, when one thinks about it, astounding question: "Where are all the women?" Apart from Simone de Beauvoir, who was included in our discussion of French existentialism, there are virtually no women in evidence in this three-thousand-year history. How could this be possible? Women think and worry and articulate and write as much and as well as men. Why are they not included in the history of philosophy? To ask a different question, Why isn't their philosophy included? Would women's philosophy be the same as men's? Would a history of women's philosophy look much the same, or very different? If there were more women philosophers, would philosophy look the same? Apart from a simple question of fairness (Why shouldn't female philosophers have their works published and recognized as do male philosophers?), serious (but traditionally unasked) questions can be formulated about the very shape of philosophy. Is it, in fact, a rather familiar male shape? And, if so, does it not fall short of its own standards of universality and all-inclusiveness?

Western philosophy has historically discussed or included women, if at all, as an afterthought. Perhaps, at best, it was simply assumed that, in matters of the mind, women were essentially the same as men, so no special mention was required. (Nevertheless, we might ask, why wasn't this confirmed by actually recording women's views and commentary?) All too often, unfortunately, the omission of women was not benign neglect but based on the assumption that women were deviant or secondary instances of human beings, and the male of the species was understood to be the paradigm. (The Roman word "virtue," to take one of many examples, is derived from the root for man, "*vir*." Even more obviously, there is the well-established use of the word "man" and "mankind" to refer to all members of the species.) The case has even been made (and not just once or twice in Western history) that women are not merely deviant or secondary but rather the inferiors of men; and their social subordination has been "justified" on the basis of their different inherent capacities, only some of which have to do with the biological fact that women give birth to babies and men do not.

In particular, it has been supposed that women are less rational and more emotional than men, and therefore less suited to philosophy. The first question, of course, is whether or not any of these claims are true. If any of them do contain an element of truth, the second question is how the difference between men and women came about. If, for example, women do seem more emotional than men, why is this? Does the treatment and education of women encourage or require them to be "more emotional"?

On a deeper level, we might challenge, as some philosophers have, the very distinction between emotion and reason and the traditional emphasis and trust that have been placed exclusively on the latter. Perhaps the heightened rationality and the systematic exclusion of emotion in most male philosophers is a liability, a symptom of inadequacy, a problem. Some feminists have suggested that "philosophy" has come to prefer methods that conform to the paradigmatic "masculine" style encouraged by our culture. If disputation and confrontation are taken to be basic philosophical methods, it shouldn't surprise us that more men than women feel comfortable in the discipline, since these modes are socially preferred in men but discouraged in women.

Whatever else it may have been, philosophy has always been a refuge, a luxury enjoyed primarily by those who have (one way or another) been free from the demands of exhausting physical labor, earning a living, cleaning and caring for a household. For that reason, it should not be surprising that most of the men we have discussed, and most of the great philosophers (except, notably, Socrates) were gentlemen bachelors (or, sometimes, priests). Consequently, very few of them talk very much about the family, and interpersonal relationships in general play an embarrassingly minuscule role in the history of philosophy. Nor do most of the philosophers (excepting notably Marx and Adam Smith) talk very much or very flatteringly about work or earning a living. Some of our great philosophers were cared for by the church or the community. Some were independently wealthy. Some were professors or ran their own institutes. But they were almost all in privileged positions, and they were able to envision the heavens in part because they did not have to sweep the floor.

Philosophy is a privilege. It is also an accomplishment, an accomplishment in which success depends not just on talent but on colleagues, teachers, an audience, publishers, readers, future students. The sad truth is that women have been shut out at virtually every level of philosophical success. Relatively few women have been allowed to even get interested in philosophy. Before this century, few women were admitted to the appropriate schools, and those who were allowed to study philosophy (some of the students of Plato and Pythagoras, for example) were rarely allowed to achieve stature. If a woman did manage to disseminate some ideas of her own and attract a following, she would rarely be recognized as "one of the boys" and she in all probability remained unpublished and unknown. And if she got published her books did not survive the destruction that has hidden so many original texts from us and spared only a chosen few. The absence of women in philosophy was not, we can be sure, for lack of talent. But no woman philosopher ever found her Plato, as did Socrates, to carry her legend to posterity. (If there was such a Plato, she probably never got published.)

Feminist philosophy, philosophy premised on the supposition that women are as important as men and that women can do philosophy as well as men, challenges the entire Western tradition (and not only that tradition). Feminist philosophers contend that the historical treatment (or omission) of women is itself a symptom of the tradition's limitations. While claiming to be universal and all-inclusive, philosophy has not even included or taken account of the woman next door. And it certainly has not asked whether she sees things differently or would ask the same questions in the same way as male philosophers.[88]

Feminism has added a new dimension to philosophy, for it insists that a person's gender importantly conditions the way that he or she approaches the world. Feminists take what Nietzsche called "perspectivism" very seriously. A philosopher, like everyone else, is situated in a social and historical context, feminists contend, as well as in a biological situation which may well make some difference in formulating philosophical problems. The same, of course, is true of men. A philosophical theory should be assessed in light of the perspective from which it is produced—and in light of considerations which that perspective obscures. How could that exclude one's gender and one's biology?

None of this is to assume, a priori, that feminine or female philosophy must in the long run be different from masculine or male philosophy. Indeed, insofar as the aim is to initiate an ongoing dialogue, we would expect there to be increasing convergence as well as more mutual understanding. (Not every feminist, we should hasten to add, takes this to be the goal.) But whether or not there is convergence or for that matter even dialogue, it is of the greatest significance that women are now entering philosophy in large numbers and publishing some of the most significant work in the field. (This is true not only in America and Europe, although some of the toughest "old boy networks" are still to be found there. It is also increasingly true in Asia as well as in the Middle East, and also in Africa and Latin America.) It remains to be seen, once women have fully defined and occupied their rightful place in philosophy, what real differences in interest, thought, and approach there might be.

Recent research has uncovered a significant number of women throughout the history of philosophy, but it is no easy matter to resurrect those who were buried, often unpublished and long ignored, and to distinguish their contributions from those of the men with whom they worked and who may have become known for their ideas. Even Hypatia (370–415), perhaps the most famous woman in the early history of philosophy, is far better known for her awful death (she was killed by a mob) than for her own (Neoplatonic) philosophy. Consequently, what we can say about women in philosophy and feminist philosophy is mostly very modern.[89]

One of the first modern works of feminist philosophy was *A Vindication of the Rights of Woman* (1792) by the British writer Mary Wollstonecraft (1759–1797). Wollstonecraft argued that women should be treated as the equals of men in education, politics, work, and mores. John Stuart Mill's treatise entitled *The Subjection of Women* (1869) insisted that women were the equals of men and called upon society to include women in political decisions. (Some feminists have argued that Mill owed many of the ideas expressed there, as well as in other works, to his longtime companion Harriet Taylor.) The political consequence of such philosophical defenses of women's rights was the development of feminist movements in nineteenth-century Europe and America. In particular, these movements sought female suffrage, a quest that succeeded only after years of struggle. Although the American suffrage movement became organized in 1848, women of the United States did not get the vote until 1920. British women got the vote in 1928; and French women got the vote only in 1944.

A new era of philosophical feminism arrived with the publication of Simone de Beauvoir's book *The Second Sex* in 1949. Beauvoir was part of the existentialist movement, and it has recently become a matter of contentious discussion to what extent she borrowed from her lifelong companion Jean-Paul Sartre's philosophy and to what extent he borrowed from her the ideas for which he became famous. Beauvoir became equally famous as a novelist and then as a feminist. Combining existentialism and feminism, she established the first philosophical beachhead from which to launch a discussion of sex and gender differences in philosophy. Her examination of women emphasizes the obstacles that obstruct a woman's affirmation of herself as an authentic, autonomous human being.

There are or have been, first of all, legal obstacles, denials of women's rights to property, to authority, to the vote, to speak in public, to run for office, to receive equal pay. But besides legal obstacles, Beauvoir analyzes the psychological "phenomenological" structures that function to limit women's freedom. She famously claims that, "One is not born a woman." Instead, Beauvoir argues, women are socialized to assume the stance of "the Other" to men. Women should attempt to free themselves from these social demands and inner restrictions that stem from them. Beauvoir argues, in keeping with the tenor of existentialism, that social structures that make it difficult for some individuals to express their freedom are also damaging everyone's freedom. Thus, she concludes, men also have a stake in women's liberation. The liberation of women would also be a liberation for men.

Beauvoir's analysis of the psychological obstructions to women's social equality inspired new interest in the ways that socialization supports sexism, the prejudicial preference of one sex over the other. Her claim that one "becomes" a woman suggested a distinction that has become basic in feminist discussion, the distinction between *sex* and *gender*. "Sex" refers to the anatomical features of one's reproductive system. "Gender," by contrast, refers to those socially constructed behaviors and roles that are assigned on the basis of these anatomical features. This distinction facilitates the recognition that sexual characteristics do not in themselves establish that a person is suited to the gender roles that the person's society considers "natural." Feminists have often used the sex/gender distinction to attack *biological determinism*, or the view that "biology is destiny," usually taken to imply that women must play certain roles (like that of motherhood) because they were born with certain kinds of bodies. Indeed, today even the "given-ness" of the biological body is being called into question. Could anatomy ultimately be a "social construct"?

Beauvoir's work also helped feminists to recognize inner obstacles that prevent women from assuming social roles of equal stature with those of men. The feminist movements that were part of the larger leftist movements within Europe and America in the late 1960s were especially concerned to overturn the social and psychological structures that subordinated women. One of the prominent debates of this era concerned whether feminist liberation was compatible with the institution of marriage or with heterosexuality (which some feminists viewed as necessarily involving a woman's assumption of the subordinate role). Another focus was the question of how a woman could overcome psychological obstacles within her own mind (for example, a cultivated "fear of failure") that prevent her from achieving first-class participation in society.

Philosophical feminists have analyzed the often unwitting ways in which sexist suppositions have affected apparently neutral historical concepts. In particular, feminists have criticized the Enlightenment ideals of universality, objectivity, and reason. The stance of universality is suspect, for it easily camouflages a demand for conformity. Too often those who have made claims to objectivity and universality have simply envisioned their own traits writ large. The result is that the "objective" stance of Western philosophy has been a white male stance. Any features that might be unique to the perspectives of women or minority groups were systematically effaced by the demand for a "universal" perspective. So, too, "objectivity" has often been defined as "value neutrality," without considering what this might eliminate or ignore.[90]

One attempt to redress the omission of women and minorities from philosophy has been the demand for a *feminist ontology* and a *feminist epistemology*, beginning with the perspectivist assumption that the perspectives of women, at least as they have contingently developed, can make unique and important contributions to the projects of coming to know reality. Beginning with similar assumptions, some feminists have sought to develop a feminist philosophy of science that would draw on women's perspectives both in determining which projects science should pursue and in determining the significance of empirical findings.[91] The social sciences and medical research would obviously be affected, and some feminists have argued that the impact would be much broader.

The feminist movement that developed in the late 1960s sought to develop a sense of "sisterhood" among women, comparable to the "fraternity" of men advocated by those Enlightenment philosophers who inspired the French Revolution. Friendships among women have been emphasized as part of this "celebration" of women. Some women have advocated feminist separatism, the development of an alternative social order that would be completely constructed and governed by women. Some theorists, worried that early feminism had developed a heterosexist bias, have sought to situate lesbians at the center of feminism. Recently, some feminists have called for a recognition that neither sex nor gender should be thought to entail that sexual desire take a particular direction. Heterosexuality has been tightly linked to the gender roles that society has required of women, they argue, and we should differentiate "desire" from both "sex" and "gender." These need not conform to the societally sanctioned package.[92]

Many feminists, concerned that feminism not lose sight of political issues in the larger society, have sought to form theoretical alliances with other schools of social and political philosophy and other political movements. Some have forged theoretical syntheses of feminism and psychoanalytic theory (as well as producing harsh critiques of traditional, especially Freudian, psychoanalysis). In the United States, such efforts have sometimes employed psychoanalytic accounts of childhood to show how the assignment of early child-rearing to women has encouraged the development of sexist attitudes. French feminists have placed more emphasis on rewriting psychoanalytic theory from a feminist standpoint, placing particular emphasis on the female bodily and maternal experience (which remained such a mystery to Freud).

Efforts to bring psychology to bear on philosophy have also had impact on feminist approaches to ethics. Psychological studies have suggested that women approach ethical problems more situationally than men, who tend to seek relevant principles in resolving moral quandaries.[94] Some feminists, accordingly, have sought to formulate a *feminist ethics* that stresses a "women's" approach to morality, focused on relationships more than principles, on caring more than consistency. What Kant defended as morality, for example, appears in this context as a peculiar male preference for impersonality and dispassion. Other feminists, however, worry that the suggestion that women have a "different" kind of morality encourages support for a double standard and the regressive tendency to think of women as less "rational" than men.

Some feminists have come to question the movement's emphasis on sisterhood. They fear that such focus on a monolithic group of "women" marginalizes many women who are different from the white middle-class women who have been leading the movement. These include lesbians and women of nonwhite ethnicity or underprivileged economic backgrounds. As a consequence, a "third wave" of feminist philosophy has developed.[95] In response to complaints that feminism is a movement of affluent, heterosexual, white women, current feminism is especially concerned with the recognition of diversity among women and the special concerns of those belonging to less privileged social classes and cultures.

Currently, feminism is being actively reconsidered and redefined from the standpoints of women from minority groups and from the third world, many of whom felt underrepresented in the largely middle-class writings of earlier feminists. Some feminists are questioning whether it is even appropriate to talk about "women" or "gender" as cross-cultural categories. Perhaps, they suggest, feminists should be more concerned with local problems as they find them and less with developing a theoretical account of women's situation everywhere. In any event, philosophical feminism is now attempting to redress the earlier marginalization of many women by avoiding the oppressive patterns in Western thought that feminism itself has sought to expose.

The Return of the Oppressed: Africa, Asia, and the Americas

The latter part of the twentieth century has witnessed an unprecedented degree of interaction, intermingling, and confrontation between different cultural groups. The world is getting smaller, transportation easier and cheaper. Natural borders and geographical boundaries are no longer formidable. Immigration and mobility between countries, whether for economic, political, personal, or cultural reasons, is staggering. (Many of the world's most prosperous societies are reeling from the influx of refugees and the complex and not always happy cultural encounters that ensue.)

The struggles of third world countries to end colonialism and economic exploitation, the continuing civil rights movement (now movements) in the United States, and nationalistic movements in Europe and elsewhere all reflect growing concerns about the way cultural groups can and should live together. Smaller ethnic and cultural communities are currently pressing to assert and maintain their identities in the face of what many see as the threat of engulfment by larger social groups and societies, while others who identify with those larger structures feel themselves threatened by what they see as pressures toward social disintegration. One of the most tangible results of this mutual intimidation is the dramatic increase in civil wars and revolutions, typically ethnic or nationalistic in origin, as smaller ethnic groups fight to distinguish themselves from larger majorities. Philosophy, often cast in the language of universal rights but carefully adapted to the local circumstances, is one of the many weapons employed in such struggles.

The most popular philosophy for this purpose, at least until very recently, has been Marxism. Soon after the Second World War, Mao Tse-tung overthrew the traditional government of China, a "peasant revolt" that has attracted the interest of all oppressed people worldwide. Marxism was successfully synthesized with local traditions and concepts (as it had been in Russia under Lenin some decades before), emerging much more powerful and (if one goes back and reads the original Marx) virtually unrecognizable. The ancient Confucianism of the Han dynasty (beginning in the third century B.C.E.), with its emphasis on supreme personal and family authority, took on new form in the new paternal structure of "communist" China with victorious father Mao. In one sense, life in China and certainly its external politics were turned upside down, but many China scholars continued to comment on the fact that Mao's China was more like than unlike traditional autocratic Chinese governments.

Like most revolutionary governments, Mao's new China took on many of the worst oppressive habits of its predecessors, and in the mid-1960s Mao's "cultural Revolution" plunged the country into chaos, both social and economic. By 1990, with the collapse of the Soviet Union, Marxist Maoism gave way to another venerable ancient Chinese Confucian tradition, what we call a business society. (For those who view what seems to be novice Chinese capitalism with an amused eye, it is worth remembering that China is among the world's oldest and most experienced business societies.) Nevertheless, the stunning example of the Maoist revolution continues to beckon to poor and oppressed peoples across the world. In a similar vein, one of the best-selling philosophy books of the century, comparable perhaps only to Mao's *Little Red Book*, is *The Wretched of the Earth*, by Frantz Fanon (1925–1961), which urges oppressed people everywhere to use violence to end their persecution. (An equally stunning contemporary contrast to Mao's violent revolution, however, was provided by Mahatma Gandhi's "nonviolent resistance" to British rule in India, which we will discuss shortly.)

Philosophy cannot but be affected by these global currents and concerns. The increasing cultural contact and conflict between groups raises momentous philosophical issues. Are there norms and standards that are indeed suited and appropriate for all cultures? (Is the language of "human rights" that is the focus of the United Nations Declaration of 1948 an attempt, in fact, to force first world ethics on third world peoples?) Is there a single concept of knowledge that is as valid in China and Nigeria as it is in Chicago and Heidelberg? (Is the reality studied by physics truly real and universal, or are the agreements in physical theory due to the language and techniques of physics?) Is there a single religion or a single sense of spirituality that underlies all religions? (Or is the very notion of "missionary work" an attempt to destroy indigenous cultures?) Is there any such category as "humanity"? Or are there only various collections and cultures of human beings?

Moreover, as part of philosophy, we should ask ourselves how cultural groups are to be identified. The fact that this question has not traditionally been recognized as deeply philosophical tends to reflect the uncritical assumption that philosophers do not speak from a cultural perspective and do not themselves embody particular ways of thinking. In contemporary African philosophy, by contrast, the question, "What does it mean to be African?" is at the core of current controversy (as "What does it mean to be Jewish?" has traditionally served as one of the focal questions of Jewish philosophy). The distinction between philosophy and culture is arguably a thing of the past.

The notion of distinctive cultural character can play a healthy role—balanced against the idea that there is something commonly human about all of us in mediating the way people come to know the world. Léopold Sédar Senghor (1906–) notably, was a spokesman earlier in this century for a new breed of philosophers who attempted to answer this question. The "negritude" movement, initially proposed by a group of African-French writers, developed the view that black people have a collective racial character that evolved from the African people's particular responses to their unique environment. Distinctive in the African character, according to Senghor, is "affective participation," an emotional involvement with objects not readily familiar to European philosophy. African art and music, he writes, are particularly illustrative of this emotional involvement, and African philosophy differs accordingly.

Senghor's views stand in striking contrast with those of American philosopher W. E. B. Du Bois (1868–1963), who developed an influential theory of African-American "dual consciousness." Black Americans, according to Du Bois, always look at themselves through the eyes of the white world that judges them, in addition to their own consciousness of themselves. Du Bois's account emphasizes the unique situation of African-Americans while making painfully clear the deep division between virtually all other American minorities and the black minority—a chasm created and widened by a long history of colonialism, mass kidnapping, and slavery.

Senghor's views have been explicitly criticized by other African philosophers for reinforcing the notion that Africans are essentially different from Europeans, a notion that has too often been employed to justify colonialism. In efforts to counter this tendency, some African philosophers have attempted to demonstrate that traditional African thought addresses questions similar to those considered in the European tradition (for example, the nature of the person and the mind/body problem). Others have argued that African philosophy has its own agenda, not because of essential differences from Europeans, but because the historical circumstances of Africa (particularly colonialism) have resulted in a particular, uniquely African set of concerns. And yet, African philosophy, in an obvious sense, is an essential part of the story of philosophy, both because of its differences and its kinship to other philosophical traditions.

Who speaks as an authority for a given ethnic or racial community, and what is the role of authority within that culture? The Western emphasis on criticism in philosophy has been met with suspicion in many authoritarian cultures where obedience and submission seem far more important and persuasive than the abstract (and as yet unproved) promises of a vigorous and socially disruptive "dialectic" that only aspires to consensus or the truth.

Such political questions touch on sensitive political issues. What protections should be established for dissidents within minority groups and what policies should be adopted regarding other sovereign states? What is the scope of "human rights" in criticizing and possibly even interfering with domestic policies and practices? (For example, consider the killing of civilians for their political or religious beliefs or tribal affiliations, the ritual maiming of young men or women in traditional ceremonies and rites of passage, or the silencing of the press.) Does it matter, for example, whether censorship is the product of corporate clout or consumer indifference rather than government sanctions? What about censorship in the name of religion? And when is a religion no longer "just" a religion but a potentially oppressive political force?

The resurgent power of "fundamentalism" raises such questions, sometimes formulated in the all-too-familiar language of mutual hatred and violence. How are we to understand one another? It is all well and good for philosophers to spin arguments about the intelligibility of mutually incomprehensible "alternative conceptual frameworks," but the more pressing philosophical problem is, how do we deal with different conceptual and cultural frameworks when we actually confront them. Philosophy itself must become political (as, perhaps, it has always been). It must not only concern itself with the relations between ideas but seek to identify the powerful interests and influences that motivate the beliefs in these ideas. It cannot simply reject separatism and violence. It must speak to those who advocate separatism and violence. Otherwise, it will become (or already is) irrelevant.

What is the optimum relationship between minority groups and larger societies? In New Zealand, for example, the white Europeans and the native Maoris have two distinct codes of justice, one based on the question of individual guilt, the other based on the assumption of family responsibility. A white New Zealand citizen accused of a crime is prosecuted and put on trial under the legal system originally imposed by the British colonizers. A Maori who commits a crime entangles his or her entire family in an exquisite system of moral and emotional (as well as, perhaps, financial) debts. Some have asked how the supposedly single legal system of New Zealand should accommodate these two different visions of law and responsibility. Similar questions are being asked by countries all over the world. It is all well and good to insist on "respect for the law," but which laws? And what about those societies that are based not on "the law" at all but rather on religious or some other authority?

Similarly, in every "multicultural" country, the question applies to every minority: should assimilation or separatism be the regulative ideal? Whether we are talking about African-Americans and Hispanics in the United States, German Turks in Germany, Koreans in Japan, or the descendants of the Incas in Latin America, the most basic questions of fairness have become unavoidable and immensely complex. To what extent should governments and educational institutions encourage ethnic solidarity? To what extent should they encourage cooperation and intermingling, the loosening of ethnic ties? Central to this debate, of course, is the pressing political question of language. Given that language has become not only the primary mode of human communication but also the arbiter of social class and economic prospects, what should be the role of an "official language" in domestic policy—and to what extent should native languages be encouraged instead or as well? Is the American ideal of the "melting pot" or the Canadian ideal of the "mosaic" a desirable goal, or should minority groups be left to develop as they choose, with the larger society making minimal demands for their conformity and minimal gestures in their support?

These questions are not, to be sure, the traditional metaphysical questions of being and becoming, not the wholesale skepticism that provoked supposedly uncompromising doubt in Descartes, but it must now be asked whether those questions themselves were regional peculiarities, problematic not because they were so profound but rather because they were so conscientiously detached from the practical wisdom and ordinary concerns of their culture. Or, from a different perspective, perhaps what went wrong with the most abstract and supposedly most "basic" questions and concepts of Western philosophy was the failure to consider alternatives, the possibility that the categories in question were not so necessary or basic at all.

For example, it has often been pointed out that Chinese thought does not have a concept like *logos,* in the sense of a stable underlying order. Accordingly, the Chinese have not shared our Western confidence in science as a discipline that can discover the underlying laws and structure of the universe. Similarly, there has never been such a strong notion of progress, including scientific progress, in China, although some of the great technological breakthroughs in human history have occurred there. Until recently, the Chinese perspective was dismissed with disdain by the majority of Western philosophers. Now, however, with the collapse of some of our most celebrated philosophical projects in the West and some new and startling developments in the natural sciences, Western philosophers are treating alternative conceptions of reality more sympathetically. Even in the sciences, there is increasing interest in philosophies that differ from, rather than simply repeat or reinforce, our own cognitive and cultural traditions.

With the emergence of philosophical (as well as political and economic) demands from Africans, Asians, and Native Americans who have too long been shut out of American philosophy and culture, specialized ethereal concerns come to seem increasingly pointless and evasive. The first philosophers were not out to escape from reality but to understand it. They coined a language of wisdom which, it turns out, is a common language in many if not most cultures of the world. It has to do with living well, and now, with living well all together. Currently, as African-American and African-based philosophies command their own prominence in the intellectual world, as Chinese and Japanese and Indian philosophy attract new attention and respect from Western philosophers, as Native American philosophy becomes more broadly known and discussed in its native land, there is an opportunity to forge a shared wisdom, a good part of which will involve respect for differences and understanding the dynamics of cultural and intellectual interaction.

Looking across the broad panorama of philosophical traditions, classic and contemporary, written and oral, religious and secular, one begins to get a glimpse of the similarities and differences, of the subtle and not-so-subtle effects of one culture's thinking on another. Perhaps there never were "pure" cultures or traditions. All societies have always been somewhat fragmented into subgroups and dissidents. Perhaps nationalism and even the idea of a "culture" has been (and still is) another philosophical myth. Perhaps there never was an entity called Germany, but only a Swabia, a Bavaria, a Franconia, a Prussia, which themselves were made of many smaller groups and identities.

Now Germany is still divided, not between east and west, but between self-declared German-born Germans and a hundred others—for example, German-born Turks and German-born Slavs—whose languages and interests are not so different that they cannot be learned and understood. Each of these groups has and has had a philosophy, an articulate outlook, a list of vital questions. Sometimes, these coincide and overlap. Sometimes they are quite different and even opposed.

Perhaps the most fascinating philosophy of all, from a cross-cultural perspective, is the philosophy *(tetsugaku)* of Japan, in some ways so similar to, but in profound ways so different from, the Western philosophy we have been examining. No Westerner who has ever visited Japan could deny that there are profound, even incomprehensible differences between the two cultures in their ways of thinking and their attitudes toward each other and the world. Like other non-Western cultures, Japan suffered shock and trauma when it opened itself up to the West. Indeed, one of the greatest modern philosophers of Japan, Nishitani Keiji (1900–), has written an entire book on the enduring problem of what he called *"nihilism"* (borrowing the term from Nietzsche), which he claimed still permeates the culture of Japan as a result of that original shock of cultural compromise and loss.

"Philosophy," understood as such, is something new in Japan, and the word itself *(tetsugaku)* refers distinctively to Western-style thinking. (Japanese universities give an enormous number of courses, for example, in Kant, Hegel, and the German idealists—indeed, more than virtually any university outside of Germany.) In addition to that imported philosophy, the Japanese also have a distinctive way of understanding themselves, and this is deeply articulate, fully "philosophical" in any meaningful sense of the term, and as systematic as a philosophy can be. That philosophy emerged from the traditional culture, from Japanese Zen Buddhism, and from the social practices of late feudalism, especially the samurai tradition. It is evident not so much in the academic philosophy of the universities but in everyday life, in such diverse activities as the Noh theater, the art of flower arranging, and the Japanese way of doing business.

Business, of course, is the ultimate Japanese victory—perhaps, it is often said, the victory that eluded them in the Second World War. The Japanese electronics and automobile industries, industries once dominated by the United States, are now the most successful in the world. Japanese banks are the largest in the world, and Japanese investments abroad, outside their tiny islands, are mind-boggling.

Capitalism as such has been "exhibit A" in the argument for universality in modern times, but Japan's economy is not just capitalism but another form—a very different one—of capitalism from that practiced in the United States. Japanese corporations are not like American corporations (as American corporations that have recently tried to imitate them have found out). Japanese corporations are not, like traditional American corporations, opposed to governmental cooperation and support, and Japanese corporations do not relate to other corporations in the same way that American corporations do. Japanese business relationships are not like American business relationships. Japanese capitalism is not the same as American, British, or German capitalism. And there are excellent studies to demonstrate that Taiwanese, Italian, and Scandinavian capitalism are something else as well.[96] Capitalism and its culture, in other words, are complex and varied, and so are the ideas and values that make modern business possible. The differences are both subtle and profound. "Business is business," goes an old American platitude. But the truth is that business is many different things, and here again it is the differences as well as the similarities that should fascinate us.

The old idea that a philosophy has to work itself out "from the inside" without consulting other traditions and without seeing itself on the larger map of the world is, we hope, becoming an idea whose time has past. It is not that other cultures and ideas are necessarily better (as many Americans seemed to think of Asian philosophy just a few decades ago). But it is just false that philosophy is essentially bound *within* a culture and concerned only with itself, rather than with reaching out and "beyond" (first of all) its cultural perspective and limitations.

For example, two of the outstanding philosophers of India in this century combined traditional Vedanta with an excellent English education to produce philosophies that have far transcended their local origins. One, of course, is Mohandas (Mahatma, "Great Lord") Gandhi (1869–1948), who applied the techniques of *Satyagraha* ("soul force") and his own exemplary ascetic lifestyle to the nonviolent expulsion of the British Raj from India. His life, beliefs, and methods have inspired millions because of both his political success and his moral example.

The other is Ghose (Sri) Aurobindo (1872–1950), who is less well known but still inspires reverence among his followers, not only in India but around the world. He introduced the concept of evolution into Vedanta. He rejected the common Indian insistence that the world is illusory and the world-negation that goes along with that belief. Accordingly, he also rejected asceticism. He attempted to reconcile Hinduism with Christianity and to establish a community (or *ashram*) in which religious mysticism and ordinary life would be integrated.

Philosophy, in the West, has until recently been treated as a uniquely Western tradition. We want to say that philosophy has appeared almost everywhere, in one form or another, and we should be open to the differences as well as the similarities among various philosophical traditions. Previously in the history of philosophy there have been occasional exchanges and cross-references but, for the most part, only neglect and mutual dismissal. Now, however, the discipline of philosophy in the West is expanding its concern to a global scale, as political and environmental pressures force us to consider ourselves citizens of the planet as well as our respective nations.

One consequence of this growing recognition of the global context is a strong move toward *multicultural* and *comparative philosophy*. Scholars and teachers from other cultures have long attended the premier schools in England, Europe, and America and carried back with them the philosophical fashions of the day. Now, the influence is turning the other way, as Western philosophers increasingly attempt to learn and teach philosophy as it has developed outside the West. A sense of shared concern is beginning to infiltrate philosophy.

Drawing from sources as diverse as Native American and African belief systems and those of the ancient Greeks, the field of philosophy has discovered new kinds of problems, which has led, for example, to the development of *environmental philosophy*. Environmental philosophy is concerned with the global problems of sustaining a good life for the world's people in the present while preserving enough of the planet's resources to support the life (both human and nonhuman) of the future. Some philosophers within (and many outside) this movement have urged that humanity extend its sense of moral responsibility not only to the entire human population but to animals as well. They advocate respect for animal rights and the adoption of political policies that reflect this respect. On an even larger scale, many "New Age" and other environmentally sensitive philosophers are pressing the importance of an all-embracing organic "Gaia" philosophy (from the Greek, for "earth"). Instead of conceiving of ourselves as isolated individuals, communities, or societies, instead of thinking of humanity as something distinct and "in dominion" over the creatures and resources of the earth, this philosophy insists that the world be considered as a living whole.

In other words, after twenty-five centuries of trying to move away from primitive animism to a more mechanical, more scientific view of the world, we have come around full circle, back to beliefs that are shared by the ancient animists and many so-called primitive peoples. Philosophy, like art, may find its way back to its original "roots," much as modern art has done. (Picasso initiated modernism when he brought the images of African masks, then on exhibit in Paris, into the iconography of traditional Western art.) Perhaps there will come a day when we philosophers, too, no longer insist on distinguishing between our own esoteric sophistication and the often-insightful ideas and feelings of more ordinary folk. Perhaps, too, global or even transglobal philosophy will one day transcend the limitations of a strictly human, earthly philosophy, but such speculations would surely venture beyond our present concerns.

From Postmodernism to the New Age

With the quick rise of feminist and multicultural philosophy and the increasing skepticism about traditional philosophical questions, one might expect there to be an effort within traditional philosophy to move beyond the tradition, to embrace these various demands for inclusion and to recognize and respect differences, to acknowledge how often force has been instrumental in imposing Western "universal" and "objective" categories on the rest of the world. This movement would benefit enormously, of course, from the fragmentation and confusion in the world, as the new millennium approaches, as the wreckage from the last world war and the cold war gets cleared away, and, last but by no means least, as the long-standing Enlightenment confidence in reason and the philosophical traditions this encouraged become exhausted, unintelligibly specialized, and technically and conceptually bankrupt.

But, what would it be called? It could not be partisan, for that would defeat its all-embracing objective. At the same time, unlike the "modernism" it attacks, it could not itself attempt to be neutral, for the pretense of neutrality is precisely what it seeks to reject in modernism. It could not be merely traditional but, nevertheless, it must certainly make reference to the tradition. It could not be overly provincial, not overtly political, and, of course, it cannot be sexist, racist, or otherwise "politically incorrect" (a phrase whose celebrity is itself a reflection of a new intellectual moralism).

So why not call it *postmodernism*? After all, say this movement's proponents, modernism—that overly Western, deceptively provincial, too exclusive movement that began with Descartes and the new science—has run its course. Philosophy, that search for a single absolute truth, no longer exists. There are only philosophies. There is no longer Truth, only "discourses," people talking, thinking, writing, broadcasting. There is no center, only rapidly expanding margins.

Postmodernism is, perhaps, the most unimaginative of names, suggesting only that it is "after," no longer "beyond," not even "here." Postmodernism, accordingly, has come to represent a ragbag of objections, accusations, parodies, and satires of traditional philosophical concerns and pretensions. It is largely negative, rarely positive, the celebration of an ending but not clearly the marking of anything new. It rejects the old philosophical confidence and assertiveness (although most postmodernists are not best known for their humility or their timidity). Postmodernists assert virtually nothing, and they quickly take that back, too (one of many assertions that they advocate "under erasure").[97]

Nevertheless, certain "postmodernist" themes keep emerging and repeating themselves, whether or not they are taken all that seriously even by their promoters. First of all, postmodernism tends to hold that there is no all-embracing, "totalizing" viewpoint, no "God's-eye view," no pure "objectivity." (To say this, accordingly, cannot itself be to assert an objective truth.) There are, according to most postmodernists, only interpretations (a thesis freely borrowed from Nietzsche). And there are many different interpretations (even, according to some postmodernists, "infinitely many"), and the differences between them cannot be adjudicated, except, some would say, by way of power. (Others would say that different views are "incommensurable," mutually unintelligible.)

The only healthy intellectual attitude, according to many postmodernists, is a vigorous skepticism, a "hermeneutics of suspicion." Postmodernists tend to have a particular suspicion of dualisms and polarities, not just of the Cartesian sort but of virtually any kind whatever. (Some of their original wrath was directed against the structuralist Lévi-Strauss, who, like his nemesis Sartre, often indulged in universal dichotomies.)

Finally, but by no means consistently, the postmodernists seem to celebrate, or in any case diagnose, a widespread fragmentation in the world. A fragmentation of cultures, a fragmentation of meaning, a fragmentation of politics, ethics, and justice, and, most basic of all, a fragmentation of self or, alternatively, the disappearance of the self. No more "I think, therefore I am," or even "We are." Postmodernists tend to think of the "self" as a fiction postulated to convince us that something stable underpins our lives. Thus, postmodern writing typically presents itself (a typical postmodern phrase) as distinctly impersonal, unfocused, even, upsettingly, when it is being most personal, even confessional. Indeed, the impersonal personal confession has become something of an orthodoxy, no small curiosity in the light of the long Western tradition (for example, Socrates and Descartes) of intimately stated absolute truths.

Perhaps because its rather overstated theses seem so ominous, postmodernism tends to reject the usual pompous, somber philosophical style of the Western tradition. It rather prefers its own rather unusual but still pompous, somber philosophical style. Postmodernists express a decided preference for "playfulness," for stylistic experiment, for an utter lack of seriousness. It rejects the argumentative mode, with its insistence on proof and dogmatic obsession with certainty, and so postmodernism does not argue or prove. Indeed, refusing to take seriously its own theses, it often relies on *ad hominem* attacks, marginal commentary, and political diatribe. Postmodern "discourse" (a favorite word) has fallen in love with the parenthesis, the dash, the slash, and other disruptive punc/ tu-a(tion). The argument often lacks a final conclusion, but that, a consistent postmodernist may contend, is just the point.

Postmodernism has invited an obscurity and a pretentiousness almost unmatched in the long, often obscure, and pretentious history of philosophy. In its attack on dogmatism, it has too often become dogmatic. In its insistence on style, it has often become "stylized," conformist, and unimaginative to the point of tedium. It sometimes seems, indeed, as if it intends to be the *reductio ad absurdum* of philosophy, a magnification of philosophy's worst faults, so as to be done with it once and for all. In its rejection of the Western tradition, postmodernism has attracted fans and followers who know nothing and acknowledge no need to know anything of that tradition, despite the fact that postmodernism's most brilliant proponents[98] are themselves masterful scholars of that tradition. However, it is the interaction between postmodernist criticism and the historical tradition that gives postmodernism—that is, as a genuine philosophical position and not as an MTV-fashionable pose—its meaning and significance.

Postmodernism is, whatever else it may be, a continuation of a tradition that is unmistakably Western. It brings out themes that have been active if sometimes latent throughout that tradition—skepticism; pluralism; an emphasis on style, irony, and indirect discourse; a rejection of dogmatism; a suspicion of such abstractions as "Truth" and "Being"; a respect for, even a fascination with, other traditions and cultures. It combines a certain suspicion of and some distancing from authority with a sense of the importance of politics in philosophy. At the same time, it remains artfully academic, quite at home with the traditional philosophical timidity about "getting one's hands dirty," unembarrassed by the fact that it remains largely unintelligible to anyone but its own advocates.

Postmodernism has found its more enduring intellectual home in America, not in France, and postmodernist themes seem to have infiltrated the culture far more in the United States as well. The postmodernists take inspiration from certain continental figures—the Germans Nietzsche and Heidegger, as well as a quick sequence of briefly fashionable French philosophers. It is a sign of continuing American and a new British insecurity, a kind of inverse pretentiousness, that our intellectuals so often look to France for philosophies that not only could but actually have been generated closer to home—for example, by William James and John Dewey. Here we will sketch only the very briefest history of postmodernism (in part because of our resolve to avoid discussing living authors and in part because the true significance of postmodernism cannot yet be determined).

The story begins in France after existentialism, with a rebellion (which its more Freudian proponents would describe as "Oedipal") against the father figure of Jean-Paul Sartre. However radical he may have seemed at the time, during the years immediately following the Second World War and the occupation, Sartre stubbornly held onto many of the central features of the traditional Cartesian and idealist philosophy: its dualism of consciousness and world, its Hegelian sense of history, its uncritical assumption of the "presence" of the world, and belief in the possibility of some anchor for knowledge. He remained an unabashedly Enlightenment philosopher, an adamant universalist.

One of Sartre's harshest critics was an anthropologist, Claude Lévi-Strauss, who initiated a brief but powerful movement called *structuralism*. Lévi-Strauss was primarily concerned with the provinciality of Sartre's philosophy—with Sartre's attempt to take what was essentially a Parisian intellectual's consciousness and extend its categories to all of humanity. Lévi-Strauss did not deny the possibility of universal structures of the mind. Indeed, the basic point of structuralism was precisely to study those basic distinctions and oppositions that can be found in all cultures and suggest that they may in fact be the built-in rules or structures of the human mind. (Kant had made a similar suggestion, except that instead of arguing from the universality of certain categories to their probable innateness he argued from the a priori neccessity of the categories that they therefore must be universal.) Lévi-Strauss's attack on Sartre was telling. It opened the eyes of a new generation to flaws that became the focal point of an attack on the entire philosophical tradition.

Some of the impetus for this attack emerged from the later writings of Martin Heidegger, who had come to question, or in any case revise, some of his own earlier work and was pushing it in a direction quite opposite Sartre's existentialism, which he rejected rather disdainfully. Sartre's Cartesianism, his emphasis on the subject (consciousness), his strong voluntarism (emphasis on choice), his insistence on freedom—all this struck Heidegger as horribly wrong. Indeed, Heidegger by this time had come to see the entire Western metaphysical tradition as an enormous mistake, beginning with Plato and going on finally until Nietzsche, whom he (dubiously) interpreted as "the last of the metaphysicians." Heidegger's misgivings inspired the new generation of Frenchmen, most of whom are still living, and so we will mention only one (who is not).

Michel Foucault (1926–1984) was a dynamic neo-Nietzschean who at one time seemed to be a structuralist (which he denied) but then became an accomplished historian, whose main thesis was that history is largely an illusion. Foucault, like Nietzsche, became keenly aware of the unacknowledged role of *power* in all human activities and relationships, but, in particular, he noticed the role of power in knowledge, especially historical knowledge. Foucault refused to accept knowledge as "objective" but rather viewed it as part and parcel of the instruments of social manipulation. The categories of knowledge, he argued, served social functions, to distinguish, to discriminate, to isolate, to incriminate, to condemn. They were by no means "morally neutral." As examples, he focused on the more marginal aspects of social existence usually ignored completely by philosophers— the prison, the mental asylum, the margins of sexuality. His point was to show how these "margins" were in fact created by the language or "discourse" of power. The implication, not clearly stated, was that "truth" in such matters was a function of social status and politics, not the "facts" of the case.

As for history, it, too, is largely a matter of our own creation, according to Foucault. It is another social construction, a device by which a story gets woven around a more or less conveniently chosen set of supposed "facts." Historians generally emphasize the continuities of history. Foucault emphasized the *discontinuities*, the breaks in the stories, the lack of any real history in the usual, linear, "objective" sense. The history of philosophy, "the tradition," accordingly, would better be seen as a convenient fiction as well, another "discourse," a story that we have made up in order to make the world intelligible and acceptable. In relating the history of philosophy, we further our own interests as protectors and heirs of that tradition. (Looking back over the present work, we can't really say that he's wrong on this point.)

Foucault's harshest attacks however, were aimed at his self-confessed (but rarely mentioned) mentor, Jean-Paul Sartre. Sartre had defended freedom as the essence of consciousness, the necessary nature of the human subject. But Sartre ignored the possibility that the core concepts of his philosophy, the concepts of freedom and consciousness, might themselves be *socially constructed*, that is, not simply found a priori or in reflection or in nature but constituted by a culture and a language. If this were so, then freedom might not be the ontological core of human existence, as Sartre argued, but rather the peculiar product of a certain kind of thinking. Furthermore, the subject—or consciousness (being-for-itself)— might not be what is essential to all of us but, again, might be something constructed, something created by culture and language or even imagined. Perhaps, the postmodernists argue, there is "really" no subject, no consciousness, no freedom, just an "interplay of forces" and our "selves" nothing but the tentative juncture of these forces.

So, where is philosophy now? Postmodernism isn't a philosophy. It's at best a holding pattern, perhaps a cry of despair. It rightly talks about world philosophy, the philosophy of many cultures, but such talk in itself is not a philosophy either. Meanwhile, academic philosophy goes on—in America, England, Holland, and Germany, as well as in non-postmodernist France, in Japan as in Argentina and India—without the postmodern sense that the enterprise is over. (Indeed, postmodernist philosophers continue to hold lifetime tenure, only occasionally acknowledging an awareness of the irony.)

What proceeds in the "mainstream" with a dull hum is increasingly technical, ever more esoteric philosophy or, rather, philosophies, much as in the schools of the late Middle Ages. The crisis in philosophy has prompted its ossification, this despite recent breakthroughs in computer research that have spawned the growth industry of "cognitive science" and "artificial intelligence." Postmodernism has already given birth to a new generation of tenured academics, and the old-guard defenders of "the tradition"—those who remain adamant about the need to read the ancients in the original Greek and Latin, those who have not given up on Cartesianism or empiricism and who are predictably horrified by the new trends—wage a stubborn war in the name of "real philosophy," often at odds with one another as well as with their colleagues down the hall.

The real losers in this confusing but ultimately stultifying squabble over what constitutes "real" philosophy tend to be the students, of course, who enter into philosophy not to gain admission into one of these exclusive schools but to ask the same old questions, or to ask their own versions of what may be a variety of varying questions—about the meaning of life, the best way to live, and whether their faith is compatible with their business or science degrees. And, we should add, the losers include the public, or that significant segment of intelligent people who still hunger for some philosophical insight, for a peek "beyond" the mundane and sometimes horrible daily grind but find little to nourish them in academic philosophy, or what little escapes the airtight walls of academe.

And, yet, the human mind abhors a vacuum, and where traditional philosophers fear to tread, others show no such timidity. It is in this context, perhaps, that we should consider the phenomenon sometimes labeled *New Age* philosophy, an amazing collection of notions that range from healthy, whole-earth thinking to loony-toons from the edge. Here the curious seeker will find everything from intriguing treatises on the environment and often bona fide alternative forms of medicine to breathless narratives recounting UFO abductions and the curious reincarnation (or "channeling") of ancient Egyptians (typically the ruling class) as late twentieth century comic actresses. To treat this collection as a single "movement" would no doubt be a serious misreading. But the evident hunger for philosophy that such New Age phenomena reveal does suggest an important prognosis for philosophy, despite the doomsday warnings from some of the postmodernists and the seemingly untouchable desiccation that has come to define so much of contemporary philosophy. What remains of the traditions is a hunger for philosophy, now much complicated by a new global awareness. Narrowly trained philosophy professors may safely pursue their narrow pursuits, but there is an urgent demand for something more, and that demand, in our (for better or worse) world of increasing free enterprise, will be satisfied.

World Philosophy: Promise or Pretense

We have tried, within our own limitations, to write a "short" history of philosophy that would include, if not all of the world's philosophy, at least an awareness of its extent and complexity. We have tried not to show our hands too obviously in our treatment of our own "Western" tradition, but it must have been evident that we share both enthusiasm and misgivings about the course that this history has taken.

As philosophers ourselves, we cannot help being excited by the bewildering variety of ideas, the dynamism of ongoing confrontations, and the sometimes profound manifestations of social sensibilities in more or less abstract philosophical terms. But, at the same time, we are disturbed by the fact that the old ideal of wisdom, the idea that philosophy is something distinctively human rather than an activity that is a peculiar professional skill, has gotten lost. In particular, philosophy has gotten increasingly precious. The dialogue is restricted, exclusive, closed to all but a handful of like-minded specialists.

It is possible, of course, that the new global philosophy will become even more specialized. Instead of Indian or Chinese philosophy serving to enrich the thought of other cultures, for example, it is imaginable that Sanskrit or Mandarin scholars will make it exclusively their own. Instead of sharing our insights with colleagues in other fields and professions, in other walks of life, it is all too imaginable that philosophy will become nothing but another academic specialty, increasingly more technical, and eventually of no interest (and with no claim for support) from anyone outside "the profession."

That would be a tragedy, in our opinion, but many of our most talented philosophers are arduously working in precisely that direction. Philosophy is wonderful, literally full of wonder. It may be a luxury, but it is a luxury everyone can afford. Indeed, it may be a necessity in times of doubt, trouble, or turmoil. To confuse philosophy with the more obscure questions that it has sometimes (with good reason) produced is to misunderstand the discipline as a whole.

What we need is not more hardheadedness but more humaneness, more openness. We need to be better listeners, not better arguers. We need to acknowledge the profound insight of some recent feminist theoreticians—that what the West has pursued as "objectivity" is not value-neutrality or impersonality but a heightened sense of social and intellectual responsibility. That, after all, is what philosophy has always been about, the effort to reach "beyond," beyond our own limitations, beyond our necessarily biased views of the world and other people. That is why Aristotle insisted that philosophy begins with—and continues as—a "sense of wonder." Anything less just isn't worthy of the name.

Notes

1. Since we will be talking about many philosophies and philosophers who were not Christians, we will use the accepted designation "B.C.E."—"before the common era"—throughout this book instead of "B.C."

2. It might be worth noting that the Greek word, *dike*, often translated as "justice," but meaning, essentially, "the right way to live," originally simply meant "the way," as well.

3. We will see a similar debate unfold in eighteenth-century Europe with the philosophy of Jean-Jacques Rousseau and other moral-sentiment theorists.

4. *Danaids*, as translated in G. S. Kirk and J. E. Raven, *The Presocratic Philosophers* (Cambridge: Cambridge University Press, 1957), p. 29.

5. See Wendy Doniger O'Flaherty, ed. and trans., *Hindu Myths: A Sourcebook Translated from the Sanskrit* (Baltimore, Md.: Penguin Books, 1991), pp. 25–26. Much of the analysis here is derived from O'Flaherty's discussion. In all of our (modest) uses of Sanskrit, we will commit the most unpardonable Sanskritist sin of omitting all diacritical marks in our Anglicized spellings. We also will do the same for Greek. Our readers, not to mention the typesetter, will be grateful.

6. "Brahmins" are the fortunate members of the highest caste in India—the aristocracy, so to speak. The verbal connection is obvious. They are the closest to the Absolute, the most knowledgeable.

7. Rg Veda, 10.129, trans., Wendy Doniger O'Flaherty (Harmondsworth, Eng.: Penguin, 1981), p. 26.

8. Ibid., 10.130, p. 33.

9. Svetasvatara Upanishad IV.6, in *The Principal Upanishads*, trans., S. Radhakrishnana (London: Allen and Unwin, 1975), p. 733.

10. Chandogya Upanishad VIII 7.1 in *The Principal Upanishads*, trans., Radhakrishnan, p. 501.

11. Kirk and Raven contend that Pythagoras was moved by a "religious or emotional impulse" rather than the search for a rational explanation of nature (p. 216). This false opposition will haunt Western philosophy throughout its history.

12. Cited in Benjamin Farrington, *Greek Science* (Harmondsworth, Eng.: Penguin 1944), p. 81.

13. This is not only true of the Western tradition, of course. The multimilennial debates in Indian philosophy make many of the debates in the West seem like transient disputes by comparison. In China, although philosophical disputation goes back to Confucius and

early Taoists, disputation as such was considered socially disruptive and discouraged, as in many authoritarian societies. One might paradoxically conclude that the virtue of always reinterpreting, reinventing, and challenging itself is, itself, one of the debatable virtues of philosophy.

14. One should cautiously note that the root of "dogmatic" is "dogma," which in religious studies means something significantly different and not at all negative or close-minded. It simply means belief or doctrine. "Dialectical" has also been misappropriated. It originally meant "conversational" and implied rigorous scrutiny and open-mindedness. But even in Greece, and much later in Marxist thought, it came to resemble the negative versions of "dogmatic"—close-minded and ideologically intransigent.

15. Fragment 12.

16. Fragment 30.

17. Kirk and Raven attribute to him "an original line of philosophical development" (p. 158).

18. The Chinese verb for "being" is *yu*. To say that something "is" does not mean that it exists but rather suggests that it is present-at-hand or available.

19. An imaginative contemporary version of this vision of time can be found in several of Kurt Vonnegut's early novels, in which he introduces a race of extraterrestrials from the planet Trafalamador. Trafalamadorians see the world as all of one moment, no before, no after, just everything happening all at once in a single, eternal *now*. Likewise, for Parmenides there is just a single, eternal now, but we, unlike the Trafalamodorians, are incapable of appreciating that fact. See, e.g., Kurt Vonnegut's classic *Slaughterhouse Five* (New York: Dell, 1971).

20. See the section "Vedas and Vedanta: Early Philosophy in India" in this book. In the oldest Vedas, these theses are already suggested. In the second century B.C.E. Buddhist philosopher Nagarajuna, these arguments are spelled out in some detail. In Buddhism, *anatman* refers to nothingness, the recognition that there is no self, no soul, no permanence; *anitya* to the transitoriness of all things; and *duhkha* to the frustration and suffering that necessarily follow.

21. Xenophon's testimony remains dubious. See Gregory Vlastos, "The Paradox of Socrates," in *The Philosophy of Socrates*, ed., Gregory Vlastos (New York: Doubleday 1971) pp. 1–4. Aristophanes wrote a play lampooning Socrates called the *Clouds*, but it is more spoof than parody and not very helpful in understanding the historical Socrates or his philosophy. See Kenneth J. Dover, "Socrates in the *Clouds*," in Vlastos, ed., *The Philosophy of Socrates*, pp. 50–77.

22. In the dialogue entitled the *Symposium*, Socrates presents his philosophy as if it had been merely dictated to him by a local muse. This was perhaps a dramatic device for Plato, but it also pointed to a deeper truth that Socrates himself often suggested, namely, that the deepest truths are presented to us. We do not "figure them out." Julian Jaynes, *The Origins of Consciousness in the Breakdown of the Bicameral Mind* [Boston: Houghton Mifflin, 1976], entertains the tantalizing thesis, that what we call "reflective consciousness" might well have been experienced thirty centuries ago as an "inner voice" rather than as our own.

23. This is obviously not true of Plato, however, who had deep affinities with both thinkers, so it is hardly probable that Socrates did not care about them as well.

24. There were other responses to Socrates, of course, not all of them so elevating. Another student of Socrates, named Antisthenes, preached poverty and an extremely ascetic (self-denying) personal morality. He was a Cynic (from the Greek word *cyne*, meaning dog). Of Diogenes, another Cynic, Plato is said to have remarked, "He's Socrates gone crazy."

25. His dying words were, "I owe a chicken [a sacrifice, a gift of thanks] to Asclepius," the god of healing.

26. The exception, again, is Pythagoras, who freely allowed women to study with him and become philosophers in their own right.

27. The rather raucous humor of the dialogue is particularly accessible in a new translation: *Plato, Symposium*, trans., Alexander Nehamas and Paul Woodruff (Indianapolis, Ind.: Hackett Publishing, 1989).

28. Aristotle calls merchants and moneylenders "parasites," and work, of course, is for slaves.

29. This is complicated by the fact that Aristotle wrote two distinct treatises on ethics, the much-read *Nicomachean Ethics* and the much less known *Eudemian Ethics*. In the former, the life of virtuous activities is emphasized. In the latter, it is the contemplative life.

30. The *peripatos* was a covered walk in the garden, giving the name "Peripatetics" to Aristotle and his school. Aristotle would pace along the walk while teaching.

31. "Hellenistic" historically refers to the period after Alexander, but, for our purposes, it might just as well mean after Aristotle. "Hellenes" was the name by which the ancient Greeks referred to themselves.

32. The reason-versus-passion debate goes back at least to the pre-Socratics. (For example, see Kirk and Raven on Pythagoras, p. 216.) Indeed, one could rewrite the history of philosophy using the dialectic of rationality and emotion as its guiding theme. (We have resisted this temptation here.)

33. *The Enchiridion*, VIII.

34. He is best known to Latin students for his blistering denunciation of his rival, Catiline, in 63 C.E., in which he presented himself as the savior of Rome.

35. Again, we will omit the diacritical marks in our Anglicized Sanskrit spellings.

36. *"Pundata"* is the Sanskrit name for "the learned."

37. One should not overemphasize this contrast between the traumatized West and the enlightened East, however. The period between 475 and 221 B.C.E. in China, for instance, is commonly referred to as the "Period of the Warring States," and the official establishment of Confucianism in the subsequent Han dynasty was certainly due in part to the reaction against the chaos of the preceding centuries. By 220 C.E. China was once again in chaos, suffering a series of successions and revolts that lasted until 581.

38. In medieval Christianity, of course, there would be a good deal of logical ingenuity expended in support of religious faith, but faith is hardly the same as mysticism.

39. For example, in the philosophy of Sri Aurobindo, who died in 1950 (see Part IV).

40. On these matters, as in all other references to Indian philosophy in this book, we are (karmically) indebted to Stephen H. Phillips. All misunderstandings are our own.

41. From *Majjhima-Nikaya*, cited by Stephen H. Phillips in *Classical Indian Metaphysics* (La Salle, Ill.: Open Court, 1995).

42. *Majjhima-Nikaya*, translated by Phillips. op. cit.

43. It might be argued that our notions of equality and inequality, however, shift their meaning when we are talking about China, because the Confucian tradition models human society as a family rather than as a contractually based civil unit.

44. The Buddhist monk to the pizzaman: "Make me One with everything."

45. According to Fung Yu-Lan, "Lao-tzu" literally means "Old Master." (See Fung Yu-Lan, *A Short History of Chinese Philosophy*, ed. Derk Bodde (New York: The Free Press, 1948), p. 93. The historical personage to whom this name was given (probably a sage named Li Tan) was probably not the author of the work we know as the *Lao-tzu*, but traditionally one refers to the author (or authors) of the *Lao-tzu* as Lao-tzu.

46. We are very aware and sensitive to the issues surrounding the masculine "He" in the designation of God, and it may well be true that many of the religions preceding Judaism, Christianity, and Islam, against which they rebelled, were matriarchal in form. But insofar as we are talking about these religions in their traditional conceptions we will employ the masculine gender.

47. It is against the background of the Hebrew abhorrence of child sacrifice that one can understand the shocking nature of the sacrifice of Jesus by His own father.

48. Although the Nazis' attempted genocide is often referred to as "the Holocaust," this term is inadequate and misleading. A holocaust is a burnt offering presented as a sacrifice to God—hardly a good description of Hitler's effort. *Shoah*, the Hebrew word for "great calamity," is perhaps a more appropriate term than "Holocaust."

49. Anthony Phillips notes that the Old Testament prophets frequently indicted their communities for failing to treat the disadvantaged with compassion. Such behavior belied their professions and rituals of religious devotion. See Anthony Phillips, *God B.C.* (Oxford: Oxford University Press, 1977).

50. Many Jews did believe, like the ancient Greeks, that the dead went to Sheol, a murky place beneath the earth. But, as in Greek philosophy, the souls that survived there were at most a pathetic shadow of their former selves. The Book of Ecclesiastes does introduce the idea of personal immortality as a possible solution to the problem of evil, but it treats this idea as merely mythic, and, in general, the idea of personal immortality was not adopted by the majority of Jews. Some sects, notably the Pharisees around the time of Christ, did embrace the idea, and although it was never part of official Jewish teachings, the idea of an afterlife no doubt always had its appeal for many Jews, long before the teachings of Jesus and Paul.

51. The Apocalypse was probably written by a different person who lived later than John the Apostle. Some recent scholars speculate, however, that all parts of the New Testament attribed to "John" may have come from a Christian community that had been close to the Apostle.

52. The enormous emphasis we now place on our personal, inner feelings, what historian Robert Stone has called "affective individualism," is our own interpretation of this historical trend.

53. Ibn Rushd, "Commentary on Aristotle's *De anima*," cited in David Knowles, *The Evolution of Medieval Thought* (London: Longman, 1962), p. 200.

54. Thomas's empiricism, however, was not as radical as Hume's was later on. Hume was skeptical of causality, claiming that our experience does not warrant our assumption that one event causes another. We experience only succession, in Hume's view, not causes. Thomas, by contrast, considered the concept of causality well grounded, contending that the mind came to this conception through its empirical experience.

55. Although Thomas's philosophy has become dominant in Catholic theology, some of his views were controversial. For a discussion of the reception of Thomas's philosophy by the Augustinians, see Paul Vignaux, *Philosophy in the Middle Ages: An Introduction*, trans. E. C. Hall (New York: Meridian Books, 1959), p. 130ff.

56. By the eighteenth century, Western "practitioners" of alchemy were primarily concerned with spiritual transformation. In this century, Carl Jung observed correlations between alchemical images and the images of dreams, and he revived interest in alchemical texts among many who are concerned with the human psyche, arguing that such texts could give us insight into humanity's collective unconscious. (See the section in Part IV entitled "Zarathustra in the Trenches: The Limits of Rationality" for a further discussion of Jung's psychological theories.)

57. The text appears in a longer work called *The Book of the Secret of Creation*, which

is attributed to Apollonius of Tyana, who lived in the first century C.E.; the versions that survive, however, come from the sixth or seventh century.

58. The Shinto religion involves elaborate ritual and mythology but is not an especially doctrinal religion. It has continued to coexist peacefully with Confucian influence and Buddhism in Japan. In the modern era Shinto was made a state religion and used to fortify nationalist sentiment. Since World War II, Shinto has been disbanded as a state religion, but it continues to be an important religious phenomenon, and its shrines and festivals are still beloved in Japan.

59. For example, slavery was practiced and was legal in New York City until 1828, less than forty years before the Civil War.

60. It is worth noting that until relatively recently the long entry "Africa, History of" in the *Encyclopedia Brittanica*, for example, consisted almost entirely of an account of the nineteenth-century exploration of the interior by European (mainly British) adventurers and missionaries. It is not as if the history of the indigenous peoples there was unknown; it is as if they never existed, waiting to be discovered.

61. There are also political and medical explanations of such dietary restrictions, of course. Politically, dietary laws serve to separate off one people from another, usually the "righteous" from the "unrighteous," the "clean" from the "unclean." For a good general discussion of such matters, see Mary Douglas, *Purity and Danger: An Analysis of Concepts of Pollution and Taboo* (New York: Praeger, 1970). "Health consciousness" today is similarly used by some people to justify their own self-righteousness. Medically, of course, there may be or have been good reason for certain prohibitions, but one would be missing the point if one tried to reduce all such rules and customs to medicine misunderstood.

62. For instance, the seventeenth-century social philosopher Grotius begins a treatise on the laws of war, *De Jure Belli*, by complaining, "Throughout the Christian world I observed a lack of restraint in relation to war, such as even barbarous races should be ashamed of . . . It is as if, in accordance with a general decree, frenzy had openly been let loose for the committing of all crimes." Quoted in Robert L. Holmes, *On War and Morality* (Princeton, N.J.: Princeton University Press, 1989), p. 153. The perspective defended here owes an obvious debt of gratitude to Stephen Toulmin, who has argued it at length in his book, *Cosmopolis* (New York: Macmillan, 1990).

63. Here is a typical example of the standard conception of the modern from philosopher Antony Flew: "The division of the history of philosophy into periods is always and inevitably more or less artificial. Yet of such divisions one of the least arbitrary is that by which modern, as opposed to ancient and medieval, philosophy begins with Descartes (1596–1650); and, more precisely, with the publication in 1637 of his *Discourse on the Method*. This brief, brilliant manifesto was in every way a portent of things to come." *An Introduction to Western Philosophy* (London: Thames and Hudson, 1971), p. 277.

64. We thank Antony Flew for pointing this out in his "Introduction," op. cit., p. 277.

65. In the *Meditations*, "this proposition: I am, I exist, is necessarily true every time that I pronounce it or conceive it in my mind" (*Meditation II*, trans. Laurence J. Lafleur [Indianapolis: Bobbs–Merrill, 1960], p. 24). If Descartes's assertion is taken to be an argument, then it would actually consist of two claims, the first of which, "I think," is self-evident; the second, "I am," follows from the first, on the assumption, "If I think, then I exist." Descartes's premise in either version is sometimes simply refered to as "the *cogito*" (Latin for "I think").

66. This "cosmological" argument for God's existence makes up the bulk of the third meditation. The "ontological" argument appears in the fifth.

67. The adjective "Cartesian," derived from the Latin for "Descartes," has a long history and applies to any of those doctrines famously to be found in Descartes.

68. Such trivia include matters of mere definition, such as "a dog is an animal." The special circumstances would be those pertaining to logic and mathematics. But these special circumstances will turn out to be very controversial indeed, and there will be a great many more of them. For example, is divine revelation, which Montaigne himself took to be the one acceptable certainty, to be considered one of these "special circumstances"?

69. One might insist, however, that some clear and distinct ideas, notably the belief in God, are "undoubtable" precisely because of the emotional investment one has in them. Descartes did not ignore the emotions, however. He was the author of one of the classic essays on emotion, *The Passions of the Soul* (1645–1646) in which he analyzes the passions as bodily "agitation of the animal spirits" and thus clearly divorces them from reason.

70. The *idea* of the individual dates back to the twelfth century or so.

71. Nothing turns here on the technical notion of substance as such. One can restate the problem in perfectly contemporary neurological and psychological terms.

72. In Persia in the previous century, Mulla Sadra (ca. 1571–1640) had similarly described nature as the continuum that unites all beings. He contended that the motion of things was essential to nature, so nature was inherently in flux. Like Spinoza, Mulla Sadra also linked this account of nature to an ethical vision. All beings have an innate desire to perfect themselves, he argued; this desire gives direction to all beings, including us. The consequence is that nature is orderly, with all its parts united and flowing in tandem.

73. A typical example of the dismissal of Pascal can be seen in D. W. Hamlyn's comment: "Pascal is not really a major *philosophical* figure, despite his contributions to knowledge in other ways." *The Pelican History of Western Philosophy* (New York: Penguin, 1987).

74. Q.E.D. stands for "*Quod est demonstratum*," the traditional Latin summation indicating a proof completed.

75. Indian mysticism offers an exception to this generalization. As we have seen, some Indian mystics, such as Nagarjuna, availed themselves of the tools of logic and argumentation precisely in order to establish the place of mysticism.

76. Antoine, the Marquis de Condorcet, *Sketch for a Historical Picture of the Progress of the Human Mind*, written while he was in prison, awaiting execution during the French Revolution.

77. See Edward Said's discussion of this phenomenon in *Orientalism* (New York: Random House, 1978).

78. The classic exchange on the matter was carried out in the correspondence of Leibniz and Locke, who were contemporaries.

79. That debate continues to this day. A few years ago, MIT linguist-philosopher Noam Chomsky and Harvard philosopher Nelson Goodman took part in a vigorous debate about what, if any, particularly linguistic (syntactic) capacities were "inborn" in the human brain. On the one hand, how would children learn to speak so quickly and have such versatility if there were not structures (or rules) already in place? On the other hand, despite the fact that there are so many languages, a child seems capable of learning virtually any of them, depending on his or her linguistic context. Thus, Chomsky suggests the *idea* of a "universal grammar," an inborn template for all natural languages.

80. The first two "estates" were the nobility and the clergy. The third estate included virtually everyone else.

81. Bishop Berkeley had also called his view "idealism," specifically "subjective idealism." In order to distinguish his view from Berkeley's, Kant calls his a "transcendental idealism," suggesting that the "external world" is real after all, but is nevertheless constituted according to the universal and necessary rules of the mind.

82. Here the important word "transcendental" means essential to the very possibility of experience.

83. The notion of "teleology" goes back to Aristotle, who similarly argued for a larger purposive picture of the cosmos.

84. The word "liberalism" has become one of the most abused and, consequently, most useless terms in our political vocabulary. The use of the term in recent American politics, in particular, as roughly equivalent to "spendthrift and mush-headed," is entirely opposed to the classical meaning, which has much in common with what today would be called "conservative" thinking.

85. James made this comment in his work *The American Scene* (1907). Du Bois's works are extensive and include *The Souls of Black Folk* (1903) and *Dusk of Dawn: An Essay Toward an Autobiography of a Race Concept* (1940).

86. Freud's basic theories are focused on male development, with female development discussed mainly as a variant of the male case.

87. About the same time, Husserl was exploring the same problem—and coming up with a similar conclusion—through his phenomenology. A musical melody, for example, cannot be broken down into atomistic instants. Even the shortest bit carries with it the preceding notes and anticipates the notes to come.

88. See, for example, Genevieve Lloyd, *The Man of Reason: "Male" and "Female" in Western Philosophy* (Minneapolis: University of Minnesota Press, 1984).

89. We have made it a principle (of arbitrary fairness, and in order to avoid some nasty personal and political issues) not to include any living philosophers in the book, except, of course, in the occasional footnote. For that reason, we will not provide much by way of the details of contemporary feminism, which is, of course, available in voluminous detail in a great many publications. For some neglected historical figures, see M. Atherton, ed. *Women Philosophers of the Early Modern Period* (Indianapolis, Ind.: Hackett, 1994).

90. See Sandra Harding, *The Science Question in Feminism* (Ithaca: Cornell University Press, 1986). See also Helen E. Longino, *Science as Social Knowledge: Values and Objectivity in Scientific Inquiry* (Princeton, N.J.: Princeton University Press, 1990).

91. It should not be thought that feminism thereby aspires to invent an alternative physics, for example, or dismiss or reject the scientific accomplishments and discoveries of the past. The demand is rather to expand science, to consider more and different kinds of evidence, particularly in the social sciences, where systematic bias can be amply demonstrated. Some recent scholars who have made such arguments include Sandra Harding, Steven Jay Gould, and Robert Procter.

92. See, for example, Judith Butler, *Gender Trouble: Feminism and the Subversion of Identity* (New York: Routledge, 1990); idem, *Bodies that Matter: On the Discursive Limits of "Sex"* (New York: Routledge, 1994).

93. See, for example, Janice G. Raymond, *A Passion for Friends: Toward a Philosophy of Female Affection* (London: Women's Press, 1985).

94. See Carol Gilligan, *In a Different Voice: Psychological Theory and Women's Development* (Cambridge, Mass.: Harvard University Press, 1982).

95. The first wave of feminism focused on the attainment of equal rights for women in legal terms. The second wave focused on the attainment of women's first-class participation in society and drew attention to the psychological and sociological barriers that prevented it, even when protective laws were in place.

96. For example, see Marco Orru's unpublished monograph "Institutional Typologies of Capitalist Economies."

97. A clever image of Jacques Derrida's, suggesting the writing of something down and then erasing it, implying both assertion and retraction.

98. For example, Jacques Derrida and Richard Rorty, both of whom are happily alive, have not been included here.

Selected Bibliography

Western Philosophy

General Introductions

Copleston, Frederick. *The History of Philosophy*. 9 vols. Rev. ed. Westminster, Md.: The Newman Press; 1946–74.

Durant, Will and Ariel. *The Story of Philosophy*. 9 vols. New York: Simon and Schuster, 1935.

Flew, Antony. *An Introduction to Western Philosophy*. London: Thames and Hudson, 1971.

Jones, W. T. *A History of Western Philosophy*. 4 vols. New York: Harcourt, Brace, Jovanovich, 1969–75.

Parkinson, G. H. R., and S. G. Shanker, eds. *The Routledge History of Philosophy*. 10 vols. London: Routledge, 1993–.

Russell, Bertrand. *History of Western Philosophy*. New York: Simon and Schuster, 1945.

Solomon, Robert C. *Introducing Philosophy*. 5th ed. Fort Worth: Harcourt Brace, 1993.

Tarnas, Richard. *The Passion of the Western Mind*. New York: Harmony, 1991.

Whitehead, Alfred North. *Adventures of Ideas*. New York: Macmillan, 1933.

PART I

Egypt

Glanville, Stephen. *The Legacy of Egypt*. Oxford: Clarendon, 1947.

Steindorff, Georg, and Keith C. Seele. *When Egypt Ruled the East*. Chicago: University of Chicago Press, 1957.

Ancient Greece

Barnes, Jonathan. *Aristotle*. New York: Oxford University Press, 1982.

Burnet, J. *Early Greek Philosophy*. 4th ed. London: Black, 1930.

We have not included classic texts, which are widely available in various editions. The books listed here are recommended for those who desire additional information on (as well as in) the history of philosophy.

Cornford, Francis M. *Before and After Socrates.* Cambridge: Cambridge University Press, 1932.

Dodds, Eric Robertson. *The Greeks and the Irrational.* Berkeley: University of California Press, 1951.

Farrington, Benjamin. *Greek Science.* Harmondsworth, Eng.: Penguin, 1944.

Findlay, John Niemeyer. *Plato and Platonism.* New York: Times Books, 1978.

Guthrie, W. K. C. *Greek Philosophy.* London: Methuen, 1950.

Kirihan, P. D. *Pre-Socratics.* Indianapolis, Ind.: Hackett, 1994.

Kirk, G. S., and J. E. Raven. *The Pre-Socratic Philosophers.* Cambridge: Cambridge University Press, 1957.

Kraut, Robert. *Socrates and the State.* Princeton, N.J.: Princeton University Press, 1984.

Mourelatos, A. P. D. *The Pre-Socratics.* Princeton, N.J.: Princeton University Press, 1993.

Ring, Merrill. *Beginning with the Pre-Socratics.* Mountain View, Calif.: Mayfield, 1987.

Ross, W. D. *Aristotle.* 5th ed. London: Methuen, 1949.

Stone, Isidor F. *The Trial of Socrates.* Boston: Little, Brown, 1988.

Taylor, Alfred E. *Aristotle.* Mineola, N.Y.: Dover, 1955.

———. *Socrates.* Garden City, N.Y.: Doubleday, 1953.

Vlastos, Gregory, ed. *The Philosophy of Socrates.* New York: Doubleday, 1971.

PART II

Zoroastrianism

Boyce, Mary. *Zoroastrians: Their Beliefs and Practices.* London: Routledge and Kegan Paul, 1979.

Malandra, William W. *An Introduction to Ancient Iranian Religion.* Minneapolis: University of Minnesota Press, 1983.

Judaism

Jacobson, Dan. *The Story of the Stories: The Chosen People and Its God.* New York: Harper and Row, 1982.

Katz, Steven T. *Jewish Philosophers.* New York: Bloch, 1975.

Kent, Charles Foster. *History of the Hebrew People.* New York: Charles Scribner's Sons, 1905.

Phillips, Anthony. *God B.C.* Oxford: Oxford University Press, 1977.

Scholem, Gershom G. *On the Kabbalah and Its Symbolism.* Translated by Ralph Manheim. New York: Schocken Books, 1965.

Christianity

Chadwick, Henry. *History and Thought of the Early Church.* London: Variorum Reprints, 1982.

Cross, F. L., and Elizabeth A. Livingstone, eds. *The Oxford Dictionary of the Christian Church.* London: Oxford University Press, 1958.

Pelikan, Jaroslav. *The Christian Tradition: A History of the Development of Doctrine.* Chicago: University of Chicago Press, 1971–89. Vol. 1: *The Emergence of the Catholic Tradition* (100–600). Vol. 2: *The Spirit of Eastern Christendom* (600–1700). Vol. 3:

The Growth of Medieval Theology (600–1300). Vol. 4: *Reformation of Church and Dogma* (1300–1700). Vol. 5: *Christian Doctrine and Modern Culture* (since 1700).
Walsh, Michael. *Roots of Christianity*. London: Grafton, 1986.

Islam

Cragg, Kenneth. *The House of Islam*. 2nd ed. Belmont, Calif.: Wadsworth, 1975.
Hourani, Albert. *A History of the Arab Peoples*. Cambridge, Mass.: Harvard University Press, 1991.
Lewis, Bernard. *Islam and the West*. New York: Oxford University Press, 1993.
Ormsby, Eric. "Arabic Philosophy." In *From Africa to Zen: An Invitation to World Philosophy*. Edited by Robert C. Solomon and Kathleen M. Higgins. pp. 125–50. Lanham, Md.: Rowman and Littlefield, 1993.
Phillips, Stephen H. *Classical Indian Metaphysics*. La Salle, Il: Open Court, 1995.
Rahman, Fazlur. *Islam*. 2nd ed. Chicago: University of Chicago Press, 1979.
———. *Major Themes of the Qur'an*. Minneapolis, Minn.: Bibliotheca Islamica, 1980.
Sepasi-Tehrani, Homayoon, and Janet Flesch. "Persian Philosophy." In *From Africa to Zen: An Invitation to World Philosophy*. Edited by Robert C. Solomon and Kathleen M. Higgins. pp. 151–86. Lanham, Md.: Rowman and Littlefield, 1993.

Medieval Philosophy

Bainton, Roland H. *The Medieval Church*. New York: Van Nostrand, 1962.
Copleston, Frederick, S.J. *Thomas Aquinas*. New York: Harper and Row, 1955.
Goodman, L. E. *Avicenna*. New York: Routledge, 1992.
Grunebaum, Gustave E. von. *Medieval Islam*. Chicago: University of Chicago Press, 1966.
Knowles, David. *The Evolution of Medieval Thought*. London: Longman, 1962.
Netton, Ian Richard. *Al-Farabi and His School*. New York: Routledge, 1992.
Runciman, Steen. *The Eastern Schism: A Study of the Papacy and the Eastern Churches During the Eleventh and Twelfth Centuries*. Oxford: Clarendon, 1955.
Vignaux, Paul. *Philosophy in the Middle Ages: An Introduction*. Translated by E. C. Hall. New York: Meridian Books, 1959.

The Protestant Reformation

Kittelson, James M. *Luther the Reformer: The Story of the Man and His Career*. Minneapolis, Minn.: Augsburg, 1986.
Whale, J. S., D.D. *The Protestant Tradition: An Essay in Interpretation*. Cambridge: Cambridge University Press, 1955.

The Renaissance

Cassirer, Ernst. *The Individual and the Cosmos in Renaissance Philosophy*. Translated by Mario Domandi. New York: Barnes and Noble, 1963.
Copenhaver, Brian P. *Renaissance Philosophy*. New York: Oxford University Press, 1992.

Kristeller, Paul Oskar. *Renaissance Thought and Its Sources.* Edited by Michael Mooney. New York: Columbia University Press, 1979.

McKnight, Stephen A. *Sacralizing the Secular: The Renaissance Origins of Modernity.* Baton Rouge: Louisiana State University Press, 1989.

Seung, T. K. *Cultural Thematics: The Formation of the Faustian Ethos.* New Haven: Yale University Press, 1976.

PART III

Allison, H. E. *Kant's Philosophy of Freedom.* Cambridge: Cambridge University Press, 1990.

Beck, Lewis White, ed. *Eighteenth-Century Philosophy.* New York: The Free Press, 1966.

———. *Early German Philosophy: Kant and His Predecessors.* Cambridge, Mass.: Harvard University Press, 1969.

Berlin, Isaiah, ed. *The Age of Enlightenment: The Eighteenth-Century Philosophers.* New York: Oxford University Press, 1979.

Breazeale, Daniel. "Fichte and Schelling: The Jena Period." In *The Age of German Idealism.* Edited by Kathleen Higgins and Robert Solomon. pp. 138–80. London: Routledge, 1993.

Cassirer, E. *Kant's Life and Thought.* New Haven, Conn.: Yale University Press, 1981.

Cottingham, John. *The Rationalists.* Oxford: Oxford University Press, 1992.

Gardiner, Patrick, ed. *Nineteenth-Century Philosophy: Hegel to Nietzsche.* New York: The Free Press, 1969.

Guyer, Paul, ed. *The Cambridge Companion to Kant.* Cambridge: Cambridge University Press, 1992.

Hamlyn, D. W. *Schopenhauer.* London: Routledge, 1980.

Hampshire, Stuart, ed. *The Age of Reason: The Seventeenth-Century Philosophers.* New York: Braziller, 1957.

Higgins, Kathleen. *Nietzsche's Zarathustra.* Philadelphia: Temple University Press, 1987.

Higgins, Kathleen, and Robert Solomon, eds. *The Age of German Idealism.* London: Routledge, 1993.

Hooker, M., ed. *Descartes.* Baltimore, Md.: Johns Hopkins University Press, 1978.

Kenny, Anthony. *Descartes: A Study of His Philosophy.* New York: Random House, 1968.

Körner, Stephan. *Kant.* New Haven, Conn.: Yale University Press, 1955.

Mackey, Louis. *Kierkegaard: A Kind of Poet.* Philadelphia: University of Pennsylvania Press, 1971.

Miller, James. *Rousseau and Democracy.* New Haven, Conn.: Yale University Press, 1984.

Nehamas, Alexander. *Nietzsche: Life as Literature.* Cambridge, Mass.: Harvard University Press, 1985.

Nola, Robert. "The Young Hegelians: Feuerbach and Marx." In *The Age of German Idealism.* Edited by Kathleen Higgins and Robert Solomon. pp. 290–329. London: Routledge, 1993.

Schacht, Richard. *Nietzsche.* London: Routledge, 1983.

Skorupski, John. *English-Language Philosophy, 1750–1945.* Oxford: Oxford University Press, 1992.

Solomon, Robert C. *Continental Philosophy Since 1750: The Rise and Fall of the Self.* Oxford: Oxford University Press, 1988.

———. *In the Spirit of Hegel.* New York: Oxford University Press, 1983.

Tanner, Michael. *Nietzsche.* Oxford: Oxford University Press, 1995.

Taylor, Mark. *Journeys to Selfhood: Hegel and Kierkegaard*. Berkeley: University of California Press, 1980.
Toulmin, Stephen. *Cosmopolis: The Hidden Agenda of Modernity*. New York: Macmillan, 1990.
Werhane, Patricia. *Adam Smith and His Legacy for Capitalism*. New York: Oxford, 1978.
White, M. *The Philosophy of the American Revolution*. New York: Oxford, 1978.
Woolhouse, R. S. *The Empiricists*. New York: Oxford University Press, 1988.

PART IV

Barnes, Hazel. *Sartre*. Philadelphia: Lippincott, 1973.
Charlesworth, Max. *The Existentialists and Jean-Paul Sartre*. London: Prior, 1976.
Dreyfus, Hubert L., and Raul Rabinow. *Michel Foucault: Beyond Structuralism and Hermeneutics*. 2nd ed. Chicago: University of Chicago Press, 1983.
Fogelin, Robert. *Wittgenstein*. London: Routledge, 1983.
Guignon, Charles, ed. *The Cambridge Companion to Heidegger*. Cambridge: Cambridge University Press, 1993.
Hylton, Peter. *Russell, Idealism, and the Emergence of Analytic Philosophy*. Oxford: Oxford University Press, 1990.
Janik, A., and S. Toulmin. *Wittgenstein's Vienna*. New York: Simon and Schuster, 1993.
Magee, Bryan. *Modern British Philosophy*. Oxford: Oxford University Press, 1988.
Miller, James. *Michel Foucault*. New York: Simon and Schuster, 1993.
Myers, Gerald. *William James*. New Haven, Conn.: Yale University Press, 1986.
Schroeder, William. *Sartre and His Predecessors*. London: Routledge, 1984.
Skorupski, John. *English-Language Philosophy, 1750–1945*. Oxford: Oxford University Press, 1992.
Sluga, Hans. *Heidegger's Crisis*. Cambridge, Mass.: Harvard University Press, 1993.
Solomon, Robert C. *From Rationalism to Existentialism: The Existentialists and Their Nineteenth-Century Backgrounds*. New York: Harper and Row, 1972.
Spiegelberg, H. *The Phenomenological Movement*. The Hague: Martinus Nijhoff, 1962.
Weitz, Morris, ed. *Twentieth-Century Philosophy: The Analytic Tradition*. New York: The Free Press, 1966.

Nonwestern Philosophy

General Introductions

Douglas, Mary. *Purity and Danger: An Analysis of Concepts of Pollution and Taboo*. New York: Praeger, 1970.
Deutsch, Eliot, ed. *Culture and Modernity: East–West Philosophic Perspectives*. Honolulu: University of Hawaii Press, 1991.
Smart, Ninian. *The Long Search*. Boston: Little, Brown, 1977.
Smith, Huston. *The Religions of Man*. New York: Harper and Row, 1958.
Solomon, Robert C., and Kathleen M. Higgins, eds. *From Africa to Zen: An Invitation to World Philosophy*. Lanham, Md.: Rowman and Littlefield, 1993.
———. *World Philosophy: A Text with Readings*. New York: McGraw-Hill, 1995.

African Philosophy

Abimbola, Wande. *Ifa: An Exposition of Ifa Literary Corpus*. Ibadan, Nigeria: Oxford University Press, 1976.
Abraham, W. E. *The Mind of Africa*. Chicago: University of Chicago Press, 1962.
Appiah, Kwame Anthony. *In My Father's House: Africa in the Philosophy of Culture*. New York: Oxford University Press, 1992.
Fanon, Frantz. *The Wretched of the Earth*. New York: Grove Press, 1968.
Fløistad, Guttorm, ed. *Contemporary Philosophy*. Vol. 5: *African Philosophy*. The Hague: Martinus Nijhoff, 1987.
Gyekye, Kwame. *An Essay on African Philosophical Thought*. New York: Cambridge University Press, 1987.
Hountondji, Paulin. *African Philosophy: Myth and Reality*. Translated by Henri Evans, with Jonathan Reé. Bloomington: Indiana University Press, 1983.
McVeigh, Malcolm. *God in Africa: Conceptions of God in African Traditional Religion and Christianity*. Cape Cod, Mass.: C. Stark, 1974.
Makinde, M. Akin. *African Philosophy, Culture, and Traditional Medicine*. Athens: Ohio University Press, 1988.
Mbiti, John S. *African Religions and Philosophy*. Garden City, N.Y.: Doubleday, 1969.
Mudimbe, V. Y. *The Invention of Africa: Gnosis, Philosophy and the Order of Knowledge*. Bloomington: Indiana University Press, 1988.
Murungi, John. "Toward an African Conception of Time." *International Philosophical Quarterly* 20:4 (December 1980): 407–16.
Okere, Theophilus. *African Philosophy: A Historico-Hermeneutical Investigation of the Conditions of Its Possibility*. New York: University Press of America, 1983.
Oruka, H. Odera. "Sagacity in African Philosophy." *International Philosophical Quarterly* 23:4 (December 1983): 383–94.
Senghor, Léopold Sédar. *Prose and Poetry*. Translated by Clive Wake and John Reed. London: Oxford University Press, 1965.
Serequeberhan, Tsenay, ed. *African Philosophy: The Essential Readings*. New York: Paragon House, 1991.
Trimier, Jacqueline, "African Philosophy." In *From Africa to Zen: An Invitation to World Philosophy*. Edited by Robert C. Solomon and Kathleen M. Higgins. pp. 187–219. Lanham, Md.: Rowman and Littlefield, 1993.
Wiredu, Kwasi. *Philosophy and an African Culture*. New York: Cambridge University Press, 1980.
Wright, Richard A., ed. *African Philosophy: An Introduction*. Lanham, Md.: University Press of America, 1984.

American Indian Philosophy

Allen, Paula Gunn. *The Sacred Hoop*. Boston: Beacon, 1986.
Brown, Joseph E. *The Spiritual Legacy of the American Indian*. New York: Crossroad, 1984.
Crow Dog, Mary. *Lakota Woman*. New York: HarperCollins, 1990.
DeMallie, Raymond J. *The Sixth Grandfather: Black Elk's Teachings Given to John G. Neihardt*. Lincoln: University of Nebraska Press, 1984.
Erdoes, Richard. *Lame Deer: Seeker of Visions*. New York: Simon and Schuster, 1976.
Jennings, Francis. *The Invasion of America*. New York: Norton, 1975.

Josephy, Alvin. *Now That the Buffalo's Gone: A Study of Today's American Indians*. Norman: University of Oklahoma Press, 1984.

Nelson, Richard. *Make Prayers to the Raven*. Chicago: University of Chicago Press, 1983.

Overholt, Thomas W., and J. Baird Calicott. *Clothed-in-Fur and Other Tales: An Introduction to an Ojibwa World View*. Washington, D.C.: University Press of America, 1982.

———. "Traditional American Indian Attitudes Toward Nature." In *From Africa to Zen: An Invitation to World Philosophy*. Edited by Robert C. Solomon and Kathleen M. Higgins. pp. 55–80. Lanham, Md.: Rowman and Littlefield, 1993.

Underhill, Ruth M. *Red Man's Religion: Beliefs and Practices of the Indians North of Mexico*. Chicago: University of Chicago Press, 1965.

Vescey, Christopher. *Imagine Ourselves Richly: Mythic Narratives of North American Indians*. New York: Crossroad, 1988.

Chinese Philosophy

Allan, Sarah. *The Shape of the Turtle: Myth, Art, and Cosmos in Early China* Albany: State University of New York Press, 1991.

Allinson, Robert E., ed. *Understanding the Chinese Mind*. Hong Kong: Oxford University Press, 1989.

Ames, Roger T. *The Art of Rulership*. Honolulu: University of Hawaii Press, 1983.

Ames, Roger T., and David L. Hall. *Thinking Through Confucius*. Albany: State University of New York Press, 1987.

———. "Understanding Order: The Chinese Perspective." In *From Africa to Zen: An Invitation to World Philosophy*. Edited by Robert C. Solomon and Kathleen M. Higgins. pp. 1–23. Lanham, Md.: Rowman and Littlefield, 1993.

Bodde, Derk. *Chinese Thought, Society, and Science*. Honolulu: University of Hawaii Press, 1991.

Fung Yu-Lan. *A Short History of Chinese Philosophy*. Edited by Derk Bodde. New York: Macmillan, 1948.

Graham, A. C. *Disputers of the Tao: Philosophical Argument in Ancient China*. La Salle, Ill.: Open Court, 1989.

Mote, Frederick W. *Intellectual Foundations of China*. New York: Alfred A. Knopf, 1971.

Wing-Tsit Chan, ed. *A Source Book in Chinese Philosophy*. Princeton, N.J.: Princeton University Press, 1963.

Indian Philosophy

Basham, A. L. *The Origins and Development of Classical Hinduism*. Boston: Beacon, 1989.

Bilimoria, Purusottama. *The Self and Its Destiny in Hinduism*. Geelong: Deakin University Press, 1990.

Daniélou, Alain. *The Myths and Gods of India: The Classic Work on Hindu Polytheism from the Princeton Bollingen Series*. Rochester, Vt: Inner Traditions International, 1991.

Deutsch, Eliot. *Advaita Vedanta*. Honolulu: East-West Center Press, 1969.

Koller, John. *The Indian Way*. Albany: State University of New York Press, 1982.

O'Flaherty, Wendy Doniger, ed. and trans. *Hindu Myths: A Sourcebook Translated from the Sanskrit*. Baltimore, Md.: Penguin Books, 1975.

Phillips, Stephen H. *Aurobindo's Philosophy of Brahman.* New York. E. J. Drill, 1906.
———. "Indian Philosophies." In *From Africa to Zen: An Invitation to World Philosophy.* Edited by Robert C. Solomon and Kathleen M. Higgins. pp. 221–66. Lanham, Md.: Rowman and Littlefield, 1993.
Potter, Karl. *Guide to Indian Philosophy.* Boston: G. K. Hall, 1988, pp. 221–266.
Zimmer, Heinrich. *Myths and Symbols in Indian Art and Civilization.* Edited by Joseph Campbell. Bollingen Series VI. Princeton, N.J.: Princeton University Press, 1946.

Japanese Philosophy

Benedict, Ruth. *The Chrysanthemum and the Sword: Patterns of Japanese Culture.* Boston: Houghton Mifflin, 1946.
Dumoulin, Heinrich. *Zen Buddhism: A History.* 2 vols. Translated by James W. Heisig and Paul Knitter. New York: Macmillan, 1989–90.
Kasulis, T. P. *Zen Action/Zen Person.* Honolulu: University of Hawaii Press, 1981.
Nishitani Keiji. *The Self-Overcoming of Nihilism.* Translated by Graham Parkes, with Setsuko Aihara. Albany: State University of New York Press, 1990.
Parkes, Graham. "Ways of Japanese Thinking." In *From Africa to Zen: An Invitation to World Philosophy.* Edited by Robert C. Solomon and Kathleen M. Higgins. pp. 25–53. Lanham, Md.: Rowman and Littlefield, 1993.
Ryusaku Tsunoda, ed. *Sources of Japanese Tradition.* New York: Columbia University Press, 1958.
Sei Shōnagon. *The Pillow Book of Sei Shōnagon.* Translated and edited by Ivan Morris. New York: Penguin Books, 1967.
Suzuki, Daisetz T. *Zen and Japanese Culture.* Princeton, N.J.: Princeton University Press, 1959.
Varley, H. Paul. *Japanese Culture.* Honolulu: University of Hawaii Press, 1973.

Latin American Philosophy

Aquilar, Luis, ed. *Marxism in Latin America.* Rev. ed. Philadelphia: Temple University Press, 1978.
Clendinnen, Inga. *Aztecs.* Cambridge: Cambridge University Press, 1991.
Crawford, William Rex. *A Century of Latin American Thought.* Cambridge, Mass.: Harvard University Press, 1944.
Dascal, Marcelo. *Cultural Relativism and Philosophy: North and Latin American Perspectives.* New York; E. J. Brill, 1991.
Dussel, Enrique. *Philosophy of Liberation.* Translated by A. Martinez and M. Morkovsky. New York: Orbis Books, 1985.
Gracia, Jorge J. E. *Latin American Philosophy in the Twentieth Century.* Buffalo: Prometheus, 1986.
Jorrin, Miguel, and John D. Martz. *Latin-American Political Thought and Ideology.* Chapel Hill: University of North Carolina Press, 1970.
León-Portilla, Miguel. *Aztec Thought and Culture: A Study of the Ancient Nahuatl Mind.* Translated by Jack Emory Davis. Norman: University of Oklahoma Press, 1963.
———. *The Broken Spears: The Aztec Account of the Conquest of Mexico.* Boston: Beacon Press, 1966.
Sahagún, Fr. Bernadino de. *The Florentine Codex: General History of the Things of New*

Spain. 12 books in 13 vols. Translated by Arthur J. O. Anderson and Charles Dibble. Santa Fe: School of American Research and the University of Utah Press, 1950–82.

Valadez, Jorge. "Pre-Columbian and Modern Philosophical Perspectives in Latin America." In *From Africa to Zen: An Invitation to World Philosophy.* Edited by Robert C. Solomon and Kathleen M. Higgins. pp. 81–124. Lanham, Md.: Rowman and Littlefield, 1993.

Zea, Leopoldo. *The Latin American Mind.* Translated by J. H. Abbot and L. Dunham. Norman: University of Oklahoma, 1963.

The Environment

Blackstone, William, ed. *Philosophy and Environmental Crisis.* Athens: University of Georgia Press, 1974.

Callicott, J. Baird. *In Defense of the Land Ethic: Essays in Environmental Philosophy.* Albany: State University of New York Press, 1989.

Elliot, Robert, and Arran Gare, eds. *Environmental Philosophy: A Collection of Readings.* University Park, Pa.: Pennsylvania State University Press, 1983.

Leopold, Aldo. *A Sand County Almanac: And Sketches Here and There.* New York: Oxford University Press, 1977.

Regan, Tom, and Peter Singer, eds. *Animal Rights and Human Obligations.* 2nd ed. Englewood Cliffs, N.J.: Prentice-Hall, 1989.

Regan, Tom, *Earthbound: Introductory Essays in Environmental Ethics.* Prospect Heights, Ill.: Waveland Press, 1984.

Sadler, Barry, and Allen Carlson, eds. *Environmental Aesthetics: Essays in Interpretation.* Victoria, B.C.: University of Victoria Press, 1982.

Sagoff, Mark. *The Economy of the Earth: Philosophy, Law, and the Environment.* Cambridge: Cambridge University Press, 1988.

Singer, Peter. *Animal Liberation.* 2nd ed. New York: Random House, 1975.

Vandeveer, Donald, and Christine Pierce, eds. *People, Penguins, and Plastic Trees.* Belmont, Calif.: Wadsworth, 1986.

Feminism

Beauvoir, Simone de. *The Second Sex.* Translated by H. M. Parshley. New York: Knopf, 1953.

Butler, Judith. *Gender Trouble: Feminism and the Subversion of Identity.* New York: Routledge, 1990.

Chodorow, Nancy. *The Reproduction of Mothering: Psychoanalysis and the Sociology of Gender.* Berkeley: University of California Press, 1978.

Dinnerstein, Dorothy. *The Mermaid and the Minotaur.* New York: Harper and Row, 1977.

Firestone, Shulamith. *The Dialectic of Sex: The Case for Feminist Revolution.* New York: Bantam Books, 1970.

Gilligan, Carol. *In a Different Voice: Psychological Theory and Women's Development.* Cambridge, Mass.: Harvard University Press, 1982.

Harding, Sandra. *The Science Question in Feminism.* Ithaca, N.Y.: Cornell University Press, 1986.

hooks, bell. *Feminist Theory: From Margin to Center.* Boston: South End Press, 1984.

Lloyd, Genevieve. *The Man of Reason: "Male" and "Female" in Western Philosophy.* Minneapolis: University of Minnesota Press, 1984.

Nicholson, Linda J., ed. *Feminism/Postmodernism.* New York: Routledge, 1990.

Noddings, Nel. *Caring: A Feminine Approach to Ethics and Moral Education.* Berkeley: University of California Press, 1984.

Raymond, Janice G. *A Passion for Friends: Toward a Philosophy of Female Affection.* London: Women's Press, 1985.

Ruddick, Sara. *Maternal Thinking: Toward a Politics of Peace.* Boston: Beacon Press, 1989.

Tuana, Nancy. *Woman and the History of Philosophy.* New York: Paragon, 1992.

Index

Abelard, Peter, 143–45, 148, 246
Abraham, v, 100, 101, 106–7, 169
Aeschylus, 19
African philosophy, 167–71, 294–95, 299–300.
  See also specific individuals
Agathon, 50–51
Ahura Mazda, 3, 99–100
Akhenaton (Amenhotep IV), v, 4, 100–101
al-Farabi, 136–37
al-Ghazali, 138
al-Hallaj, 134
al-Kindi, 135–36
al-Razi, 136–37
al-Suhrawardi, 152
Albert the Great, 145, 150
Alchemists, 149–51
Alcibiades, 43, 56
Alexander the Great, 57, 67, 69, 112, 168, 309
  n. 31
'Ali, 132
American Indian philosophy. *See* Native
  American philosophy
American philosophy, 235–41, 259–63, 294–96.
  See also specific individuals
Analytic philosophy, 252–3. *See also* specific
  individuals
Anaxagoras, 29, 36–37
Anaximander, 29, 31–32, 33, 36, 62
Anaximenes, 29, 32, 62
Andersen, Hans Christian, 228
Animism, 171
Anselm, St., 137, 143, 184
Antisthenes, 66, 309 n. 30
Aphrodite, 19, 54
Aristophanes, 55, 308 n. 21
Aristotle, 10, 25, 29, 30, 35, 36, 39, 56–69, 71,
  87, 92, 93, 135–38, 141, 142, 144–46, 149,

157, 164–65, 176, 189, 217, 231–32, 246,
  265, 308 n. 27, 309 nn. 28,31
Arjuna, 14
Atman, 23, 88
Atomists, atomism, 29, 70, 166
Augustine, St., 3, 21, 68, 122–26, 128–29, 133,
  143, 146–48, 157, 176, 184, 278
Aurobindo, Ghose (Sri), 298, 309 n. 39
Austin, J. L., 285–86
Averroës. *See* Ibn Rushd
Avicenna. *See* Ibn Sina
Ayer, A. J., 276
Aztecs 172–73

Bacon, Francis, 165–66, 177
Barth, Karl, 277
Beauvoir, Simone de, 282, 286, 289–90
Bentham, Jeremy, 230
Bergson, Henri, 265–66, 267
Berkeley, Bishop George, 188, 195–96, 209
Bhagavad-Gita, 14, 88–89
Bradley, F. H. 249
Brahman, Brahmanism, 2, 13, 15, 19, 21, 22,
  23, 24, 75–76
Bruno, Giordano, 150, 164
Buber, Martin, 277
Buddha, 2, 4, 31, 72, 75–77, 86
Buddhists, Buddhism, 13, 15, 16, 21, 24, 75–
  77, 80, 83, 84–91, 96–99, 133, 152–54, 184,
  224, 308 n. 20
Butler, Judith, 313 n. 92

Caligula, 72, 74
Calvin, Calvinism, 158–59, 200, 257
Camus, Albert, 277, 278, 279–80
Carlyle, Thomas, 205
Chang-tzu, 98–99